WITHDRAWN

Puškin

TODAY

Puškin

TODAY

Edited by

DAVID M. BETHEA

Indiana University Press
BLOOMINGTON AND INDIANAPOLIS

© 1993 by Indiana University Press
All rights reserved

The paper used in this publication meets the minimum requirements of American National Standard for Information Sciences—Permanence of Paper for Printed Library Materials, ANSI Z39.48-1984.

TM

Manufactured in the United States of America

Library of Congress Cataloging-in-Publication Data

Puškin today / edited by David M. Bethea.
   p. cm.
   Includes bibliographical references and index.
   ISBN 0-253-31161-6
   1. Pushkin, Aleksandr Sergeevich, 1799–1837—Criticism and interpretation.   I. Bethea, David M., date.
PG3356.P89   1992
891.71'3—dc20   92-7861

1 2 3 4 5 96 95 94 93

Contents

Contributors

DAVID M. BETHEA   (University of Wisconsin-Madison)
SERGEJ DAVYDOV   (Middlebury College)
PAUL DEBRECZENY   (University of North Carolina at Chapel Hill)
CARYL EMERSON   (Princeton University)
GEORGE GUTSCHE   (University of Arizona)
WILLIAM HARKINS   (Columbia University)
SIMON KARLINSKY   (University of California, Berkeley)
LESLIE O'BELL   (University of Texas, Austin)
DANIEL RANCOUR-LAFERRIERE   (University of California, Davis)
STEPHANIE SANDLER   (Amherst College)
J. THOMAS SHAW   (University of Wisconsin-Madison)
VICTOR TERRAS   (Brown University)
WILLIAM MILLS TODD III   (Harvard University)
WALTER VICKERY   (University of North Carolina at Chapel Hill)

A Note on Transliteration and Editions

In the interests of precision, the International Scholarly System of translit-
eration is used throughout this volume. For the nonspecialist reader we
provide the following table:

Cyrillic	Library of Congress	International Scholarly
ж	zh	ž
й	i	j
х	kh	x
ц	ts	c
ч	ch	č
ш	sh	š
щ	shch	šč
ъ	”	”
ы	y	y
ь	’	’
э	e	è
ю	iu	ju
я	ia	ja

Unless otherwise indicated, the "large Academy" edition of Puškin's
works (1937–59, 17 vols., Moscow: Akademija Nauk) is the one normally
cited, with the abbreviation "PSS" (*Polnoe sobranie sočinenij*). Several
authors have preferred to use the system in *The Dictionary of Puškin's
Language* (Slovar' jazyka Puškina, 1956–61, ed. V. V. Vinogradov, 4 vols.,
Moscow: Gosudarstvennoe izdatel'stvo inostrannyx nacional'nyx
slovarej), where, for example, "EO.I.50" refers to the "large Academy"
edition of *Evgenij Onegin* (Eugene Onegin), Chapter I, Stanza 50.

Puškin

TODAY

DAVID M. BETHEA

Introduction

It is difficult if not impossible to put into words what the Puškin phenomenon means to the Russian national psyche. Discourse on "Puškin" (the
cultural myth) can soon be overcome by a kind of abulia or loss of bear-
ings—what has prevented more than one Puškinist, having spent a lifetime
preparing for the task, from writing *the book*. Simple verbal constructs no
longer seem adequate to the task; they either descend into platitude and
sweeping generalization or—probably the wiser approach—they avoid the
subject altogether. Phrases such as "national poet" and "fountainhead of
modern Russian literature" are by now so *de rigueur* that one employs
them with reverse, Aesopian logic: they are worked into one's argument as
straw men, but they *are* worked in nonetheless. Here the most prudent
strategy is to let others speak for you. As M. O. Geršenzon, one of the most
brilliant of early twentieth-century Puškinists, once remarked in a letter to
the poet V. F. Xodasevič, "In difficult days I know of no greater joy than to
read Puškin and to make little discoveries about him."[1]

In a word, Puškin is not merely a multi-faceted writer whose experiments at the boundaries of genre have never been equaled, or a historical
figure whose fate became for all educated Russians coming after the quint-
essential "life of the poet," or an ever-emerging cultural myth and point of
origin to which other writers have had to return, almost hypnotically, in
order to resolve the "anxiety of [his] influence." More than all this, Puškin
has been the haven, the safe port, where the intelligentsia has gone to
protect its sanity during the periodic inclement weather that has marked
Russian politics during the last two centuries. Geršenzon meant to say that
his world, which could be (and was) falling apart on the outside, was kept
intact by "the little discoveries" that went on inside his mind and in those
of his fellow *puškinisty*. This was the salubrious "wisdom" of Puškin that
entered into the title of Geršenzon's finest book, *Mudrost' Puškina* (The
Wisdom of Puškin, 1919). And one has to assume that, perhaps more than
anything, it was the special joy of finding some nugget buried deep within
the seemingly inexhaustible lode of Puškiniana that inspired, and continues to inspire, generations of Russian/Soviet scholars, including such
names as M. P. Alekseev, D. D. Blagoj, S. G. Bočarov, S. M. Bondi, M. A.
Cjavlovskij, G. A. Gukovskij, N. V. Izmajlov, N. O. Lerner, Ju. M.
Lotman, B. S. Mejlax, B. L. Modzalevskij, P. E. Ščegolev, A. L. Slonimskij,
B. V. Tomaševskij, Ju. N. Tynjanov, V. E. Vacuro, S. A. Vengerov, V. Veresaev, V. V. Vinogradov, and numerous others.

Volumes such as this usually begin with the requisite *topos*: Puškin's genius is real, but it is linguistically grounded and therefore virtually untranslatable; our study aims to clarify a historically skewed Western perspective by chipping into this verbal bedrock and exposing it as if "for the first time" to non-native eyes and ears. Fortunately for us, this preemptive appeal to the non-specialist reader is at long last becoming an anachronism, for American Puškin studies have, as these essays richly demonstrate, fully come of age over the past thirty-five years. The amount of criticism and scholarship on Puškin done in this country has been, especially recently, increasing in an almost geometric progression, as have the number and quality of translations of his works; moreover, the approaches to Puškin have become more diversified and theoretically adventuresome.

The occasion for our collection was a national conference held in Madison, Wisconsin, on April 24–26, 1987, to mark the sesquicentennial anniversary of the death of Aleksandr Sergeevič Puškin (January 29, 1837).[2] The conference, entitled "Puškin Today," was generously supported by grants from the National Endowment for the Humanities, the Knapp Bequest, and the Anonymous Fund of the University of Wisconsin. Its senior director was Professor J. Thomas Shaw of the University of Wisconsin, a scholar who has devoted more than forty years to the study of Puškin and whose concordances, rhyme dictionaries, multi-volume edition of Puškin's letters, and numerous articles are well known to both the American and the Soviet scholarly communities. The ostensible reason for our gathering was the sesquicentennial celebration, but its genuine *raison d'être* was to take stock of where American Puškin studies had come over the post-war period and, equally important, where it seemed to be going, that is, *which* approaches to Puškin distinguished our national undertaking from others and how our contributions could be seen to define themselves against those of, say, our Soviet colleagues. It is the underlying premise of the conference and of the papers issuing from it that there is something to be said for studying the central figure of a national literature from a position "on the outside."

The contributors to this volume represent the full spectrum of American Slavic studies: they come from different generations, gender perspectives, academic backgrounds, institutional affiliations, geographical areas, and critical methodologies. A number have devoted significant portions of their academic careers to date to the study of Puškin; they have produced the books and articles that have in large part defined the field of *puškinovedenie* (Puškin studies) to the American audience. Others, mainly from the "younger" generation, have written dissertations and articles on Puškin, and several of these have books in press. To cite only the major publications of our group with a Puškin "focus": Paul Debreczeny's (University of North Carolina) *The Other Pushkin: A Study of Alexander Pushkin's Prose Fiction* (1983) and his translations of *The Complete Prose Fiction* (1983); Caryl Emerson's (Princeton University) *Boris Godunov: Transpositions of a Russian*

Theme (1986); Simon Karlinsky's (University of California-Berkeley) *Russian Drama from Its Beginnings to the Age of Pushkin* (1985); Leslie O'Bell's (University of Texas-Austin) *Pushkin's "Egyptian Nights": The Biography of a Work* (1984); Stephanie Sandler's (Amherst College) *Distant Pleasures: Alexander Pushkin and the Writing of Exile* (1989); J. Thomas Shaw's (University of Wisconsin-Madison) *The Letters of Alexander Pushkin* (1963, 1967), *Pushkin's Rhymes* (1974), and *Pushkin: A Concordance to the Poetry* (1985); William Mills Todd III's (Harvard University) *The Familiar Letter as a Literary Genre in the Age of Pushkin* (1976) and *Fiction and Society in the Age of Pushkin: Ideology, Institutions, and Narrative* (1986); and Walter Vickery's (University of North Carolina) *Pushkin: The Death of a Poet* (1968) and *Alexander Pushkin* (1970). Several of these works are generally regarded as being "seminal" (not only to Puškin studies but to Slavistics in general) for the theoretical and conceptual issues they raise.

Puškin Today is divided into two parts. Part One ("Puškin: Contemporary Critical Views") is intended to introduce the American audience to the wealth of critical methodologies now being applied to the study of Puškin. Here the reader finds chapters centering around a text or texts and a dominant methodology: *Eugene Onegin*/literature as social institution (William Mills Todd III); "The Queen of Spades"/reader response criticism (Caryl Emerson); religious poems of 1836/structuralism (Sergej Davydov); *Eugene Onegin* and Bestužev-Marlinskij's *Journey to Revel'*/intertextuality (Simon Karlinsky); *Bronze Horseman*/psychoanalysis (Daniel Rancour-Laferriere); *Eugene Onegin*/rhetoric (William Harkins); *Bronze Horseman*/cultural mythology (David M. Bethea). None of these methodologies is assumed to be sufficient (or hermeneutically "totalizing") in its own right; only when counterposed and read "against one another" do they indicate the sense of healthy pluralism and dialogue (perhaps "round table" is the more operative term) now present in our field. Needless to say, this pluralism is the beneficiary of the solid scholarly accomplishments of the early and intermediate post-war years.

Part Two of *Puškin Today* is entitled "Puškin: Text and Context." It is here that some of the most vexed issues—what medievalists call *temnye mesta* (dark spots/obscure passages)—in the "text(s)" of the poet's life and works are thoroughly and ingeniously broached, if not in every case resolved: Puškin's "African heritage" in the context of his life and art (J. Thomas Shaw); the Odessa love lyrics and their troubled poet-persona (Walter Vickery); the complex design of *Eugene Onegin* (Leslie O'Bell); the use of soliloquy and its implications for the "loneliness" of Puškin and his play *Boris Godunov* (Stephanie Sandler); the ambiguous notion of "politics" as it relates to Puškin's famous poem "Stanzas" (George Gutsche); Puškin's growing reputation as "national poet" as seen through the optic of his nineteenth-century journal reception (Paul Debreczeny); and Puškin's legacy as the "father" of Russian realist prose (Victor Terras). If the focus in Part One was largely methodological, then the focus in these essays is more practical and "contextual," and demonstrates the extent to which these American Slavists have mastered (and in their own ways "domesticated") the enormous secondary literature on Puškin.

PART ONE

In " 'The Russian Terpsichore's Soul-Filled Flight': Dance Themes in *Eugene Onegin*," William Mills Todd III builds on the methodological assumptions found in his *Fiction and Society in the Age of Pushkin*: (1) that the various orders of a culture (aesthetic, intellectual, behavioral) may be analyzed as *institutions* in terms of their conventions, functions, and signifying processes; (2) that these cultural orders may interact with each other in ways that are accessible to semiotic analysis; and (3) that an individual work of literature may incorporate other cultural orders, using the resources of literary conventions and devices, not as isolated items in a thematic repertoire but as strategies for guiding the reader's production of meaning. Todd traces dance developments in early nineteenth-century Russia, paying particular attention to its multiplicity of forms (balls, ballets, popular dances) and growing professionalization. He then shows how these contextual issues function within the syncretic world of the novel, how they shape the reader's understanding of both the "fictional level" (characters performing the rituals of their culture) and the "fiction-making level" (the author-narrator's artistic maturation).

Caryl Emerson is well known for her studies of Mixail Baxtin and their application to one of Puškin's most vexed works, the drama *Boris Godunov*. Her central thesis in " 'The Queen of Spades' and the Open End" is that Puškin intended to attract precisely "decoders and system-builders" as readers of his tale. She identifies four basic categories of reader-critics in the literature on "The Queen of Spades": those that concentrate on the mechanics and ideology of gambling (Lotman, Rosen); psychological and generational treatments (Murray and Albert Schwartz, Burgin); linguistic and syntactic studies (Vinogradov, Faletti); and numerological analyses (Leighton). Although each of these approaches succeeds in decoding part of the puzzle, the integrating move that will crack the code forever is always missing, leaving the reader in the role of Germann. Emerson's conclusion is that in "The Queen of Spades" Puškin was in fact exploring the *true* spirit of gambling, namely, that there is no system. The reader is provided neither with a code nor with total chaos, but with *fragments* of codes, codes that tantalize but do not quite add up and cannot therefore be "solved."

Few scholars have written more intelligently about the structure of Puškin's poetic and prose language, especially in its paronomastic guises, than Sergej Davydov. "Puškin's Easter Triptych: 'Hermit fathers and immaculate women,' 'Imitation of the Italian,' and 'Secular Power' " is no exception. In the first part of his essay, Davydov argues ingeniously for a

version of the Stone Island cycle of poems written in the last year of Puškin's life that is based on the events of Holy Week. The "forbidden" subject of Puškin's religious beliefs after 1825 is here addressed in a
straightforward manner that, historically at least, has been glaringly absent
from Soviet treatments.[3] Davydov then analyzes the three middle poems of
the cycle as a "triptych" united formally and structurally by the theme
Easter. Projected on the calendar of Easter events, "Hermit fathers," with
its Lenten prayer of Efrem Sirin, brings the reader through the "sad days of
the Great Fast" [i.e., Lent] to Holy Week (Wednesday); "Imitation of the
Italian" takes us to the betrayal of Christ and the suicide of Judas (Thursday and Friday morning); and "Secular Power" reenacts the crucifixion
scene (Friday) and exposes the subsequent betrayal of the divine mystery
by worldly powers.

Simon Karlinsky has written widely on leading figures and epochs of
Russian literature, including celebrated studies of Gogol', Čexov, Marina
Cvetaeva, and Russian drama. His contribution to *Puškin Today* is primarily intertextual and involves the discovery of a little-known, though significant, subtext for *Eugene Onegin* and *Poltava*. Aleksandr Bestužev-
Marlinskij's *Journey to Revel'* was first published in February 1821 in the
journal *Contender* (Sorevnovatel') and then reissued in book form in the
summer of the same year. Although the work was patterned on the then
popular travelogues of Sterne, Dupaty, and Karamzin, it differed from its
forebears by its interlarding of prose passages with verse. Karlinsky demonstrates elegantly that not only did *Journey to Revel'* bear the imprint of
Puškin's work written prior to 1821 (e.g., *Ruslan and Ljudmila*), but, more
intriguing, its early verse portions provided lexical, syntactic, and rhyming
models for some of the poet's mature works, including *Eugene Onegin* and
Poltava.

Puškin studies and psychoanalysis are joined in the provocative work
of Daniel Rancour-Laferriere. Rancour-Laferriere admits that a basic rule
(*Grundregel*) of psychoanalysis is frequently broken in its application to
the study of literature: if the deep meaning of an utterance is to be sought
in a speaker's spontaneous/uncensored/"free" associations, how are a dead
poet and his carefully conceived (and "concealed") artistic discourse to be
"psychoanalyzed"? The answer, according to Rancour-Laferriere, is to re-
sort to a "compensatory tool": awareness of the various phonological, morphological, syntactic, subtextual, narrational, and rhetorical devices that
function, like the clinical knowledge of a patient's patterns of free association, to point the way to unconscious motivation. "The analysand's stories
and those found . . . in literary works of art contain intricate mixtures of
revelation and concealment. . . . [A] structural parallel [therefore exists]
between the material investigated by the clinical analyst and the subject
matter of the worker in applied analysis" (Kohut). Thus, for example,
in *The Bronze Horseman* the acoustic "encoding" of *poln* (full)/*voln*
(waves) rhymes contains the theme of couvade (male childbirth, paternity-

maternity) that is central to both Peter's undertaking (the creation of a city
out of the "waters") and Puškin's undertaking (the creation of a poem
about Peter).

In "The Rejected Image: Puškin's Use of Antenantiosis" William Harkins examines one of the lesser-known rhetorical figures in *Eugene Onegin*.
As opposed to the more common litotes and antithesis, antenantiosis involves an elaborate construction that is at once negated: "the poet's fantasy
is let loose, so to speak, on a chain of inappropriate images or characterizing
epithets." Harkins's rhetorical approach is particularly useful for the insight
it provides into Puškin's characterization in *Eugene Onegin*. Whereas antenantiosis is found relatively infrequently in those passages depicting Onegin
and Lenskij (to present the protagonist and antagonist through a *negative*
trope would be, for Puškin, too obvious), it is strategically foregrounded
when the author's favorite heroine, Tat'jana, enters the narrative. Telling us
that the young Tat'jana is *not* like other provincial maidens in the early
scenes of country life creates a state of suspense at the prospect of this absence; on the other hand, telling us that she lacks something in the climactic
scene describing her salon and her triumph as *grande dame* serves only to
reinforce her moral superiority and heroic stature.

David M. Bethea's "The Role of the *Eques* in Puškin's *Bronze Horseman*" is the last essay in Part One. It is a study of the cultural mythology of
Falconet's equestrian statue and the latter's role in the symbolic structure
of Puškin's poem. Bethea begins with a contextualization of Falconet's
work within the Western European tradition of *Reiterstandbild*. The main
issue here is that the *eques*, at least in the West, was a symbol of imperial
control, of "reining" and "reigning" the "body politic," whereas in Russia
this same symbol was fraught with contradictions and not so easily trans-
plantable. Indeed, implied in Falconet's *concetto*, which was borrowed
from Bernini, another Westerner, was an unconscious parody of one of
"old" Russia's most sacred iconographic and heraldic images—St. George.
In the second half of his essay Bethea adduces several related Puškin texts
to show that an earlier confrontation between "heraldic lion" (emblem of
Jurij Dolgorukij, founder of Moscow) and "democratic ass" (parody of the
new social structure under Peter) is in fact a rehearsal for the tragic duel(s)
between Evgenij and Peter, "sacred" Moscow and "pagan" Petersburg, in
The Bronze Horseman.

PART TWO

One of the perennial problems in dealing with biographies, particularly
Puškin's, is that much of the material is based on memories written down
decades after the event. How accurately did *anyone* come to know Puškin,
who remained chary about revealing himself even to those closest to him?
"Puškin on His African Ancestry: Publications during His Lifetime," by
J. Thomas Shaw, examines the references to the poet's black ancestry in

works that he published, or attempted to publish, during his lifetime: "To Jur'ev," *Eugene Onegin* (verse and note), "To Jazykov," "To Dawe, Esq.," "Chapter IV" and "Assembly" of the uncompleted *The Blackamoor of Peter the Great*, the note on *Poltava*, "My Genealogy," and "Table Talk." It is interesting that during 1828-31 Puškin wrote and published (or republished) *all* the allusions to his great-grandfather (Peter's "blackamoor") that appear in his works, a fact of considerable import in light of the journalist Bulgarin's unprincipled attacks (1829-31) on the literary "aristocrats" in general and on Puškin in particular. Thus, as Shaw concludes, the theme of Puškin's African heritage is not only fascinating in its own right, a vital element of the poet's "exotic" nature, but it is also a revealing index of how that "genealogy" was perceived, depending on who the speaker was (friend vs. foe) and the forum he had chosen (public vs. private).

Walter Vickery's study "Odessa—Watershed Year: Patterns in Puškin's Love Lyrics" is based on a close examination of sixteen Puškin love lyrics written in the seven-year period of 1823-30. These lyrics are all believed to be addressed to (or implicitly to refer to) women in whom Puškin became interested during his stay in Odessa (1823-24). Most scholars have been interested primarily in the identity of the addressees, but Vickery takes a different approach. He divides the poems into four groups, according to their dates of composition: 1823-24 (Odessa), 1824-26 (Mixajlovskoe), 1829 (Caucasus and probably Petersburg), and 1830 (Boldino). It is his contention that, irrespective of the addressees, a pattern in the poet's attitude toward love emerges: 1823-24 (current love), 1824-26 (past love remembered), 1829 (sublimation and release), 1830 (farewell). Two allied points also surface during discussion, namely, that the poet's diverse emotions appear to be "non-viable" from the standpoint of enduring love, and that he repeatedly performs the role of "supplicant" seeking to prolong a relationship which the woman addressee is breaking off. Thus Puškin's feeling that he was not made for love (or rather, that love was not made for him) may be more accurate than heretofore acknowledged.

Leslie O'Bell takes Jurij Lotman's provocative *mot* as the starting point for her essay on *Eugene Onegin*: "*Onegin* was begun by the writer of *Baxčisaraj Fountain*, continued by the creator of *Boris Godunov*, and completed by the author of the *Little Tragedies*." The "magic crystal" metaphor of *Onegin* is for O'Bell more than a figure of speech: the novel is in a real way embedded in the larger and slowly developing crystal of Puškin's other works which accompany and nurture it. The ideal reader, which O'Bell implicitly posits, should take *Onegin* chapter by chapter, retelling it against the counterpoint of the works that form its context. This, then, is the first sustained attempt to bring together all previous studies which relate *Onegin* to one or another of Puškin's individual works with the aim of seeing what latent picture they form and of coordinating them with our best understanding of the inner dynamic of the novel. O'Bell identifies four major thematic or conceptual nodes into which *Onegin* has alternately been fit: the demon, the man of the world, the journey, and the farewell and homecoming. In fact, the four elements continually dovetail as aspects of Puškin's ongoing preoccupation with one character, the man of the world in his demonic hypostasis, compelled to wander but doomed to nostalgia for his lost home. What the "magic crystal" ultimately reveals is that *Onegin* is a long farewell and the slow preparation of a nemesis.

One of Puškin's most problematic works is the subject of Stephanie Sandler's essay "Solitude and Soliloquy in *Boris Godunov*." In an approach which resonates with Caryl Emerson's study of the "open end" in "The Queen of Spades," Sandler is interested in why so many scholars, while explaining away the play's lack of popular success with reference to stage construction, political climate, or audience, have themselves failed to penetrate to its deeper indeterminacy. She submits that *Boris Godunov* keeps readers "at a distance" in ways that are themselves worthy of analysis, and she focuses on those scenes or speeches (especially Boris's soliloquies) where language *obstructs communication*. In the Tsar's first soliloquy, for example, he places rhetorical obstacles before himself that undermine his attempts to speak with emotional authenticity; and in the second he uses images which, if taken literally, identify him with his adversary, the Pretender, and thus further erode his authority. Finally, Sandler considers Puškin's own situation in exile during the time *Boris Godunov* was written (1824–25); in her reading, the discontinuities, isolated utterances, and failed instances of communication in the play are representative of Puškin's "anxieties of audience" during the last stages of his exile.

The precise nature of the poet's political convictions in the post-Decembrist era has always been a controversial issue in Puškin studies, especially when those convictions are read against the background of his earlier "freedom-loving" verse. In "Puškin and Nicholas: The Problem of 'Stanzas,' " George Gutsche investigates a much-analyzed poetic text in light of the September 1826 meeting between Tsar Nicholas I and Puškin, at which time the poet was "forgiven," allowed to return from exile, and "liberated" from official censorship. Puškin indeed had reason to believe that Nicholas would soon be embarking on far-reaching reforms to rival those of Peter the Great, and it is in this spirit of hope that he composed his poem. Throughout his study Gutsche manages a delicate balance between text and context. He points out the ways in which the work has left itself open to diverse interpretation, and he analyzes its competing voices—on the one hand, the hope that Nicholas will achieve the "glory" and "good" associated with Peter's reign (panegyric); on the other, the counsel on how this process of emulation is to come about (didactic). In Gutsche's view, "Stanzas" is above all a *pragmatic* solution to concrete problems facing Puškin at this critical time in his career. Puškin could not remain Puškin if he broke entirely with the liberal ideals of his youth, yet neither could he help those Decembrist friends in exile without finding some still-dignified *modus vivendi* for dealing with the tsar and his government.

Paul Debreczeny, the first American scholar to write a comprehensive book on Puškin's prose, turns his broad knowledge to the question of the poet's reception in "Puškin's Reputation in Nineteenth-Century Russia: A Statistical Approach." The underlying assumption of his study is that it is possible to measure an author's reputation by counting associative references to him in literary periodicals (Rosengren). "Associative references" is used here in the sense of a "mention" of the author in articles or essays not directly devoted to him or to his work. Hence the fact that a critic cites one author in connection with another suggests that the first is viewed as a "standard," that his name is sufficiently in the foreground of cultural consciousness to be called up from memory through certain associations. The combined references of a number of critics can add up to a network of codes shared by at least a segment of society. Debreczeny examines five Russian journals from differing ideological camps and periods spanning the nineteenth and early twentieth centuries: *European Herald*, 1820–28; *Son of the Fatherland*, 1820–29; *Contemporary*, 1862; *Annals of the Fatherland*, 1882; and *Russian Treasures*, 1902. His statistical survey shows that Puškin was much more in the forefront of his own and later (ideologically inimical) periods' cultural consciousness than other Russian "classics" and that by 1902 he had become an integral part of the "personality" of the educated class.

Victor Terras's "Puškin's Prose Fiction in a Historical Context" takes stock of Puškin's legacy in prose from the viewpoint of a distinguished Dostoevskij scholar. It is a deliberately provocative attempt to put the contents of our volume "in perspective" by a member of the "opposition party." Quoting Belinskij, Terras advances the argument that Puškin's prose (i.e., the stories) was mainly a "post horse" en route to the novel form, and that judgment of it by subsequent generations was unavoidably colored by the fact that Puškin was (or was fast becoming) Russia's national poet. Such writers as Dostoevskij, in his reaction to "The Stationmaster" (in *Poor Folk*), and Apollon Grigor'ev, in his thesis of the seminal role of Ivan Petrovič Belkin as prototype of the "meek Russian," were ultimately, according to Terras, responsible for the discovery of Puškin as prose fiction writer. Terras also links Puškin's progress from committed *poet* of the aristocratic Decembrist movement to uncommitted *littérateur* of the 1830s to certain qualities of his prose: its terse and objective narrative style, irony, and "dummy narrator." Perhaps, concludes Terras, Adolf Stender-Petersen was correct to suggest that Puškin's stories were "stages on the road to a great realistic novel": the notion that Russian realist prose "came straight from Puškin" is at least as suspect as that according to which it "came straight out of Gogol's 'Overcoat.' "

In sum, *Puškin Today* is the first systematic attempt by non-native scholars to evaluate and analyze the remarkable variety and compass of a figure who by all accounts is absolutely central to Russian culture, even

"Russianness" itself. It has been written and compiled with several audiences in mind: Puškinist, specialist in Russian literature, non-specialist Western reader. Its primary aim is to demonstrate the current state of American Puškin studies, including the latter's hard-earned "maturity." Its unity lies in its diversity, in the many ways it approaches and rediscovers what, in the Soviet context, has often become a monolithic cultural icon. This seems right and necessary for many reasons, not the least of which is the acknowledged "protean" nature of Puškin himself. To study Puškin's religion or his African heritage without resorting to ideology or to apply a Freudian lens to certain of his problematic works could—and probably will—be seen by our more traditionalist Soviet colleagues as something bordering on *lèse majesté*. Be that as it may, this pluralism and willingness to engage multiple viewpoints and disciplines in order to get closer to a real "Puškin" is precisely what distinguishes our endeavor from the otherwise fine historical and textual studies of Soviet Puškinists. The reader will surely recognize in the pages that follow some of the most prominent names in American Slavistics. Fortunately, however, each voice does not participate as coloratura soloist, but rather performs "in concert" as a member of a chorus whose unique vocalizations gather past, present, and perhaps even a little of the future in *Puškin Today*.

Part I

PUŠKIN: CONTEMPORARY
CRITICAL VIEWS

WILLIAM MILLS TODD III

"The Russian Terpsichore's Soul-Filled Flight"

Dance Themes In *Eugene Onegin*

Belinskij's characterization of *Eugene Onegin: A Novel in Verse* as an "encyclopedia of Russian life" (Belinskij 1953 VII: 503) has more merit than is generally acknowledged. A diligent researcher, using the *Dictionary of Puškin's Language* as an index to the novel, could rapidly locate a variety of illuminating entries on Russian life of the early nineteenth century: "cuisine," "estate management," "feet," "marital fidelity," "novels," "reading habits," "roads," "Russian winter, attitudes toward," and many others. Social and intellectual historians might require some other reference tools and sources, but Puškin's novel and its drafts do not disappoint the student of dance, who finds references to audience responses, ballet theaters (in Petersburg and Moscow), ballet techniques (entrechat), choreographers (Didelot), dancers (Istomina, Lixutina), folk dances (choral forms, the squat-jig, the *Trepak*), roles (cupids, demons, nymphs, serpents), and social dances (cotillon, galop, Mazurka, minuet, waltz). A few aspects of Russian dance do remain untouched, among them the serf ballets that were proving too expensive for their owners by the early nineteenth century, and the work of A. P. Gluškovskij, who was the first to choreograph a ballet based on a Puškin poem (*Ruslan and Ljudmila, or The Overthrow of Černomor, the Evil Wizard*, December 1921). It is, nevertheless, fair to claim that only the novel's references to literature cover more thoroughly the syncretic wealth of early nineteenth-century Russian culture with its autochthonous and foreign elements, its folk, gentry, and aristocratic levels.

Using *Eugene Onegin* in this way as a dance encyclopedia serves a number of purposes: documenting Puškin's acquaintance with and interest in the dance, suggesting the nature of dance connoisseurship in the early nineteenth century, and testing our hypotheses (developed from the study of non-literary sources) about the place of various dance forms in Russian culture of Puškin's time. We can supplement these insights with material from his other works, especially his lyrics, letters, and criticism.

But this plundering of Puškin's novel for discrete references to individual cultural phenomena precludes what may be for the history of Russian culture a no less important reading, and one that would do more justice to Puškin's novel as a work of imaginative literature. Such a reading would follow the dance references as they unfold in the novel, each successive one having the potential to modify a reader's understanding of the ones that preceded it and to encourage a reader to expect more references that will be important elements in plot, characterization, and thematic reverberation. This reading would remain cognizant of the novel's two ontological levels, each with its own "reality" and plot development: a *fictional level* of the text, on which the characters perform the rituals of their culture during the years 1819–25, and a *fiction-making level*, on which the omnipresent author-narrator makes them perform, as he himself undergoes a prolonged course of artistic maturation while writing *Eugene Onegin* (1823–31).[1] Read this way, the dance elements would be related to the world of early nineteenth-century Russia as elements of a fictional narrative which would itself, in its entirety as a literary work, refract various cultural orders, including the dance. The dance elements would be shown to help constitute aspects of the novel, ones involving the development of the characters, the relationship between the characters and their setting, and the very act of writing the novel. The dance elements, then, are not merely material in a repertoire but one of the text's strategies for structuring its reception (Iser 1978: 53–103). For the dance in *Eugene Onegin* represents, first and foremost, an important moment in the cultural process by which the novel's characters, including the author-narrator and the readers he projects, order and make sense of their lives.

The first mention of dance in *Eugene Onegin* illustrates some of these linkages. It occurs almost immediately after the novel opens, during the introduction of the hero:

> Fresh from a blameless state career,
> His father lived on IOU's,
> He used to give three balls a year,
> Until he had no more to lose. [I.3][2]

As an encyclopedia entry this quotation has little to offer, only an indication that dance in its ballroom version was one of the gentry's social rituals. Yet the terseness which makes this passage uninteresting in isolation is of thematic significance within the novel. The balls, given on name days and on festive occasions, appear as conventional, perfunctory pastimes for the gentry, like state service and bankruptcy. The author-narrator underscores this by calling our attention to the regular appearance of the balls; there is nothing sufficiently unusual about them to make them eventful and, therefore, deserving of commentary. The rest of the stanza, devoted to Eugene's education, reinforces the sense of insouciant superficiality that these lines convey.

The following stanza, however, makes a qualitative point, as it begins to describe the hero's involvement in the dance: "He danced Mazurkas well and bowed / Without constraint or affectation" [I.4]. This falls within the bounds of the conventional, but on a level of excellence that matches Eugene's mastery of other social arts, speaking French and arranging amorous triangles. The deftness (*legko*—"lightly"—in the original) with which he dances the strenuous Mazurka and the ease that he communicates with his polished bow bespeak not only ability but also professional training in an era in which the connection between "ballet" and "ball" was not yet merely etymological.

The tentative image of Eugene and his milieu that a reader draws from these initial dance references will be magnified and modified in many ways by ensuing dance references. Eugene's deftness will be implicitly compared with Istomina's virtuosity, his nonchalance with the author-narrator's enthusiasm for the dance, his conventional responses with Didelot's inspiration and "poetry." Each setting will be contrasted with other settings (Petersburg, the countryside, Moscow) by the type and quality of social dancing that characterize it. And references to dance will join with references to other cultural orders as Puškin unfolds the first work of Russian literature to explore the wealth of possibilities for creativity and confusion that were made possible by Russia's relatively recent entry into Western Europe.

For purposes of analysis, I shall examine references to ballet and to ballroom dancing separately, although, as we shall see, these two aspects of the dance were never far apart during the Alexandrine era of Russian culture. In any event, *Eugene Onegin* will not let us forget their proximity. I shall begin the investigation by outlining some contextual issues, biographical and historical; at times it will be appropriate to use the novel as a dance encyclopedia. But I shall focus on the thematic aspects of dance in Puškin's text, since *Eugene Onegin* is the work in which Puškin himself devoted the most attention to the place of the dance in his culture and in his own creative development.

Puškin, like the hero of his verse novel, came of age in Petersburg during the second decade of the nineteenth century. Arriving in the capital in 1811, he began his schooling at the newly founded Imperial Lycée. Onegin's future creator and "friend" was soon caught up in the dance's artistic and social spheres. Before leaving Moscow, he had taken dance lessons and attended the "children's balls" that were arranged by F. A. Iogel', dance instructor at Moscow University (Cjavlovskij 1951 I: 15; Čirejskij 1975: 163, 405, 420). Now, in Petersburg, not only could he continue to learn social dances, but he could share in the city's fashionable enchantment with the ballet. Dance was everywhere. Ballets were mounted for all theatrical performances, even for tragedies. Comic operas regularly included folk dancing. Dancers played roles in dramatic works, tragediennes danced (Krasovskaja 1958: 82–85). The balletomane emperors of Puškin's

time did not limit their choreographic fantasies to the parade ground
(Lotman 1973: 65); in 1836 Nicholas I set aside his designing of uniforms in
order to choreograph military drills for the harem girls in Titus's *Uprising
in the Seraglio* (Krasovskaja 1958: 202).

The lycée trained Puškin and his schoolmates to take an active part in
this continuing dance festival. Dance was one of the social skills that they
would need as they climbed the rungs of the imperial bureaucracy, for
which the lycée was preparing them. A succession of dance teachers provided regular lessons. The septagenarian Huard instructed his pupils in the
gavotte, the minuet, and other stately dances of his time. Several years
(and another Frenchman) later, his place was taken by I. F. Eberhardt, a
notable professional dancer and ballet teacher. Although the official records remain silent on the point, Puškin's family legends report that the
poet received excellent marks for his dancing (Slonimskij 1974: 14).

One does not have to exaggerate either the quantity or the quality of
this training to realize the background that it would have given Puškin for
appreciating the techniques of ballet. Six years of weekly dance classes in
the lycée were not equivalent to the six-year course to which Didelot sub-
jected his dancers, and Puškin's elder contemporary Aleksandr Turgenev
drew a justifiably sharp distinction between recreational and theatrical
dance on the basis of technique and difficulty (Turgenev 1810: 212).[3] Noble
amateur dancers and professionals would no longer mingle in performance
as they had once done at the court of Louis XIV; but the two forms of
dance used similar music and similar basic techniques: *battements*, the five
positions, the minuet with its bows, steps, and graceful arm movements
(Slonimskij 1974: 16–17). Professional dancers served as instructors of ballroom dance. All of this could give an attentive enthusiast the vocabulary to
appreciate the innovations of a choreographer or the technical perfection
of a dancer. The participation of lycée teachers in the Petersburg ballet—
Eberhardt as dancer and Val'vil' (the fencing instructor) as arranger of
combat scenes (Tomaševskij 1956: 267)—would have helped bring the
pupils even closer to the world of theatrical dance.

A young Petersburg gentleman, such as Puškin or his creature Eugene,
would not be drawn to the ballet merely to sit in the audience and appreciate the technique of the dancers on stage. It was fashionable for young men
to cross the audience/backstage/offstage boundaries socially and erotically,
visiting ballerinas backstage or in their quarters, hovering around the
younger dancers, occasionally "protecting" those who had finished their
course of training. Puškin captures this in an unpublished essay on the
theater (1820):

Before the beginning of an opera, tragedy, or ballet a young man strolls among
all ten rows of the stalls, stepping on everyone's feet, conversing with all acquaintances and strangers. "Where have you come from?"—"From Seme-
nova's, from Sosnickaja's, from Kolosova's, from Istomina's." "How lucky

you are!" "She is singing today—she is performing, she is dancing—let's clap for her—let's call her out! How nice she is! What eyes she has! What feet! What talent! . . . " (PSS XI: 9)

The poet, who would later admit to having chased Istomina himself (PSS XIII: 56) and who had earlier made her the leading actress in a puerile epigram (PSS II: 37), draws the obvious conclusion: "can one rely on the opinion of such judges" (PSS XI: 9)? Hardly, when "talent" comes last in the young man's list of attributes.

Advertising the first chapter of *Eugene Onegin* as, in part, a "description of the social life of a young man in Petersburg at the end of 1819" (PSS VI: 638), Puškin included all of these possible relationships to the dance in his description: skilled social dancing (as we have already seen), appreciation of virtuosity, dutiful attendance at the theater. There are, however, two important young men in the novel at this point in the first chapter, Eugene and his creator, and their reactions to the dance are sharply differentiated as Puškin begins to evade a subsequently identified Byronic penchant for labeling a self-portrait with a protagonist's name [I.46].

The lines that propel Eugene toward the theater predict the level of his appreciation of the dance, as his fashionable French timepiece calls him to a new ballet from a fashionable restaurant:

> Their thirst for yet more goblets clamors
> To douse the sizzling cutlet grease,
> But the repeater's jingling hammers
> Bid them to the new ballet piece. [I.17]

Neither here nor in the remaining lines of the stanza does Eugene distinguish himself from the fond admirers of female stage performers that Puškin described in his article. Appreciation is limited to female parts, to isolated bits of virtuosity, to offstage familiarity.

> The stage's arbiter exacting,
> Who to the charming queens of acting
> His fervent, fickle worship brings
> Established freeman of the wings,
> Eugene, of course, must not be missing
> Where everyone without *faux pas*
> Is free to cheer an *entrechat*,
> Jeer Cleopatra, Phèdre, with hissing,
> Call out Moïna (in a word,
> Make sure that he is seen and heard). [I.17]

The initial characterization ("arbiter exacting") receives a satiric tinge from the lines that follow, as Eugene's arrival is seen as merely conventional ("of course"), and as Eugene disappears into the collective "everyone." The reader hardly needs biographical parallels to sense the author-narrator's irony, but it is appropriate in this context to recall that in December 1819 Puškin taunted and nearly fought a duel with an officer whose appreciation of ballet was limited to applauding pirouettes (Slonimskij 1974: 31).

The next stanzas cast Eugene's conventional attitudes in even sharper relief, as the author-narrator covers the same ground, but with enthusiasm and insight. Values that Puškin will reassert throughout the novel join in a stanza on the Russian theater: daring, freedom, emotion, genius, wit [I.18]. Among the artists and playwrights of the Russian stage that Puškin celebrates, there appears but a single foreigner, Didelot, "crowned with glory." Puškin russifies him with the Cyrillic alphabet, as he had not done with the amateurs' ballet terminology in the preceding stanza (*"entrechat"*). Puškin gives the French balletmaster's work an important part in the development of Russia's syncretic culture, but the dandy's superficial appreciation remains unassimilated and stands outside of significant cultural experience.

The author-narrator, like Eugene, has spent his time in the wings [I.18], and he, too, pays his tribute to the leading ladies of the stage:

> My goddesses! Speak, have you vanished?
> Oh, hearken to my plaintive call:
> Are you the same? Have others banished
> And barred, yet not replaced you all?
> Will yet with choral part-song capture,
> With aerial spirit-flight enrapture
> Our Russian-born Terpsichore? [I.19][4]

Yet there are important differences between the author and Eugene. The elegiac tone is occasioned by Puškin's exile from the capital, an event to which he has earlier alluded [I.2]. Eugene will never give another thought to the ballet, once he has left Petersburg, but the dance will remain in the poet's thoughts thousands of miles away. Indeed, as this stanza demonstrates, it will inspire his poetry. The goddesses, Terpsichore, and the enchantment that figure in this stanza—rusty accouterments of neoclassical verse—acquire a fresh luster of significance as poetic recollections of Didelot's mythological and Anacreontic ballets and of Istomina's inspired and innovative technique.[5] Replacing the translator's phrase "with aerial spirit-flight / Our Russian-born Terpsichore" with a more literal rendition of "russkoj Terpsixory dušoj ispolnennyj polet" yields "the Russian Terpsichore's soul-filled flight," where "soul" connotes "feeling," "inspiration," "spirit." This more literal version captures Puškin's tribute to the synthesizing power of poetic imagination as it acts upon a wealth of cultural possibilities. Puškin's lines are couched both in the Russian language and in the international imagery of classical antiquity, and they articulate another creative unity, one of soul (in a broad sense) and technique ("flight"), for the use of mechanical "flights" (*polety*) to swirl the dancers through the air was one of Didelot's innovations. In the poet's perception of the dance there are no isolated techniques, but the recognition of animated, meaningful movement, the equivalent in another artistic medium of the stated goal of the author-narrator's own writing, a "union of magic sounds, thoughts, and feelings" [I.59].

This particular contrast between the author's delight and his hero's indifference continues for two more stanzas. The author's imagination outraces Eugene, who has lingered over his cutlet, to the theater and finds it "boiling" with excitement as the curtain rises. The lines that describe the ballet, among the best known and loved in Russian poetry, were, in fact, the very first lines from the novel to be published (without Puškin's approval or knowledge, in Bulgarin's *Literaturnye listki* [Literary Pages], 1824):

> There stands ashimmer, half ethereal,
> Submissive to the magisterial
> Musician's wand, amid her corps
> Of nymphs, Istomina—the floor
> Touched with one foot, the other shaping
> A slow-drawn circle, then—surprise—
> A sudden leap, and away she flies
> Like down from Aeol's lip escaping,
> Bends and unbends to rapid beat
> And twirling trills her tiny feet. [I.20]

How feeble is the dandy's recognition of an entrechat by comparison with the acuteness of these verses, whose concreteness has inspired a number of attempts to translate them into ballet terminology.[6] Together with this concreteness, one might notice the similarity that Puškin has drawn between his art and Istomina's: he is as obedient to the exigencies of his medium (iambic tetrameter, the *Onegin* stanza) as she is to the string solo accompaniment ("smyčku volšebnomu poslušna"—"Submissive to the magisterial / Musician's wand") and to the grammar of dance. The tempos and vertical movements that she achieves parallel the effects that he uses to capture them in verse, as he varies his own rhythms, syntax, and alliteration to match her performance. Just as Didelot creates a moment of dynamic stasis by raising the curtain on a still ballerina, Puškin creates a pregnant syntactic tension by making the reader wait for his grammatical subject (Istomina) until the end of a four-line period, an effect which Professor Arndt's translation handsomely reproduces. As she begins her movements, the poet calls attention to them by increasing the number of stressed syllables well beyond his usual density. No fewer than four of these lines carry four stressed syllables; only one has as few as two.[7] A series of striking consonantal alliterations and word repetitions mirror the precision and rhythm of her dancing: "stoit Istomina"; "i vdrug pryžok, i vdrug letit, / Letit kak legkij pux ot ust Eola"; "to stan sov'et, to razov'et, / I bystroj nožkoi nožku b'et."

Istomina's magic unites the entire theater, save Eugene, in delight. He finally arrives at the theater, having missed this scene, and enters, like the young man in Puškin's article, by stepping on the feet of the people in the stalls. The stanza that follows completes the contrast between hero and creator by circling back to the situation of two stanzas before. There the author-narrator imagined himself at a future time elegiacally lamenting replaced ballerinas, casting a disenchanted lorgnette about the theater, and yawning as he would remember the past [I.19]. Eugene, who had fallen behind the author in reaching the theater, now surges ahead in disenchantment:

> Applause all round. Onegin enters,
> And threads his way from toe to toe.
> His double spyglass [lorgnette] swoops and centers
> On box-seat belles he does not know.
> All tiers his scrutiny embraces,
> He saw it all: the gowns and faces
> Seemed clearly to offend his sight;
> He traded bows on left and right
> With gentlemen, at length conceded
> An absent gaze at the ballet.
> Then with a yawn he turned away.
> And spoke: "In all things change is needed;
> On me Ballets have lost their hold;
> Didelot himself now leaves me cold." [I.21]

Here the poet consigns the roving lorgnette, the yawn, and the boredom to his hero. Onegin comes to experience what the poet had imagined, but he does so without first knowing the sense of creative identification with the ballet that the author has come to celebrate. The two young men are separated here not by a difference of taste, but by life experience and by the poet's ability to participate to the fullest in their common culture. The sullen rake's call for "change" (*smena*) reminds the reader of the poet's graceful play on words, "smeniv, ne zamenili vas" ("barred, yet not replaced you all") to Eugene's disadvantage.

The poet concludes this important moment in the characterization of himself and his hero with a footnote that rebukes Eugene for his comment on Didelot: "a trait of chilled sentiment worthy of *Childe Harold*. Mr. Didelot's ballets are filled with liveliness of inspiration and unusual charm. One of our Romantic writers found much more poetry in them than in all of French literature" (PSS VI: 191). A draft version of this footnote identified the "Romantic writer" as Puškin himself (PSS VI: 529). The note was published together with the separate first edition of the novel's opening chapter in 1825, when the balletmaster was beginning to experience some of the difficulties that would drive him from the stage; Puškin retained it in the first complete edition of the novel (1833), which appeared after Didelot had "retired." Thus the footnote stands not merely as a rebuke to the fashionably Byronic Eugene, who would fail in all attempts at poetry [I.7, I.43, VIII.38], but as an aesthetic manifesto, and as a bold expression of gratitude to Didelot for occasioning the ballet stanzas, with their liveliness and their significance that transcends mere virtuosity.

In these stanzas, as we have seen, Eugene alone will not join in appreciating the dance; the boxes, orchestra, stalls, and gallery with their different economic and social groups have participated in the celebration of Didelot, Istomina, and the new ballet [I.20–21]. Now the author-narrator directs the reader's attention from Eugene to a new contrast:

> While yet the cupids, devils, monkeys
> Behind the footlights prance and swoop;
> While yet the worn-out grooms and flunkies
> Sleep on their furs around the stoop. . . . [I.22]

With a deftness that recalls Pope's "Rape of the Lock," the author-narrator locates the fairy-tale world of the unidentified Didelot ballet in a world of social and economic inequality. The footmen, resting on their masters' robes, and the coachmen, clapping their hands to keep warm, belong to the order which made it possible for Eugene to be inside, yawning. As the novel continues, groups that are not party to the cultural advantages of Petersburg and of the urban nobility will be assigned a relationship to the dance, but ballet themes will virtually disappear from *Eugene Onegin* as its author turns to more sober styles and motifs. Puškin dropped a subsequent reference to Istomina from the fifth chapter (PSS VI: 609, 650). Although he sent his provincial heroine, Tat'jana, to a Moscow ballet in Chapter VII, he specified neither the choreographer, nor the dancers, nor the ballet, nor its roles. Theatrical dance remains outside Tat'jana's range of cultural experience, and it becomes relegated to the interests of the matured poet's youth:

> But where Melpomene's fine raving
> Reverberates both long and loud,
> Where her bedizened drapes are waving
> Before a less-than-frenzied crowd,
> Where dear Thalia's gentle napping
> Deaf to her champions' friendly clapping,
> Where youth reserves exclusive fee
> Of worship to Terpsichore
> (As was the case, too, when we knew her,
> When you and I were youngsters yet). . . . [VII.50]

The interest and the memories remain, but the balletmaster no longer helps to choreograph the poet's lines.

Dance, now banished from the novel's theatrical stages, continues to appear in the ballroom, and in no less broad a context of social conven-

tion, sensual desire, and aesthetic creativity. For a ball was no less a manifestation of Russia's cultural syncretism than a ballet mounted by a French
balletmaster for Russian dancers on themes from classical antiquity. Peter
the Great had introduced balls (then called "assemblies") to Russia a century before the opening of Eugene Onegin, as part of his campaign to
create a Western European civilization for Orthodox Muscovy, and he
began to establish the necessary conventions for a nobility that had there-
tofore sequestered its women and looked askance at Russia's own rich
tradition of folk dancing. In a short time the balls became strictly organized manifestations of gentry life, with sequences of dance forms, types of
conversation, and set activities (Lotman 1983: 79–89).

Among the sources of Puškin's knowledge about these developments
was an 1823 essay, "On the First Balls in Russia," by Aleksandr Kornilovič.
The essay outlines the evolution of balls during the eighteenth century, but
most important for our purposes is the persistent vision of ritualistic conjunction that it conveys. Social distinctions, economic status, civil service
ranks, even sex differences disappear or transform themselves as the eighteenth-century balls join their participants in harmonious community.
Commoners dance with the royal family, forgetting their rank; Russians
dance with captive French officers and are trained for the dance by Swedish ones; the empresses dance both the minuet and Russian folk dances;
men disguise themselves as women, and vice versa (Kornilovič 1960:
201–204).[8] Competitive games—first chess and draughts, later cards—
would be included in the evening's festivities, but the winners and losers
that these produced did not (at least in Kornilovič's idealization) destroy
the sense of common pleasure.

By Puškin's time, satires and novels would come to challenge this vision of ritual harmony. Griboedov's Woe from Wit (1822–24), which Puškin quotes in Eugene Onegin, achieves its climax in a ball scene that brings
incompatibility into the open, ruins reputations, exposes an imposter, and
leaves the hero calling for his carriage. In Baratynskij's narrative poem The
Ball (1828), the heroine commits suicide rather than attend a ball at which
her former lover will be present. Lermontov's A Hero of Our Time (1840)
transforms the ball from an event of communal concord into one of vicious competition; the first ball scene of Gogol"s Dead Souls (1842) brings
the society of that novel properly together, but the final ball witnesses an
explosion that breaks nearly all ties—friendship, infatuation, business acquaintance, even the connection between signifier and signified. Other examples abound. In all of these cases, the ideal civilizing function of balls
serves as the background against which a reader would perceive the actual
disasters of individual heartache or social fragmentation.

Puškin's writings, including Eugene Onegin, capture both possibilities,
harmonious and disjunctive, and balls figure in a number of his texts. For
every youthful poem that celebrates a ball, there is a letter that describes
his boredom at these gatherings and shows the poet dozing off, or eating

ice cream and complaining about his lowly court rank that required him to attend. Where literary convention conveys personal experience and where it does not in his epistolary treatment of balls is not easy to determine. Memoirs differ on the quality of his dancing and on the extent of his enthusiasm for balls. In any event, his family and school trained him to dance and to analyze the appropriate dances, as we have seen. His fiery temperament and remarkable eye for physical details prepared him both to participate in and to observe creatively these social functions that combined dancing, gaming, dining, and attendant pursuits—seduction, writing malicious epigrams, dueling. One thing is clear: in none of his works are the social dances and balls so thoroughly detailed as in *Eugene Onegin*. In these passages, as in the ballet stanzas, the dance plays an important part in characterization, plot, and cultural contrast.

In the first chapter the transition from ballet to ball is provided by Eugene, who rushes from the one to the other, paying more attention to his toilet than he had to the new Didelot ballet. A series of images join ball and ballet—Eugene arrives late at each; the "crowd" of nymphs surrounding Istomina is replaced by a "crowd" of dancers; Istomina's deft feet yield to the feet on the ballroom floor that set off a famous pedal digression of five stanzas [I.30–34].

Unlike the Istomina passage, with its opening of pregnant motionlessness [I.20], distinguishing the disorderly audience from the deliberate artists on stage, the ball scene is all motion, as forms of the verb "to fly" appear three times in the initial stanza:

> Now he has passed the liveried sentry,
> Skipped up [*vzletel*] by every other stair
> And, pausing at the marbled entry
> To realign a straying hair,
> Has entered. The great hall is swarming,
> The band benumbed by its own storming,
> In hum and hubbub, tightly pent,
> The crowd's on the Mazurka bent,
> Spurs ring, sparks glint [*letajut*] from guardsmen's shoulders,
> Belles' shapely feet and ankles sleek
> Whirl by [*letajut*], and in their passing wreak
> Much flaming havoc on beholders,
> And fiddle music skirls and drowns
> Sharp gibes of wives in modish gowns. [I.28]

The insistence on flying is even clearer in the original, where the verb appears anaphorically at the beginning of the tenth and twelfth lines. Sound, too, in this stanza is more disorderly than in the ballet scene, as the "magic wand" of the theater orchestra's violinist yields to storming, hum, hubbub, ringing spurs, and the skirling fiddle.[9]

Inspired by this chaos of sounds and movement, the poet abandons his hero's plot line and is swept away in an exhaustive, exhilarating series of digressions that are as appropriate for the ball scene as was the poet's disciplined, precise account of Istomina's dancing for the ballet stanzas: "When ardent dreams and dissipations / Were with me still, I worshipped balls" [I.29]. The "madness" of this worship ("Ja byl ot balov bez uma") has its erotic, amorous implications, and so Puškin adds, with mock indignation, moral chaos to the general uproar, before he resumes his obsession with feet—through reminiscences that encompass seasons, climates, and landscapes until, at last holding a lady's stirrup, he feels a dainty foot in his hands and his "imagination boils" [I.34].

The erotic and the poetic achieve this climax simultaneously, but Puškin has not let the reader forget—amidst this chaos of sounds, memories, and desires—that achieving it has been a culturally mediated process. He emphasizes this in a passage that focuses on the conventionality of poetry, the dance, and desire itself:

> The breast of Dian, I adore it,
> And Flora's cheek to me is sweet!
> And yet I would not barter for it
> Terpsichore's enchanting feet.
> For they, the captive gaze ensnaring
> With pledge of bliss beyond comparing,
> Inveigle with their token charm
> Desires' unbridled, wanton swarm. [I.33][10]

The magic and enchantment of the ballet passage [I.17, I.18, I.20], generally replaced by chaotic "madness" in this ball scene [I.29, I.31], return here, as Puškin underscores the aesthetic ("Terpsichore") and conventionally significant ("token"—*uslovnyj*) aspects of the dance. The conventional allusions to classical mythology are each paired with an object of erotic fascination (Diana's breast, etc.) to reinforce this union of culture and desire, which is further strengthened by the association of the ballet role of Flora (and possibly of Diana) with Istomina, "the Russian Terpsichore."[11]

Turning to the first stanza of the ball passage [I.28] quoted above, one can see that the ball is, in fact, fulfilling its ritual function of "putting at the service of the social order the very forces of disorder that inhere in man's mammalian constitution" (Turner 1977: 93). The energies and desires of the throng are channeled into a polite social form, the ball, which permits these energies to be harmlessly dissipated in hours of exhausting physical activity. Jealous gibes and whispers that might have sown discord are drowned by the fiddle music. Even Eugene, who has been unable to join in the public enthusiasm for the ballet, disappears totally into the festivities. After the poet sends him running into the ball, we are not permitted another view of him until he emerges nearly eight hours later, "worn out by the ballroom's clamor" [I.36]. One might infer that there has been nothing eventful in his behavior, as there had been at the ballet.

Eugene will soon forsake this conventional attraction to the Petersburg balls, however. His fashionable spleen comes to preclude it. The author-narrator, unwilling to share Eugene's disenchantment with the ballet, now steps onto the fictional level of the novel to befriend his hero and to join him in shutting his ears to "society's clamor" (*sveta šum* [I.37]).[12] Yet the madness and noise of balls and social dancing will not disappear from the remaining seven chapters as will the enchantment and magic sounds of the ballet. For the poet and his characters will encounter them as indelible expressions of each cultural setting in the novel, be it urban or rural, gentry or folk. Some mention of these forms of dancing will appear in each of the remaining chapters—if only in metaphor or memory—as Puškin continues to examine the dance for its conjunctive and aesthetic functions.[13]

The central chapters of the novel find the exiled poet and his hero in the countryside. Here the syncretic complexity of Russian culture acquires a new dimension, one of folk tradition. The rural gentry, poised between the culture of its serfs and that of the Westernized urban aristocracy, had rich opportunities for drawing on each, and Puškin makes this an essential part of the gentry's life experience. The novel's heroine and her family will order and comprehend their lives according to cultural patterns of both folk and Western European origin.

The folk's choral dance (*xorovod*) dominates the dance theme in these early chapters, to the extent that the poet, viewing a sunrise through his heroine's eyes, will choreograph the stars in this roundelay form [II.28]. In the lyrics of his youth, Puškin had used the term *xorovod* to signify any choral dance—Greek, Circassian, imaginary. Here, for the first time in Puškin's work, the term takes on Russian folk specificity in contrast to other dance forms in the novel. The *xorovod* becomes one of the many aspects of age-old Russian culture that the Larins, members of the gentry, preserve:

> Their peaceful life was firmly grounded
> In the dear ways of yesteryear,
> And Russian *bliny* fair abounded
> When the fat Shrovetide spread its cheer.
> Two weeks a year they gave to fasting,
> Were fond of games and fortune-casting,
> Of roundelay [*xorovod*] and carrousel. . . . [II.35]

Had Puškin given the Larins more wealth, or had he set the novel a few decades earlier, he might have given them a troupe of well-rehearsed serf dancers to perform the *xorovod* in highly polished fashion and in lavish costumes.[14] Given the family's more modest circumstances and the fall from fashion of such troupes, it is most likely that on the Larin estate the *xorovod* was a dance for serfs that the gentry took pleasure in observing, but which preserved its festive, recreational nature. So it will seem when

Tat'jana takes an evening stroll in spring 1821 [VII.15] as the choral groups are breaking up for the evening.

A serf's life was not all dancing, of course, and the peasants obviously served less to entertain than to feed the gentry. The most detailed and poignant reference to the *xorovod* in *Eugene Onegin* occurs in this context. The *xorovod* could take many forms; it could perform entire dramatic scenes and pantomimes to the accompaniment of singing. Typical themes might include field work, a girl's desire to enjoy herself with a young man, or an attempt by a young man (dressed as a hare) to break out of the circle (Krasovskaja 1958: 9–10, 12). But at the end of Chapter III the dance component is taken out of the serf-girls' *xorovod*, and they are forced to sing the song, which Puškin adapted from folk motifs, while they pick berries, so that they will not be able to consume the fruit. The conditions of their work do not restrain the frolic, charm, and independence of their song, but their crafty masters' love of the *xorovod* [II.35] has led them to find not only aesthetic but also material uses for it, and, in so doing, to constrict its movement.[15]

The provincial gentry find practical uses for their own dances as well, matchmaking foremost among them. The longest ball scene of the novel is occasioned by Tat'jana's name day, and the guest list includes eligible suitors for this marriageable young lady. Her female relatives (not knowing that Eugene has already rejected Tat'jana's love) make certain that he is invited [IV.49]. Puškin takes every opportunity to explore the event as art and ritual. He assembles all of the novel's major characters (except himself) for it, and he uses it to separate the characters irrevocably from each other through the heartache, duel, and death that proceed directly from it. Ol'ga, Tat'jana's sister, will leave her family; Tat'jana will be parted from Eugene; Ol'ga's engagement to Lenskij will never lead to marriage; Eugene will kill Lenskij in a duel.

The scene begins as the guests assemble for the festival, and Puškin lists with relish the unlikely material that will be harmoniously united in feasting and the dance, giving each guest a comic surname. Only two participants fail to lose themselves in the general celebration: Tat'jana, painfully embarrassed by Eugene's presence; and Eugene, angry at having been tricked into attending such a large, noisy gathering. Their emotions remain unnoticed, however, as food, drink, and a poem of clumsy scansion occupy the throng. The author-narrator stresses the harmony of the evening by presenting the obligatory card games not as disjunctive competitions, but as a means of circulating the guests, who change partners before each rubber, in orderly fashion [V.36].

As the guests leave their teacups to begin the dancing, the author-narrator digresses from the description of it momentarily and transfers our attention to the second plot level of the novel, that of his poetic maturation. Recalling his pedal digression from the Petersburg ball in Chapter I, Puškin promises to become more sensible and correct by purging this fifth chapter of such digressions [V.50]. His ironic promise—he must digress to make it—has the effect of ensuring that the reader will perceive these ball scenes *thematically*, comparing one with the other, not viewing them in isolation, without relationship to each other. Puškin will insist on such a contrastive thematic reading even more emphatically two stanzas later when he compares the old-fashioned rural Mazurka with the modish urban variation.

This explicit ordering of our ideations invites the reader to note similarities and differences between the two dance scenes. First of all, the poet takes greater interest here in describing the dances themselves. His account begins with a waltz:

> As unreflecting and unfading
> As life's young pulse that never halts,
> Pair after wheeling pair parading,
> Revolved the pulsing, stirring waltz. [V.41]

The first line contains two adjectives and a conjunction in the original, "odnoobraznyj i bezumnyj" (lit. "monotonous and mad"). The second of these adjectives recalls the poet's relationship to the Petersburg balls. Here "madness" seems to bear some of the erotic overtones that it did in the earlier passage, especially since it is the Petersburg dandy, Eugene, whom we see sweeping Ol'ga away in the waltz. But Puškin also stresses the persistent rhythm of the waltz with the heavily stressed lines that follow (three stresses, four, and three, respectively). The heaviness of these stresses, the pounding alliterations, and the twofold word repetitions (pair-pair, pulse-pulsing) would seem inappropriate to a modern reader, used to the gliding three-step waltz. But, as Jurij Slonimskij has noted, Puškin is re-creating (and quite adequately) with the sound patterns of his verse a more swiftly revolving *valse deux temps* (Slonimskij 1974: 11).[16]

The country Mazurka yields nothing in vigor to this waltz:

> Now the Mazurka . . . Where it pounded
> Its thunderous beat in former days,
> The ballroom end to end resounded
> As stamping heels shook the parquets
> And set the startled windows ringing;
> Now, lady-like, demurely swinging,
> On lacquered boards we slide and curve,
> And other country towns preserve
> The pristine glories duly polished:
> High heels, mustachios, saltos bold
> Grace the Mazurka as of old
> Where they have never been abolished
> by Fashion's tyranny, the prime
> Disease of Russia in our time. [V.42]

Here is none of the deftness of the Petersburg Mazurka that Eugene had
learned [I.3]. The poet momentarily becomes a dance historian to record
the evolution of this proud, vigorous dance from its rural, folk origins to its
refined, social variation (which could, nevertheless, still set spurs clanging
and dainty feet flying in Chapter I, as we have seen). The edition of Chapter V that Puškin published separately in 1828 continued the Mazurka for
another stanza, in which he described some of the solo improvisations that
this dance licenses (PSS VI: 610).

Perhaps Puškin omitted this second Mazurka stanza from complete
editions of the novel in order not to distract the reader's attention unduly
from his plot, which at this point in the novel is producing another important contrast with the ball scene in the first chapter. There spitefulness in
jealous whispers and incipient seductions figured in the ball scene, but the
whirl of the ball could drown out the whispers and exhaust the amorous
play to no ill effect, except occasional boredom. But the rural festival in
Chapter V features scheming that goes beyond the innocent play of matchmaking.

The Larins' ball seems to fulfill its ritual harmonizing function success-
fully, especially when Tat'jana overcomes her emotion and performs as all
expect her to. But the text complicates this situation by introducing an
element of competitiveness into the event. Eugene, irritated that he has
been tricked into attending a large function, seeks to slake his anger by
declining an opportunity to dance with Tat'jana, dancing instead exclusively with Ol'ga and striking up a casual flirtation with her, to the amaze-
ment of all present [V.41]. In this way he frustrates the Larins' expectations
that he will court Tat'jana, and he enrages Lenskij by competing for the
attention of his frivolous fiancée. Lenskij's casually conveyed invitation is
repaid with casual teasing by Eugene that comes to bore both him and
Ol'ga, but when neither Lenskij nor Ol'ga can deal with this maneuver, the
tragic violence of a duel provides the dénouement. Competitive card
games can be assimilated into the conjunctive process of a ball, but not an
unwanted form of amorous play, and the country ball, for all the vigor of
its dances, ultimately proves too inflexible to serve its ritual purpose.

The failure of this ball to produce a fiancé for Tat'jana forces her
family to try its luck on the Moscow marriage mart—a round of dinners,
theater visits, and balls, all functions of the "hollow *monde*" [VII.48].
These scenes are colored by Tat'jana's heartache and, on his level of the
plot, by the poet's growing inclination toward "austere prose" [VI.43]. The
ball that Tat'jana attends at the Russian Assembly of the Nobility, like the
ballet to which she is taken, is granted a certain vitality by the poet, but
little detail. As befits this city in which the rural gentry and the aristocracy
could meet more readily than in Petersburg, the ball combines features of
the novel's earlier ball scenes: "Where hubbub, heat, the music's gale / The
whirling couples' swish and swagger / The senses all at once assail"
[VII.51]. Here the whirling couples recall the description of the country

waltz [V.41]; the Russian uses identical vocabulary—*vixor'* ("whirlwind") and *mel'kat'* ("to flash"). The "thundering" hussars that "fly" out of the stanza conjure up images that invite the reader to remember the Petersburg ball of Chapter I: "Here flock hussars on leave, invading / This one-night stage, to bluster on [*progremet'*], / To glitter, conquer, and be gone [*vletet'*]" [VII.51]. The list of dances is similar to those of the previous balls, as we would expect from the conventionality of this social form: galop, mazurka, waltz [VII.53]. But Puškin shows the passage of time between the earlier scenes and this by introducing a new dance, the galop, into this Moscow scene. A lively round dance in two-in-a-measure time, it was rapidly gaining popularity all over Europe, but could not have been expected to have reached the provinces or the Petersburg of Chapter I.

Tat'jana's inviolable inner world commands the poet's attention throughout these stanzas, and he does not set her to dancing in this world, whose agitation she hates [VII.53]. Although her mind is far away from the dancing, the Moscow ball does its conjunctive work. Tat'jana is finally noticed by a stout general [VII.53], who will (we are invited to assume) reappear as her husband in the last chapter of the novel [VIII.14]. The "fate" [VIII.47] that has found her is the institution of marriage, in which balls played a significant role.

No dancing lightens the final chapter of the novel with flashing feet, thundering heels, or soul-filled flights. This is no casual oversight on the part of the author-narrator; he characterizes the dominant social gathering here as a "rout" and then defines the word in a footnote, lest the reader miss his point: "an evening assembly without dances" (PSS VI: 195). The author and his characters have matured and grown sober, relegating the whirlwind of the dance to memories of youth [VIII.3]. The role of bringing the members of society into harmonious relationship with each other is no longer played by balls, and another conventional form fulfills this function, the salon. As Puškin presents these two forms in his novel, a salon differs significantly from a ball in assigning its hostess a more responsible, creative role. Following conventional patterns of supper, cards, and dancing, the balls in the novel have more or less organized themselves.[17] Who hosted the balls in the first and seventh chapters? The poet does not tell us. What role did Tat'jana's mother play in the ball in Chapter V? None. But a salon or a rout depends more upon the personal qualities of the person who organizes it. The rout that Puškin's muse admires at the beginning of the final chapter has a hostess [VIII.6, VIII.14]; Tat'jana transcends her dislike of society and forms a salon that is aesthetically pleasing and, in its civility, morally effective [VIII.23]. In imposing this aesthetic order upon the unpromising materials that society offers her, she has come to play the most creative role available to a gentlewoman of her time. It is, therefore, appropriate that Puškin approaches her with the same title of adoration, "goddess" [VIII.27], that he had previously reserved for Istomina and her fellow stage performers [I.19]. Where their feats had inspired his youthful verse, Tat'jana's social-cultural creativity now serves as an "ideal" for the novelist.

Despite the gradual disappearance of dance themes from *Eugene Onegin*, one may still conclude that the dance has fulfilled important functions in nearly every aspect of Puškin's novel. Dance occasions bring the characters together and drive them apart. The dances of each setting in the novel, and the uses to which these dances are put, help the reader to understand distinctions that Puškin draws between the various spheres of Russian culture. Similarly, ways in which the characters (including the author-narrator) join in the dancing help us to understand them and to draw distinctions between them; for "character" in Puškin's novel is manifestly a relationship to cultural possibilities, a manner of choosing between them, and not an inner essence that the text pretends to define.

The dance itself can embody many of the novel's highest values—creativity, beauty, vitality, and poetry (the imaginative and significant fusion of meaning and technique). Although dance is not a verbal art form, it can convey meaning in *Eugene Onegin* because, like literature or social behavior, it has a place in culture's network of conventional signifying processes. Depending on their own and their audience's skill, knowledge, and ideation, the characters express soul, emotion, desire, and liveliness of imagination through the language of dance. Indeed, the ballet, the most demanding and imaginative dance form in *Eugene Onegin*, is granted a magic power to enchant its audience. It certainly has the power, at the opening of the novel, to inspire the poet's search for an artistic union of "magic sounds, feelings, and thoughts."

Nevertheless, Puškin's verse novel remains an account of the poet's maturation, as he moves from the fairy-tale world of *Ruslan and Ljudmila* [I.2] to "austere prose" [VI.43] and the novel, coming to see life itself as a novel in the last stanza of *Eugene Onegin* [VIII.51]. Thus the poet's attention turns from an enchanting ballerina and her "poetic" balletmaster to a young woman, Tat'jana, whose life and thought would be shaped by her reading of novels. The charming feet of the ballerina or ballroom dancer yield the parquet to the resounding spurs of Tat'jana's husband, tolling an end to sentimental dreams and proclaiming a novelistic world of social relationships, family, and irreversible decisions. To be consistent with the traditions of the novel as a genre, *Eugene Onegin* had to banish all forms of magic and enchantment, including the ballet.

And banish them it did. But the "retirement" of Didelot and Puškin's "goddesses" during these very same years gave the dance-bereft eighth chapter of the novel a historical analogue. The absence of dance from its final chapter makes *Eugene Onegin* less of a straightforward dance encyclopedia, perhaps, but no less significant an evocation of dance developments in Russian culture during the 1820s.[18]

CARYL EMERSON

"The Queen of Spades" and
the Open End

In Puškin, however, the idea of
fate, fate acting with the speed of light-
ning, is deprived of any of the strictness
and purity of religious doctrine. Chance
is that point which casts the idea [of
fate] in a position of faceless and vacil-
lating indeterminateness, an indeterminateness which nevertheless retains the
right to pass judgment over us. . . .
Chance chops fate off at the knee and
constructs it on a new scientific basis.
Chance is a concession to black magic
on the part of precision mechanics,
which had discovered in the tiresome
hustle and bustle of atoms the origin of
things, and right under the nose of the
distraught church had craftily managed
to explain the world order as disorder.
. . .
    Homelessness, orphanhood, loss of
an aim and a purpose—all the same,
blind chance, elevated to a law, suited
Puškin. In that idea the enlightened
century preserved untouched, for the
nonce, a taste of that mystery and trick-
ery dear to the poet's heart. In it there
was something of the card games that
Puškin loved. Chance meant freedom—
the freedom of fate transfigured by
some lapse of logic into arbitrary li-
cense, and the freedom of human inse-
curity, torn to shreds like a drunkard. It
was an emptiness fraught with catastro-
phes, holding out promise of adventure,
teaching one to live by faking it, by taking risks. . . . With the ascension of
freedom, everything became possible.
    —Abram Terc, *Progulki s Puškinym*
(Collins-London: Overseas Publications Interchange, 1975), 37–39.

Of the many controversies surrounding Puškin's "Pikovaja dama" (The Queen of Spades), one of the most persistent has centered on its almost seamless fusion of the fantastic with the realistic.¹ On the one hand, the tale is saturated with unexplained—indeed, inexplicable—coincidence and supernatural events, very much in the Gothic (and later the Gogolian) tradition. On the other hand, the work is remarkably precise in historical and topographical detail, with a sober, reportorial narrator who documents by the day, hour, and minute the uncanny and the mundane with apparently equal confidence. As one student of the tale has remarked, this neutral narrator "does not moralize, does not issue warnings, does not terrify, but permits the readers themselves to assess characters and events" (Poljakova 1974: 385).

Given the uncertain genre of the tale, this burden on readers to "assess characters and events" through their own efforts has presented a challenge. "The Queen of Spades" both invites logical decoding and appears to frustrate it. In this essay I will suggest that such a dual—and ultimately contradictory—invitation to the reader constitutes a deliberate strategy on Puškin's part, Puškin's extension, as it were, of his own profound and endlessly inventive categories of parody into a realm we would today call reader-reception aesthetics.

First, a few words on the sorts of parody one finds in Puškin. On the most elementary and playful level there is outright blasphemy, as in *Gavriiliada*. And then there are Puškin's famous inversions of moral scenarios or literary cliché, such as the fate of the Prodigal Son theme in "Stancionnyj smotritel'" (The Stationmaster) or the mockery of feuding families and civilizing the natives in "Baryšnja-krest'janka" (Mistress into Maid). But one of Puškin's most sophisticated sorts of parody can be found, it seems, at a level *above* that of specific theme or plot. Here I draw on Gary Saul Morson's discussion of parody in his book *The Boundaries of Genre*: "Parodies are usually described and identified as being of (or 'after') a particular author or work, but the parodist's principal target may, in fact, be a particular *audience* or *class of readers*" (Morson 1981: 113). With *Shamela* as his case in point, Morson suggests that Fielding, like many parodists, "implies that readers must not be too ready to accept the invitations authors extend, and that reading is an action which, like any action, can be performed responsibly or irresponsibly" (1981: 114).

Precisely this target—readers who are "too ready to accept the invitations authors extend"—seems to me a defining characteristic of this final category of parody of Puškin. What is parodied is the reader's search for a system or a key, and in this search, the more numerous the partial hints and tantalizing fragments provided by the author, the more challenging and irresistible the search becomes. We glimpse the method in *Evgenij Onegin* (Eugene Onegin). In that novel the formal symmetry governing the action and fates of the heroes encourages us, along with Tat'jana, to seek a "key" to Onegin's personality. When Tat'jana asks, alone in Onegin's library (Book Seven, XXIV), "ne parodija li on?" (Is he not a parody?), that parody could have several targets. Not the least of these targets is the reader or analyst of the novel, who persists in the attempt to make all of Onegin's disparate segments add up to a psychologically satisfying explanation.[2]

The strategy is even more boldly present in *Boris Godunov*. There the presence of a real-life, documented historical event beneath the dramatic plot greatly increases the possibility and range of parody. Puškin takes Karamzin's well-known, providential, over-determined story and reworks it so that only the open-ended, indifferent characters win—characters with infinitely malleable biographies, like the Pretender. The seemingly disjointed structure of the play, in which all the major action is offstage, encourages the audience to seek a *hidden* unity. But precisely that search can be seen as part of the target of the parody. The absence of unity in Puškin's historical drama is more than a "Shakespeareanism." It can be read as a comment on the nature of history itself—in which, we know, Puškin always respected the element of *chance*, "that powerful, instantaneous tool of providence."[3]

Indeed, as Puškin surely divined, the very idea of historical unity distorts. Contemplating a historical event, later generations do not need to impose a unity on it. They already know how the story will end. Thus the "unity" that we perceive in any account of the past has no necessary connection with logic, system, or causality; it simply reflects the outrageous privilege of historical perspective. One possible way of exposing that false unity would be to confront the audience of historical drama with an event on stage as it might have looked in its own time and on its own chaotic, present-tense terms to its participants. With canonized historical plots such as that of Boris Godunov, this sense of radical openness is exceedingly difficult to transmit. Part of what Puškin parodies in *Boris Godunov*, I suggest, is audience gullibility: historical themes, when clothed in a present-tense form like drama, can never be honest to the event. That event will always appear chaotic and open-ended to those living it, and somehow inevitable and predetermined to those re-creating it or witnessing it later in narrative art.

If *Boris Godunov* has provoked its share of searches for hidden unity and keys to its meaning, those searches are meager and amateurish fare when compared to the studies devoted to the decoding of "The Queen of Spades." My purpose here is not to survey the extremely rich and clever secondary literature in any detail, but merely to offer some general categories of classification.

To state first the obvious: The spare, efficient, dense, and objectively cold prose in this tale encourages the reader to assume that someone is in control. Meaning appears to be distributed by some higher power, or at least by a higher narrative perspective. The critical search for this unified meaning seems to fall into four basic categories or strategies. Each strategy erects a symbolic system in the text that relates to some narrative or visual patterns—in behavior, plot, language, or number; these patterns are then interpreted as tying together all the details of the story.

There are, first, the socio-literary studies that focus on the mechanics and ideology behind gambling in Puškin's era. Exemplary here might be Jurij Lotman's discussion of card games and gambling in nineteenth-century Russia (Lotman 1975) and Nathan Rosen's classic essay on the meaning of the three magic cards (Rosen 1975). As Lotman points out, the concept of *chance* (and the challenge presented by games of chance) involves both a negative and a positive aspect: what is rational collapses into the chaotic and the anomalous, but at the same time what is dead becomes animate, mobile, changeable. Gambling is a metaphor for multiple, *co-existing* codes in a society and in a text. The impulse to coordinate, rank, and crack these codes has been the motivation behind much of the criticism on "The Queen of Spades."

A second category would be the psychoanalytical-generational treatments. These include the vision, by Murray and Albert Schwartz (1975), of Germann as a sexual impotent who seeks through gambling the prerogatives of parenthood, and also Diana Burgin's ingenious hypothesis (Burgin 1974) that the Countess revealed the secret of the three cards to Čaplickij because he was her natural son by St. Germain and also (once he grew up) her lover. Burgin suggests that this taboo-ridden family cabal exercises a fatal attraction for Germann; he tries obsessively to gain entry but fails, and can only imitate its patterns hopelessly unto death.

On a different level of analysis are the linguistic and syntactic studies, of which V. V. Vinogradov is the illustrious founder. Representative of this approach would be Heidi Faletti's inquiry into the frequency of parataxis in the text (Faletti 1977), and her suggestion that this tendency to bunch together clauses without conjunctions has a thematic significance: it is the linguistic expression of a plot "organized largely on the basis of juxtaposition" (1977: 133).

Finally we have the various erudite numerological studies. Prototypical here is Lauren Leighton's "Gematria in 'The Queen of Spades': A Decembrist Puzzle" (1977). Leighton reveals a multitude of anagrams, chronograms, cryptograms, cryptonyms, and logogriphs that suggest Masonic allusions and references to the executed Decembrist Kondratij Ryleev. This final category is perhaps the most quantified of the searches for a "key to the work." But critics in all categories would probably ascribe to Diana Burgin's comment in the paragraph of her essay that opens a subchapter entitled "Questions: Clues to the Solution of the Mystery": "It is up to the reader to speculate on the implications of the text, piece together the information they offer, and come up with the solution to the mystery. Let us begin this task by examining four passages" (1974: 47). The primary responsibility of the reader is to uncover a system that will explain the work.

In the midst of these many mysterious codes, the question inevitably arises: Who is the reader of all this hidden material? If Puškin is parodying the code-breaking efforts of an audience, on what level does this audience exist? In a recent essay, "The Ace in Puškin's 'The Queen of Spades,'" Sergej Davydov assumes that the audience parodied is *internal* to the text; that is, it is Germann himself: "Puškin settles his own account with Germann. . . . He surrounds him with mysterious events, teases him with anagrams and cryptograms which the calculative engineer repeatedly failed to solve" (1989: 130). This idea of internal audience is intriguing. But it seems to me equally—if not more—plausible that the audience parodied by Puškin is in fact the reader *external* to the text, and for a reason quite opposite to the "failure" Davydov detects in Germann. Puškin might well be parodying his readers precisely because of their success and skill at reading codes.

Support for this hypothesis (albeit grudging support) can be found in even the most severely puzzle- and key-oriented criticism. For much of it ends on an oddly indeterminate note. After prodigious code-cracking efforts, Leighton asks "what functions gematria serves in the tale" (1977: 464). And he modestly concludes that it adds interest, zest; it "enriches the style by enlarging the tale's lexical means, expanding its semantic fields, and adding to its morphological and syntactic texture. . . . It helps to unify the tale's parts into a gracefully organic whole, and it makes for a greatly intriguing, and therefore greatly entertaining, narrative." The puzzle, in other words, is not cracked; it is only elaborated. Several other studies conclude in much the same way (Davydov, Poljakova): despite all the apparent overcoding, something in the text is always missing; the integrative move that will cap the deed is forever deferred. It is either the elusive ace, or the absence of resolution in the debate over realistic versus supernatural motivation, or the lack of a single literary prototype that the heroes of the tale might be parodying. As Paul Debreczeny points out, there appear to be many diluted prototypes for both characters and scenes. "Puškin used details of literary models only as so many tiny building blocks," Debreczeny concludes (1983b: 202). What, then, do these blocks actually build?

In answer, I would suggest that the codes we get in this story, wonderfully crafted as they are, were designed by Puškin *not* to build any single unified structure, or to solve any single puzzle. Scholars have long noted this strategy on a blunt compositional level, in Puškin's choice of epigraphs. The epigraphs to "Queen of Spades" rarely summarize but rather comment ironically on their chapters, defining "the chapter's tonality— sometimes, to be sure, against the spirit of its content" (Poljakova 1974: 410). But it would seem that the irony of structures in this tale is not confined to a dialogue between epigraph and text. That irony is itself a clue to a larger disjunction. For just as the self-contained scenes in *Boris Godunov* do not add up to the dramatically resolved whole that was expected of tragedy, so the mysteries in "The Queen of Spades" are not really solvable by a single code—by the sort of code we would seek, say, in a good detective story. And yet the evidence for crackable codes is so overwhelming in "The Queen of Spades" that we, along with Germann, are almost flung into the search. This passion on the part of the reader to explain the whole by a single key might well be the real target of Puškin's parody.

With this hypothesis, yet another reading of the story becomes possible: Puškin provides us not with a code, and not with chaos, but precisely with the *fragments* of codes, codes that tantalize but do not quite add up. He teases the reader with partial keys—because the reader, like Germann, does not really want to gamble. The reader wants to *decipher*, to study the past so that it will reveal the future, to predict patterns of behavior and events. We know from the very plot of the tale, however, that only desperately passionate true gamblers—people willing to stake everything on *true* chance, like St. Germain, the Countess, Čaplickij—can be privy to true secrets (Burgin 1974: 53).

In this reading, the key passage in the text has nothing to do with threes, sevens, numerology, or cryptography. It is, rather, the Countess's final words to German: "Eto byla šutka" (it was a joke)—*not*, note, a riddle, which has an answer already implied in the asking. Simply a joke, non-repeatable and non-systematizing, randomly successful in one context and perhaps a complete fiasco in some other time and place. Naturally Germann cannot read this reponse properly, because his whole life is one of calculation. When he answers the Countess with "Etim nečego šutit'" (This is no joking matter), it is clear to what extent his entire being is alien to the lesson of *real* gambling, namely, that there *is no system*.[4] As Lotman points out in his essay on the card game, Faro is a model of fate. And, Lotman continues, "the external world, which possesses an inexhaustible supply of time and unlimited possibilities of resuming the game, inevitably outplays every individual" (1975: 477–78).

This wisdom, which is routinely applied to Germann, could apply to code-crackers outside the text as well. For Puškin always promises system, but it is a trap. In this connection it is worth mentioning the excellent essay by Michael Shapiro on Puškin's "semiotic dominant" (Shapiro 1979). Shapiro suggests that the one truly characteristic feature of Puškin's work is its *definition by negation*. And the essential negated value in "The Queen of Spades," I suggest, is the search for system. As Shapiro points out, it is not the supernatural that drives Germann mad, but chance itself, the most everyday and natural randomness of events. As Shapiro concludes his reading of the tale: "The element of chance which irrupts into the conclusion just when success is nearest is conditioned by the preternatural, by that whole realm of the (private) imagination which is opposed to reality as its negation. The reversal is all the more powerful since all of the events leading up to the moment of potential success are themselves accidents" (1979: 125).

There is, in short, a philosophy of history in this tale, just as there clearly is in *Boris Godunov*. The means are different because the problem that time poses in each work is different. In the play, Puškin parodies our search for system in the past; in the story, he parodies our search for system in the future. *Blindness to the present*—Germann convinced of his ace and confronted by a Queen—is common to both works. If Dmitrij the Pretender survives because he is so thoroughly a product of contingency, then Germann, in contrast, perishes because he cannot live in that sort of world once the *promise* of code has been offered him. In the seductive fragments of an explanation that are strewn around his story, we glimpse what might be the real logic of the tale: an allegory of interpretation itself. In "The Queen of Spades" Puškin appears to be celebrating the spirit of the true gambler, whom chance can impoverish but could never drive mad.

SERGEJ DAVYDOV

Puškin's Easter Triptych

"Hermit fathers and immaculate women," "Imitation of the Italian," and "Secular Power"

During the last year of his life, Puškin wrote relatively few poems. The most important were completed on Kamennyj ostrov (Stone Island) in the summer of 1836 and included "Mirskaja vlast'" (Secular Power; 5 July), "Podražanie italijanskomu" (Imitation of the Italian; 22 June), "Iz Pindemonti" (From Pindemonte; 5 July), "Otcy pustynniki i ženy neporočny . . . " (Hermit fathers and immaculate women; 22 July), "Kogda za gorodom, zadumčiv, ja brožu . . . " (When I, pensive, roam beyond the city; 14 August), and "Ja pamjatnik sebe vozdvig nerukotvornyj . . . " (Exegi monumentum; 21 August). By the end of July, Puškin had marked the first four poems with roman numerals. He intended to publish them separately, as a lyrical cycle, perhaps in his own journal, *Sovremennik* (The Contemporary). However, Puškin's numeration reveals that the entire Stone Island cycle should have consisted of six poems:

  I   unknown
 II   "Hermit fathers and immaculate women"
III   "Imitation of the Italian"
IV   "Secular Power"
  V   unknown
VI   "From Pindemonte"

The two empty positions and their precise location leave no doubt that the cycle took a very concrete shape in Puškin's mind. It should also be noted that when Puškin conceived the idea of this cycle and sketched its outline, two major poems, "When I, pensive, roam beyond the city" and "Exegi monumentum," were not yet written; they were completed in August.[1]

Leaving aside for the moment the speculation on the place of the missing poems and the hypothetical shape and unity of the entire cycle, I would like to focus on the three middle, contiguous poems which Puškin marked with roman numerals II, III, and IV. "Hermit fathers . . . ," "Imitation of the Italian," and "Secular Power" form a micro-cycle of their own, sharing a number of common features. None of the three poems is Puškin's original creation; they are based either entirely or partially on some text of foreign origin. "Hermit fathers . . . " contains a paraphrase of the "Prayer of St. Ephraem the Syrian," "Imitation of the Italian" is based on Francesco Gianni's sonnet about Judas, which Puškin knew from a French translation by Antoni Deschamps, and "Secular Power" partially reproduces the New Testament account of the Crucifixion, interspersed with motifs from the Easter liturgy. All three poems are lyrical meditations on the relationship between the powers and laws that rule this world, the *jus humanum* and *jus divinum*.[2] The cycle is also formally unified: the poems are written in Alexandrine lines, with a caesura after the third foot, and with alternating feminine and masculine pairs of rhymes. Most important, the three poems are united by the theme of Easter. Projected on the calendar of Paschal events, "Hermit fathers . . . ," with its Lenten prayer, falls on the "mournful days of Lent" (dni Velikogo posta); "Imitation" brings us to Holy Thursday, the betrayal of Christ, and the suicide of Judas; while "Secular Power" re-enacts the Crucifixion scene of Good Friday and exposes the subsequent betrayal of the divine mystery by secular powers.[3]

Written as the last of the three poems, on 22 July, "Hermit fathers . . . " opens the Easter cycle:

II

1 Отцы пустынники и жены непорочны,
2 Чтоб сердцем возлетать во области заочны,
3 Чтоб укреплять его средь дольних бурь и битв,
4 Сложили множество божественных молитв;
5 Но ни одна из них меня не умиляет,
6 Как та, которую священник повторяет
7 Во дни печальные Великого поста;
8 Всех чаще она мне приходит на уста
9 И падшего крепит неведомою силой:
10 Владыко дней моих! дух праздности унылой,
11 Любоначалия, змеи сокрытой сей,
12 И празднословия не дай душе моей.
13 Но дай мне зреть мои, о Боже, прегрешенья,
14 Да брат мой от меня не примет осужденья,
15 И дух смирения, терпения, любви
16 И целомудрия мне в сердце оживи. (PSS III: 421)

Hermit fathers and immaculate women,
so as to soar in their heart to remote realms,
and strengthen it in the midst of earthly storms and battles,
composed a multitude of divine prayers.
But none moves me more
than that which the priest repeats
during the mournful days of Lent;
it comes to my lips more often than the rest
and bestows the fallen one with mysterious strength;

> Lord of my days! Do not grant my soul
> the spirit of despondent idleness,
> ambition, that concealed snake,
> and vain talk.
> But grant me to see, o Lord, my trespassings,
> may my brother be not condemned by me,
> and the spirit of humility, patience, love,
> and chastity revive in my heart.

Projected on the calendar of Easter events, this poem falls on the days of Lent. The last seven lines of the poem paraphrase the prayer of the fourth-century church father and saint Ephraem the Syrian, which is said during the weeks of Lent until the Wednesday of Holy Week:

> Господи и Владыко живота моего, духъ праздности, унынія, любоначалія и празднословія не даждь ми. Духъ же целомудрія, смиренномудрія, терпенія и любве, даруй ми рабу Твоему. Ей, Господи Царю, даруй ми зрети моя прегрешенія, и не осуждати брата моего, яко благословенъ еси во веки вековъ. Аминь. (Molitvoslov 1907: 139)

> Lord and Master of my life, grant me not a spirit of slothfulness, despondency, ambition, and vain talk. Bestow on me, your servant, the spirit of chastity, humility, patience and love. Yea, Lord and King, grant that I see my own sins, and not judge my brother, for you are blessed forever and ever, Amen.

In "Hermit fathers . . ." Puškin revisited for a moment an old theme from his blasphemous youth, only to retell it in a very different key. In Puškin's first narrative poem, "Monax" (The Monk, 1813), the fourteen-year-old disciple of Parny and Voltaire teased the hermit father Pankratij with a woman's skirt, eventually corrupting him. The same "mournful days of Lent" which inspired Puškin's pious meditation provoked in 1821 only a gastronomic rebellion, a veritable "crie de ventre":

> А мой ненабожный желудок
> "Помилуй, братец,—говорит,—
> Еще когда бы кровь Христова
> Была хоть, например, лафит . . .
> Иль кло-д-вужо, тогда б ни слова,
> А то подумай, как смешно!—
> С водой молдавское вино".
> Но я молюсь—и воздыхаю . . .
> Крещусь, не внемлю сатане . . .
> А все невольно вспоминаю,
> Давыдов, о твоем вине . . . ("V. L. Davydovu"
> [To V. L. Davydov], 1821; PSS II: 179)

> And my impious stomach
> says, "Have mercy, my dear,
> if only the blood of Christ

> were, let's say, Lafite . . .
> or Clos de Vougeot, then there'd be no question,
> but here—think of it, how ludicrous!—
> Moldavian wine diluted with water."
> But I pray, and sigh . . .
> cross myself, do not heed Satan . . .
> Though I can't help but remember,
> Davydov, your wine . . .

In a letter to Del'vig of the same year, we find a direct parody of St. Ephraem's prayer:

I wish him [Kjuxel'beker] in Paris the spirit of chastity, in the chancellery of Naryškin the spirit of humility and patience; I am not worried about the spirit of love, he will not be lacking in that; I say nothing of the idle talk—a far-off friend cannot be too talkative. (23 March 1821; PSS XIII: 24; Shaw 1967: 82)

Keeping in mind the spiritual distance between the young Puškin of the blasphemous *Gavriliada* and the poet in the last year of his life, I return to the prayer "Hermit fathers. . . . "

"Dlja molitvy post est' to že, čto dlja pticy kryl'ja" (Fasting is to a prayer what wings are to a bird)—Puškin copied down this sentence in 1836 from a sermon of the Russian Archbishop Georgij Koniskij (PSS XII: 14). In the last year of his life, Puškin frequently turned to religious subjects in his journalistic ventures also. The articles "Sobranie sočinenij Georgija Koniskogo, Arxiepiskopa Belorusskogo" (The Collected Works of the Belorussian Archbishop Georgij Koniskij), "Ob objazannostjax čeloveka: Sočinenie Sil'vio Pelliko" (On Man's Obligations: The Works of Sylvio Pellico), and "Slovar' o svjatyx" (Dictionary of Saints), published anonymously that year in *The Contemporary*, testify to Puškin's new interest in the Christian tradition and his admiration for the fathers of the church, the Russian saints, and the Book of Books: "That book is called the Gospel and its eternally new charm is such that when we, oversatiated with the world or overcome with despondency, chance to open it, we no longer are capable of resisting its sweet attraction and spiritually immerse ourselves in its divine eloquence" (PSS XII: 99)

Christ's preaching receives the highest praise: "There were few chosen ones (even among the first shepherds of the Church) . . . whose meekness of spirit, sweetness of eloquence and infant-like simplicity of heart would approximate the sermons of our heavenly teacher" (PSS XII: 99).

The prayer of St. Ephraem had for Puškin similar appeal. Its incorporation into his own poem is Puškin's way of paying homage to the spiritual and poetic gifts of the church father. Puškin reproduced the prayer almost verbatim and without quotation marks. By doing so, the poet subscribed to the ancient principle of sacred writing where *imitatio* rather than *innovatio* is the ideal. Puškin eloquently justified this time-honored principle in his defense of Sylvio Pellico's religious writings:

One of the most common charges of the critics is: "That is no longer new, that has already been said." But everything has already been said, all ideas have been expressed, and repeated, in the course of the centuries—what follows from that? That the human spirit no longer produces anything new? No, we aren't going to slander it; the mind is as inexhaustible in the assimilation of ideas [*v soobraženii ponjatij*] as language is inexhaustible in the combination of words [*v soedinenii slov*]. All words are in the dictionary; but the books which are constantly being published are not mere repetitions of the dictionary. (PSS XII: 100)

The same words can be applied to Puškin's rendering of St. Ephraem's prayer. Although Puškin faithfully paraphrased its text, his poem differs from the model in several respects. Some changes were motivated by simple stylistic considerations. Old Church Slavonicisms have been replaced with contemporary words: "ne dažd' " with "ne daj," "daruj" with "daj," the composite word "smirennomudrija" with the simple "smirenija"; the change of "života moego" to "dnej moix" avoids the comical effect. Other changes, such as the addition of three metaphors—"zmei sokrytoj sej" (qualifying "ljubonačalie"), "duše moej" (instead of "ne dažd' mi"), and "v serdce oživi" (instead of "daruj mi")—are genuinely liturgical and as such do not present a major distortion of the prayer; they interrupt its enumerative sequences. The prayer's coda—"jako blagosloven esi vo veki vekov. Amin' "—was also dropped, as it is a standard formula and thus not peculiar to St. Ephraem.

The reduction of the double address "Gospodi i Vladyko" and "Gospodi Carju" to a single "Vladyko" or "Bože" is less significant than the omission of "rabu Tvoemu." Puškin once proudly declared (paraphrasing Lomonosov): "I can be a subject, even a slave [*daže rabom*],—but I won't be a bondman and jester even to the heavenly Lord" (Diary 10 May 1834; PSS XII: 329). Puškin's delicate personal touch has also altered St. Ephraem's sequence of the Christian virtues. In Puškin's version, "love," as could be expected, precedes "chastity," which comes as the last of the four virtues.

The sin of idle talk ("prazdnoslovie") calls to mind the words "A moljas', ne govorite lišnego, kak jazyčniki: ibo oni dumajut, čto v mnogoslovii svoem budut uslyšany" (When ye pray say nothing superfluous as the heathen do, for they think that they shall be heard for their much speaking) (Matt. 6:7). Moreover, the vice of "idle talk" has far-reaching implications for the poet's use of words. Puškin disclosed its biblical and poetic meaning in the 1826 poem "Prorok" (The Prophet), based on Isaiah 6:1–13, in which a six-winged Seraph appears before a dying man and "tears out of his throat the sinful, idle, and deceitful tongue." It is important to stress that after this poem, the frivolous treatment of religious themes disappears entirely from Puškin's works. In this sense, "The Prophet" can be seen as a watershed separating the deluge of "idle talk" of Puškin's blasphemous youth from the verbal terseness of his later lyrics. To reproduce verbatim an ancient prayer in one's own poem is, no doubt, a

safe method of avoiding the sin of idle talk. Yet, whatever loss of originality Puškin incurred on the surface, he fully compensated for on the deeper
level of the poem's structure.

"Hermit fathers . . . " has an intricate poetic form. Although the poem
is not divided into stanzas, it consists of three thematic segments: lines 1–4
address the creators of the various prayers; in lines 5–9, marked by the
conjunction "no," Puškin singled out one prayer among many; while lines
10–16 contain the prayer itself. The poem is characterized by a progression
from impersonal to personal mode, revealed on the pronominal level. The
first segment lacks any reference to the lyrical subject; the second has two:
"menja" and "mne," while the third, the most personal segment of the
poem, containing the prayer itself, has seven: "moix," "moej," "mne,"
"moim," "moj," "menja," and "mne." In this process the prayer becomes
internalized, the "alien word" becomes one's own.

Puškin's Alexandrines are regular, even monotonous, as befits the so-
lemnity of the prayer. But the regular rhythmical pattern is interrupted in
line 10 where four stresses meet (iamb and spondee, separated by a caesura): "Vladyko dnej moix! Dux prazdnosti unyloj. . . . " The unexpected
stress marks the beginning of the prayer, making line 10 with its six stresses
the most highly stressed line of the entire poem. Significantly, the prayer
concludes with the lowest stressed line of the poem (three stresses): "I
celomudrija mne v serdce oživi." Thus, after the initial staccato, the prayer
ends on a calm line pronounced as if in one breath.

The impression produced by the poem's sound is one of an uninter-
rupted flow resembling liturgical reading. The sound orchestration of the
stressed vowels, however, divides the poem into three distinctive segments
corresponding to the threefold thematic division. Each of the segments is
successively dominated by one stressed compact vowel, "o," "a," or "e,"
while the frequency of the remaining two drops significantly. Contrasted
with the neutral distribution pattern of Russian stressed vowels, the results
are as follows:

	o	+81.4%	
I	a	-64.6%	"o"-segment (lines 1–4)
	e	-42.9%	

	a	+107%	
II	o	-45%	"a"-segment (lines 5–9)
	e	-39%	

	e	+67.4%	
III	a	-38%	"e"-segment (lines 10–16)[4]
	o	-70%	

The sound and theme in this poem are linked in one more meaningful
way. The transition from silent meditation to the actual articulation of the
prayer is paralleled on the level of sound by the shift from the back vowel

"o" to the mid "a," and to the front "e." Significantly, this vocalic shift is accompanied by an increase of the bilabial consonant "m" (+47.6% in the entire poem, +110.7% in the prayer section). Thus the sound orchestration enhances the transition from meditation to articulation and beautifully illustrates what Puškin stated in line 8: "Vsex čašče mne ona prixodit *na usta*" (It comes to my lips more often than the rest).

For the Romantics, who often perceived art as a form of religion, a poem was equivalent to a prayer. In "Hermit fathers and immaculate women . . . " Puškin almost verbatim and without quotation marks reproduced St. Ephraem's prayer. By doing so, the poet was following the medieval canon of sacred art, the principle of imitation, while the hidden and highly intricate structure of the poem's rhythm and sound reveals the full extent of Puškin's creative innovation. Having faithfully reproduced the ancient words, and while letting the non-verbal elements of the poem speak so meaningfully from within, I believe, Puškin avoided the sin of "idle talk" without betraying his poetic calling.

Prayers, Puškin states at the beginning of his poem, were composed to strengthen the human heart for earthly storms and battles, and for the spiritual ascent to heavenly realms: "čtob serdcem vozletat' vo oblasti zaočny, / čtob ukrepljat' ego sred' dol'nix bur' i bitv." But, since prayers are offerings in addition to being spoken, they have to be received. In his article on the Archbishop Georgij Koniskij, written not long before this poem, Puškin quoted a passage about a prayer said amidst a storm at sea by a godless man:

> When during a strong and dangerous storm all sailors turned to prayer and one godless man began to articulate something too, the helmsman stopped him with these words: "You had better keep silent; perhaps God does not know you are among us and therefore there is hope in despair, but once He hears your holy prayer, we are lost." (PSS XII: 16)

Is Puškin's prayer any different? I believe so. The fact that "Hermit fathers . . . " (which Puškin himself referred to as "Molitva" [Prayer]) does not stand alone in his oeuvre is, together with its highly intricate structure, the best refutation of the alleged "organic inability for religion" which, according to D. S. Mirskij (1934: III), Puškin preserved until his last days:

> Along with his conformism in matters of daily life and ideology, Puškin made attempts to "master" religion. But his nature found it more difficult to reconcile itself with god than with the tsar. And while the court could claim *Poltava* for its own, Puškin's religious verses (such as the once famed "Prayer") stand out for their low quality. (Mirskij 1934: 112)

Puškin did not undergo a spiritual conversion, like Gogol', Dostoevskij, or Tolstoj; his path from the Parnassian atheism of his youth, which culminated in 1821 with *Gavriiliada* (Gavriliada), toward the religious spirituality of the 1836 cycle was a gradual one. The most significant landmarks on this path were "Podražanija Koranu" (Imitations of the Koran, 1824), "Prorok" (1826), "Angel" (1827), "Vospominanie" (Recollection, 1828), "V časy zabav . . . " (In hours/times of amusement, 1830), and "Strannik" (Pilgrim, 1834). If one were to telescope the development of the religious theme in Puškin, one might choose these three quotations:

Ум ищет божества,
А сердце не находит.

The mind seeks divinity
but the heart fails to find it.
("Bezverie" [Unbelief], 1817; PSS I: 243)

И внемлет арфе серафима
В священном ужасе поэт.

And to the Seraph's harp
the poet harkens in sacred awe.
("In times of amusement . . . ," 1830; PSS III: 212)

Веленью Божию, о Муза, будь послушна . . .

Obey God's will, o Muse . . .
("Pamjatnik" [Monument], 1836; PSS III: 424)

The development of the religious theme culminated in the cycle written during the last year of Puškin's life. With the poem "Otcy pustynniki i ženy neporočny," Puškin has humbly added to the "multitude of divine prayers" created by the hermit fathers and immaculate women a prayer of his own making, thus repeating in his inspired art their spiritual feat.

III
(Подражание италиянскому)
1 Как с древа сорвался предатель ученик,
2 Диавол прилетел, к лицу его приник,
3 Дхнул жизнь в него, взвился с своей добычей смрадной
4 И бросил труп живой в гортань геенны гладной . . .
5 Там бесы, радуясь и плеща, на рога
6 Прияли с хохотом всемирного врага
7 И шумно понесли к проклятому владыке,
8 И сатана, привстав, с веселием на лике
9 Лобзанием своим насквозь прожег уста,
10 В предательскую ночь лобзавшие Христа. (PSS III:418)

(Imitation of the Italian)
When the traitor-disciple fell from the tree,
the devil flew in, pressed himself against his face,
breathed life into him, [then] soared up with his stinking booty
and cast the living corpse into the maw of starved Gehenna . . .
There demons, rejoicing and clapping,

took with guffaws the universal foe on their horns
and noisily carried him to their accursed lord.
And Satan, half-rising, with glee on his countenance,
charred with his kiss the lips
which on that treacherous night had kissed Christ.

Although he wrote it before "Hermit fathers . . . " Puškin marked
"Imitation of the Italian" with the roman numeral III. "Imitation" continues the theme begun in "Hermit fathers . . . " through contrast between
humility and hubris: the faith and devotion of the "hermit fathers and
immaculate women" are opposed to the lack of faith and the betrayal of
the disciple Judas—lips soothed by prayer as opposed to lips burned
through in Satan's kiss. Projected on the calendar of the Paschal events,
"Imitation" moves us to Thursday of Holy Week, to the betrayal of Christ
and the suicide of Judas (Matt. 27:1–5).

As the title indicates, "Imitation of the Italian," like the rest of the
poems in this cycle, is based on a foreign subtext. The poem is rooted in
Catholic tradition. In 1855, P. V. Annenkov identified its source as the
sonnet "Sopra Iuda" by the Italian *improvisatore* Francesco Gianni
(1760–1822).[5]

Allor che Giuda di furor satollo
Piombò dal ramo, rapido si mosse
L'instigator suo Demone, e scontrollo
Battendo l'ali come fiamma rosse;

Pel nodo che al felon rettorse il collo
Giù nel bollor delle roventi fosse
Appena con le scabre ugne rotollo
Ch'arser le carni, e sibillaron l'osse;

E in mezzo al vampa della gran bufera
Con diro ghigno Satana fu visto
Spianar le rughe della fronte altera:

Poi fra le braccia se recò quel tristo,
E con la bocca fumigante e nera
Gli rese il bacio, ch'avea dato a Cristo.

When Judas, satiated with fury,
plunged from the bough,
his Demon tempter moved quickly against him,
beating red wings like a flame.

By the noose that wrung the felon's neck,
he hurled him down with his ragged claws
into the boiling red-hot pits
that burned his flesh and made his bones sizzle.

At the center flame of this fire-storm,
with dire grimace, Satan was seen

to smooth the furrows of his proud brow.

Then [Judas], that wretched one, entered [Satan's] embrace
and with his smoldering and black mouth,
returned to him the kiss he had given unto Christ.

However, as B. V. Tomaševskij has demonstrated, Puškin was familiar
not with the Italian original of the sonnet but with a French translation by
Antoni Deschamps (1800–69), who was best known for his 1829 translation
of Dante (Tomaševskij 1930: 79–80). Puškin had Deschamps's translation
of Dante in his library as well as his *Dernières Paroles* (Paris, 1835)
(Modzalevskij 1910: #218, 867), where in the section "Études sur l'Italie" we
find "Sonnet de Gianni: Supplice de Judas dans l'enfer":

> Lorsqu'ayant assouvi son atroce colère
> Judas enfin tomba de l'arbre solitaire,
> L'effroyable démon qui l'avait excité
> Sur lui fondit alors avec rapidité.
> Le prenant aux cheveux, sur ses ailes de flamme,
> Dans l'air il emporta le corps de cet infâme,
> Et descendant au fond de l'éternel enfer
> Le jeta tout tremblant à ses fourches de fer.
> Les chairs d'Iscariote avec fracas brulèrent
> Sa moëlle rotit et tous ses os sifflèrent.
> Satan de ses deux bras entoura le damné,
> Puis, en le regardant d'une face riante,
> Serein, il lui rendit de sa bouche fumante
> Le baiser que le traître au Christ avait donné.

Deschamps appended to his translation of Gianni the concluding lines of
the Italian original, and Puškin could have formed an impression of the
Italian improviser's style. However, Tomaševskij, who compared all three
versions, has convincingly shown that Puškin was following Deschamps
rather than Gianni (Tomaševskij 1930: 78–81). I would like to add to
Tomaševskij's comparison several observations about Puškin's version of
the Judas sonnet.

In Gianni and Deschamps, the infernal forces were represented by the
Demon and Satan. Puškin added to them a third force, devils (*besy*), thus
creating an "infernal trinity" consisting of *besy*, *diavol*, and *satana*.[6] Although all three are emanations of the same principle, there is a clear
hierarchy among them, and Puškin distributed their respective roles accordingly.

The lowest rung on Puškin's ladder is occupied by the grotesque creatures *besy*. The terror of Satan was so great that the imagination of medieval man had to cut him down to size and occasionally endowed him with
comic, carnivalesque features. Thus the Satan of demonology became the
devil prankster of folklore. Puškin was most original in the depiction of

these playful imps in league with the *diavol* and *satana*. There is nothing
glamorous about them; they perform menial tasks and chores. Their appearance and antics introduce a grotesque note into the poem, which was
absent in Gianni and Deschamps, but can be traced back to Dante, Goethe, Hoffmann, and folklore. These thoroughly unmajestic "devilkins" are
often found in Puškin's early poetry. In "Nabroski k zamyslu o Fauste"
(Sketches to a project on Faust, 1825) they are Satan's domestic servants
preparing the celebration of their master's saint's day [*sic*]:

> —Сегодня бал у сатаны—
> На именины мы званы—
> [Смотри, как эти два бесенка
> Усердно жарят поросенка],
> А этот бес—как важен он,
> Как чинно выметает вон
> Опилки, серу, пыль и кости. (PSS II: 381)

> —There is a ball at Satan's today,
> we are invited to his saint's day—
> Look how these two devilkins
> are diligently frying a piglet,
> and this devil—what an important air he puts on,
> how ceremoniously he sweeps out
> the sawdust, sulphur, ashes, and bones.

In the fragment "I dale my pošli" (And we went further, 1832), written in
terza rima and calling to mind Dante's vivid imagination, Puškin presented his *besy* at their most impish:

> Бесенок, под себя поджав свое копыто,
> Крутил ростовщика у адского огня.
> Горячий капал жир в копченное корыто,
> И лопал на огне печеный ростовщик. . . .
> И бесы тешились проклятою игрою . . .
> А бесы прыгали в веселии великом . . . (PSS III: 281–82)

> A little devil, squatting on his hoof,
> was turning a pawnbroker on a spit at the hellish fire.
> The hot lard dripped into a soot-caked trough,
> and the roasted pawnbroker burst in the fire.
> . . . And the devils were enjoying their accursed game:
> . . . And the devils were leaping in great merriment.

Puškin's introduction of these cheerful creatures into the "Judas sonnet"
provides for comic relief before the wretched dénouement, a device employed, for example, by Dante in Canto XXII of the *Inferno*, where a
squabble among the devils ensues. However, their merry nature should not
obscure the fact that they are inflicters of pain. "There demons [*besy*],

rejoicing and clapping, / took with guffaws the universal foe *on their horns* / and noisily carried him to their accursed lord."

The more solemn tasks, such as the communication between this and the nether world, Puškin entrusted to the *diavol*. Puškin did not equip this hypostasis with material attributes such as claws (Gianni), pitchfork (Deschamps), or flaming wings (both). Nor does his *diavol* inflict physical pain; his tasks are of a spiritual rather than a menial nature: he *resurrects* Judas. Puškin's diction is accordingly dignified where the *diavol* is concerned: "Diavol priletel, k licu ego prinik, / Dxnul žizn' v nego, vzvilsja s svojej dobyčej smradnoj / I brosil trup živoj v gortan' geeny gladnoj" (The devil flew in, pressed himself against his face, / breathed life into him, soared up with his stinking booty, / and cast the living corpse into the maw of starved Gehenna).

At the top of the infernal hierarchy presides the "prokljatyj vladyka": *satana*.[7] Puškin depicted "the accursed lord" of the universe, rising from his throne, in full satanic splendor. The "mirth" on his countenance is a remote and solemn echo of demons' lowly "guffaws." "I satana, privstav, s veseliem na like / Lobzaniem svoim naskvoz' prožeg usta, / V predatel'skuju noč' lobzavšie Xrista" (And Satan, half-rising, with glee on his countenance, / charred with a kiss the lips / which on that treacherous night had kissed Christ).

The introduction of the infernal trinity enabled Puškin to present the events in three steps, each intensifying the ordeal. First, Puškin resurrected Judas, before subjecting him to torture. In Deschamps, Judas remains a corpse throughout the ordeal. Next, Puškin replaced Deschamps's "iron pitchfork" (absent in Gianni) with the less threatening and more familiar "horns." Puškin also spared Judas the infernal flames: no roasting of flesh, no hissing bones; there is even laughter in Puškin's Hell, which was absent in Gianni and Deschamps. While Puškin underplayed the pyrotechnic effects in the first two episodes, he raises the heat in the final scene. Puškin's Satan "charred with a kiss the lips," whereas Gianni's and Deschamps's Satan merely kisses Judas. To Judas, after having been transported on flaming wings, impaled on a pitchfork, and had his flesh, bones, and marrow incinerated, Satan's kiss must have come as a relief at the end of Gianni's and Deschamps's poem. In Puškin, common sense and good measure prevail. Had Puškin followed his predecessors, his Judas would have had no lips left for the final kiss. In projecting the excruciating physical pain into Satan's kiss, Puškin perhaps followed Dante, whose Satan chews Judas's head in the last canto of the *Inferno*.

Where Puškin mostly departs from Gianni and Deschamps is in the intricate dualistic structure of his poem. "Imitation of the Italian" is based on an oxymoron in which the infernal and the divine orders are continually juxtaposed. Puškin exploited this duality on several levels. Judas's suicide, resurrection, and descent to Hell repeat in a perverted form the mystery of the crucifixion, resurrection, and ascension of Christ. It suffices to replace Judas with Christ, the Demon with the Angel, Hell with Heaven, Satan with God, death with life, and the sinister mirror image of the divine mystery becomes evident.[8]

In "Imitation" Puškin and Satan enact a pseudo-divine mystery, embellished with sham attributes of genuine mystery. In doing so, Puškin followed the Orthodox teaching of the Antichrist, the false Christ who claims to act in the name of Christ. (For similar reasons, Milton had his Satan quote from the Gospels.) The oxymoron of the infernal and the divine perhaps goes back to the belief that Satan is a fallen angel who dared to raise his brow against his creator (Isa. 14:11–15, Luke 10:18, Rev. 12:9). Satan too desired to create, but he was not a true creator. In his demiurgic hubris, Satan plagiarized the divine creation, but the result was a perversion of the original act, a caricature of it. In Satan's creation everything becomes its opposite: a kiss becomes the instrument of betrayal, ascension becomes descent, life is turned into death, reward into punishment, love into hatred.

This paradox affects even the smallest elements of the poem. Phrases, words, even morphemes seem to belong to two realms at once, simultaneously pointing to both antonymic referents, the satanic and the divine. Such word combinations as "predatel' učenik," "trup živoj," "prokljatyj vladyka," and "lobzaniem prožeg" (traitor-disciple, living corpse, accursed lord, charring kiss) carry within themselves their own negation. The use of words in an improper context results in a diabolic perversion of the sacred meaning. The word "Vladyka" (Lord), which referred in "Hermit fathers . . . " to God ("Vladyko dnej moix!"), is applied to Satan. Satan's face, for example, is referred to as "lik"—a term usually reserved for the countenances of saints on icons. The word "drevo," referring to the tree on which Judas hanged himself, will be used in the next poem of the cycle to designate the Holy Cross: "Togda po storonam životvorjašča dreva . . . " (then, by the sides of the life-bearing tree). Likewise, the words "predatel', predatel'skaja" (traitor, treacherous), applying to Judas, reappear in the next poem in an opposite, positive meaning, referring to Christ's self-sacrifice: "Xrista, *predavšego* poslušno plot' svoju" (Christ, who meekly surrendered/betrayed his flesh). Likewise, the cacophonic word "dxnul" (breathed into) can be seen as another diabolic perversion of the sacred meaning contained in such words as "dux, duša, vdoxnut' " (spirit, soul, inhale), and by implication "vdoxnovenie" (inspire) ("I, priznak Boga, vdoxnoven'e" [And the sign of God, Inspiration] from "Razgovor knigoprodavca s poètom" [Conversation between Bookseller and Poet]). It is fitting that in a poem about betrayal, words continually betray their original, positive meaning.

The corruption of the divine harmony can already be observed on the sub-lexical level. In a poem entitled "Imitation of the Italian" one would expect euphony to dominate the sound structure, as was the case in so many Italianate stylizations of Puškin's time. Puškin, too, admired the melodious quality of the Italian language. Commenting on Batjuškov's line "Ljubvi *i oči, i* lanity," with the characteristic hiatuses on the vocalic word boundaries, Puškin exclaims: "Zvuk*i i*talijanskie! čto za čudotvorec ètot Batjuškov" (Italian sounds! What a miracle worker is this Batjuškov) (PSS XII: 267). Batjuškov, who was renowned for his dislike of harsh Russian sounds, strove to avoid consonantal clusters in his poetry: "čto za Y, čto za šč, šIJ, ščIJ, PRI, TRY? O varvary!" (Batjuškov 1934: 30). However, in Puškin's "Podražan*ie i*talijanskomu," only the title lives up to Batjuškov's mellifluous ideal, whereas in the poem itself, Puškin accumulated more consonant clusters (triple and quadruple) than perhaps anywhere else in his poetry. The effect is definitively cacophonic: "Ka*k s dr*eva . . . diavo*l pr*ilete*l k l*icu ego prini*k, dx*nul *ž*izn' *v n*ego, *vzv*ilsja *s sv*oej dobyče*j sm*radnoj . . . brosi*l tr*up živo*j v* gortan' *g*eeny *gl*adnoj . . . s xoxoto*m vs*emirnogo vraga . . . *k pr*okljatomu vladyke . . . privsta*v, s v*eseliem . . . lobzanie*m s*voim na*skvoz' pr*ožeg usta . . . *v pr*edatel'skuju noč' . . . " Lines 3–4, in which the satanic resurrection takes place, stand out as the most cacophonic of the entire poem; Puškin accumulated here seven clusters of three consonants, followed by a triple alliteration: "*Dxnul ž*izn' *v n*ego, *vzv*ilja *s sv*oej dobyče*j sm*radnoj / I brosi*l tr*up živo*j v g*ortan' *g*eeny *gl*adnoj."

These two lines of seven and six ictuses are also the most heavily stressed in a poem whose lines average four ictuses. Significantly, the only supranumerical stress falls on the hunchback of a word "dxnul" (breathed into), which consists of four consonants and the dark vowel "u." This spondee is responsible for the only metrical deviation in the entire poem.

In passages such as this, Puškin's language seems to have descended to the very "cerchi di Giuda"—"that is the lowest and most dark place of all, / Farthest from the Heaven that moveth all" (*Inferno* 9: 27–29). Dante, too, resorted to cacophony in many passages of *Inferno* to produce a similar effect. This device of deliberately corrupting the euphonic norm is present to a degree in Gianni (line 8) but, surprisingly, is entirely missing in Deschamps, who was the translator of Dante. In this sense, Puškin's "Imitation" stands closer to the original Italian poetic tradition than to the French version which he used as a model.

It should not come as a surprise that in the poem about Hell, the word "ad" (Hell) reverberates in a number of key words: "smr*AD*noj, gl*AD*noj, r*AD*ujas', xox*OT*om, proklj*AT*omu vl*AD*yke," and most importantly in "s*AT*ana." Including the title, "P*OD*ražanie italijanskomu" contains eight anagrams of the word "ad."[9] In some words such as "smr*AD*noj, gl*AD*noj, proklj*AT*omu" (stinking, starved, accursed) we deal with a semantic parallelism between the word and the anagram. But in words such as "r*AD*ujas' " and "vl*AD*yka" (rejoicing, lord), the anagram has an oxymoronic effect, corrupting the positive meaning of the host word.[10]

Dissecting Puškin's "Imitation of the Italian" reveals how the central theme of betrayal has penetrated the smallest components of the poem's anatomy. On a higher level of meaning, the poem is a philosophical meditation on the relationship between the powers of man, Satan, and God, and on the nature of evil. Christian theology opposes Manichaean dualism;

Satan too is a creation of God, and as such possesses free will from which evil originates. Satan first betrayed God and then seduced men into doing the same. Judas betrayed Christ and was in turn betrayed by Satan. By returning to Judas the kiss he had given to Christ, Satan, paradoxically, punishes his disciple. Free to pursue his own aims and influence man's choices, Satan cannot help but fulfill his part in a universal design. By his returning the kiss, the circle of justice is completed; Satan fulfilled the will of God, rather than his own.[11]

Perhaps even more important for Puškin the poet is that Satan was denied the gift of creation. All he is capable of doing is plagiarizing and temporarily corrupting the divine design by bringing discord into that harmony. "Imitation of the Italian," whose intricate structure so faithfully reproduces the mechanism of the satanic subversion, concludes by affirming the primacy of the supreme design. The apostasy is turned into theodicy; the last word of the poem about Judas is "Xristos."

Christ is the central theme of the next poem, "Mirskaja vlast' " (Secular Power), which concludes the Easter triptych. Although it was written as the first poem that summer (on Friday, 5 June), Puškin marked it with the roman numeral IV.

IV
"Мирская власть"

1 Когда великое свершалось торжество
2 И в муках на кресте кончалось Божество,
3 Тогда по сторонам животворяща древа
4 Мария-грешница и Пресвятая Дева
5   Стояли две жены,
6 В неизмеримую печаль погружены.
7 Но у подножия теперь креста честнаго,
8 Как будто у крыльца правителя градскаго,
9 Мы зрим поставленных на место жен святых
10 В ружье и кивере двух грозных часовых.
11 К чему, скажите мне, хранительная стража
12 Или распятие казенная поклажа,
13 И вы боитеся воров или мышей?
14 Иль мните важности придать Царю Царей?
15 Иль покровительством спасаете могучим
16 Владыку, тернием венчанного колючим,
17 Христа, предавшего послушно плоть свою
18 Бичам мучителей, гвоздям и копию?
19 Иль опасаетесь, чтоб чернь не оскорбила
20 Того, чья казнь весь род Адамов искупила,
21 И, чтоб не потеснить гуляющих господ,
22 Пускать не велено сюда простой народ?[12] (PSS III: 417)

"Secular Power"
When the fulfillment of the great triumph drew near,

and God lay dying on the cross in agony,
then, by the sides of the life-bearing tree—
the sinner Mary and the Blessed Virgin—
  there stood two women,
immersed in immeasurable grief.
But now, at the foot of the hallowed cross,
as if at the porch of the city mayor,
we see in place of the holy women
two fearsome sentinels with rifles and in shakos.
Tell me, what is the purpose of this guard?
Can it be that the crucifixion is the property of state,
and you are afraid of thieves or mice?
Or do you imagine you add status to the King of Kings?
Or are you saving with your mighty patronage
Our Lord, whose head is wreathed in a crown of thorns,
Christ, who meekly surrendered his flesh
to the tormentors' whips, nails, and spear?
Or are you vexed that the rabble might offend
the one whose death redeemed the tribe of Adam,
and so as not to crowd the masters in their revelry,
it was decreed to bar the common folk?

"Imitation of the Italian" and "Secular Power" are complementary poems juxtaposing sin and virtue, hubris and humility. The former opened with the tree on which Judas hanged himself, the latter opens with the "life-giving tree," the Holy Cross. Projected on the calendar of the Paschal events, "Secular Power" brings us to the hours of the Crucifixion on Good Friday.

Both poems are meditations on the betrayal and death of the traitor and the betrayed. "Imitation" traces the posthumous ordeal of Judas and his subsequent betrayal by Satan; "Secular Power" traces the postmortem betrayal of Christ and of the symbol of the Crucifixion. Each poem challenges and judges the transcendental and secular powers involved in that betrayal. Thus Judas, whom Puškin calls "vse*mir*nyj vrag" (universal foe), is linked to "*mir*skaja vlast' " (worldly power) in more than just an alliterative sense.

As Prince Vjazemskij pointed out, "Secular Power" is a poetic reflection on a concrete event. The poem was written "because in the Kazanskij Cathedral on Good Friday, armed soldiers stood guard at the shroud of Christ" (PSS 1959–62 II: 749) to preserve order. However, the presence of the sentinels at the sacred place at such a moment provoked Puškin's invective against this, albeit unintentional, profanation of the divine mystery by secular forces. The poem dramatizes the conflict between the two powers and underscores its pointlessness.

Like the previous two poems, "Secular Power" has a threefold structure. The first segment (lines 1–6) re-enacts the original moment of triumph: "Kogda velikoe sveršalos' toržestvo / I v mukax na kreste končalos' božestvo." Both verbs "sveršalos' " (was coming to fulfillment) and "kon-čalos' " (was dying) designate finiteness, yet their imperfective aspect paradoxically creates the impression of something non-finite and atemporal. Also the unusual "Kogda . . . togda" (when . . . then), expressing simultaneity rather than sequentiality of the events, has a similar effect of atemporality. Unlike mystery, which takes place in eternity, history takes place in time. The second segment (lines 7–10) transfers us into the present, into history proper ("teper' . . . my zrim" [but now . . . we behold]), where the corruption of the mystery occurs. The third segment (11–22) contains Puškin's invective in which the discrepancy between the worldly and the divine power is heightened through a series of mocking rhetorical questions, all implying negative answers.

Like the rest of the poems of this cycle, "Secular Power" is based on a subtext from the Gospels and from the text of the Paschal service. But in contrast to the canonic texts, where three Marys appear by the cross (John 19:25), Puškin leaves out the third woman. The omission is a deliberate one, motivated by the considerations of symmetry. The place of the two holy women will be usurped in the second segment of the poem by the two sentinels. Ironically, the achieved symmetry is purely formal, and no true equation between the two events exists. The disproportionate length of the two segments (6 lines vs. 4 lines) reveals the disparity between the authentic event and its sham version. At the same time Puškin's two women evoke the visit to the Holy Sepulcher by "Mary Magdalene, and the other Mary" (Matt. 27:61, 28:1). The armed guards, placed at the entrance to the sepulcher, were to prevent the disciples from "stealing away" Christ's body and saying to people "He is risen from the dead" (Matt. 27:64), cf.: "I vy boitesja vorov ili myšej?" (Or is it thieves or mice you fear?)[13]

The attempt of secular power to protect or usurp the divine triumph is mocked by Puškin in a series of ironic similes and metaphors in which the holy symbols are desecrated by profane images. "Krest čestnoj" (hallowed cross) is mockingly compared to the mundane "kryl'co" (porch), while God (Božestvo, Car' Carej, Vladyka, Xristos) is reduced to "city mayor" (gradskoj pravitel'). The two holy women are replaced by two sentinels, calling to mind the Roman guards or the two thieves. "Raspjatie" (Crucifixion), which is also referred to as "kazn' " (execution), is reduced to "*kazen*naja poklaža" (state property). (Both words call to mind the *Kazan*skij Cathedral, where the profanation took place.)

Puškin's rhymes also participate in the exposé of this sham substitution. In the first segment which reproduces the genuine event, all rhymes semantically harmonize and are enriched by alliteration, thus producing a certain homophonic effect: "tor*žestvo*-bo*žestvo*, *dreva-deva*, *ženy*-pogru*ženy*" (triumph-God, tree-Virgin, women-immersed). The rhymes in the second and third segments which deal with the sham version are all non-alliterative and produce a semantically dissonant effect, bordering on grotesque: "kresta čestnago–pravitelja gradskago, svjatyx-časovyx, myšej-carej, mogučim-koljučim, plot' svoju–kopiju, oskorbila-iskupila, gospod-narod" (hallowed cross–city mayor, holy women–sentinels, mice-King, mighty-thorny, flesh-spear, offend-redeem, masters-folk).

Like the other poems of this cycle, "Secular Power" is written in regular Alexandrines. The only verse that deviates from this pattern is the truncated line 5, which Puškin graphically isolated in the text. This elliptic line from which the third Mary is missing is actually a hemistich. Its isolation within the poem can be seen as a graphic metaphor for the abandonment, while its incompleteness evokes a sense of loss. The only other metrical irregularity found in the poem is the supranumeric stress in line 10: "V ruž'e i kivere *dvúx gróz*nyx časovyx." The ostentative spondee rhythmically marks off the two poised sentinels, and links this line to the only other irregular line, the hemistich "Stojali dve ženy," whose place has been usurped by the sentinels.

The third segment (lines 11–12) shifts into direct speech, which consists of rhetorical questions. It differs from the rest of the poem through its intonation, and it introduces a new rhythmical pattern, characterized by pyrrhics before the caesura (lines 11–19). The column of pyrrhics divides the third segment vertically, as it were, into two rhythmical and intonational columns. Each rhetorical question in this segment presupposes a negative answer: "K čemu?" "Ni k čemu!" The sarcasm of the questions in combination with the implied negative answers completes the exposé of the sham event. The liturgical lines "Vsue xraniši grob, kustodie, / Ne uderžit bo raka Samosuščuju žizn' " (In vain are you guarding the tomb, custodian, / The shrine won't keep the Self-sustaining life) characterize best the failure of the secular powers to usurp the sacred event.

"Secular Power" concludes Puškin's poetic liturgy which I call the Easter triptych. Its last two poems are directly linked to the sin of Judas, hubris and betrayal. In "Imitation" Christ was betrayed in life, in "Secular Power" he is betrayed in death. Both poems share the theme of death: the suicide of the traitor, and the Crucifixion of the betrayed. More important, the attempts to subvert the divine order backfire in both poems, and the hubris is punished. The kiss which Satan gives Judas is a punishment meted out in accordance with a higher design. Likewise, the attempt by the secular powers to usurp the divine triumph fails, and the primacy of *civitas Dei* over *civitas mundi* is upheld in accordance with Christ's words: "My kingship is not of this world" (John 18:36).

It can be added that Puškin's poem about the crucifixion flanked by two sentinels turned out to be fatidic. It calls to mind the circumstances surrounding his own funeral, only a few months ahead. Prince Vjazemskij described this event:

It may be said without exaggeration that more police than friends collected about the bier. I do not speak of the soldiers picketing the streets. But against whom was arrayed this military force which filled the home of the deceased during those minutes when a dozen of his friends and closest comrades gathered there in order to render him their last homage? (Simmons 1971: 426)

Admission to the funeral service at the Royal Stables Church was restricted to those who held tickets. From there, at midnight on 3 February, the sleigh with the poet's body hastily departed for the Svjatogorskij Monastery in the Pskov province. The infamous role of the sentinels fell to the gendarme Rakeev, who accompanied the sleigh (and 25 years later came to arrest N. G. Černyševskij), whereas the place of the two Marys was taken by Puškin's friend A. I. Turgenev and Nikita Kozlov, the poet's old valet.

The last question that remains to be answered concerns the hypothetical shape and unity of the entire "Stone Island" cycle, which was to consist of six poems. There can be little doubt that the three contiguous poems marked by Puškin II, III, IV, and straddled by the two empty slots, I and V, form a thematically unified minicycle which I have called the Easter triptych. However, when by the end of July Puškin sketched the outline of this cycle, two major poems, "Kogda za gorodom, zadumčiv, ja brožu . . . " (When I, pensive, roam beyond the city . . .) and "Ja pamjatnik sebe vozdvig . . . " (Exegi monumentum), were not yet written; they were completed only on 14 and 21 August, respectively.

Puškin did not live to realize his project, but the eventual shape of the cycle has become the subject of an engaging academic discussion. N. V. Izmajlov (1954: 555; 1958: 29), for example, proposed "Exegi monumentum" as the opening poem of the cycle, while "When I, pensive, roam . . . " was to fill the fifth place. N. L. Stepanov (1959: 32) and M. P. Alekseev (1967: 124) were against the inclusion of "Exegi monumentum" in this cycle, though Stepanov accepted Izmajlov's suggestion that "When I, pensive, roam . . . " might be the fifth poem of the cycle.

In my opinion the hypothetical place of "When I, pensive, roam . . . " and "Exegi monumentum" should be determined according to the same principle which governed the inner triptych. The remaining two poems seem to continue the hours of the Easter week: after the Lenten prayer (II) and the poems about Judas's suicide (III) and the crucifixion (IV) could follow Puškin's sepulchral meditation in "When I, pensive, roam . . . " Projected on the Paschal calendar, "When I, pensive, roam . . . " would correspond to the time of the tomb (Saturday). The contrast between the death of Judas and Christ which was established in the previous poems is echoed in "When I, pensive, roam . . . " in the opposition of two postmortem abodes—the obnoxious, grotesque public (city) cemetery, reminding one of Hell, and the heavenly ancestral (country) graveyard. Christ's descent to Hell on Saturday would be a befitting context. The entire cycle would then conclude with "Exegi monumentum," in which Puškin proudly raised the claim of his poetic immortality, while humbly subordinating his

Muse to the will of God. Projected on the Easter calendar, "Exegi monumentum" points toward the day of Resurrection (Sunday).

In order to complete the hypothetical shape of the cycle, one last conjecture is necessary. If "Exegi monumentum" were to conclude the cycle, then "From Pindemonte" would have to be shifted to the unfilled first position. The two poems have several features in common: the proud declaration of independence before the secular powers and the rejection of the *vox Caesaris* and *vox populi* in favor of some supreme power. In "From Pindemonte" it is the "divine beauty of nature and the creations of art," in "Exegi monumentum" it is the poet's Muse and the will of God. However, there is a substantial difference between the two poems which would justify the shift. The invocation of the divine in "From Pindemonte" has polytheistic overtones, which places the poem into the pagan tradition of the Roman republic: "Ja ne ropšču o tom, čto otkazali *bogi*, / Mne v sladkoj učasti osporivat' nalogi" (I do not fret because the *gods* refuse / to let me wrangle over revenues). The grammatical plural in this crucial word disqualifies "From Pindemonte" as the concluding poem of the cycle, which by now had taken a distinctly Christian turn. Moreover, in "From Pindemonte" the divine beauty of nature stands on equal footing with the man-made beauty of art:

> По прихоти своей скитаться здесь и там,
> Дивясь божественным природу красотам,
> И пред созданьями искусств и вдохновенья
> Трепеща радостно в восторгах умиленья.
>   —Вот счастье! Вот права . . . (PSS III: 420)

> At one's own whim to roam here and there,
> at nature's divine beauties to marvel,
> [all the while] trembling joyously in tender ecstasies
> before works or art and inspiration.
>   —This is happiness! These are rights . . .

In the quasi-Christian "Exegi monumentum," this equation is shifted in favor of the divine: "velen'ju Bož'ju, o Muza, bud' poslušna" (obey God's will, O Muse). It therefore makes more sense to see the aloof, whimsical ("po prixoti svoej"), and definitely pre-Christian "From Pindemonte" as a poem preceding the Easter triptyph, which "Exegi monumentum" would then conclude on a rather humble note: unlike Horace in his "Exegi monumentum," Puškin is not demanding Delphic laurels from his Muse. Instead the poet submits his Muse, and through her his poetic immortality, to the will of God.

"Exegi monumentum" thus beautifully reflects the internal movement of the entire cycle, which alternated between the expressions of hubris and humility. In "From Pindemonte" the poet aloofly rejects the "much vaunted" democratic rights and freedoms offered by society yet reverts to rapture and "umilenie" when facing creation, divine and human. In "Hermit fathers . . . " the poet, following the example of saintly men and women, creates a prayer through which he asks that the spirit of humility ("dux smirenija") be revived in him. The poem about Judas and Satan represents supreme hubris. It is followed by the example of Christ and the two Marys, whose meekness is contrasted with the hubris of the secular powers. The meditation over the graves in "When I, pensive, roam . . . " juxtaposes posthumous hubris to humility, the pretentiousness of the public urban cemetery to the humbleness of the ancestral country graveyard. The last poem of this cycle brings us from the two cemeteries to Puškin's own monument in "Exegi monumentum." The contemplation about one's posthumous destiny in "Exegi monumentum" proceeds from hubris toward humility, from "Net, ves' ja ne umru" (Not all of me shall die) to "Velen'ju Bož'ju, o Muza, bud' poslušna" (Obey God's will, O Muse). "Exegi monumentum" thus repeats and concludes the inner development of the entire Stone Island cycle, whose hypothetical arrangement I propose as follows:

  (I) "From Pindemonte"
  II "Hermit fathers and immaculate women"
 III "Imitation of the Italian"
 IV "Secular Power"
 (V) "When I, pensive, roam beyond the city . . . "
(VI) "Exegi monumentum"

The Horatian subtext of "Exegi monumentum" gives additional support to my arrangement, since Puškin might have wanted to conclude his cycle not only with a Horatian ode but also in accordance with Horace's compositional design: Horace placed *his* "Exegi monumentum" at the end of the third book of his *Carmina*.

SIMON KARLINSKY

Bestužev-Marlinskij's
Journey to Revel' and Puškin

Aleksandr Bestužev (1797–1837) acquired his literary reputation as a romantic critic and fiction writer during the years 1822–25 when, jointly with Kondratij Ryleev, he edited the annual miscellany *Poljarnaja zvezda* (North Star). A participant in the Decembrist rebellion, he was exiled first to Siberia, then to the Caucasus. National fame as the foremost Russian romantic novelist came to Bestužev during those years in exile, when he signed his work with the pen name A. Marlinskij (after a pavilion called Marly in Peterhof where he once lived). During the 1830s and early 1840s, multi-volume collections of his stories, novels, and essays appeared in numerous printings (Muratova 1962: 162). He was the first Russian writer whose work was widely translated into foreign languages (Vengerov 1892 III: 176–77). Then, by circa 1850, the murderous reviews by Vissarion Belinskij of 1840, 1842, and 1847 (Muratova 1962: 165) gradually turned the general admiration into contempt for what came to be termed "Marlinism." Semën Vengerov was the only commentator of the late nineteenth century to assert that the Belinskij-derived view of Bestužev-Marlinskij as the epitome of everything false, verbose, and stilted was neither fair nor true (Vengerov 1892: 148–49).

Belinskij's curse was lifted from Bestužev's name only after the 1930s, when the Decembrists were admitted into the revolutionary pantheon of the USSR. Unpublished in his country since 1847, Bestužev's fiction made a comeback in 1937 (Bestužev-Marlinskij 1937). The year 1948 saw the appearance of his collected poetry in the *Biblioteka poèta* series (with a second edition in 1961). In 1958 a two-volume collection of his novels, stories, essays, and poetry was published. None of these editions included Bestužev's first major publication, the travelogue in prose and verse *Poezdka v Revel'* (Journey to Revel') (though the first six lines of its prefatory poem were cited by Nikolaj Mordovčenko in his introduction to the *Biblioteka poèta* collection of verse). The travelogue was published in February 1821 in the journal *Sorevnovatel'* (Contender) (Golubov 1960: 78), and it appeared in book form in the summer of that year (the authorization to publish, signed by the censor Ivan Timkovskij and dated June 25, 1821, is reproduced on the reverse of the title page in Bestužev 1821).

Aleksandr Bestužev began his literary activities in 1818–19 as a literary critic who championed nascent Russian romanticism. His attacks on stylistic archaisms and neoclassical poetics in Pavel Katenin's translation of Racine's *Esther* and Aleksandr Šaxovskoj's comedy *Lipeckie vody* (The Lipetsk Spa) created a considerable stir and made Bestužev's name known in St. Petersburg literary circles (Vengerov 1892: 153; Golubov 1960: 55–60). At the end of 1820 Bestužev traveled from St. Petersburg to the capital city of Estonia, Tallinn, which was then called Revel' in Russian, Reval in German and other Western languages, and had borne the name of Kolyvan' in the earlier Russian tradition.

The journey, which lasted less than two weeks (from the end of December 1820 to January 10, 1821), was undertaken with the transparent purpose of writing a book of travel impressions. Bestužev must have read a number of history books on the Baltic region. He was particularly fascinated by the recurrent occupation of Estonia by its various neighbors—the German knights of the Livonian Order, the Swedes, the Danes, and the Russians—with the resultant mixture and conflict between the varying cultures.

Bestužev had three literary models for his travelogue, all of which are mentioned in its text. All three were highly admired representatives of that genre: *A Sentimental Journey* by Laurence Sterne (1768); *Lettres sur l'Italie* by Charles-Marguerite-Jean-Baptiste-Mercier Dupaty (1785), a work that was still much valued and reprinted in France during the first three decades of the nineteenth century; and Nikolaj Karamzin's *Pis'ma russkogo putešestvennika* (Letters of a Russian Traveler) (1791).[1] Like these predecessors, Bestužev recorded the sights and conversations of his trip and his own emotional, typically sentimentalist reactions to them. He also incorporated into his text a literary discussion he had had with his brother, in which he made it clear that the most important contemporary writers for him were Karamzin and Krylov among the older generation and Baratynskij and Puškin among the younger. (*Ruslan i Ljudmila* [Ruslan and Ljudmila] was published in the summer of 1820, a few months after Puškin's departure for his southern exile in May. Baratynskij's first *poèma*, *Piry* [Feasts], was read and discussed at the December 13, 1820, meeting of the literary society Vol'noe obščestvo ljubitelej rossijskoj slovesnosti [Free Society of Lovers of Russian Literature], of which Bestužev became a member on November 15 of the same year.) (Golubov 1960: 74; Bazanov 1949: 347)

Journey to Revel' also contained two interpolated novellas of the kind that were to bring Bestužev his later fame for his narrative prose: a contemporary society tale with mistaken identities, a duel fought to defend a woman's honor, and a happy dénouement ending in marriage (Bestužev 1821: 5–13); and a historical tale of knightly adventure (1821: 124–41) which was the progenitor of the series of Bestužev's cloak-and-dagger stories of 1822–25 that were set in the Baltic region and are now known as his

Livonian Cycle (Leighton 1972: 258 and 1975: 70). The opening paragraph of the second novella, incidentally, is a compact summary of the reign of Boris Godunov from the death of Ivan the Terrible to the coronation of the False Dimitrij, the historical territory later to be traveled by Puškin and A. K. Tolstoj.

Unlike the sentimentalist travel accounts on which *Journey to Revel'* was patterned, its text is interlarded with passages in verse. Although as a poet Bestužev must be assigned a secondary rank, the poems included in *Journey to Revel'* are among his most remarkable ones, both in their own right and for their special intertextual relationships with the poetry of his predecessors and contemporaries. (Lauren G. Leighton's two surveys of Bestužev's poetry [1969a: 309–22 and 1975: 117–33] do not mention the poems in *Journey to Revel'*.)

It has long been noticed that one of the best-known lines in the whole of Russian poetry, "Beleet parus odinokij," was borrowed by Lermontov from Bestužev's narrative poem "Andrej, knjaz' Perejaslavskij" (Andrej, Prince Perejaslavskij), first published in 1828 and 1830. But Lermontov was by no means the only poet to incorporate lines from Bestužev's poetry into his own, as we shall see. For his part, Bestužev often appropriated lines, phrases, or the entire tone of a poem from other poets. To give one random example, the first line of his love lyric "Aline" (To Alina), dating from 1827 or 1828, "Ešče, ešče odno lobzan'e!" (Bestužev-Marlinskij 1961: 75), is an unconcealed, though slightly garbled, quotation from Puškin's *Cygany* (The Gypsies), line 431: "Ešče odno . . . odno lobzan'e."

In *Journey to Revel'*, the elegy on pages 4–5 evokes Konstantin Batjuš-kov's elegy "Ten' druga" (The Shade of a Friend; cf. Bestužev 1821 and Batjuškov 1964: 170–71). The two extended poems about the waterfall at Narva (121–22, 123) could stand comparison with the poems called "Vodopad" (The Waterfall) by Deržavin (which antedated Bestužev's two poems), Baratynskij (1821 and thus almost contemporary with *Journey to Revel'*) and Jazykov (1830). Most uncanny of all in intertextual terms are the two first poems of Bestužev's book, the prefatory one, in the form of a dedication of the book to the poet's friends, and the poem about military maneuvers on page 3. These two poems are interesting not only because they show what Bestužev had learned from his contemporaries Puškin and Baratynskij, but also because the first one predicts the diction and the vocabulary of *Evgenij Onegin* (Eugene Onegin) and the second one adum-brates *Poltava*, two works by the mature Puškin that did not yet exist when Bestužev's travelogue was published. There is still another poem in *Journey to Revel'*, a satirical one on pages 32–33, which compares the St. Peters-burg balls to an informal social gathering the narrator attended in Revel'. This poem's intertextual ties to several passages in *Eugene Onegin* (I.27–28, II.25–44, VIII.14–16 and 23–26) are quite complex and would merit a separate study.

For several years now, I have amused myself by showing a xerox of the first poem in *Journey to Revel'* to some of my colleagues and asking them to guess what it might be. Among the written replies from scholars particularly concerned with Puškin studies, I can cite the following descriptions of this poem: (1) "a real encyclopedia of the imagery of both Puškin and Baratynskij in the mid-1820s"; (2) "a hitherto undiscovered earlier draft of *Eugene Onegin*"; and (3) "a clever imitation of Puškin that uses his typical imagery, lexicon, and diction." This Puškinian flavor of the prefatory poem was so easily grasped by the colleagues I addressed that one has to marvel as to why the poem was not included in the recent editions of Bestužev's verse or why it was not mentioned in any of the prefaces to the publications of his other writings.

With the appearance of J. Thomas Shaw's dictionary of Puškin's rhymes in 1974 and his later, even more indispensable concordance to Puškin's poetry (1985a), we now have the precise scholarly equipment with which to measure the Puškinian effect these two poems produce. Since none of the poems in *Journey to Revel'* bears a title, I shall henceforth refer to the first of them (Bestužev 1821: 1–2) as the prefatory poem and to the second one (1821: 3) as the military poem. (Please see the attached texts reproduced from the 1821 edition and their English translations by the author of this essay, with the added numbering of lines.)

The prefatory poem is dated "Revel', 29 December 1820." It consists of thirty-four lines of irregularly rhymed iambic tetrameter. Although the rhymes never form an Onegin stanza, they freely alternate the three kinds of rhyming typical of it: quatrains of cross-rhymes and of adjacent and enclosing ones are present. Thus a pattern is produced which suggests to the reader, if only half-consciously, the sonorities of Puškin's novel in verse. The opening quatrain of the poem reads:

> Желали вы—я обещал,
> Мои взыскательные други!
> Чтоб я рассказам посвящал
> Минутных отдыхов досуги.

The rhyme *drugi-dosugi* in this first quatrain immediately brings us to Puškin. True, as J. Thomas Shaw's dictionary of rhymes (1974) demonstrates, Puškin did not get around to rhyming these words in their plural form until 1835, in a draft of a response to his friends who advised him to write a sequel to *Eugene Onegin*. But the singular forms, *drug-dosug* and *drug-nedosug*, were a constant feature of Puškin's verse from as early as his 1815 poem "Gorodok" (Small Town), where these combinations are to be found at several points. As Tamara Xmel'nickaja suggested (1966: 58), when Andrej Belyj attempted a stylization in the manner of Puškin's *Eugene Onegin* in certain portions of his autobiographical *poèma Pervoe svidanie* (First Encounter, 1921), he wrote a quatrain with the enclosing rhyme *drug-dosug*.

But the beginning of the prefatory poem reminds us of Puškin also because these lines show the impact of the "Posvjaščenie" (Dedication) to *Ruslan and Ljudmila*, which Bestužev could have read during the preceding summer. His close familiarity with this *poèma* is attested by the prose meditation (Bestužev 1821: 27), where the narrator is caught in a blizzard and reflects on the transience of human existence. The prose passage and the four lines of verse that end it,

> Промчатся веки в след векам
> За улетающим мгновеньем,
> И смерть по жизненным путям
> Запорошит наш след забвеньем!

> Centuries after centuries will pass
> Following the fleeting moment,
> And death will obliterate our traces
> Along the paths of our lives!

follow fairly closely Ruslan's apostrophe to the battlefield covered with remnants of dead warriors and overgrown with *trava zabven'ja* (III.178–91). Puškin dedicated *Ruslan and Ljudmila* to beautiful women, *krasavicy*, while Bestužev's prefatory poem is addressed to his "demanding friends," *vzyskatel'nye drugi*. The prefatory poem repeats two ideas about writing poetry from the dedication of *Ruslan and Ljudmila*: poetry is created during the hours of leisure ("V časy dosugov zolotyx"), and it should be playful (*igrivaja*). Compare lines 4 and 7 of "Dedication" with lines 4 and 15 of the prefatory poem, where Puškin's "moj trud igrivyj" is echoed in Bestužev's "Poèzii vsegda igrivoj." This last epithet was also applied to poetry twice in Puškin's verse epistle "K Batjuškovu," published in 1815 (S:I.20.24 and S:I.20.43).[2]

Other Puškinian echoes in the prefatory poem are more problematic because they involve Puškin's poems that antedate *Journey to Revel'* but were not published until after Puškin's and Bestužev's deaths in 1837. Two of Bestužev's biographers assume that Puškin and Bestužev must have been close friends during the period 1818–early 1820 (Vengerov 1907–15: 153; Golubov 1960: 62–63). But this supposition is nowhere attested or in any way documented. Mixail Alekseev (1930: 241–51) and Lauren G. Leighton (1983: 351–82) were right to insist that the two writers had never met in person. Their correspondence of 1822–25, when Puškin was a contributor to Bestužev's and Ryleev's *Poljarnaja zvezda*, begins with Puškin's highly formal letter (*Milostivyj gosudar'* [Gracious Sir]) in reply to a lost one by Bestužev (Puškin 1982 I: 458–59). The form of address and the tone of the letter imply that the two writers were strangers when this correspondence began. However, it is conceivable that Bestužev had access to the two poems in question in hand-written copies through Baratynskij or some other literary man that he is known to have met prior to his Revel' journey.

Be that as it may, line 7 of the prefatory poem, "čtob ja, pitomec prazdnoj leni," follows the pattern of line 34 from Puškin's then-unpublished "Naezdniki" (The Riders), "Užel' nevol'nik prazdnoj negi" (S:I.69.34). Similarly, Bestužev's line 20, "I s krov'u rezvoju kipelo," calls to mind a line from Puškin's "Monax" (The Monk), "U ženixa krov' sil'no zakipela" (S:I.2a.85). Line 19, "Kogda zvezdilosja Ai," with its neologistic verb *zvezdit'sja*, is a clear allusion to Baratynskij's *Piry*:

> Свое любимое Аи.
> Его звезящаяся влага
> Недаром взоры веселит. (Baratynskij 1957: 224)

> . . . His favorite Ay.
> Its star-sparkling liquid
> Not for nothing makes the gaze rejoice.

The frequent evocations by the Russian poets of Puškin's time of the champagne brand Ay might ultimately be traced, as Nabokov has suggested, to Voltaire's example (Nabokov 1975 II: 480). Puškin had mentioned it in his 1819 verse epistle "Vsevoložskomu" (To Vsevoložskij, pub. 1826). Ay is brought up in Puškin's poetry a total of six times. The last time it appears is in "Otryvki iz putešestvija Onegina" (Excerpts from Onegin's Journey). Its context, "Kak zašipevsego Ai / Struja i bryzgi zolotye," in the eulogy to the music of Rossini, seems to combine Voltaire's *écume pétillante* (as cited by Nabokov) with Ay's starry sparkle, praised by both Baratynskij and Bestužev in 1820.

So far, only the possible impact of Puškin (and to a lesser degree Baratynskij) on Bestužev's opening poem has been examined. What about the reverse influence—the impact of the first two poems in *Journey to Revel'* on Puškin? Although Puškin spoke of a few of Bestužev's novellas and essays in his correspondence, the travelogue and its highly Puškinian first poem are nowhere brought up (Bogoslovskij 1934: 620). Yet he must have kept it in his mind for many years, consciously or not, because its rhymes, rhythms, intonations, and whole lines keep reverberating through the pages of the mature Puškin of *Eugene Onegin* and *Poltava*.

The remarkably long breath of the prefatory poem encompasses one continuous sentence in its initial sixteen lines. The syntactic structure of this sentence is built on the enumeration of the things the poet had promised his friends to write—*ja obeščal* of the first line. This enumeration is reinforced by the anaphoric reiteration of *Čtob ja*, which begins lines 3, 7, and 11 and which may have been in the back of Puškin's mind when he composed the even more anaphoric fourteen-line listing of Mazepa's vices in Canto One of *Poltava*, where more than half of the lines begin with *Čto* or with *Čto on* . . . :

> Не многим, может быть, известно,
> Что дух его неукротим,

Что рад и честно и бесчестно
Вредить он недругам своим;
Что ни единой он обиды
С тех пор как жив не забывал

Perhaps not many know
That his spirit is indomitable,
That he is happy to harm his enemies
In both honorable and dishonorable ways;
That he has not forgotten a single offense
Since the beginning of his life

and so on for eight more lines (*Poltava* I.228–42). A similarly anaphoric series of lines beginning with *čto* is found in *Eugene Onegin*, VIII.11. In the dedicatory poem of *Eugene Onegin* we find that the lines "Poèzii živoj i jasnoj" and "Prostonarodnyx, ideal'nyx" recall lines 11 and 15 of Bestužev's dedication: "Poèzii, vsegda igrivoj" and "čtob ja bylova [*sic*] s ideal'nym." Both texts qualify their authors' manner of writing poetry by the adjective *nebrežnyj* ("Ruka nebrežnaja pisala" in Bestužev and "Nebrežnyj plod moix zabav" in Puškin). Neither Batjuškov nor Baratynskij, Bestužev's other possible models, connected the adjectives *igrivyj* or *nebrežnyj* with their creative endeavors (Shaw 1975a, 1975b).

Line 25 of the prefatory poem, "Skvoz' nabljudatel'nyj lornet," must be the progenitor of a series of similar lines in *Eugene Onegin*: "Razočarovannyj lornet" (I.19.11), "I nevnimatel'nyj lornet" (VII.51.11), and, in "Otryvki iz putešestvija Onegina," the line closest of all to Bestužev, "A razyskatel'nyj lornet." The first of these *lornet* lines repeats Bestužev's rhyme for it, *svet*. In his fine commentary on *Eugene Onegin*, Ju. M. Lotman devoted a whole page to explaining the significance of the lorgnette in Puškin's time. Lotman cited several eighteenth-century works as the probable source of these lines (Lotman 1983: 151–52).

Lines 27–30 of Bestužev's prefatory poem form a quatrain that features a typical Puškinian device: a group of dots that replace an unprintable word. The number of dots (eight) and the context point to at least three Russian adjectives, all of them translatable into English as "shitty." But it is the next quatrain, lines 31 and 34, that seems a veritable hatchery for future Puškin lines and intonations:

За тем напутный мой рассказ
Без пиитических прикрас
Рука небрежная писала;
И так, друзья — н а ч н е м   с н а ч а л а.

Although there is a four-foot iambic line in *Ruslan and Ljudmila* that ends with the words *moj rasskaz* (VI.361), the first line of Bestužev's last quatrain seems closer to the final line of the prologue to *Mednyj vsadnik* (The Bronze Horseman), "Pečalen budet moj rasskaz." The second line of this quatrain, "Bez piitičeskix prikras," consisting as it does of the negative *Bez*, followed by a five-syllable adjective and a two-syllable noun in genitive plural which the adjective modifies, may have served as a model for some of the most expressive lines in *Eugene Onegin*. In VI.44 we find "Užel' i vprjam i v samom dele / Bez èlegičeskix zatej / Vesna moix promčalas' dnej," and in VIII.14, at the description of Onegin's first glimpse of Tat'jana as a married society woman, there is a sequence of four lines (7–10), all anaphorically beginning with *Bez*, which culminates with "Bez podražatel'nyx zatej," echoing both Bestužev and the cited line from VI.44.

The Puškinian significance of line 33, "Ruka nebrežnaja pisala," has already been mentioned. The final line of the prefatory poem explodes with Puškinian associations that fly in all directions. Its first half, "I tak druz'ja," also forms the beginning of the last line of the False Dimitrij in Scene 11 of *Boris Godunov*, "Itak, druz'ja, do zavtra, do svidan'ja." (Line 21 of Bestužev's prefatory poem, "Teper' sovsem drugoe delo," would later be echoed in Mnišek's rhymed speech at the end of *Boris Godunov*'s Scene 12, "Teper' ne to, ne to čto prežde bylo.") The second half of line 34, which Bestužev emphasized by spacing out its letters (*razrjadka*), was apparently the point of departure for all four instances when Puškin used the word *načnem* that are recorded in Professor Shaw's concordance: "Načnem ab ovo" of the unfinished "Ezerskij" (1832–33) and the shorter poem related to it, "Rodoslovnaja moego geroja" (Genealogy of My Hero, 1836); the beginning of the narration proper that follows the initial digression on versification in *Domik v Kolomne* (Little House in Kolomna), "Teper' načnem."—"žila-byla vdova"; and the poignant moment in *Eugene Onegin* when the two male protagonists are about to start shooting at each other: "čto ž, načinat'?"—"Načnem, požaluj" (Shaw 1985a II: 609).

The prefatory poem from *Journey to Revel'* so clearly presages the diction of *Eugene Onegin* that even the *magičeskij kristall* of *Onegin*'s penultimate stanza, through which the poet dimly distinguishes the contours of his future novel, seems to be foreshadowed by Bestužev's lines 11–14:

> Чтоб я былова с идеальным
> Разнообразные черты,
> Воображением хрустальным
> Одел в блестящие цветы
> Поэзии всегда игривой.

Therefore, it is curious to note that when Chapter I of *Onegin* was published in February 1825, Bestužev thought it insignificant and unworthy of Puškin. His oft-quoted letter to Puškin of March 9, 1825, with its invidious comparison of Puškin's description of St. Petersburg to that of Byron in *Don Juan* and Puškin's able defense of his *magnum opus* in his reply of

March 24 (Puškin 1982: 471–78), indicates that neither writer was aware of any connection between *Onegin* and Bestužev's poem written five years earlier. (On Bestužev's view of *Onegin*, see Leighton 1969a: 200–201 and 1983: 351–52.).

Bestužev's military poem, which follows the prefatory one after sixteen lines of prose, does not have the Puškinian rhythm or sonority. A somewhat sloppily versified fifteen lines that mix iambic tetrameter, pentameter, and hexameter and have no regular rhyming pattern, the poem seems far from Puškin's habitual craftsmanship and precision. And yet, its lexicon, its rhymes, and some phrases somehow found their way into Puškin's later work. The poem's very first word, the inchoative *Byvalo*, has become almost a Puškin trademark. There is one example of it in a Puškin poem that antedates *Journey to Revel'*, the epigram "Na Rjabuškina" (On Rjabuškin, pub. 1815). But this initial position of *Byvalo* is especially frequent in the mature Puškin of *Poltava* (two instances), *Domik v Kolomne* (also two), and, significantly, *Eugene Onegin*, where six stanzas, mostly in the later chapters, begin with this word.[3] In the fifteenth stanza of "Otryvki iz putešestvija Onegina," "Byvalo, puška zorevaja" is an amalgam of the first two lines of Bestužev's military poem: "Byvalo tam, kogda Priroda v sne, / Gremela puška zarevaja." (Bestužev misspelled the word *zorevaja*; *puška zorevaja*, according to *Slovar' jazyka Puškina* 1957 II: 159, was a cannon shot that announced the reveille, *zórja*.) To quote Xmel'nickaja once more on Andrej Belyj's stylistic disguise as Puškin in portions of his *Pervoe svidanie*, "At times, the very choice of words takes us back to the lexical coloration of the poetry of Puškin's time" (Xmel'nickaja 1966: 58). As an example of what she means, Xmel'nickaja cites two lines from Belyj's poem: "Byvalo, ja zvonilsja zdes' / Otdat'sja piršesvennym negam . . ."

The rhyme of line 3 of the military poem, *na kone*, is common enough in Puškin, whether in amphibrachic lines (as in "Černaja šal' " [The Black Shawl] and "Pesn' o veščem Olege" [Song of the Prophetic Oleg]) or in iambic ones. Yet, of the fourteen instances cited in the dictionary of rhymes (Shaw 1974), not a single one repeats Bestužev's rhyming it with *sne*. But the line that follows, "Skakal, oružiem sverkaja," has several memorable associations with Puškin, including *Onegin*, "vzorami sverkaja" from Tat'jana's dream (V.18.12), and "Stal'noj ščetinoju sverkaja" from the 1831 poem "Klevetnikam Rossii" (To the Slanderers of Russia; S:III.190.41). This line of Bestužev's has somehow found its way into a popular Russian song with words and music by V. A. Sabinin, first published in Kiev in 1915 and frequently heard in Russian émigré restaurants during the period between the two world wars (Černov 1949 I: 145; Ivanov 1969 II: 216–17):

Оружьем на солнце сверкая,
Под звуки лихих трубачей,

По улице, пыль поднимая,
Проходил полк гусар-усачей.

Their weapons sparkling in the sun,
To the sound of the jaunty buglers,
In the street, raising dust,
There marched a regiment of mustachioed hussars.

In line 5 of the military poem, the intertextual relationship is reversed, because that line is a paraphrase of a line from Puškin's early poem "Vospominanija v Carskom Sele" (Recollections in Carskoe Selo, pub. 1815). Compare Puškin's "Za stroem stroj tečet [. . .]" (S:I.24.99) with Bestužev's "I vdrug stekalsja k stroju stroj." There are also two comparable wordings in *Ruslan and Ljudmila*, "Tam rubitsja so stroem stroj" and "I s voplem stroj na stroj valitsja" (VI.260 and VI.302). But in the lines that follow, 6–9:

Перун послышав боевой: —
Пехота двигалась стенами,
Смыкались латников полки
И налетали козаки,

we find ourselves again in future Puškin poems.

Bestužev's rather archaic "Perun [. . .] boevoj" was repeated by Puškin in a strange, fragmentary poem about the confrontation between Tsar Alexander I and Napoleon. Written in 1824 but couched in an eighteenth-century odic manner, the poem begins with the words "Nedvižnyj straž dremal." In its line 51, the gaze of Napoleon is described as "Kak boevoj perun, kak molnija sverkal" (S:II.209.51). This line of Puškin's thus combines lines 4 and 6 of Bestužev's poem. The other three lines cited above generated some of the imagery and vocabulary of the description of a battle in Canto Three of *Poltava*. "Pexota dvigalas' stenami" is recognizable in "Volnujas' konnica letit; / Pexota dvižetsja za neju" (*Poltava* III.164–65). "Smykalis' latnikov polki" reappears in *Poltava* as "Polki rjady svoi somknuli" (III.158). Four lines at various points in *Poltava* end with the word *polki*, and two of these lines rhyme this word, as Bestužev did, with *kazaki* (Bestužev spelled it *kozaki*). The whole contour of two of Puškin's lines in *Poltava*, "Ne pogibali kazaki" (I.189) and "Koj-gde garcujut kazaki" (III.193), follows that of Bestužev's "I naletali kazaki."

The remaining lines of the military poem (lines 10–15) might offer a few more, somewhat less certain examples of Bestužev-to-Puškin intertextuality. Line 11, "Ulanov približalsja roj," has the shape and sonority, though certainly not the visual impact, of Puškin's "Prelestnic obnažennyj roj" in *Baxčisarajskij fontan* (Baxčisaraj Fountain) (87). "I luč dennicy zolotoj" (line 12) offers a particularly intriguing instance of who-got-it-from-whom. Puškin has the line "V časy dennicy zolotoj" in his lengthy verse epistle "Poslanie k Judinu" (Epistle to Judin), written in 1815, but not published in his lifetime. If we assume that Puškin read *Journey to Revel'* at the time of its first publication in February 1821,[4] then the combination *luč dennicy* could come from Bestužev. We meet it in Puškin in a serious context in the elegy "Grob junoši" (The Grave of a Youth), written a month or two after the publication of Bestužev's travelogue. The wording in the elegy is "Naprasno bleščet luč dennicy."

The most familiar instance of this phrase is, of course, in Lenskij's elegy in Chapter VI of *Eugene Onegin*, later made universally popular through Petr Čajkovskij's heartstring-tugging setting of these words in Lenskij's aria of his best-known opera, where he turned Puškin's parody into a war horse for sweet-voiced tenors.

> "Блестнет заутра луч денницы
> И заиграет яркий день;
> А я, быть может, я гробницы
> Сойду в таинственную сень . . . ." (VI.22.1–4)

> "The morning star's ray will beam tomorrow
> And the vivid day will begin to sparkle;
> And I, perhaps I will descend
> Under the mysterious canopy of the tomb. . . . "

Neither Vladimir Nabokov (1975 III: 24–31) nor Jurij Lotman (1983: 296–300), both of whom made a thorough search in their respective commentaries for every possible foreign and Russian source for Lenskij's cliché-ridden elegy, had anything to say about earlier precedents for *luč dennicy*. Could it be possible that all those tenors have for over a century been singing a phrase ultimately traceable to Aleksandr Bestužev-Marlinskij, of whom none of them surely had ever heard?

The answer is, unfortunately, no, because Bestužev's "luč dennicy zolotoj" is a verbatim quotation from Batjuškov's 1810 adaptation of Evariste Parny's poem "Le Revenant." Called "Prividenie" (The Apparition) in Russian, this is a poem which Puškin is known to have particularly admired (Batjuškov 1964: 119–20, 282). Batjuškov's and Bestužev's wordings are practically identical. Puškin must have read "Prividenie" when the two-volume edition of Batjuškov's verse and prose appeared in 1817 (Puškin's marginal notes to its second volume are usually included in academic editions of his collected writings, and they are assumed to date from ca. 1830). Chapter VI of *Onegin* was written in 1826. The reminiscence of Batjuškov's line, cited by Bestužev in 1821, was most likely unconscious when Puškin placed these words in Lenskij's elegy. Let's just say that when those tenors project the by-now hackneyed words "Blestnet zautra luč dennicy," they are citing three well-known Russian poets: Konstantin Batjuškov, Aleksandr Bestužev-Marlinskij, and Vladimir Lenskij. Simultaneously.

It has long been known that great poets may borrow plots, style, or particular turns of phrase from their lesser contemporaries. This applies to Puškin as much as to anyone. Commentators have pointed out his borrowings from a wide array of foreign and Russian sources. There have even been special studies of Puškin's so-called plagiarisms (Geršenzon 1926: 114–22; Gippius 1930: 37–46). In an earlier work I tried to show the importance for Puškin of the neoclassical verse comedies by Russian playwrights of the early nineteenth century, especially Nikolaj Xmel'nickij (Karlinsky 1985: 312–37).

In 1935, Sergej Bondi (1935 VII: 652) demonstrated the dependence of Puškin's *Sceny iz rycarskix vremen* (Scenes from Knightly Times), dating presumably from as late as 1835, on the Bestužev-Marlinskij novella "Revel'skij turnir" (Tournament at Revel') (based, in part, on the interpolated novella about knights in *Journey to Revel'*). As this essay has sought to show, there is an even more important debt that Puškin owes to Bestužev: the earliest formulation of the style and diction of Puškin's own mature poetic manner, to be sounded later with much greater significance and perfection in *Eugene Onegin* and *Poltava*.

The Prefatory Poem

<Из «ПОЕЗДКИ В РЕВЕЛЬ»>

ПИСЬМО ПЕРВОЕ

Ревель, 20 декабря 1820 года.

1 Желали вы, — я обещал,
2 Мои взыскательные други,
3 Чтоб я рассказам посвящал
4 Минутных отдыхов досуги
5 И приключения пути
6 Вам описал, как Дюпати;
7 Чтоб я, питомец праздной лени
8 И пестун прихотей ее,
9 Ловил крылатых мыслей тени
10 Под сонное перо мое;
11 Чтоб я былого с идеальным
12 Разнообразные черты
13 Воображением хрустальным
14 Одел в блестящие цветы
15 Поэзии, всегда игривой,
16 Или веселости шутливой;
17 Я обещал, друзья мои,
18 И уверительно, и смело,
19 Когда звездилося *Аи*
20 И с кровью резвою кипело.
21 Теперь совсем иное дело:
22 Мечты сокрылись, былей нет,

23 И я, грызя перо с досады,
24 Напрасно устремляю взгляды
25 Сквозь наблюдательный лорнет:
26 Здесь люди — люди, свет, как свет,
27 А на <гвардейские> петлицы
28 (Замечено из-под руки)
29 Не вьют цветочные венки
30 Парнаса милые сестрицы;
31 Затем напутный мой рассказ
32 Без пиитических прикрас
33 Рука небрежная писала;
34 Итак, друзья, н а ч н е м   с н а ч а л а.

JOURNEY TO REVEL'

FIRST LETTER

Revel', December 20, 1820

1 You have wished it [and] I promised,
2 O my demanding friends!
3 That I should devote to stories
4 The leisure of my brief repose,
5 And describe to you like Dupaty
6 The adventures of the journey;
7 That I, a disciple of idle leisure
8 And the mentor of its whims,
9 Would catch the shadows of winged thoughts
10 Under my drowsy pen;
11 That I, with my crystal imagination,
12 Should dress the varying features
13 Of the past and of the ideal
14 In the glittering flowers
15 Of poetry, always playful,
16 Or of jocular merriment;
17 I promised [this], O my friends,
18 Both affirmatively and bravely,
19 When the Ay star-sparkled
20 And seethed like [our] frisky blood;
21 Now things are quite different:
22 Dreams disappeared, there are no true stories,
23 And I, biting my pen with vexation,
24 In vain cast my gaze
25 Through the observant lorgnette:
26 Here, people are people, society is society.
27 And the dear muses of Parnassus
28 Do not weave flowery wreaths
29 (As was slyly noticed)
30 For [shitty] military collars.

31 This is why my careless hand
32 Wrote my parting story
33 Without poetic adornments;
34 And so, my friends, let's begin at the b e g i n n i n g.

[The Military Poem]

1 Бывало, там, когда природа в сне,
2 Гремела пушка заревая,
3 И всадник по полю, рисуясь, на коне
4 Скакал, оружием сверкая,
5 И вдруг стекался к строю строй,
6 Перун послышав боевой,
7 Пехота двигалась стенами,
8 Смыкались латников полки
9 И налетали казаки,
10 И, тихо вея флюгерами,
11 Уланов приближался рой;
12 И луч денницы золотой
13 Дробился на штыках граненых
14 И на доспехах вороненых.
15 Вот слышим: «Смирно! По местам!»

The Military Poem

1 There it used to happen, while Nature was asleep,
2 The reveille cannon thundered
3 And the horseman, silhouetted against the field on his steed
4 Galloped, his weapons sparkling.
5 And suddenly a formation would join a formation,
6 Hearing the thunder of battle: —
7 Infantry moved like a [solid] wall,
8 Regiments of armored men closed up
9 And Cossacks attacked;
10 And their pennants quietly fluttering
11 A swarm of uhlans approached;
12 And the ray of the golden dawn
13 Was refracted on their faceted bayonets
14 And on their blue-steel armor.
15 Now we hear: Attention! To your places!

DANIEL RANCOUR-LAFERRIERE

The Couvade of Peter the Great

A Psychoanalytic Aspect of *The Bronze Horseman*

> *The Bronze Horseman* is certainly the
> most suggestive and poetically pregnant
> of Pushkin's poems.
> —D. S. Mirsky

It is perhaps difficult to imagine that anything more of interest could be said about Puškin's *Mednyj vsadnik* (The Bronze Horseman), given that several large-scale studies of the poem already exist (Knigge 1984; Puškin [Izmajlov] 1978; Lednicki 1955; Makarovskaja 1978). Yet none of the previous studies is psychoanalytic in approach, and the possibilities for psychoanalyzing the poem are legion.

This study will focus on just one psychoanalytic aspect of Puškin's multi-layered and complex poem. Basically, what I am going to suggest is that Puškin's characterization of Peter the Great contains hidden fantasies of male childbirth. Reproductive success is a concern of the various representatives of Peter in the poem.

That the founding of Petersburg was an act of "creation" on Peter's part has of course already been recognized by various scholars. Anciferov (1924: 65) calls Peter a "Kosmokrator." Gregg says that Peter is a "god-like Creator" who "has brought Cosmos out of the watery Chaos" (1977: 168). Èpštejn (1981: 107) speaks of the "acts of creation" that Peter prepares for as he contemplates the waters. Makogonenko (1982: 168) refers to the "fruitfulness" ("plodotvornost' ") of Peter's idea of building a city that would benefit the Russian people. Banerjee (1978: 52) calls Puškin's Peter a "thaumaturgic creator." And so on.[1] But these characterizations do not go much beyond what Puškin's own Evgenij shouts at the statue: "Dobro, stroitel' čudotvornyj!" (All right then, wonder-working builder!) What the psychoanalyst looks for is a little farther below the surface than this. Peter is obviously a creator. But what does his creativity *mean* in the context of the poem? With what other surface structures of the poem does it associate? With what deep structures of the psyche does it resonate?

We can begin to answer these questions, I think, if we consider first the prevalence of water imagery in the poem. Briggs (1976: 233) says that most of the poem's similes and metaphors concern the Neva River and its flooding. Puškin's friends referred to *The Bronze Horseman* as "the poem about a flood" (Blagoj 1929: 295). The poem is bathed, as it were, in the waters of the Neva. At the beginning Tsar Peter contemplates the Neva's desolate waves and decides to build a city on its shores. A hundred years later Petersburg stands proud and tall where once the humble Finnish fisherman had cast his nets. But the river still dominates the environment. Huge and imposing as the city may be, it is still vulnerable to the whims of the beastly Neva:

> Нева вздувалась и ревела,
> Котлом клокоча и клубясь,
> И вдруг, как зверь остервенясь,
> На город кинулась. (PSS V: 140)

> Nevá swelled and roared,
> Gurgling and welling up like a cauldron,
> And of a sudden, bristling like a beast,
> Rushed on the city.

As the flooding intensifies, the Neva is transformed from a merely animate being ("zver' ") into a human being; i.e., it is personified: "zlye volny, / *Kak vory*, lezut v okna" (. . . the angry waves / *Like thieves* climb through the windows). The personification of the river as a kind of kleptomaniac is extended in subsequent images of a "greedy flood" lapping at Evgenij's feet, and a gang of thieves dropping plunder:

> Нева обратно повлеклась,
> Своим любуясь возмущеньем
> И покидая с небреженьем
> Свою добычу. Так злодей,
> С свирепой шайкою своей
> В село ворвавшись, ломит, режет,
> Крушит и грабит; вопли, скрежет,
> Насилье, брань, тревога, вой!. . . .
> И грабежом отягощенны,
> Боясь погони, утомленны,
> Спешат разбойники домой,
> Добычу на пути роняя. (PSS V: 143)

> Nevá drew back,
> Reveling in the turmoil she had made
> And abandoning with heedlessness
> Her booty. Thus an outlaw

With his ruthless gang
Having burst into a village, will shatter, slash,
Smash and loot; shrieks, gnashing,
Rape, cursing, panic, howls!
And [then], with plunder weighed down,
Fearing pursuit, exhausted,
The robbers hurry homeward,
Dropping their plunder as they go.

Even after the Neva has calmed down and Evgenij has realized that the
river took away his beloved Paraša, the image of a thief remains:

Торгаш отважный,
Не унывая, открывал
Невой ограбленный подвал,
Сбираясь свой убыток важный
На ближнем выместить. (PSS V: 145)

The plucky tradesman,
Undaunted, was opening up
The cellar looted by Nevá,
Preparing to recoup his grave loss
At his neighbor's cost.

This is accusatory social commentary, of course. The "plucky tradesman"
is not a true victim of the Neva's thieving fury. Rather, Evgenij is. It is
Evgenij who has really been robbed, been made poor in the profoundest
sense of the word: "bednyj, bednyj moj Evgenij" (my poor, poor Eugene).
This "bednjak" (wretch, poor one) does not even have his sanity anymore,
much less his possessions or his Paraša. His poorness now consists in his
very lack of a mind, for the narrator alliteratively and tautologically calls
him a "bezumec bednyj" (poor madman).

But Evgenij's insanity has certain advantages. He is a madman whom
no one has bothered to lock up. He is free both to roam the streets of
Peter's city and to think the most subversive thoughts. He can return to the
scene of the crime and re-live the experience which originally drove him
mad.

Only the scenes do not quite match. Whereas when he went mad he
was standing at the spot where his beloved's hut had been washed away,
when he explodes at Peter the Great he is standing near the Bronze Horseman:

"Добро, строитель чудотворный! —
Шепнул он, злобно задрожав, —
Ужо тебе! . . . " И вдруг стремглав
Бежать пустился. Показалось
Ему, что грозного царя,
Мгновенно гневом возгоря,

> Лицо тихонько обращалось . . . .
> И он по площади пустой
> Бежит и слышит за собой —
> Как будто грома грохотанье —
> Тяжело-звонкое скаканье
> По потрясенной мостовой.
> И, озарен луною бледной,
> Простерши руку в вышине,
> За ним несется Всадник Медный
> На звонко-скачущем коне;
> И во всю ночь безумец бедный,
> Куда стопы не обращал,
> За ним повсюду Всадник Медный
> С тяжелым топотом скакал. (PSS V: 148)

"All right then, wonder-working builder!"
He whispered with a shudder of spite,
"I'll [show] you . . . !" And suddenly full tilt
He set off running. It seemed
To him that the dread Tsar's face,
Instantly aflame with wrath,
Was slowly turning . . .
And he runs down the empty square
And hears behind him,
As if it were the rumbling of thunder,
A heavily-ringing gallop
Over the quaking pavement.
And twilit by the pallid moon,
Arm reaching forth on high,
There speeds after him the Bronze Horseman
Upon the clangorously galloping steed;
And all night, wherever the wretched madman
Might turn his steps,
Behind him everywhere the Bronze Horseman
Was galloping with heavy clatter.

Phonologically, this is one of the most successful examples of expressive alliteration and repeated rhyme in all of Russian poetry (cf. Brjusov 1929: 91). Clinically, the passage describes an attack of paranoia (Gregg 1977: 174). Bronze statues do not chase people. But paranoia is not the only misperception here. The passage is also a misplaced resolution of Evgenij's feelings. The thieving Neva, not Peter, took his Paraša away (cf. Gregg 1977: 172; Slonimskij 1963: 295). Evgenij should be shouting at the river, not at the statue. He should imagine the waves coming after him, not the Bronze Horseman.

Why is it that Evgenij runs (*bežit*) before the galloping tsar, just as earlier the people had run before the threatening waves of the Neva ("Vse pobežalo"—cf. Belyj 1929: 203)? There must be, as Èpštejn has already

noticed, "a kind of secret commonality of intentions" between the river
and the Bronze Horseman (1981: 105). That secret needs to be brought out
into the open. The equivalence between Peter and his river needs to be
explored.

The poem begins with a grandiose Peter and his grand river in stark
juxtaposition:

> На берегу пустынных волн
> Стоял он, дум великих полн,
> И вдаль глядел. Пред ним широко
> Река неслася. . . . (PSS V: 135)

> Upon a shore of desolate waves
> Stood *he,* of lofty musings full,
> And gazed afar. Before him broadly
> The river rolled. . . .

A most masculine tsar this is, says the hypermetrically stressed "Stojal *on*"
(Stood *he*). And a most feminine river, says the feminine noun "Reka" and
the subsequent feminine personification of the river in "V granit odelasja
Neva" (Neva has been clad in granite). Yet the equivalence of these apparent sexual opposites is inescapable. Where would Peter be without his
Neva? *His* intention of breaking a window to the West cannot be accomplished without the *river.* The narrator adores the "*Nevy* deržavnoe
tečen'e" (Neva's majestic flow), but makes this expression rhyme with the
similarly inverted "*Petra* tvoren'e," thereby leading the reader to accept
the river as "Peter's creation." Even the Neva's epithet *deržavnoe,* because
it means "sovereign" as well as "powerful," suggests that the Neva stands
in for Peter (when in fact Peter had merely clothed the river in granite).
Still later in the poem, Puškin uses this epithet in its nominal form to refer
to Peter himself: " . . . Bezumec bednyj . . . / . . . vzory dikie navel / Na
lik *deržavca* polumira" (The poor deranged man . . . / . . . cast fierce
glances / Upon the countenance of the *ruler* of half the world).

On the phonological level, the confrontation of Peter and his river in
the poem's opening is accompanied by a powerful rhyme: "voln"/"poln,"
where the first element is an attribute of the river, the second an attribute
of Peter. Reinforcing this rhyme is an almost perfect parallelism of the
opening couplet's ictic vowels:

Ictus

Line	I	II	III	IV
1	/-	u	i	o
2	a	u	i	o/

The effect of such phonemic similarity is to enhance the semantic similarity of the Neva (described in the first line) to Peter (described in the second
line).

The most interesting suggestion that the Neva is the equivalent of Peter comes after the worst of the flooding is over:

> Но торжеством победы полны
> Еще кипели злобно волны,
> Как бы под ними тлел огонь,
> Еще их пена покрывала,
> И тяжело Нева дышала,
> Как с битвы прибежавший конь. (PSS V: 143)

> But full of the triumph of victory,
> The waves still seethed angrily,
> As if beneath them fire were glowing,
> Still foam covered them,
> And heavily Nevá was breathing,
> Like a charger that has galloped up from battle.

The rhyme of "polny" (full) with "volny" (waves) reminds the listener of the powerful opening rhyme, "voln"/"poln." But whereas the opening rhyme involved Peter contemplating the Neva, this one involves just the Neva.

Or does it? The Neva seems to have taken on some of Peter's characteristics. The fullness of her waves ("polny") is the fullness of Peter's brain all over again ("poln"). Her malice ("kipeli *zlobno* volny") reminds the reader of Peter's own hostility toward his neighbor ("Na *zlo* nadmennomu sosedu"). The flame ("ogon'") which smolders in her depths seems to be the same as the fire in Peter's horse ("A v sem kone kakoj ogon'!"). And of course, once "ogon'" is mentioned at the end of a line, a rhyme with "kon'" soon follows—*both* in the passage describing the Neva, as we have seen, and in the passage describing Peter on his horse ("Kuda ty skačeš', gordyj kon' . . . ?" [Whither do you gallop, haughty steed . . . ?]). Not without reason does Belyj ask the rhetorical question: "Is not the Neva the steed of the Bronze Horseman chasing after the madman?" (1929: 186).

The Neva, then, like Peter's horse, is his equivalent and/or his instrument. She seems to do his will. She is not merely contiguous to the Bronze Horseman but is tied to the Horseman in some essential way. The two *belong* together:

> . . . И прямо в темной вышине
> Над огражденною скалою
> Кумир с простертою рукою
> Сидел на бронзовом коне.

> Евгений вздрогнул. Прояснились
> В нем страшно мысли. Он узнал
> И место, где потоп играл,
> Где волны хищные толпились,
> Бунтуя злобно вкруг него,
> И львов, и площадь, и того,

Кто неподвижно возвышался
Во мраке медною главой,
Того, чьей волей роковой
Под морем город основался . . . . (PSS V: 147)

And straight, in his dark eminence,
Above the railed-in crag
The Idol with his arm stretched forth
Was seated on [his] steed of bronze.

    Eugene shuddered. Fearfully clear
Became his thoughts. He recognized
The place where the flood had sported,
Where the preying waves had crowded,
Rioting viciously about him,
And the lions, and the square, and him,
Who motionlessly loomed,
His brazen head in the dusk,
Him by whose fateful will
The city by the sea was founded . . .

At the very least the Bronze Horseman is inseparable from the Neva because he is a statue and is therefore immovable ("nepodvižno vozvyšalsja"). But the Horseman and the waters are linked by a vertical axis of
semantic relations as well. If he is *high* above the square ("v temnoj
vyšine," "Kto . . . vozvyšalsja"), the waters ("potop," "volny") are down
below. The city he founded is also very low, too low, in fact. This judgment
against Peter had already been made in Nikolaj Xmel'nickij's dramatic
fragment *Arzamasskie gusi* in 1829: " . . . Petr Alekseevič! byl umnyj car', /
Da k morju čeresčur pod"exal blizko. / Kak v jame stroit'sja, kogda est'
materik?" (Peter Alekseevich was a clever tsar, / But he approached the sea
too closely. / Why build in a hole, when you have dry land?)[2] Puškin's
phrase "Pod morem" is usually translated "By the sea." But the preposi-
tion "pod" basically means "under," so the phrase "Pod morem" suggests
that the city is not so much by the sea as below sea level, or even underwa-
ter (cf. Epštejn 1981: 105; Corbet 1966: 129). What is more, it was Peter's
own intention that the city be built at such a low level: "Togo, *č'ej volej
rokovoj* / Pod morem gorod osnovalsja" (Him by whose fateful will / The
city by the sea was founded). The antonymous rhyme of this last line with
"vozvyšalsja" (loomed) further emphasizes the vertical contrast of Peter
with all that is below him.

    This vertical configuration pitting high against low[3] may be dia-
grammed as follows:

HIGH (*verx*)	*Kumir . . . na bronzovom kone.*
	Evgenij. ploščad'. potop. volny.
	———————————————————— water level
LOW (*niz*)	Pod morem *gorod* osnovalsja.

If Peter willed that the city be built at such a dangerously low level, then, in effect, he willed that it be flooded. The river's waves ("volny") which so terrified Evgenij were already present in Peter's opening meditation ("Na beregu pustynnyx *voln*" [Upon a shore of desolate *waves*]). The waters of the Neva were already in motion in front of Peter's eyes ("Pred nim široko / Reka *neslasja*. . . . " [Before him broadly / The river *rolled*]), just as Peter himself moved after poor Evgenij from behind ("Za nim *nesetsja* Vsadnik Mednyj" [There *speeds* after him the Bronze Horseman]). The powerful current, "deržavnoe tečen'e," which the narrator claims is Peter's creation, "Petra tvoren'e," was already quite powerful and quite fast in "široko" and "neslasja."

We saw earlier that the flooding Neva was extensively personified as a thief or as a gang of thieves ("zlodej, / S svirepoj šajkoju svoej"). Assuming that, at one level, the Neva represents Peter, then Peter is a thief. The two most important things Peter steals from Evgenij are his intended bride, Paraša, and his sanity ("Bezumec bednyj"), i.e., his one reproductive asset (children were planned) and his ability to behave rationally. It is as if Peter's own ability to be rational, purposeful, or intentional enough to construct a city were a form of bride-capture aimed at producing offspring.

In essence, Peter gets the blame for the unhappy fate of poor Evgenij because he wants the credit for the flow of the Neva. But he wants credit for the flow of the Neva, and especially the flooding of the Neva, because such a rush of waters is a metaphor for birth. The flooding of Saint Petersburg is one manifestation of the couvade of Peter the Great.

Couvade is a phenomenon familiar to anthropologists and physicians. It may be defined as a male's conscious or unconscious imitation of the properly female process of childbirth. For example, in our culture when a man's wife is about to deliver, the man may develop abdominal pains. In some cultures the husband will don his wife's clothing, take to his bed, and groan in ritualized labor. There is an enormous literature on couvade, which I have reviewed elsewhere (Rancour-Laferriere 1985: 362ff.). Here I would just like to mention a couple of the psychoanalytic sources on this subject, such as Bettelheim (1954) and Zilboorg (1944). Bettelheim says that couvade is a "pretense" in which the man

> copies only the relatively insignificant externals and not the essentials, which, indeed, he cannot duplicate. Such copying of superficialities emphasizes the more how much the real, essential powers are envied. Women, emotionally satisfied by having given birth and secure in their ability to produce life, can agree to the couvade which men need to fill the emotional vacuum created by their inability to bear children. (1954: 211)

Zilboorg includes an example which would appear to be relevant to the behavior of Peter in Puškin's poem:

> There is little doubt that this identification with the gravid and parturient woman has a deeper, magic wish-fulfillment value of earlier, more primitive

strivings. I am inclined to believe that these strivings are coupled with envy and hostility—hence identification through illness—and that the same dynamic factors are responsible for the myth according to which Zeus took from the burning body of Semele the six-months-old fetus of Dionysus, sewed it up in his own loin, bore it to full term, and gave birth to the young god. Similarly, *the birth of Athena from the head of Zeus is but another form of identification on the basis of the same type of envy.* It is known that schizophrenics occasionally believe, and neurotics not infrequently have dreams, that a baby comes out of the penis—or the head. (1944: 289, emphasis added)

Just as Athena sprang fully armed from the head of Zeus, so Petersburg springs from the full-to-bursting brain of Peter (cf. "dum velikix poln" [of lofty musings full] and "Kakaja duma na čele!" [What thought upon his brow!]). But the price of such hubris, such couvade, is great: "I vsplyl Petropol' kak triton, / Po pojas v vodu pogružen" (And afloat was Petropolis, like Triton / Steeped to the waist in water) (PSS V: 140). The image of a watery Triton is most appropriate. One of the epithets of Athena was *Tritogeneia* (Hammond and Scullard 1970: 138). The warlike nature of Peter's city—it is a threat to the Swedes, it is decked out in fields of Mars, it is a "voennaja stolica" (martial capital)—is also apt, for the most conspicuous functions of Athena were connected with war (1970: 138).

But the point is not merely that the myth of Athena is one of the subtexts for *The Bronze Horseman*.[4] Rather, it is that Peter, who happened to be like Zeus bearing Athena, was practicing a form of couvade when he conceived of his brainchild on the low banks of the Neva.

Early in the poem Peter says that he (i.e., the royal "we") was fated *by nature* to build a city: "Prirodoj zdes' nam suždeno / V Evropu prorubit' okno" (PSS V: 135). There is an interesting motherliness about the feminine noun "priroda" (nature) here, and again a few lines later when the humble fisherman is described as a "stepson of nature." By motherliness I mean some of the typical lexical associations with "priroda" given in the Academy dictionary: "priroda-mat' " (or: "mat'-priroda"); "ditja prirody" (cf. Puškin's "pasynok prirody"); "na lone prirody"; "ot prirody" (= "ot roždenija"), etc. (ANSSSR 1950–65 XI: 704–705). There is also the obvious morphological relationship of the verb for giving birth, "*rodit*'," with "pri*rod*a." Although Peter is the one who gives birth to the idea of building a city on the Neva, he shifts *some* of the blame (or credit) for the idea onto mother nature: "Prirodoj . . . suždeno" (by nature . . . destined). This makes sense not only because it helps him rationalize the terrible thing he is about to do to the Finns, to the slaves who will build his city, and to the environment, but also because it is more acceptable for a woman than for a man to be represented as giving birth.

As the narration moves along, Peter makes use of another maternal figure, the Neva, to accomplish his goals. We saw earlier that Peter is repeatedly equated with the Neva. The Neva is a body of water, and it is in flood for much of the duration of the poem. The poem is literally awash in images of Peter's river.

Psychoanalysts have observed that in dreams, mythology, folklore, etc., water imagery is very often associated with birth. Otto Rank discusses this association at length in his classic study *The Myth of the Birth of the Hero* (1964 [1914]). King Sargon of Babylon, for example, was set afloat in a reed vessel on the Euphrates River right after being born. The infant Moses was found floating in an ark of bullrushes. So also was the infant Karna, according to the ancient Hindu epic *Mahabharata.* Oedipus was exposed on the waters of the Cithaeron before being saved. While the King Cyrus of Persia was being born, his mother dreamt that "so much water passed away from her that it became as a large stream, inundating all Asia, and flowing as far as the sea" (Rank 1964: 38). In the Grimms' tale "Dame Holle's Pond," newborn children were said to come from a well. Nor should we forget Puškin's own Prince Gvidon who, as an infant, is placed in a barrel with his mother and cast onto the sea. Examples of this association of water imagery with birth/infancy are numerous in the psychoanalytic literature (see also Freud 1953–65 V: 399–402; Niederland 1956–57; Laferriere 1977: 113).[5] The flood sequences in the Mesopotamian myths (which Anciferov [1924] has related to the flood in *The Bronze Horseman*) would themselves be psychoanalyzed as birth fantasies. When the flow of waters achieves mythic proportions in the collective memory, the thought of another kind of "waters" is activated in personal memory.

In Puškin's poem the Neva is frequently characterized by the plural noun "vody" (waters): " . . . Brosal v nevedomye vody / Svoj vetxoj nevod. . . . " (Used to cast into unknown waters) (PSS V: 136) // " . . . Mosty povisli nad vodami . . . " (Bridges are suspended over the waters) (PSS V: 136) // " . . . Vody vdrug / Vtekli v podzemnye podvaly. . . . " (the waters suddenly / Flowed into cellars underground) (PSS V: 140) (etc.). One of the meanings of "vody" is the fluid accumulating around the fetus (ANSSSR 1950–65 II: 494; cf. English "waters," i.e., the amniotic fluid). This, of course, is not the overt meaning of "vody" in Puškin's poem. But the repeated use of the plural noun to describe the flooding of the Neva hints at another, covert meaning. "Volna," too, occurs often in the poem, usually in the plural form.

The narrator says that among the objects floating down Petersburg's inundated streets are "Lotki pod mokroj pelenoj. . . . " (Pedlars' trays under sodden cover) (140). In the plural the last word would refer to the swaddling clothes in which Russian infants were traditionally wrapped. Semantically, the "lotki" enshrouded by the "pelena" *are* plural. The related verb "pelenat' " means 'to swaddle.'

At one point the narrator quite explicitly discusses the birth of an infant. A connection is made, moveover, with the flow of the Neva:

> Люблю, военная столица,
> Твоей твердыни дым и гром,
> Когда полнощная царица

Дарует сына в царской дом,
Или победу над врагом
Россия снова торжествует,
Или, взломав свой синий лед,
Нева к морям его несет,
И, чуя вешни дни, ликует. (PSS V: 137)

I love, martial capital,
Your citadel's smoke and thunder,
When the Empress of the North
Presents a son to the imperial house,
Or Russia once again celebrates
A victory over the foe.
Or, having broken her blue ice,
Nevá bears it to the seas,
And scenting vernal days, exults.

The grammatical parallelism of {-ova-} verbs embedded in this passage is revealing:

1. полнощная царица *дарует* сына (the Empress of the North gives birth)
2. Россия *торжествует* победу (Russia celebrates a victory)
3. Нева *ликует* (the Neva *exults*)

The parallelism not only confirms our suspicion that the violent flow of Peter's river is analogous to giving birth (1/3), but also suggests that victory over an enemy is like giving birth (1/2). Two pages earlier that enemy is mentioned: "I dumal on: / Otsel' grozit' my budem švedu. . . . " (And he thought / From here we shall threaten the Swede) (PSS V: 135). Building Petersburg is an act of spite against a foreign power. But victory over an internal enemy, Moscow, seems to be just as important:

И перед младшею столицей
Померкла старая Москва,
Как перед новою царицей
Порфироносная вдова. (PSS V: 136)

And before the younger capital
Old Moscow has faded,
As before a new empress
The dowager in purple robes.

Moscow, personified as an aged dowager, is now clearly past her reproductive prime. She fades before Peter's young new queen-city ("pered novoju *caricej*"). Therefore, when we later encounter the words "polnoščnaja *carica* / daruet syna," it seems in retrospect that Peter's city, certainly as much his representative as are the waters of the Neva, has given birth.

Brett Cooke, in his interesting dissertation on Puškin's creativity (including Puškin's fantasies of male childbirth), says that the opening lines

of *The Bronze Horseman* describe the "creative frame of mind" that Puškin himself experienced when writing: "It seems to be no coincidence that
Puškin had used the same 'voln' / 'poln' rhyme to describe the inspiration
of the hero of 'Poèt' " (1983: 508). In the latter poem the rhyme occurs in
the following context:

> Но лишь божественный глагол
> До слуха чуткого коснется,
> Душа поэта встрепенется,
> Как пробудившийся орел.
> Тоскует он в забавах мира,
> Людской чуждается молвы,
> К ногам народного кумира
> Не клонит гордой головы;
> Бежит он, дикой и суровый,
> И звуков и смятенья полн,
> На берега пустынных волн,
> В широкошумные дубравы . . . (PSS III: 65)

> The moment, though, the word divine
> Impinges on his sentient hearing,
> The poet's soul ruffles (its feathers),
> Like an awakened eagle.
> He frets amid the world's amusements,
> From human speech he shies away,
> To the national idol's feet
> He does not bow his proud head;
> He runs, uncouth and grim,
> Replete with sound and with perturbance
> To shores of desolate waves,
> To broadly-murmuring wildwoods . . .

The penultimate line is almost identical to the opening line of *The Bronze
Horseman*. For Puškin the process of poetic creativity and the act of con-
ceiving Petersburg were clearly similar (cf. Banerjee 1978: 54). Puškin could
capture the couvade of Peter the Great so well because he, as a poet, knew
a bit about couvade himself. Cooke (1983: 247) quotes a passage from "A
Conversation between Bookseller and Poet," which graphically illustrates
the poet's kind of couvade: "I tjažkim, plamennym nedugom / Byla *polna*
moja glava; / V nej grezy čudnye *roždalis'* " (And with heavy, flaming
discomfort / My head was full; / In it marvelous dreams were born) (PSS
II: 325). Here, as in *The Bronze Horseman*, the head is "full," and birth is
inevitable.[6]

Perhaps the creation of *The Bronze Horseman* was itself accompanied
by symptoms of couvade. At about the time he started composing *The
Bronze Horseman* during the second Boldino autumn of 1833, Puškin
wrote to his wife: "Really, *aren't you with child?* Why are you so touchy?

Farewell, darling. I'm somehow not very well today. *My little stomach aches*, like [P. K.] Alexandrov's" (Shaw 1967: 614, emphasis added).[7]

To say that Puškin's great poem about Petersburg contains hidden fantasies of male childbirth is by no means to exhaust all the psychoanalytic possibilities. A complete psychoanalysis of the poem would have to deal, for example, with the enmity between Peter and the Neva (cf. Makogonenko 1982: 175ff.), not only the alliance between them or their similarity to each other. Likewise, both Evgenij's hostility to Peter and his numerous similarities to Peter would have to be dealt with (for example, he sits astride a lion as Peter sits astride a horse; his head is as full of "dumy" as is Peter's at the beginning of the poem; when he is about to confront Peter he is described by means of majestic, Petrine Slavonicisms, etc.). Gutsche says that Evgenij "identifies himself with the statue" (1986: 30). For both the Neva and Evgenij, some form of identification with the aggressor (Peter) seems to be taking place.

Evgenij appears to be involved in positive Oedipal competition with the paternal Peter for the maternal Paraša (cf. Gutsche's "Parasha/ mother" in 1986: 157) and, like any child in such a situation, both hates and identifies with the father. Evgenij revolts against the image of Peter which, although it has been translated into socio-political terms (a mistreated class rises up against oppressive authority—e.g., Blagoj 1929: 263–328; Xarlap 1961) and into biographical terms (the personal hostility of Puškin to Nicholas I—e.g., Belyj 1929; Corbet 1966), has yet to be fully translated into the psychoanalytic language of son-father conflict.[8]

The psychoanalyst would also want to comment on the negative or inverted side of Evgenij's Oedipal relationship with Peter, that is, on the homosexual aspect. Monas speaks of the "phallic thrust" of Falconet's famous statue (1984: 390). Perhaps it is precisely the thought of phallic aggression which sparks Evgenij's sudden paranoia. Here it should be noted that the relationship of paranoia to latent homosexuality is just as obvious to a psychoanalyst (Freud 1953–65 XII: 63) as the relationship of Russian to Protoslavic is obvious to a Slavist.

Then there is the deep ontogenetic background of the poem. *The Bronze Horseman* was written by a poet who had a history of intense emotional conflict with his father. That conflict has to some extent been examined in a psychoanalytic light by Kučera (1956: 283–84) and Proffer (1968: 352–53), but the relevance of the conflict to *The Bronze Horseman* has not been explored. Can the oft-noted contradictory attitudes toward Peter in the poem (e.g., "Ljublju tebja, Petra tvoren'e" [I love you, Peter's creation] vs. "Užo tebe!" [I'll show you!]—see especially Corbet 1966, Lednicki 1955, and Knigge 1984) be related to Puškin's strongly ambivalent attitude toward his father? What do the specifically demonic and supernatural aspects of Peter have to do with the poet's feelings about his father?

In short, much psychoanalytic work remains to be done. The future probably holds yet another big book about Puškin's little masterpiece.

WILLIAM E. HARKINS

The Rejected Image: Puškin's Use of Antenantiosis

While reading through Puškin's *Evgenij Onegin* (Eugene Onegin) recently with a class, I noticed a recurrent type of literary figure involving a more or less elaborated construction that was at once negated: an image that did not apply, so to speak, and which the poet therefore had to reject. The interesting feature of this figure was the degree of elaboration, sometimes quite extensive, as well as its content: the poet's fantasy is let loose on a chain of inappropriate images or characterizing epithets.

Casting about for a name for this figure, I happened upon the term *antenantiosis*, a rare word which appears in neither Webster nor the Oxford Dictionary, but which does appear in Richard A. Lanham's *Handlist of Rhetorical Terms* (1968: 9), transplanted there from the Hellenistic rhetoricians. Liddell and Scott's *Greek-English Lexicon* lists the term, which it defines as "a positive statement made in a negative form" (1940: 151). A common source cited by both these works is Alexander Numenius's treatise *De figuris*, a second-century B.C. manual of rhetorical terms. The distinction between antenantiosis, as I employ the term, and the better-known litotes is at best tenuous, but litotes seems generally to be used to denote assertion either by understatement or by negation: its burden is rather the irony of understatement of positive qualities. An example of litotes, using negation and chosen from *Eugene Onegin*, is: "Da pomnil, xot' ne bez grexa, / Iz Èneidy dva stixa" (And he remembered, if not without error, / Some two lines of the *Aeneid*) (PSS VI: 7).

In the following passage, describing Tat'jana in her role as *grande dame*, we have something quite different from litotes:

> Она была нетороплива,
> Не холодна, не говорлива,
> Без взора наглого для всех,
> Без притязаний на успех,
> Без этих маленьких ужимок,
> Без подражательных затей. . . . (PSS VI: 171)

> She was unhurried,
> Neither reserved nor talkative,
> Without brazen look,

Without any pretensions to success,
Without mincing grimaces,
Without mimicking endeavors. . . .

Here we have a catalogue of traits and mannerisms from which Tat'jana, in her new calling, is entirely free. The irony is one not of understatement but of purity or freedom from what might have been expected, either by us or by some other reader. The device we are scrutinizing here bears, then, a relation to the projected "ideal reader" for whom Puškin wrote and what such a reader's expectations of the text might have been, and plays with those expectations.

Before going on, we ought to consider whether there may not be other negative rhetorical figures which largely lack the irony characteristic of our figure. We should exclude from consideration the *antithesis*, a figure that denies one thing to settle on another which is thus emphasized: not he but she, not town but country, etc. This seems to be a rhetorical device of emphasis or selection, and may be employed at times, at least, entirely without irony.

The key to the difference seems to be one of poetic logic and poetic development. The following two passages from *Eugene Onegin* are both figurative and ironic, at least potentially so, but they are hardly developed, and in their rhetorical form they could be classed as mere simple negation. The antenantiosis, as we will use the term, requires at least minimal positive development along with negation.

Не мог он ямба от хорея,
Как мы ни бились, отличить. (PSS VI: 8)

However hard we tried to teach him,
He could not tell an iamb from a trochee.

На северном, печальном снеге
Вы не оставили следов. . . . (PSS VI: 18)

On that northern, mournful snow
You left no traces. . . .

The first passage treats Onegin as a potential poet, but the image is kept strictly in hand, perhaps because a real poet (like Puškin himself) needs to do much more than distinguish iambs and trochees. It opens with the negation, it should be noticed. The second example is also ironic and witty enough: the reference is to a pair of "Eastern" feet, i.e., an unidentified woman's, so that, "cradled in Eastern bliss, you left no traces" (a pun, since "feet" are meant here, and not just "influence," which the Russian word *sledov* also implies) "on that northern, mournful snow." Although rhetorically this passage is again simple negation, still it does permit a complex, ironic image to unfold, and we must classify it at least as a marginal case of antenantiosis.

There is, of course, the well-known Russian folk poetic image which the textbooks once misleadingly labeled "antithesis," and which contemporary theoreticians now designate as "negative comparison." Patricia Krafcik, in her article on the subject, has chosen the term "negative simile" (Krafcik 1976: 18–26).[1] Puškin imitated the device in the opening to his *Brat'ja razbojniki* (The Robber Brothers):

Не стая воронов слеталась
На груды тлеющих костей,
За Волгой, ночью, вкруг огней
Удалых шайка собиралась. (PSS VI: 145)

No flock of ravens assembled
On the heaps of rotting bones,
Beyond the Volga, at night, around campfires
A band of bold lads came together.

Puškin also used this device in his *Poltava* and occasionally in short poems of folk character. The curious thing is that the negative comparison only looks like our figure; its semantic content is entirely different, even opposite. For we are talking about "rejected images": the negative comparison offers us a "rejected image," but one rejected only in terms of syntax; in terms of semantics it is accepted as supremely appropriate. Thus, in the example quoted above, the "band of bold lads" coming together at night does indeed resemble, at least metaphorically, a flock of ravens, and this is the image's point.

The negative comparison serves to remind us that in literary style, just as, as it is said, in the world of the Freudian id, the negative does not exist; everything is asserted. There are no real "rejected images," then; every image creates a figure that is perceived: some of these figures may survive only for a moment, while others go on to survive the work of literature itself. Hence, our "rejected images" are in a sense every bit as positive as any of the images in *Eugene Onegin*, and as self-sufficient. Still, there may well be inner reasons that inclined Puškin to use negative imagery in his *Eugene Onegin*, and (since such images are not very common elsewhere in his poetry) it would seem fruitful to search for their logic in the characters he was portraying; most of our examples are elements of character portrayal, it should be noted.

Eugene Onegin is peopled with types later popularly known as *lišnie ljudi*, "superfluous people." Onegin and Lenskij both clearly belong to this category, while Tat'jana in childhood is depicted as wanting and "incomplete" (even in later life in Petersburg she remains unfulfilled and in a sense still incomplete). Of course, a negative image could just as well express virtue by rejecting vice, strength by negating weakness. (The litotes often functions in this way, though with its implicit irony the effect is to diminish, not underline, positive qualities.) There is something quite appropriate in the poet's use of his negative imagery to depict negative characteristics: loss, inadequacy, superfluity. Before we reject this possibly too glib thesis, let us look at the evidence.

The great bulk of our examples from *Eugene Onegin* do indeed relate to the characters, and do express limitation, lack, or want. Chapter I describes Onegin's lack of scholarly ambitions, as well as his inability to become a poet:

> Он рыться не имел охоты
> В хронологической пыли
> Бытопицсания земли. . . . (PSS VI: 7)

> He had no taste for delving
> In the chronological dust
> Of world history. . . .

> И не попал он в цех задорный
> Людей, о коих не сужу,
> Затем, что к ним принадлежу. (PSS VI: 23)

> And he didn't end up in the perky guild
> Of those whom I will refrain from judging,
> Since I belong to them.

Near the end of the book, in Chapter VIII, Puškin again echoes this theme of the unmade poet; perhaps the author was obsessed with his relation to his hero, or with the idea that Eugene should have been a poet: "I on ne sdelalsja poètom, / Ne umer, ne sošel s uma" (And he didn't become a poet, / Didn't die, didn't lose his mind) (PSS VI: 164).

This is all the material relevant to Eugene, and it seems very little. But we should remember that outside Chapter I and Chapter VIII, Puškin keeps Eugene somewhat at a distance and for the most part does not enter into his mental processes (as he does with Lenskij or Tat'jana in the intervening chapters).

Concerning Lenskij, the poet offers us a long catalogue of occupations and temptations that will not serve to distract him from his love:

> Ни охлаждающая даль
> Ни долгие лета разлуки,
> Ни музам данные часы,
> Ни чужеземные красы,
> Ни шум веселый, ни Науки
> Души не изменили в нем. . . . (PSS VI: 40)

> Neither the refreshing expanse,
> Nor the long years of separation,
> Nor the hours devoted to the Muses,
> Nor the charms of other lands,

> Nor the merry bustle, nor his studies
> Could affect or change his soul. . . .

And after Lenskij's death, an interesting passage makes the ironic point that he will never have to put up with the boredom, worries, or sorrows of married life: "Gimena xlopoty, pečali, / Zevoty xladnaja čreda / Emu ne snilis' nikogda" (The cares of matrimony, the griefs, / The yawns in cold succession / Never came to his dreams) (PSS VI: 94). These images serve to suggest, perhaps, a complete split within Lenskij between the poet and the lover: the lover and his love are unworthy of the poet.

It is Tat'jana with whom the device of antenantiosis is most closely linked. The characterization of the young country girl carries a whole series of images setting her off, not only against her elder sister Ol'ga but also against the village girl of the typical reader's expectation, the "ordinary" child of the country. Our first example vividly contrasts her to her sister and also suggests that, as a country girl, she is alone and unique in aloneness:

> Итак она звалась Татьяной.
> Ни красотой сестры своей,
> Ни свежестью ее румяной
> Не привлекла б она очей. (PSS VI: 42)

> So she was called Tat'jana.
> Neither with her sister's beauty,
> Nor with her fresh red cheeks
> Could she attract men's gazes.

Next comes one of our most felicitous examples: through an arrangement of syntax in which the negation is delayed, the poet creates an image that is rejected only at a point when it is almost complete:

> Ее изнеженные пальцы
> Не знали игл; склонясь на пяльцы,
> Узором шелковым она
> Не оживляла полотна. (PSS VI: 43)

> Her delicate fingers
> Had never known needles; bent over the embroidery frame
> She failed to enliven
> The linen with a silken pattern.

The same delay of negation characterizes our next example:

> Но куклы даже в эти годы
> Татьяна в руки не брала;
> Про вести города, про моды
> Беседы с нею не вела. (PSS VI: 43)

> But even in those years
> Tat'jana held no doll,

With whom she might discourse
About town gossip, or the fashions.

These images serve, of course, to depict the life of the typical country girl, to which Tat'jana cannot and will not conform, as do several others:

Играть и прыгать не хотела,
И часто целый день одна
Сидела молча у окна. (PSS VI: 42)

She didn't play or jump about,
But often all day long
She sat in silence at the window.

\---

Она в горелки не играла,
Ей скучен был и звонкий смех,
И шум их ветреных утех. (PSS VI: 43)

She didn't play catch,
Loud laughter bored her
As did the noise of frivolous pleasures.

This established pattern of the "typical" maiden versus Tat'jana is broken, however, with our next example:

Нейдет она зиму встречать,
Морозной пылью подышать
И первым снегом с кровли бани
Умыть лицо, плеча и грудь:
Татьяне страшен зимний путь. (PSS VI: 52)

She doesn't go out to greet the winter,
To breathe the powdery frost,
To wash her face, shoulders and breast
With the first snow from the bathhouse roof:
Tat'jana feared the wintry walks.

The point here is not that Tat'jana does not love winter; we know very well that she does. But now she is making preparations to go to Moscow, and her customary life is broken off, never to be restored. There is pathos here as well as irony.

Next comes perhaps our wittiest and cruelest example:

Не обратились на нее
Ни дам ревнивые лорнеты,
Ни трубки модных знатоков
Из лож и кресельных рядов. (PSS VI: 161)

The ladies' envious lorgnettes
Weren't turned toward her,

Nor were the monoculars of the modish connoisseurs,
In their boxes and their parterre rows.

If the negative imagery associated with Tat'jana's childhood applied to her purely as an individual, here for the first time we learn how the world regards her (or rather, how it ignores her). Here, almost for the first time, Puškin injects a note of suspense and even melodrama; it is at this point we leave Tat'jana, to meet her again as the *grande dame* of Petersburg society of Chapter VIII. The example quoted above at the outset of the essay depicts her in this new role. It contrasts sharply with the negative images given for Tat'jana's childhood; for the first time negative imagery has a clearly positive function and implies a heroic characterization rather than mere poverty or deprivation. We are thus reassured that, despite her new success, Tat'jana has not been spoiled; she has not yielded to the lure of the new life she has accepted for herself.

This last example may well supply a clue concerning Puškin's preference for using the device more frequently in portraying Tat'jana than for Eugene or Lenskij. Perhaps the men were too obvious, too negative; a statement of total rejection for them would have been an overstatement, a device that Puškin did not often employ. In the case of Tat'jana, however, the negated images accomplish a double purpose: (1) they imply a sought-for positive—Tat'jana's lack of indulgence in childish pastimes may imply deeper spiritual concerns, for instance, even though we are not told very much concerning these; and (2) they create a certain melodramatic suspense, since their implication is so strongly negative that we are left unprepared for the heroine's ultimate triumph. To be sure, this total lack of preparation for the change could be perceived as a fault, as certain of Puškin's contemporaries already supposed. But if we recollect that Tat'jana's negative behavior may point to a deeper spiritual reality within her, we cannot object to Puškin's treatment.

Apart from these three chief characters, examples of negative imagery are rare. The minor characters, including Ol'ga and Mme. Larina, do not seem to have any. Rare (and rare in Puškin's lyric poetry as well) are lyric uses of the device. An eloquent example that constitutes an exception is Puškin's witty description of an absent moon: "I vod veseloe steklo / Ne otražaet lik Diany" (And the waters' merry glass / Does not reflect Diana's aspect) (PSS VI: 24). There is a comic suggestion here that the mechanism of the water's mirror has broken down and is not functioning.

The change of seasons also brings absence and deprivation, and enables the poet to parody the imagery of pastoral poetry:

На утренней заре пастух
Не гонит уж коров из хлева,
И в час полуденный в кружок
Их не зовет его рожок. . . . (PSS VI: 90)

At dawn the herdsman
No longer drives the cattle from the barn,
And at noon his horn
Does not call them to form their circle. . . .

Recollecting the importance of metapoetry both in *Eugene Onegin* and in Puškin's poetry in general, we should ask, Are there any metapoetic passages that can be classified as showing negative imagery? One passage does indeed recall for us Puškin's custom of doodling in the margins while writing, presumably when poetic inspiration deserted him:

Пишу, и сердце не тоскует,
Перо, забывшись, не рисует,
Близ неоконченных стихов,
Ни женских ножек, ни голов;
Погасший пепел уж не вспыхнет. . . . (PSS VI: 30)

I write, and my heart does not grieve,
My pen does not forget itself and draw,
Amidst the unfinished verses,
Women's feet, or their heads;
No more will the cold ashes blaze. . . .

There is a sharp satiric attack on Moscow society:

В бесплодной сухости речей,
Расспросов, сплетен и вестей,
Не вспыхнет мысли в целы сутки,
Хоть невзначай, хоть наобум;
Не улыбнется томный ум,
Не дрогнет сердце, хоть для шутки. (PSS VI: 160)

In the barren aridity of talk,
Of queries, slanders and gossip,
No ideas spark for days at a time,
Even by chance, even at random;
The infirm mind cannot smile,
The heart cannot tremble, even in jest.

The following passage is technically an antithesis, since it rejects B for A. But within the A part an image arises that must be negated:

Нет, не пошла Москва моя
К нему с повинной головою.
Не праздник, не приемный дар,
Она готовила пожар
Нетерпеливому герою. (PSS VI: 155)

No, my Moscow did not go to him
With bowed head.

> No holiday, no gift,
> But rather a conflagration it prepared
> For the impetuous hero.

The reference here, of course, is to Napoleon's entrance into Moscow and the great fire of Moscow which "answered" that entrance.

Curiously, Puškin made relatively little use of antenantiosis in his other poetry. I have listed below a few of the more interesting examples. The first is from *Ruslan and Ljudmila*, and is a rare instance (in Puškin) of an extended nature description carried out in largely negative terms:

> Кругом все тихо, ветры спят,
> Прохлада вешняя не веет,
> Столетни сосны не шумят,
> Не вьются птицы, лань не смеет
> В жар летний пить из тайных вод. . . . (PSS IV: 80)

> All is silent all around, the wind sleeps,
> The vernal cool does not blow,
> The age-old pines do not rustle,
> The birds soar not, the doe dares not
> Drink from a secret spring in the summer heat. . . .

There are several instances of the device in the comic narratives *Graf Nulin* (Count Nulin) and *Domnik v Kolomne* (Little House in Kolomna), as we might predict, since one possible use of irony is humor. Here is a long and striking example from *Graf Nulin*:

> А что же делает супруга
> Одна в отсутствии супруга?
> Занятий мало ль есть у ней?
> Грибы солить, кормить гусей,
> Заказывать обед и ужин,
> В амбар и в погреб заглянуть.
> Хозяйки глаз повсюду нужен:
> Он в миг заметит что-нибудь.
>
> К несчастью, героиня наша
> ---
> Своей хозяйственною частью
> Не занималася, затем,
> Что не в отеческом законе
> Она воспитана была,
> А в благородном пансионе
> У эмигрантки Фальбала. (PSS V: 4)

> And what does his spouse do
> All alone, when her spouse is absent?
> Is there too little for her to do?
> She can salt mushrooms, feed the geese,

Plan for dinner and supper,
Inspect the barns and cellars.
Her watchful gaze is always useful:
It can ferret out trouble in a second.

Alas, our heroine

Was little concerned
For housekeeping work;
She was not instructed by the village priest,
But raised in a school for well-born young ladies,
Run by a Frenchwoman, Mme. Falbalas.

This technically is antithesis, too, but before the negation a long series of images of household life and chores the heroine ought to perform (but does not) is built up.

Another satiric example comes from Puškin's poetic genealogy, "Moja rodoslovnaja":

Не торговал мой дед блинами,
Не ваксил царских сапогов,
Не пел с придворными дьячками,
В князья не прыгал из хохлов,
И не был беглым он солдатом
Австрийских пудренных дружин. . . . (PSS III: 1: 261)

My granddad didn't sell pancakes,
He didn't wax the tsar's boots,
He didn't sing with the court clerks.
He didn't rise from serf to prince,
Nor was he a soldier who escaped
From Austrian brigades of powdered comrades. . . .

Here Puškin underlines his removal from courtly favor by poking fun at the favorites to tsars and tsarinas: Peter the Great's Menšikov, supposedly once a seller of pancakes, or the court scrivener who was the lover of the Empress Elizaveta Petrovna.

These examples might lead us to inquire whether the negative image of ironic wit ought not to have appeared more frequently in the poetry of Puškin, celebrated for its irony. Yet, perhaps we do have sufficient wit in the examples already given. Onegin the non-scholar and non-poet is surely witty, as is the water's failure to reflect the image of the moon. In the first instance Onegin's would-be pretensions contrast with the writer Puškin's actual achievements. The second image is comical because the sentence form employed suggests a failure of a "mechanism," in this case the mirror, to function. Less funny are the passages connected with Tat'jana, but this is quite natural in terms of their inverse seriousness and their suspense-making function.

Examples of antenantiosis in Puškin's lyric poetry can hardly be found, though negative rhetorical constructions are fairly common. Either the negative is asserted as such, without irony (e.g., "Ne daj mne bog sojti s uma"—PSS III: 322), or we are dealing with an antithesis ("Net, ja ne l'stec"—Puškin's abject apology for his loyalty to Tsar Nicholas—PSS III: 89). Even when the first element of the antithesis is fairly well extended, it always remains clear within the poem's context that its ultimate resolution will arrive (e.g., "Ne tem gorožas' "—PSS II: 2: 49). Perhaps the short lyric poem did not offer Puškin the poetic space essential to the rhetorical development of the antenantiosis, and prefers the balder, sharper outline of the antithesis.

In closing, we should pose the question, From where might Puškin have taken this ironic device? Its use was sufficiently widespread, of course, that a specific answer to this question will scarcely be possible. It is enough to suggest here, I believe, that Puškin did not lack sources.

In classical literature the obvious, though hardly the unique, source might well be Horace. Horace was probably Puškin's favorite classical poet, and in fact examples of our device abound in his poetry. I quote two fairly extended instances from the *Odes*:

> Nondum subacta ferre iugum valet
> cervice, nondum munia camparis
> aequare, nec tauri ruentis
> in venerem tolerare pondus.
>
> Circa virentis est animus tuae
> campos invencae, nunc fluviis gravem
> solantis aestum, nunc in udo
> ludere cum vitulis salicto praegestientis. (Smith 1952 II: 5)

> Not yet can she bear, with supple neck, the yoke,
> Nor yet with any other let herself be paired;
> Immature for the duties of breeding,
> And the fiery embraces of the bull.
>
> The heifer confines her heart
> To the fields, now pausing
> To slake summer heat in the stream,
> with young steers yet younger at play. . . .

This is actually an antithesis, of course, but the opening series of negative images describing the heifer's immaturity and unfitness for love is developed as an independent chain of images.

> Non semper imbres nubibus hispidos
> manant in agros aut mare Caspium
> vexant inaequalis procellae
> usque, nec Armeniis in oris. . . . (Smith 1952 II: 9)

'Tis not ever the fields that become rough in the rain
Nor the Caspian ever harried by storm;
   Nor each month in the year
   When the ice stands intent on Armenian shores. . . .

This could be read minimally as simple negation (which it is rhetorically), but Horace seems to extract a good deal of irony from describing nature images that are not "typical" or expected. This makes his use of the device approximate that of Puškin, though of course his images are much more lyric than most of Puškin's (compare, however, the image quoted above from Puškin's *Ruslan and Ljudmila*).

If we turn to the Russian poet who was, more than any other, a follower of Horace (and, of course, a predecessor of Puškin), Deržavin, we find striking examples of the device. Here is a negative chain of images from the fourth stanza of *Felica*:

> Не слишком любишь маскарады,
> А в клоб не ступишь и ногой;
> Храня обычаи, обряды,
> Не донкишотствуешь собой;
> Коня парнасска не седлаешь,
> К духам в собранье не въезжаешь,
> Не ходишь с трона на Восток;
> Но кротости ходя стезею,
> Благотворящею душею,
> Полезных дней проводишь ток.

> You're not too fond of masquerades,
> You won't set foot within a club;
> Preserving customs, rituals,
> You don't turn into a Quixote;
> You don't desert the throne to go East [i.e., to Masonic lodges]
> You don't join the spirits [i.e., Masons] in their meetings,
> But treading the path of meekness,
> With charitable soul,
> You pass the span of useful days.

This is no doubt more labored than Puškin, but it does show much of the ironic wit of certain of Puškin's examples.

Curiously, though Byron's *Don Juan* gave so much to the original conception of *Eugene Onegin*, examples seem to be rare in that work. But Byron's *Beppo* does have an extended example that is outstanding and very funny: a negative description of those women whom Byron punningly calls "Musselwomen," i.e., the women of Musselmen (Moslems, in the terminology of Byron's day):

> No chemistry of them ["Musselwomen"] unfolds her gases,
> No metaphysics are let loose in lectures,

No circulating library amasses
Religious novels, moral tales, and strictures
Upon the living manners, as they pass us;
No exhibition glares with annual pictures;
They steal not on the stars from out of their attics,
Nor deal (thank God for that!) in mathematics. (1935: 76)

I do not suggest, however, that Puškin took the device from Byron; it was too general, and in any case such a hypothesis would leave us without an explanation for the example quoted above from *Ruslan and Ljudmila*.

As the two examples quoted from Horace and the one from Puškin's *Ruslan and Ljudmila* would confirm, Puškin could have made our negative device one that combined lyricism and irony. But his finest lyric poetry is too direct for this and generally eschews irony. Instead Puškin employed it in those longer works, in particular *Onegin*, in which there is much irony, often tinged with humor. Puškin is no doubt the ironic poet *par excellence* in Russian verse, and it is clear that he integrated our device with the tone, imagery, and lexicon of his well-known, even celebrated ironic manner.

DAVID M. BETHEA

The Role of the *Eques* in
Puškin's *Bronze Horseman*

After Belinskij, Valerij Brjusov was one of the first to see an emerging
shape to scholarship on Puškin's *Mednyj vsadnik* (Bronze Horseman).[1] He
outlined three dominant tensions responsible for the ideological meaning
of the work: collective versus individual will, paganism versus Christian-
ity, and rebellion versus despotism (Brjusov 1909 III: 456–57). These tensions, which subsequent generations of readers have tended to resolve by
accenting one or the other member of the opposing pairs, correspond
roughly to interpretations on the "social," "religious," and "political"
levels. Of the three levels, it is the religious that has for obvious reasons
received short shrift in this century, especially since 1917. With the exception of Merežkovskij, who is cited by Brjusov, there has been little effort to
locate the *poèma* within the broader context of *metaphysical* concerns
characterizing the poet's last years. That is to say, the growing sophistication of Puškin's "historical consciousness" did not necessarily, as the
scholarly record seems to indicate, exclude the possibility of some form of
religious conviction.[2] Soviet scholars especially have remained content to
look past compelling internal evidence in his later works and to leave him
in the role of irreverent Voltairian, a role he had by the mid-thirties long
since outgrown. This oversight is even more striking when one takes into
account the fact that it is precisely the metaphysical/religious implications
of the work that were most significant to the Symbolists writing on the eve
of the October Revolution.[3] Not all of these implications, as I shall argue in
this essay, were *read into* the work by a generation of impressionable mys-
tics looking for signs and symbols out of the past to predict the imminent
future. Some were surely planted there by Puškin himself.

The purpose of the present study is to focus attention on one image,
that of the *eques*, within the complex of potential religious/historical meanings that the later Puškin would have imputed to the confrontation between the Bronze Horseman and Evgenij. After establishing a context by
examining the dual traditions of European statuary and Russian heraldry
on which Puškin drew for his presentation of the "duel" between the
Bronze Horseman and Evgenij, I will turn to the internal evidence offered
by the poem and attempt a reinterpretation of its symbolic structure.

THE TRADITION OF EUROPEAN
STATUARY

Imperially, the steed set the ruler or the aristocratic knight (*eques*) apart from the common man.[4] If the ancient Egyptians discerned something undignified about seating their ruler on horseback and thus preferred the chariot, the Greeks had no such scruples and in fact placed great emphasis on horsemanship. One aspect of Alexander's "greatness" that has come down to us was his prowess on horseback (it was said that his horse Bucephalus would accept no other rider), including his discomfiting of Darius from his chariot as depicted in a famous mosaic. Thereafter, the steed continued to acquire symbolic meaning, becoming the attribute not simply of the *eques* but, especially during the Roman Empire, of the *emperor* as well: witness the famous equestrian of Marcus Aurelius that was first erected on the Capitol as a symbol of his majesty and authority and that was later preserved during the Christian era only because it was rechristened "Constantine" (thus linking the notion of papacy to empire) and moved to the Lateran. After a hiatus of almost a millennium, the equestrian reemerged in the monuments of Donatello, Verrochio, Bologna, Mochi, and Bernini, and in the sketches of Leonardo. Most intriguing about the Renaissance treatment is the fact that the *concetto* (the conceit or "spark" for the entire project) for the *Reiterstandbild* underwent gradual change: the horse and rider were slowly *separated* as part of an ensemble decorating a ducal tomb (e.g., that of Congrande [1330] in Verona); the *eques* now no longer had to be a sovereign, but could be a mere *condottiere*, or captain of mercenary forces (e.g., Donatello's *Gattamelata* [1448–50] in Padua); and the steed became more animated and full of latent power until the point where, in Leonardo's sketches and especially in Bernini's sculpture of Constantine the Great (1654–70), it finally *reared up on its hind legs*.[5] Bernini's equestrian occupies such a prominent place in this genealogy because it is located on the Scala Regia (the main landing of the Vatican), thereby becoming the first image of papal authority that a visitor encounters, and because Constantine is presented at that moment of revelation—the "moving stasis" of the rearing horse captures this *concetto* perfectly—when he sees the cross in the sky and prepares himself to conquer in its name. And it is this first completed statue of a horse reared on its hind legs which would become, significantly, the model for the Louis XIV equestrian at Versailles, which in turn would influence Falconet as he worked on the Bronze Horseman for Catherine (Janson 1974: 159–87).

Bernini had originally wanted to show Louis XIV on a rocky summit, "in full possession of that Glory which . . . has become synonymous with his name" (Janson 1974: 166–67), an idea which Catherine and her advisers felt was justifiably transposable to the Russian context. Moreover, the snake being trampled underfoot was an allegorization of defeated envy (see Kaganovič 1975: 86–92). But the Russian time-space in which this allegory was erected soon altered its meaning. The tsar as Marcus Aurelius or Marcus Curtius did not arguably mean much to the Russians, but, as shall be pointed out in what follows, the tsar as Christ-like St. George slaying the serpent (pagan forces) of history did. Long before this, in the late sixteenth century, foreigners visiting the court of Ivan the Terrible's son Fedor Ivanovič mentioned the existence of "a golden medal portraying St. George mounted on a horse," which was worn on the sleeve or hat of the recipient as a sign of "the highest honor that can be bestowed for any service whatsoever."[6] In any event, the *apocalyptic* connotation of the horse and rider is very much in evidence on one of the extant flags of Ivan the Terrible, where we find Jesus Christ, mounted on a white charger, surrounded by twenty-seven angels on horseback, and escorted in front by the archangel Michael on his winged steed. The official order of St. George—of which Puškin was well aware (see below)—the most popular of all Russian military medals and the only tsarist decoration to migrate (in altered form, of course) into Soviet times, was instituted in 1769, that is, some thirteen years before the unveiling of Falconet's statue on Senate Square in Petersburg. So while Peter and his followers had endeavored to secularize the imperial iconography,[7] the religious/mythic link between St. George and the Moscow horseman continued well into Puškin's time and beyond to have a secret life of its own—even perhaps in Falconet's *borrowed concetto*.[8] It is conceivable that, to those who saw Russia's historical mission in terms of an apocalyptic confrontation between Moscow, the Third Rome, and St. Petersburg, the Western city of the Antichrist, the transpositions in Falconet's *kumir* (pagan "idol"—see below) were particularly ominous: the Moscow horseman had moved to the city of Peter, St. George had traded his lance for an arm pointed imperiously into Russia's future, and the serpent impaled by the lance had become a snake trampled underfoot by the tsar's steed.

Whether its rider was Christ or Antichrist, bearer of light or bearer of darkness, the majestic steed became *the* symbol of Russia raised on her haunches between the old and the new. Lednicki has argued that Peter's steed is not in actuality caught in a full standing position (*na dyby*), but "is galloping smoothly," with "the seat of the rider . . . relaxed and comfortable" (1955: 35–36). This may be true to the foreign observer, but the fact that Puškin chose in the climax of his poem to underscore the *raising up* of Russia into a stance of fatal equipoise ("Ne tak li ty nad samoj bezdnoj, / Na vysote, uzdoj železnoj / Rossiju *podnjal na dyby*?" [Was it not thus, aloft hard by the abyss, / that with curb of iron / you reared up Russia?[9]] [PSS V: 147]) means that he at least saw horse and rider engaged in more than unimpeded forward progress. If writers such as Puškin did not, for reasons of artistic temperament or historiosophical conviction, choose to make the connection between the monument and the apocalyptic *end* of Russian history (that connection would be seen to later), the reason was not for any lack of eschatological tradition.[10] As Falconet's correspondence with Catherine, Diderot, and others indicates, the tension between what the "enlighteners" (particularly Beckij, the official administrator of the project) felt the statue should do to legitimize their position and what the sculptor felt were the unique artistic injunctions guiding him was real (Levitine 1972: 54–57). The "antiquomaniacs" within the court wanted a statue in the manner of the Marcus Aurelius on the Capitoline because such a piece would presumably confer on Peter's project to change Russia—make it *new*—a classical authority, a bloodline in the *old*. However, the Marcus Aurelius had none of the modern dynamism that Falconet had inherited from Bernini and the latter's ill-fated equestrian of Louis XIV. It was simply "the image of a triumphant horseman mounted on a powerful steed, majestically *advancing at a walking pace* on the *flat* surface of a *geometrically shaped* pedestal"; the horse itself, according to Falconet, was unsightly not only because of "its bovine head, its thick ugly neck, and, in general, its unpleasant proportions, but . . . also . . . because of its anatomical inadequacies and its *unrealistic* movement—a real horse, for instance, would never lift its foreleg to a horizontal position" (my emphasis; Levitine 1972: 54, 56). Moreover, these views were apparently shared by some of Puškin's colleagues. Batjuškov, for example, remarked in his *Progulki v Akademiju Xudožestv* (Strolls in the Academy of Arts) that there is something ponderous and "unpleasant" about the copy of the Marcus Aurelius found in the Museum of the Academy of Fine Arts in St. Petersburg, whereas "modern artists are much more successful with horses. We have before our eyes the work of Falconet, this marvelous horse, living, flaming, graceful, and *so boldly stanced . . .* " (my emphasis; cited in Lednicki 1955: 34).[11]

Falconet gradually came to agree with Voltaire's view, as it was to be enunciated in the latter's projected *Histoire de l'Empire Russe sous Pierre le Grand*, that Peter's greatest role was that of *reformer* and legislator (as opposed to conqueror), ally of the *philosophes*. The outstretched hand of the tsar was not meant to be that of the victor at Poltava, but a *main protectrice* (Lednicki 1955: 33). Indeed, Falconet confirmed his debt to Voltaire in a twice-published (1770 and 1781) letter to Diderot. Yet, to reiterate, in the Russian context there was little tradition of Western "reform" and incremental change.[12] What the term actually meant to those native Russians who wore hair shirts beneath the Western dress forced on them by their tsar was *revolution*. Thus Peter could be, and indeed was, viewed by the enlighteners as a secular St. George stamping out ignorance and obscurantism so that Russia could leap into a better future or by the sectarians as a man-god who had betrayed his role as tsar to become emperor and hence Antichrist. Regardless, however, of one's *a priori* beliefs about the direction of Russian history, Peter on horseback came to signify a radical and total shift in time-space relations, the visual equivalent of his new calendar. That this tradition was later undermined by other equestrians,[13] notably Paolo Trubeckoj's satiric monument to Alexander III in which Peter's spirited charger comes to resemble a hippopotamus, should not be seen to challenge seriously the remarkable potency of Falconet's work or Puškin's poetic deployment of it.

It is also worth recalling that the Western tradition of equestrian statuary takes its roots from the notion of controlling, of "reining" and "reigning," a wild and passionate "body politic" (Watson 1983: 275–79; see also Giamatti 1976 and Rowland 1965–66). This, after all, is the notion of noble horsemanship from which, etymologically and culturally, the *chivalric* tradition grew. He who could control his own steed and unhorse his opponent was the ideal knight, and victory in combat was all the evidence needed to establish one's nobility and chosen status. Hence in Western literature as in statuary it was essential *to keep distinct* the notions of horseman and horse, rider and ridden. In Russia, however, where a tsar such as Peter was associated by a significant segment of the population, including Puškin, with what was *new* and *revolutionary* and the people with what was *old* and *orthodox*, this Western formula could not be so easily transplanted.[14] If Catherine and her German "enlighteners" could insist on viewing Falconet's work as an expression of Peter's proud design to control the elements (and, by implication, the wild force of the people), then those of another generation could also see the tsar as that figure who, turning Russia westward and upsetting the status quo, *unleashed* rather than reined in the passions of his people. Mickiewicz apparently had this more ominous interpretation in mind when he wrote in *Pomnik Piotra Wielkiego* (Monument to Peter the Great) that "Car Piotr wypuszczał rumakowi wodze, / Widać, że leciał tratując po drodze; / Od razu wskoczył aż na sam brzeg skały [His charger's reins Tsar Peter *has released* [my emphasis—DMB]; / He has been flying down the road, perchance, / And here the precipice checks his advance" (Mickiewicz 1944: 350; cited in Lednicki 1955: 29).

Puškin himself seems to have been well aware of the tradition of the *eques*, of the favored one who rose above the people and who signified that status with a steed. In an early poem entitled "K Liciniju" (To Licinius, 1815), he describes how the haughty and insouciant Vetulius rides into the crowd on his chariot:

Лициний, зришь ли ты? на быстрой колеснице,
Увенчан лаврами, в блестящей багрянице,
Cпесиво развалясь, Ветулий молодой
В толпу народную летит по мостовой.
Смотри, как все пред ним усердно спину клонит,
Как ликторов полки народ несчастный гонят. (PSS I: 111)

Licinius, do you behold? on his swift chariot,
crowned with laurels, in refulgent purple,
haughtily reclining, the young Vetulius
flies along the road into the crowd of people.
Look how everything zealously bends its back before him,
how regiments of lictors disperse the wretched folk.

Vetulius's "elevation" above the *hoi polloi*, though Puškin's sarcasm suggests that it is unearned, is both physical (he reclines from his position "above" while the crowd bends its back in an obsequious bow from "below") and social/political (the crown of laurels[15] and the shining purple of the ruling class). His Caesar-like *hubris* is underscored in his relationship with the people, who look up to him as though receiving "the blessing of a wondrous god."[16]

But all this flattery and adulation is, to the freedom-loving young Puškin, unhealthy and corrupting. Following the archetypal course laid out by Phaeton, the chariot and driver that rise above the common man can, and inevitably do, *fall*:

> О Рим! о гордый край разврата, злодеянья,
> Придет *ужасный*[17] день—день мщенья, наказанья;[18]
> Предвижу грозного величия конец,
> *Падет, падет* во прах вселенныя венец!
> Народы дикие, сыны свирепой брани,
> Войны *ужасной* меч прияв в кровавы длани,
> И горы, и моря оставят за собой
> И хлынут на тебя кипящею рекой.
> Исчезнет Рим. . . . (My emphasis; PSS I: 113)

> O Rome! o proud land of depravity, wickedness,
> a terrible day will come—a day of vengeance, punishment;
> I foresee the end of dread grandeur,
> the universe's crown will fall, fall into the dust!
> Wild peoples, sons of fierce war,
> taking the terrible sword of battle into their bloody hands,
> will leave the mountains and seas behind them
> and pour down on you in a seething river.
> Rome will vanish. . . .

This notion of the steed of state racing out of control with "disastrous" (lit. falling "from the stars") consequences for all concerned will be addressed again in *Bronze Horseman*. There, however, the argument will be almost entirely *implicit*, since on the most obvious level Puškin is polemicizing with Mickiewicz and the latter's image, largely sarcastic and Russophobic, of the "charger's reins" that "Tsar Peter has released." Puškin's Peter *reins in* his steed *nad samoj bezdnoj* (at/above the very abyss), but he does so in a question which the climax of his poem begs rather than resolves. Finally, Puškin seems to have been genuinely intrigued by the image of equine-driven doom, returning to it in works as different as "Pesn' o veščem Olege" (Song of the Prophetic Oleg, 1822) and "Besy" (The Devils, 1830).

THE RUSSIAN HERALDIC TRADITION

Falconet's Bronze Horseman was a statue created by a foreigner to honor Peter's proud design "v Evropu prorubit' okno" (to hack a window through to Europe). As Jakobson has pointed out, however, the repeated use of the word *kumir* (idol) by Puškin to describe the monument had, "in a world of Orthodox customs . . . saturated with *the symbolism of the Eastern Church*," an "undeniably pagan association" (1975: 40). Nicholas clearly felt the potential for this sort of "magnetized" reading: in his role as censor, for example, he consistently crossed out the lines of the poem where the word appeared. In other words, as far as the tsar was concerned, there was something unseemly and even *irreverent* in Puškin's apparent attempt to telescope the notions of Petrine reform and pagan idolatry. The linkage raised the very issue that had vexed Russia from the time of the Great Schism—Peter was seen as the Antichrist by the Old Believers precisely because he had placed himself *above* God, had become a *zemnoj bog* (earthly god),[19] rather than God's chosen representative:

> The historical logic . . . is quite clear: the Russian prince, saintly in his person, became, with the rise of the State, the guardian of orthodoxy and thereby the guarantor of salvation for each Russian; hence the saintliness of the ruler, expressed in his piety, was of direct concern to each Russian, for it determined not only the existence of the tsar, but of Russia as well. *The impious tsar could not be a true tsar, but what did this mean for the fate of Russia?* Time and again the answer is given by the many men who claimed, in private and in public, that *Peter was the Anti-Christ.* (My emphasis; Cherniavsky 1961: 76)

Interpreters as varied in orientation as Merežkovskij, Brjusov, Xodasevič, Mirskij, and Jakobson have noted the "pagan" elements in *The Bronze Horseman*; no one, however, has adequately focused attention on what, metaphysically speaking, that pagan element is *opposed to*. *The Bronze Horseman*, after all, centers on the duel between Peter and Evgenij. Is Evgenij simply the hapless victim, the *pharmakos*,[20] or do his background and field of action enter into a value system that is more than political and that, in terms of the poem, makes the old-new, Moscow-Petersburg, orthodox-pagan oppositions more understandable? To answer this question we need to investigate Puškin's views on the Russian heraldic tradition, for it is this tradition, as I hope to demonstrate, with which the poet "armed" his hero in the latter's confrontation with the mounted "idol."

To recapitulate for a moment, the tradition of European statuary, although ancient and "classical" in origin, was in the context of late eighteenth- and early nineteenth-century Russia something "new," since in this case it served to eulogize the Petrine reforms and all their "diabolical" ramifications. (Recall that invariably Avvakum and his followers were on the side of the *old* belief against the *new*. "On Russian soil, sculpture was closely associated with whatever was unchristian, even antichristian, in the spirit of the Petersburg tsardom" [Jakobson 1975: 40].) Against the relative "newness" of the *kumir na bronzovom kone* (idol on a bronze steed) Puškin juxtaposes several related cultural themes—"old" Moscow (and thus the Russian state before Peter), the "old" nobility (with lineages that antedate by centuries Peter's "meritorious" nobility), and "old" coats of arms, that is, the necessary *proof* of the antiquity of one's nobility.

Whenever Puškin mentions *gerb* (coat of arms) in his writings,[21] he invariably places the word within a certain "semantic field." For example, in "Poslanie Del'vigu" (Epistle to Del'vig, 1827) we find:

> Барон в обители печальной
> Доволен впрочем был судьбой,
> Пастора лестью погребальной,
> *Гербом гробницы феодальной*
> И эпитафией плохой. (My emphasis; PSS III: 69)

> The baron in his sad abode
> was with his fate content however,
> [as was he with] the pastor's funereal praise,
> the coat-of-arms of his feudal tomb,
> and his poor epitaph.

Here the "coat of arms," the "tomb" (*grobnica*), and "feudal" (*feodal'nyj*) are joined grammatically in one phrase and semantically in one meaning unit—the "old," "ancient," "dead." This same semantic complex, which is repeated a little later in "Epistle to Del'vig" (PSS III: 71), was also anticipated in *Baxčisarajskij fontan* (Baxčisaraj Fountain, 1824):

> Тиха Мариина светлица . . .
> В домовой церкви, где кругом
> *Почиют* мощи хладным *сном*,
> С *короной*, с княжеским *гербом*
> Воздвиглась новая *гробница* . . . (My emphasis; PSS IV: 161)

> It is quiet in Marija's room . . .
> In the domestic church, where all around
> repose in cold sleep [ancestral] remains
> with crown, with princely coat-of-arms,
> a new tomb is erected . . .

The parallels between these verse passages are striking: all three (PSS III: 71 is not cited) contain etymologically related "houses for the dead" (*grob* vs. *grob*nica) and single out the accouterments of knighthood (*gerb, korona*) in that context; the latter two (PSS III: 71 and IV: 161) employ the high-style verb "to sleep the sleep of the dead" (*počit'*) in an instrumental construction involving *son*[22] and make explicit reference to the high-born status of the deceased (*vysokorodnyj baron* vs. *knjaž*eskij gerb).

The connotations associated with *gerb* do not in themselves tell us a great deal. After all, one would expect a reference to a family coat-of-arms, if the latter were genuine, to conjure up images of ancient noble origins and medieval quests. The fact that these same semantic invariants entered into Puškin's polemic with Bulgarin and the "new" men of letters of the

1830s is, on the other hand, telling. Puškin was extremely proud of his six-hundred-year-old noble ancestry, and yet he also acknowledged that the mere presence of a pedigree did not guarantee the *artistic* merit of his or anyone else's work: "No one holds in higher esteem the true hereditary nobility—whose existence is so important in a governmental sense—than our [society]. But in the peaceful republic of learning what do we care for *coats-of-arms and dusty documents* [kakoe nam delo do gerbov i pyl'nyx gramot]?" ("Otryvok iz literaturnyx letopisej" [Excerpt from Literary Chronicles] [1829]; PSS XI: 80).

And yet, as Puškin said soon thereafter in direct reference to Bulgarin's underhanded attempt to blacken his family name on his mother's side (the anecdote about Puškin's great-grandfather Gannibal being bought by a drunken skipper for a bottle of rum), the obverse is also untrue: the absence of pedigree or, what is worse, the conferral of a recently contrived pedigree based on "meritorious service" does not guarantee a work's high quality or, for that matter, a writer's high-mindedness.

Some gentlemen journalists in government service took it into their heads to attack one of their confreres because he was not a nobleman. Other men of letters permitted themselves to ridicule the intolerance of these noblemen-journalists. They made bold to ask who are these *feudal barons* [*feodal'nye barony*], these unknown knights, proudly demanding *coats-of-arms and documents* [*gerbov i gramot*] of our humble brotherhood? And what did they answer? After a short silence the gentlemen journalists in government service objected heatedly that in literature there can be no nobility, that to boast of one's nobility before one's brotherhood (especially if one is a petty bourgeois within the nobility) is killingly funny, and that six-hundred-year-old *documents* [*gramoty*] won't help a genuine nobleman in the case of bad prose or mediocre verse. What an awful "Eat it [e.g., the fig] yourself!" (My emphasis; "Oproverženie na kritiki" [Rebuttal of criticisms] [1830]; PSS XI: 151–52)

Here, in a passage edged with heavy sarcasm, we find the same terms of the already familiar semantic field (*feodal'nye barony, gerby i gramoty,* etc.), but they are undercut by the surrounding context of modifiers: the slightly archaic or official sounding *sii* (these) together with the "unknown" knights who are "proudly demanding" documentary evidence of high birth. The irony, however, is double-edged; the sarcastic voice of the Bulgarin camp, which is clearly aimed at Puškin (note the references to "petty bourgeois" and "six-hundred-year-old documents"), is turned on itself when one realizes that the *new* documents attesting to one's place in a nobility of merit are also no safeguard against "bad prose" or "mediocre verse." This, of course, is the "awful 'Eat it yourself!' " the indecent remark (an English equivalent would be something like "You're one too!") with the added connotation of hoisting oneself on one's petard, of which Puškin speaks. That he has Bulgarin and his group in mind is confirmed a few sentences later with the reference to *figljarstvo* (i.e., activities appropriate to Figljarin) and with the recounting of the anecdote about the bottle of rum on the next page (PSS XI: 152–53; cf. "Moja rodoslovnaja" [My Genealogy] PSS III: 263).

Before proceeding to the text of *Bronze Horseman*, I would like to suggest more specifically how the notions of coat-of-arms and heraldry (*geral'dika*) might enter into the text and context of Puškin's narrative poem. Coats-of-arms must by definition represent something, usually a symbol or series of symbols which tell in telegraphic form a narrative *mythos* associated with a given family, town, or state. Historically, Russia had no medieval chivalric tradition; her coats-of-arms derived primarily from ancient emblems amd figures found on seals, coins, and battle standards (Speransov 1974: 8). The Puškin family possessed coats-of-arms on both the paternal and the maternal sides. However, Puškin's quarrel with the new men of letters was not simply a family affair. Rather it had to do with changes in the status of the old nobility that went back to the Petrine reforms. Likewise, Evgenij's duel with the Bronze Horseman is not only over his personal right to domestic happiness and to the "little place" (*mestečko*) he plans to create with Paraša. It is such larger issues as old vs. new, Moscow vs. Petersburg, hereditary nobility (*stolbovoe dvorjanstvo*) vs. "tiers-état," and ultimately orthodox vs. pagan, that, I shall argue in a moment, Puškin wishes to raise by building into his poem allusions to Russia's heraldic tradition.

Let us make discussion more concrete by citing two important stanzas from "Rodoslovnaja moego geroja" (Genealogy of My Hero, pub. 1836). This "excerpt from a satirical poem" was the only part of the unfinished *Ezerskij* (written in late 1832 and early 1833) which Puškin later reworked and saw into print. Puškin took drafts of *Ezerskij* with him to Boldino in 1833, and it is clear that *Ezerskij*, if not actually part of *Bronze Horseman* as Annenkov once asserted, entered into the poet's thinking as he conceived his poem (see Puškin [Izmajlov] 1978: 165–83). Annenkov, for example, who had good critical intuition, was convinced enough by the textual parallels between "Genealogy" and *Bronze Horseman* that he felt justified in claiming that "both the excerpt and the poem were conceived together" (1984 I: 381–86). But the primary reason that *Ezerskij* and "Genealogy" are essential for the present study is that they are both much more *specific* about the hero's origins—and at the same time much more *autobiographical*—than Puškin was willing to be in *Bronze Horseman*.

The sixth stanza of "Genealogy" raises a number of themes already familiar to readers of "Rebuttal of Criticisms."[23] The speaker takes pride in the fact that, though ridiculed by "colleagues" for his aristocratic pretensions, he is in reality a "petty bourgeois" (*meščanin*), one who has to earn his own way, and in this sense a true "democrat" (PSS III: 427). Here too we find the love for antiquity which the poet associates with the world of his Muscovite grandmother and her oral history of kinfolk. But that world is passing, and one can now climb from the old nobility into the *tiers-état* through *sobstvennye zaslugi*, the "personal merits" demonstrated by active and loyal service to the state. It is immediately after this, in stanza seven, that Puškin introduces the motif of heraldry which, I suggest, has a direct bearing on a central passage of *Bronze Horseman*:

> Мне жаль, что тех родов боярских
> Бледнеет блеск и никнет дух;
> Мне жаль, что нет князей Пожарских,
> Что о других пропал и слух,
> Что их поносит и Фиглярин,
> Что русский ветреный боярин
> Считает грамоты царей
> За пыльный сбор календарей,
> Что в нашем тереме забытом
> Растет пустынная трава,
> Что *геральдического льва*
> *Демократическим копытом*
> Теперь лягает и *осел*:
> Дух века вот куда зашел! (My emphasis; PSS III: 427–28)

> 'Tis a pity that from those boyar clans
> the spirit flags and splendor fades;
> 'tis a pity that the Prince Požarskijs are no more,
> that about others there is no word,
> that they are abused by Figljarin,
> that [today's] empty-headed Russian boyar
> considers the documents of tsars
> a dusty collection of calendars,
> that our abandoned tower
> is overgrown with grass,
> that the heraldic lion
> by the ass's democratic hoof
> now too is being kicked:
> this is how far the spirit of the age has gone!

The Onegin stanza (which Puškin did *not* use in *Bronze Horseman*) is an ideal formal vehicle for leading up to the "punch line" about the "heraldic lion" and the "hoof" of the "democratic ass." The old Moscow families (the Požarskijs) have fallen out of sight and prominence, to be pilloried by Figljarin; the current nobleman cannot distinguish the real documents and charters of the tsars (including, presumably, their *gerby*) from a pile of old calendars; and the *terem* (tower-chamber), which was such a prominent institution within high-born families before Peter, seems now, in the wake of Catherine, both linguistically and socially obsolete.[24]

Yet all of these juxtapositions (Požarskij-Figljarin, historical documents–calendars, etc.), which serve collectively to point up the fall of old Moscow and the rise of new Petersburg, are in a sense secondary to the final confrontation between the lion and the ass. Puškin implies such a crescendo effect with his punctuation: after the first two lines, there is no full stop in the entire stanza until the colon at the end of the penultimate line. Instead there are a series of dependent clauses beginning with *čto* and governed by the main clause "Mne žal' " ('Tis a pity) and separated by a comma. The comparison between the lion and the ass is the last of these, placing it in a marked or "strong" position. Only after this ultimate comparison can the poet exclaim, in wry exasperation, "This is how far the spirit of the age has gone [that is, taken us]!"

The heraldic lion is a crucial image in this context because it is the first instance in which Puškin actually shows us what might be on one of the coats-of-arms he has earlier associated with feudal barons and the world of pre-Petrine Russia. And in fact the earliest recorded[25] Russian landed (as opposed to family) coat-of-arms is that of a lion *raised up on its hind legs* holding a silver *cross* in its right paw. It belonged to the town of Vladimir but owes its origins to the sign of Jurij Dolgorukij (founder of *Moscow*), which dates to the twelfth century (Speransov 1974: 24–25). That the lion had an *Orthodox* mission is attested to by the presence of the cross. Without the Christian coloring it is simply a traditional symbol of courage, strength, fury, and, on occasion, magnanimity (Speransov 1974: 16). The defeated lion, which is the more accurate symbol in this instance, is, on the other hand, representative of impotence and fallen, trampled glory. Puškin obviously could not have read later commentators on the heraldic tradition such as Lakier, Lukomskij and Tipol't, and Speransov, but he could have learned something of the sort from the "gossip" (*tolki*) of his "Muscovite grandmother" or from his own investigations into his family tree.

The lion is being kicked by the "democratic hoof" of the ass, a lower, parodic version of the steed. That is to say, this duel between lion and ass is a rehearsal for the duel in *Bronze Horseman* between Moscow and Petersburg, Evgenij and Peter, sacred and secular horseman. The second oldest recorded Russian landed coat-of-arms, and one with which every native subject with the least interest in national history would be familiar, is that of the *Moscow horseman*, who by Puškin's time had also become synonymous with *St. George*. This emblem first began to appear on Russian soil shortly after the Battle of Kulikovo and can be found in seals that were attached to late fourteenth- and early fifteenth-century *gramoty* (Speransov 1974: 24). It depicted a mounted warrior who defeats in combat a winged serpent. The warrior's mount is *raised on its haunches* over the serpent, and the rider has plunged his lance into the beast's mouth or heart. Soviet commentators are quick to assert that the emblem of the Moscow horseman did not originally have any religious connotation, that it was intended rather to show the native warrior freeing his country from the forces of the Tatar Yoke: "These changes in the [interpretation of] the ancient emblem [as St. George] took place because of [*po vine*] foreigners who were invited to work at the Chancery of Russian Heraldry and who didn't understand Russian national symbolism, but who did know the legend of the fantastic feat of 'St.' [*sic*] George" (Speransov 1974: 26). Be this as it may, such a "reinterpretation," which Speransov suggests occurred at the beginning of the eighteenth century (that is, *during the reign of Peter*!), was a fact of cultural life by the time of Puškin.

To sum up, both the lion and the horseman possessed *sacred* variants linked with the fate and holy mission of Muscovite Rus'. It is quite likely that Puškin himself would have known this (or else why would he make specific mention of the "*heraldic* lion"?). Finally, these symbols, taken together, provide a logical, artistically economical (and "ancient") foil to the *Bronze Horseman*, the universally recognized symbol of "new" Petersburg. In this regard, it is ironic that Petersburg's official coat-of-arms shows two anchors in the shape of an "X" with a gold scepter lying vertically over the point of intersection. Any "sacred" meaning (e.g., the St. Andrew's cross) has apparently been "secularized" out of the emblem, with the result that its function as totem or tutelary spirit has, for many natives at least, been preempted by that of Falconet's equestrian statue.

BRONZE HORSEMAN

Our analysis of *Bronze Horseman* will focus on the two confrontations between Evgenij and the Bronze Horseman. *Bronze Horseman* is similar to a number of other works by Puškin in that it is constructed around a pair of confrontations or "duels" (actual or psychological) that are themselves separated in time by some significant event: Tat'jana and Evgenij before Lenskij's death and after Tat'jana's marriage in *Eugene Onegin*, Silvio and the Count before and after the Count's marriage in "The Shot," Germann and the Countess before and after the Countess's death in "The Queen of Spades," Grinev and Pugačev before and after the outbreak of the Pugačev Uprising in *The Captain's Daughter*, etc. In such instances Puškin is apt to suggest important shifts in the status quo by enforcing a *reverse* parallelism; that is, the principals may be meeting for a second time, but the *tables are turned*. Thus on this occasion Evgenij sends a letter *to* Tat'jana and goes to see *her*; Mazepa is awakened by Marija (the voice of conscience and judgment) as Marija was earlier awakened by her mother on the morning of her father's execution (*Poltava*); Grinev is now in a position to *receive*, rather than offer, a gift to Pugačev, etc. A similar shift in status quo will be suggested by the seemingly minor, but in actuality crucial, changes in the descriptions of the two confrontations in *Bronze Horseman*.

Puškin sets the stage for the confrontations between Petersburg and Moscow "horsemen" by introducing, in muted fashion, the themes we have already noted elsewhere. In the "Introduction," "old" Moscow is said to have paled before the splendor of the "youthful capital": "I pered mladšeju stolicej / Pomerkla staraja Moskva, / Kak pered novoju caricej / Porfironosnaja vdova" (And before the younger capital / old Moscow has faded, / as before a new empress / the dowager in purple robes) (PSS V:

136). And Evgenij's origins, while greatly generalized from the drafts and
from the "trial runs" in *Ezerskij* and "Genealogy," still bear a strong lexical and semantic resemblance to earlier mentions of the ancient nobility,
their traditions and distinguishing characteristics (including *gerby*):

> Оно [имя «Евгений»—DMB], быть может, и блистало
> И под пером Карамзина
> В родных преданьях прозвучало;
> Но ныне светом и молвой
> Оно забыто. Наш герой
> Живет в Коломне; где-то служит,
> Дичится знатных и не тужит
> Ни о почиющей родне,
> Ни о забытой старине. (PSS V: 138)

> It [Evgenij's name—DMB] may perhaps have shone
> and by the pen of Karamzin
> have rung out in native legends;
> but nowadays by society and fame
> it is forgotten. Our hero
> lives in Kolomna; he works in some office,
> shies away from the eminent and worries his head
> neither about buried kin
> nor about forgotten times of yore.

Puškin is quick to distance himself from any facile autobiographical
link through his use of "perhaps"—that is, all of these already non-specific
details about Evgenij's past may be simply conjecture. On the other hand,
they are all the reader has at his disposal to flesh out a preliminary portrait
of the hero. And here, it is true, all emphasis seems to be on oldness,
antiquity, tradition, historical memory: the bygone times, the historian's
pen, the native legends. However, these values are now forgotten, and the
fact that the hero avoids those of his class and no longer bemoans his
"sleeping/deceased kinfolk" is revealing (note that Puškin's choice of
words is very close to what was seen in "Epistle to Del'vig," *Baxčisaraj
Fountain*, "My Genealogy," and "Genealogy of My Hero"). To repeat,
Puškin removes as much as possible any concrete connection between
himself and his hero. Now, for example, he can (or will) *not* say, as he did
in "My Genealogy," that "Pod *gerb*ovoj moej pečat'ju / Ja kipu gramot
sxoronil / I ne jaksajuš' s novoj znat'ju, / I krovi spes' ugomonil" (Under
the seal of my coat-of-arms / I've hidden away a pile of [ancient] documents; / I don't keep company with the new nobility / and have stilled the
haughtiness of my blood) (my emphasis; PSS III: 262–63).

Evgenij's first confrontation with the statue is during the flood, directly after the description of the people's fear of divine retribution and
Alexander's admonition that it is not for man, even if he be tsar, to compete with the divine elements (PSS V: 141). The introduction of a specifi-

cally *divine* element into this tale about the effects of one man's attempt to secularize Russian history makes the sudden appearance of Evgenij, that history's lone and unlikely paladin amid the chaos of the flood, all the more foregrounded and laden with meaning. This fact is indeed made explicit by the poet's decision to begin a new verse paragraph, the next-to-last of Part One, at this point:

> Тогда, на площади Петровой,
> Где дом в углу вознесся новый,
> Где над возвышенным крыльцом
> С подъятой лапой, как живые,
> Стоят два льва сторожевые,
> На звере мраморном верхом,
> Без шляпы, руки сжав крестом,
> Сидел недвижный, страшно бледный
> Евгений. Он страшился, бедный,
> Не за себя. (PSS V: 141–42)

> [It was] then [that] on Peter's square,
> where in a corner a new house had risen tall,
> where over [its] lofty porch,
> paw[s] upraised, like live [creatures],
> stand two guardian lions,
> astride on the beast of marble,
> hatless, arms crossed,
> sat motionless, terribly pale,
> Evgenij. He was in terror, poor [soul],
> not for himself.

Part One of the poem has been dominated thus far by the great movement and force of the storm. But now all action halts momentarily as the camera eye, so to speak, fixes on the hero, who *sits* "immobile, terribly pale," on the stone lion. Puškin is always meticulous when using landmarks, and this description is no exception: the stone lions *do* in fact exist at the entrance to the house of Prince A. Ja. Lobanov-Rostovskij (built in 1817–19 by the architect Montferrand).[26] Moreover, Puškin in all likelihood was familiar with the anecdote, circulating throughout Petersburg and later retold in the notes of A. V. Kočubej, about a certain Jakovlev who saved himself from the flood by climbing onto one of the lions ("Dokumental'nye materialy," in Puškin [Izmajlov] 1978: 123–24). In other words, this entire scene *could* be motivated by the poet's knowledge of the actual details surrounding the flood (recall that he chided Mickiewicz in one of his own notes for some of the inaccuracies in the latter's presentation) and therefore have no other "figurative" meaning.

Still, it can be argued that Puškin's choice of the lions (especially in the wake of the *geral'dičeskij lev*) and, equally important, Evgenij's pose on one of them (when Kočubej's version of the anecdote makes no mention of this) is marked in context. The lions do not merely appear in passing, but are one of the salient leitmotifs in the poem; they are presented in almost identical poetic lines during both confrontations (cf. PSS V: 147), thus becoming, *as stone beasts*, the only other force in the poem to compete with the "idol on bronze steed." Their front paws *are raised*, again a fact of no little consequence when one considers that the poet chose to underscore this as a distinguishing feature. Evgenij is sitting "astride" (*verxom*) the lion, a word which has obvious equestrian associations in the Russian context. And finally, his arms are folded in the shape of a cross (*krestom*)—the cross over the breast of St. George or St. Andrew?—a sign of his Orthodox affiliation.[27]

But the confrontation is not, of course, equal. Evgenij, unarmed, is turned into a parody, a stonelike double ("immobile," versus the "unshakeable" [*nekolebimyj*] Peter) of the Petersburg horseman (see Alpatov 1937: 371). He has been transferred to Peter's territory ("Peter's square"), frozen as the guardian spirit of a *newly* erected house (as opposed to the "old little house" [*vetxij domik*] of Paraša and her mother that he would prefer to be protecting). The lions should be guarding the traditions of "old" Russia, but in fact they too have been transplanted to the camp of the enemy. Puškin creates the effect of *two* equestrian statues locked in fatal confrontation through his *raising up* of Evgenij (the mark of the *eques*) onto the *elevated* (*vozvyšennoe*) portico above the flood and through his transformation of the human hero into a stone monument seemingly impervious to the natural (and by implication social/political) storm. This, after all, had been the collective result of Peter's colossal efforts to turn the wheel of state: people had been turned into so many stone objects.

The confrontation between subject and tsar, however, is not only unequal, it is not even real. The Moscow horseman is thinking not of himself ("He was in terror, poor [soul], / not for himself") but of Paraša and all that she represents for his (and thus his clan's) plans for survival into the future. Yet he sits on his steed as though "bewitched" (*okoldovan*), "riveted" (*prikovan*) to the marble and to his role as victim. True to form, the Bronze Horseman does not acknowledge his existence, but sits with his back turned on the "little man" and hence on the possibility of a genuine meeting:

> И обращен к нему спиною
> В *неколебимой вышине*,
> Над возмущенною Невою
> Стоит с простертою рукою
> Кумир на бронзовом коне. (My emphasis; PSS V: 142)

> And, with [his] back turned to him,
> in unshakeable eminence,
> over the tumultuous Neva
> stands with outstretched hand
> the idol on [his] bronze steed.

Part One ends in the suspended animation of a stand-off, with the two
stone horsemen looking out into the distance at their very different versions of the future (Paraša and her little house versus Peter's extended
arm). And all of this frozen stasis will be launched into motion only when
that future enters the present, becomes known, and "turns the tables" on
Peter's plans and ultimately on the shape of Russian history.

Part Two is structurally the mirror opposite of Part One. Now the
flood has abated; now Evgenij, who was separated from Paraša by the
raging waters, is able to learn her fate; now the hero has a second, *genuine*
confrontation with the Bronze Horseman. The effect of Paraša's death on
the hero not only is devastating psychologically, but, equally important, it
turns him into an eternal *strannik*, a pedestrian with *no place* to go, with
no future and therefore no past worth remembering or preserving (PSS V:
146). He moves about constantly in the climax of Part Two, whereas in Part
One he was limited to his role as fixed parodic horseman. This is another
way of saying that by this point in the drama Evgenij is *cut off*, freed from
his function as heroic paladin, savior of Moscow and her traditions. Puškin consciously brings his hero back to the site of the first confrontation in
order to set in greater relief *the contrast* between the man and the statue:

> Вскочил Евгений; вспомнил живо
> Он прошлый ужас; торопливо
> Он встал; пошел бродить, и вдруг
> Остановился—и вокруг
> Тихонько стал водить очами
> С боязнью дикой на лице.
> Он очутился под столбами
> Большого дома. На крыльце
> С подъятой лапой, как живые,
> Стояли львы сторожевые,
> И прямо в темной вышине
> Над огражденною скалою
> Кумир с простертою рукою
> Сидел на бронзовом коне.
>   Евгений вздрогнул. Прояснились
> В нем страшно мысли. Он узнал
> И место, где потоп играл,
> Где волны хищные толпились,
> Бунтуя злобно вкруг него,
> И львов, и площадь, и того,
> Кто неподвижно возвышался
> Во мраке медною главой,
> Того, чьей волей роковой
> Под морем город основался. . . . (PSS V: 146–47)

> Evgenij jumped up; he vividly recalled
> the former horror; hastily
> he rose, went off to roam, and of a sudden

came to a halt—and round about
he gingerly allowed his eyes to wander,
wild apprehension on his face.
He found himself beneath the pillars
of a great house. Upon the portico
with upraised paw, as though alive,
stood lions sentinel,
and straight, in his dark eminence,
above the railed-in crag
the idol with his arms stretched forth
was seated on [his] steed of bronze.
          Evgenij shuddered. Fearfully clear
became his thoughts. He recognized
the place where the flood had sported,
where the preying waves had crowded,
rioting viciously about him,
and the lions, and the square, and him,
who motionlessly loomed,
his brazen head in the dusk,
him by whose fateful will
the city by the sea was founded . . . .

Instead of being raised up like his adversary, Evgenij walks around *at ground level* to confront the statue of Peter brazenly *en face* (still, of course, looking *up*). He is empowered with the same wild abandon as the flood waters when he hurls up his famous challenge.[28] He has, in effect, joined forces with the opposition, which up to now has been symbolized by the swirling Neva—and the chaotic *hoi polloi*—threatening to trouble the "sleep" of the unshakeable bronze statue. And whereas earlier his "desperate glances" (*otčajannye vzory*) were directed toward Paraša, now his "wild glances" (*vzory dikie*) are fixed on "the countenance of the ruler of half the world" (PSS V: 142, 147–48). Terror has been replaced by madness, the staid pose of the *eques* by the restless, peripatetic circling of the man in the streets, the tutelary function of St. George by the rage of the revolutionary.

All of this makes Puškin's famous question of the Bronze Horseman— "Was it not thus, aloft hard by the abyss, / that with curb of iron / you reared up Russia?"—even more ambiguous and vexed. Framed by the "before" and "after" of Evgenij's *cognitio*, and reinforcing the dread potency of the Petrine myth ("Awesome [užasen] [is] he in the surrounding gloom! / What thought upon his brow! / What power within him hidden! / And in that steed, what fire!" [PSS V: 147]), this query catches the *eques* at the point—both verbal and visual—of maximum equipoise even as it asks *where* this force will go once it hits the ground and the "turning-point" is passed ("Whither do you gallop, haughty steed, / and where do you plant your hooves?"). Futurity, as it were, is embedded in the present (a potentially apocalyptic notion). If it could be said that, generally speaking, the "Introduction" of *Bronze Horseman* foregrounds an eighteenth-century,

"panegyric" treatment of Peter and his "Northern Palmira,"[29] and Parts
One and Two show an increased interest in the *déclassé* hero of emerging
nineteenth-century prose, then this passage, coming as it does directly before Evgenij's challenge, is a climax in several senses. Most important,
however, it is the point at which each character, hero and anti-hero,
changes his "mode of address" toward his adversary.[30]

As was suggested in our prefatory remarks, all too often Evgenij has
been cast in the role of wretched victim. The most significant fact about
the climax of Puškin's poem is not that the hero perishes—he had, in
effect, already perished with the loss of Paraša—but that the "unshakeable" statue is provoked into motion by the *words*, the "Just you wait!"
(*Užo tebe*), of the little man. The defining characteristic of the Petrine
myth had been its supreme inevitability, its refusal to acknowledge the
existence of anything else save the tsar-conqueror's inviolable design. Thus
not only has Evgenij ceased to be St. George, the Moscow horseman, but
Peter (or his spirit) has also ceased to be the imperturbable bronze *eques*,
the Petersburg horseman. The argument that this final episode, including
the horseman's pursuit of Evgenij, may simply be the hallucination of a
madman, and therefore to be discounted as any *real* shift in the status quo
is, one might submit, a moot point. If this new Peter, concerned enough
with the verbal assaults of the little man to leap off his pedestal, exists in
the mind of Evgenij, the potential revolutionary, then he exists in fact. And
his punishment of Evgenij becomes, in a circular logic of which the author
was certainly aware, a self-indictment and a self-judgment.

This essay has attempted to demonstrate how two distinct equestrian
traditions, that of European statuary and that of Russian heraldry, might
be seen to enter into dialogic confrontation in *Bronze Horseman*. There is
no victor, which fact accords with the studied irresolution of Puškin's
poem, the combined sense of splendor and cruelty that permeates Peter's
design and the poet's artistic presentation of it. Puškin incorporated in his
hero many of his most cherished values at the same time that he distanced
himself from him (the hero), and from them (the values). The religious/
mythic link with St. George and old Moscow was one of these. And although *Bronze Horseman* cannot be said to be "apocalyptic" in any explicit sense—the notions of a fatal parallax involving biblical *Endzeit*,
national myth, and revolutionary movements would have to await a writer
of a completely different temperament such as Dostoevskij—one can say
with certainty that Puškin himself was keenly aware of how the Petrine
reforms contained the germs of future social unrest. As he reminds us in
the famous lines of an unpublished chapter of *The Captain's Daughter*,
"May God preserve us from a Russian rebellion—senseless and merci-
less." His way, however, was better suited to the verbal equipoise, the
"moving stasis," of what many believe to be his greatest creation. For only
in a work such as *Bronze Horseman*, in which the concept of "turning-
point" becomes a crucial element at every level (style, structure, theme,

etc.), can the reader truly experience the paradox of Peter's Russia. Reigning and "reining," the greatest of tsars would one day *unleash* the forces of recalcitrant nature and man; the "revolutionary" monarch would become, to another generation, the apocalyptic horseman signaling the fiery end of old Russia, of monarchy and Orthodoxy itself.

Part II

PUŠKIN: TEXT AND CONTEXT

J. THOMAS SHAW

Puškin on His African Heritage
Publications during His Lifetime

Puškin was proud of both sides of his family genealogy. At the same time, he was sensitive about each of them. Any consideration of his African heritage and his attitude toward it must be undertaken in the context of his Russian heritage and his attitude toward it. This essay will focus on the direct reflection of Puškin's African ancestry in works published during his lifetime, particularly those he himself completed and published (or wished to publish). It would require an extensive monograph to examine with any adequacy all aspects of the relationship of Puškin to his African heritage—how that ancestry affected him as man and writer. That would have to include not only his public life as writer and man of society, but his private life as well; it would need to include consideration of works he began but did not complete, the indirect effects of that heritage on his work and personality, and the testimony of contemporaries to these points in such things as letters and memoir literature. Here we shall concentrate on what Puškin said about his African ancestry for the perusal of the reading public of his day and the effects of these publications on his own career. I have found no previous study that has approached the question from this angle.

There has been much study of Puškin's ancestry on both sides of his family, and recently there has been great interest in his African great-grandfather and his descendants in Russia.[1] Puškin was particularly proud of Abram Petrovič Gannibal (or Annibal), as he came to be known, and one of his sons, Ivan Gannibal. Abram Gannibal was obtained for Peter the Great in Constantinople; he became godson, ward, and favorite of Peter, who took Gannibal on expeditions with him and sent him to France for a time. However, Peter the Great died suddenly in 1725, not long after Gannibal's return from France. After that, Gannibal was out of favor until Peter's daughter Elisabeth came to the throne in 1741. He was recalled to active duty in the army and promoted to the rank of general. Under the system set up by Peter the Great, his rank gave him and his family the status of members of the hereditary Russian nobility. However, Gannibal's appeal for the recognition of noble status was made on the basis of his father's being a local ruler in Africa. No action was ever taken on this petition. Abram's son Ivan also eventually became a full general in the army, and served with distinction, especially during the Greek Archipelago Campaign of 1770, when, as the commander of a landing party, he defeated Turkish forces on the Greek mainland at Navarino; he was in charge of fire control in the naval battle of Chesma in the same year. Ivan Gannibal acted as sponsor of Puškin's mother at her social debut, which led to her marriage to Puškin's father.

Any treatment of Puškin's African heritage with regard to both his published works and his life must concern itself also with terminology and the overtones of words used in Russia at the time. The relevant terms are *Negro* (for Russian *negr*, French *nègre*), *blackamoor* (for *arap*), and *mulatto* (*mulat, mulatka*). Puškin himself, in a letter written during the last year or so of his life, clearly presented his view of the difference between the homonyms *arap* and *arab*, emphasizing an orthographic distinction that is not always observed in memoirs about him.

> *Arab* (does not have a feminine), a dweller or native of Arabia, an Arabian. *Karavan byl razgrablen stepnymi arabami* [The caravan was plundered by the Arabs of the steppes].
> *Arap* [blackamoor], feminine *arapka*; this is what negroes and mulattoes are usually called. *Dvorcovye arapy*, negroes serving in the palace. *On vyezžaet s tremja narjadnymi arapami* [He is leaving with three finely dressed blackamoors]. (Letter to P. A. Vjazemskij, second half of 1835 or in 1836; PSS XVI: 208;[2] Shaw 1967: 783)

Neither Puškin (as the above passage shows) nor other Russians of his time made any distinction between *negr* and *arap*, that is, between blacks from different parts of Africa. Later on, ethnographers classified northern Africans as "Hamitic" and "Caucasoid," and Africans south of the Sahara as "Negroid." This distinction has usually been made in studies of Puškin since D. I. Anučin's "anthropological study" (1899)—both in Russia and abroad (for example, in Simmons 1937, Lotman 1983, Fejnberg 1983). By *arap* or *negr* or *mulat(ka)* Puškin included *all* black Africans. When he spoke of "my brethren the Negroes,"[3] he included not only blacks from Egypt or Tunis but also the black slaves then in the New World (that is, blacks from south of the Sahara, now classified as Negroid, as well as the blacks now considered Caucasoid).

It should be emphasized that there is nothing to indicate that Puškin's having a black ancestor hindered his acceptance as a Russian man of letters. On the contrary, when his first Romantic verse tale, *The Prisoner of the Caucasus*, appeared in 1822, his publisher, N. I. Gnedič, obviously thought it would help sales to have a frontispiece emphasizing Puškin's black heritage; Gnedič provided such a lithograph without consulting the author.[4] Furthermore, there is no evidence that Puškin's African ancestry hindered his acceptance in Russian society, though neither his father's nor his mother's heritage gave him immediate entry to the highest circles of it.

Curiously enough, it was not the Puškin (or the Gannibal) family connections, or Puškin's genius as a writer, that, after his marriage, resulted in his having access to the "great world around the throne," but rather his wife's beauty and her family connections.

No work of Puškin's deals exclusively with his African ancestry. Mentions of, or allusions to, that ancestry always occur in a larger context; they form only *passages* or *parts* of longer works, even when the entire work is a short lyric. They are listed in Table I, along with date of composition, of publication, and of republication, if any, during his lifetime. There are ten of them, five in verse and five in prose. The first was published in 1825, and between 1828 and 1831, *all* that were published or widely circulated during his lifetime either appeared for the first time or were republished. This time of concentrated publication includes Puškin's most productive literary period, and it coincides with his period of courtship with a view to marriage and the first year of his married life.

TABLE 1

		Written	Published	Republished
1.	"To Jur'ev"	V 1820	1829	
2.	*EO*.I.50 verse	V 1823	1825	1829, 1833, 1837
3.	*EO*.I.50 note	P 1824	1825	1829; rev. 1833; 2nd rev., 1837
4.	"To Jazykov"	V 1824	1830	1832
5.	"To Dawe, Esq."	V 1828	1828	1829
6.	"Chapter IV"	P 1827	1828	1834
7.	"Assembly"	P 1827	1830	1834
8.	Note on *Poltava*	P 1830	1831	
9.	"My Genealogy"	V 1830		
10.	"Table-Talk"	P 1835-36		

Note. V = in verse; P = in prose.

The first two that Puškin published appeared in the first chapter of his novel in verse, *Evgenij Onegin* (Eugene Onegin): he mentions his African ancestry specifically both in the verse and in a rather lengthy note in prose. Four individual lyrics allude to his African ancestry.[5] Puškin published separately two individual chapters of his uncompleted novel *The Blackamoor of Peter the Great* about his black great-grandfather (though he is not explicitly named in the part Puškin himself published). Puškin's African heritage may be considered to be implied in two notes in which he mentions Othello, the most famous Moor in literature: one of them was in the Note on *Poltava*, the other in his "Table-Talk"; the second of these was written during the last year or so of his life, and he did not live to see it in print. *Both* sides of Puškin's ancestry are dealt with in a lyric, "My Genealogy," which was not printed but was widely circulated in handwritten copies.[6]

Thus publication and/or republication of all of Puškin's works that deal with his African heritage and appeared in print during his lifetime was concentrated in the years 1828–31: every one of them was published or republished during these years. And the wide circulation of "My Genealogy" constituted an obviously deliberate kind of publication.

1. *Evgenij Onegin*, Chapter I, Stanza 50, and Note

The most important of Puškin's publications on the subject of his African heritage during his lifetime is part of a "flight of the imagination" at the end of the first chapter of *Evgenij Onegin*. This chapter appeared as a separate publication early in 1825. At the time of its writing (1823), Puškin was in exile in Kišinev and then Odessa, under the guise of a transfer in government service, because of "liberal" (Russians say "revolutionary") poems. When he published it, he had been dismissed from the service and was in open exile and disgrace (*v opale*) on his mother's estate of Mixajlovskoe. Under the censorship of the time, direct mention of his exile was impossible in print, and the notion of his actually "fleeing" from Russia could not have been published. One could, however, present a poetic flight of the imagination. In the *Onegin* passage, the first such "poetic flight" is to Italy (EO.I.49). The second, in the following stanza, is to "my Africa." This second "flight of the imagination" is so important and relevant that it should be quoted, and the note he appended to it as well:

Придет ли час моей свободы?
Пора, пора! — взываю к ней;
Брожу над морем, жду погоду,
Маню ветрила кораблей.
Под ризой бурь, с волнами споря,
По вольному распутью моря
Когда ж начну я вольный бег?
Пора покинуть скучный брег
Мне неприязненной стихии,
И средь полуденных зыбей,
Под небом Африки моей,
Вздыхать о сумрачной России,
Где я страдал, где я любил,
Где сердце я похоронил. (EO.I.50)

[Will the time of my freedom come? It's time, it's time! I call to her; I wander along the shore, I await good weather, I beckon the sails of ships. When shall I begin my free flight under the canopy of storms, contesting with the waves, over the free crossroads of the sea? It is time to abandon the boring shore of the element hostile to me, and amid southern billows under the skies of my Africa, to sigh for gloomy Russia, where I have suffered, where I have loved, where I have buried my heart.]

The point of view expressed here is paradoxically and typically Puškinian: he will take a "free flight" from the Russian shore where the sea is "hostile to me," to the friendly southern billows under the skies of "my Africa." However, once there, he will sigh for Russia. The important themes include "poetic flight" (for one whose actual fleeing would have constituted a crime), travel to the south, memory of Russia from afar (from south to north), and "my Africa."

In a long footnote Puškin explained the term "my Africa" and gave information about his great-grandfather. During his lifetime, he published the stanza four times, with no changes in the verse. In the 1829 reprint of the first chapter, the appended note remained almost identical in form to that published in 1825. However, in the last two reprintings of the first chapter (when all the chapters of the novel were published together, in 1833 and 1837), the note was sharply cut. Here we shall focus on the long form of it.

Here follows my translation of the note as it originally appeared (the only changes in 1829 are the transposition of the last two paragraphs and the incorporation of the square-bracketed note into the text). It is curious that he here cites his great-grandfather's surname as "Annibal," instead of the form "Gannibal," which he uses later.

The author, on his mother's side, is of African extraction. His ancestor Abram Petrovič Annibal in his 8th year was abducted from the shores of Africa and taken to Constantinople. The Russian ambassador, after rescuing him, sent him as a present to Peter the Great, who had him christened at Vil'no. A brother of his came to get him, first to Constantinople, and then to Petersburg, proposing a ransom for him; but Peter I did not agree to return his godson. Until deep old age Annibal still remembered Africa, his father's luxurious life, 19 brothers, of whom he was the youngest; he remembered how they would be led to their father with hands bound behind their backs, while he alone was free and would go swimming under the fountains at his father's house; he also remembered his favorite sister, Lagan', who swam from a distance after the ship on which he was departing.

At 18 years from his birth, Annibal was sent by the Tsar to France, where he began his service in the army of the Regent; he returned to Russia with a broken head and the rank of a French lieutenant. From that time, he was constantly in attendance upon the Emperor. During the reign of Anna, Annibal . . . was sent to Siberia under a plausible pretext. Bored with the absence of human life and the severity of the climate, he returned to Petersburg without authorization. . . . Annibal departed to his own estates, where he lived during all Anna's reign, while being considered as being in the service and in Siberia. Elisabeth, upon ascending the throne, showered him with favors. A[bram]. P. Annibal died only in the reign of Catherine, freed from the important occupations of the service, with the rank of full general (*general-anšef*), in the 92nd year from his birth. [We hope, in time, to publish his full biography. *Puškin's note.*]

In Russia, where the memory of noteworthy people soon disappears for reason of lack of historical memoirs, the strange life of Annibal is known only from family traditions.

His son Lieutenant-General I[van]. A. Annibal belongs indubitably among the most outstanding people of the age of Catherine (he died in 1800). (PSS VI: 654–55)

Puškin had written the stanza in Odessa in fall 1823. The note was written in fall 1824 in Mixajlovskoe, the estate his mother had inherited from his great-grandfather's property, where his great-grandfather had lived in "deep old age," still remembering his childhood in Africa.

Other points which seem not to have been sufficiently emphasized hitherto are the themes (1) of exile under the guise of transfer in the service, and (2) of Gannibal's voluntarily breaking exile to return to Russia proper. In the *Onegin* passage in verse, Puškin, utilizing a "poetic flight" of the imagination, is hinting at voluntarily breaking that kind of exile in order to flee to "my Africa."

It is worth emphasizing that Puškin's biographical note including information about his great-grandfather's return without permission from Siberia to St. Petersburg was not only published in late March 1825, six months before the Decembrist Uprising, but also reprinted in 1829, four years after it.

2. "To Jazykov"

Puškin's friendly poetic epistle "To Jazykov" ("K Jazykovu"), a fellow poet, was written in September 1824, some months after the *Onegin* passage, and a month or so before he wrote the accompanying prose note. Part of the poem was published in 1830, as "To Jazykov (Fragment of a Poem)," ending with Puškin's invitation to his fellow poet to visit him at Mixajlovskoe, which the poem alludes to directly as having formerly been part of the estates of his great-grandfather Abram Gannibal. The location and year of composition were both stated explicitly: Mixajlovskoe, 1824. Here follows the relevant part of the poem in the form in which Puškin published it twice.

> В деревне, где Петра питомец,
> Царей, цариц любимый раб
> И их забытый однодомец,
> Скрывался прадед мой Арап,
> Где, позабыв Елизаветы
> И двор и пышные обеты,
> Под сенью липовых аллей
> Он думал в охлажденны леты
> Об дальней Африке своей,
> Я жду тебя. (S:II.218.25–34.)

[In the village where Peter's ward, the servant [*rab*] beloved of tsars and tsaritsas and the forgotten one who had lived in the same house with them, my ancestor the Blackamoor concealed himself, where, having forgotten the court and the splendid solemn promises of [Tsaritsa] Elisabeth, under the shade of linden lanes he thought in cool summers of his far-off Africa—I await you.]

In the verse passage in *Eugene Onegin*, Puškin imagined himself in "my Africa" remembering Russia—in memories going from south to north. In "To Jazykov," he imagines his great-grandfather in Russia, remembering "*his* Africa," with memories going from north to south.[7]

In the passage, Puškin uses the specific term *rab*, literally "slave," in speaking of his great-grandfather. Under the autocracy in Russia, particularly under Peter the Great, anyone could be treated as a "slave." One of the burning questions in Puškin's time was that of serfdom: the word *slave* could not then be applied in print to a serf except by the serf himself; Puškin's reference in print to his great-grandfather as *rab* meant that he was not really a slave. One way of alluding to serfdom as slavery was to speak of the condition of blacks elsewhere, as Puškin himself did in 1836 (review of the autobiography of an American, John Tanner; see Shaw 1966). One may compare this use of *rab* as servant to the Tsar to the term *xolop, xolopij*, which is used in the meaning "vassal, vassal's," as a boyar applies it himself with regard to Peter the Great in *The Blackamoor of Peter the Great* (PSS VIII: 26; in Chapter V, which Puškin did not publish): in modern Russian, the word *xolop* is pejorative and means something like "flunky." As we shall see, Puškin's speaking of his great-grandfather's coming from Africa, and his term *rab* (slave) provided the journalist Bulgarin with a bludgeon with which to beat him.

3. Chapters from *The Blackamoor of Peter the Great*

All posthumous editions of Puškin's works include in the prose fiction all he wrote of his uncompleted historical novel, called by editors *The Blackamoor of Peter the Great*, a fictional story based on the life of Abram Gannibal. Puškin wrote six chapters in 1827 and the beginning of a seventh in early 1828, before dropping it. He himself published only parts of two chapters of this work, one in 1828 and the other in 1830, and republished both in 1834. In the part Puškin chose to publish, little is explicitly about his great-grandfather, though more is implied.

The first of these chapters to be published came out under the title "Chapter IV from a Historical Novel." Gavrila Afanas'evič (his surname is not given in the passage), the head of the "old Russian" family, compares one K- unfavorably with the "Tsar's blackamoor": "of all the young people educated abroad (God forgive me), the Tsar's blackamoor is the one that most resembles a man" (Debreczeny 1983a: 29; PSS VIII: 22). To anyone who had read the note to the first chapter of *Onegin*, the term "Tsar's blackamoor" might have revealed that G- (as he was called in the "Chapter" as it was published and republished during Puškin's lifetime [see PSS VIII: 533]) was Gannibal—though in the *Onegin* note he was called "*An-nibal*."

The other passage Puškin published, actually part of the preceding Chapter III in the manuscript, was called "An Assembly at the Time of Peter I." Here the Frenchified K- is punished for unknowingly breaking the "rule" at Peter's "Assembly" that the lady ask the gentleman to dance the minuet, and is made to suffer the punishment allotted for it. Then the young lady, at her father's behest, asks G- to dance.

The focus of the parts of the novel Puškin published is not at all on G- (Gannibal), but on the manners and mores of the time, including Peter the Great's personal manners and his method of operating in the state, his construction of St. Petersburg, and G-'s setting to work to help Peter in the undertaking.

4. "To Dawe, Esq."

In the late 1820s two more Puškin lyrics were published that directly concern his African ancestry, though they do not mention specifically his great-grandfather. The first was a little poem addressed to a portrait painter, with title in English: "To Dawe, Esq." The portrait (if one was made) has not survived. The poem was written and published in 1828 (and republished in 1829, in the first volume of Puškin's collected poetry [*Stixotvorenija*]). The first stanza reads as follows:

> Зачем твой дивный карандаш
> Рисует мой арапский профиль?
> Хоть ты векам его предашь,
> Его освищет Мефистофиль. (S:III.59.1–4)

[Why is your marvelous pencil sketching my blackamoor profile? Though you entrust it to the centuries, Mephistopheles will hiss it off the stage.]

The remainder of the poem suggests that the artist should, instead, dedicate his talents to painting a beautiful woman such as O- (identified after Puškin's death as Anna Olenina, whom Puškin was courting at the time; his suit was rejected). The contrast of the poem is between O-'s beauty and the implied lack of beauty of his own "blackamoor profile."[8] The poet-persona suggests himself as not presenting the possibility of being converted into a handsome Faust, so that Mephistopheles would "hiss him off the stage."

5. "To Jur'ev"

In 1829, another poem including the theme of Puškin's African ancestry appeared in print—this one without his approval and against his wishes. It includes specific mention of black ancestry, and "ugliness" is an explicit theme. This poem was written in 1820 in a friendly poetic epistle ("To Jur'ev"). It describes a handsome man and his exploits with the ladies, and ends with comment in the first person about the poet-persona himself:

> А я, повеса вечно-праздный,
> Потомок негров безобразный,
> Взрощенный в дикой простоте,
> Любви не ведая страданий,

Я нравлюсь юной красоте
Бесстыдным бешенством желаний;
С невольным пламенем ланит
Украдкой нимфа молодая,
Сама себя не понимая,
На фавна иногда глядит. (S:II.94.21–32 [end])

[But I, an eternally idle rake, ugly descendant of Negroes, brought up in wild simplicity, not knowing the sufferings of love, I please young beauty with the shameless frenzy of desires; [thus] sometimes, with an involuntary flame on her cheeks, a young nymph, not understanding herself, looks stealthily at a faun.]

The relevant themes here are, in my literal translation, "ugly descendant of Negroes," and how young beautiful women are pleased "with the shameless frenzy of [his] desires" like a nymph involuntarily aroused by watching a faun while remaining unseen. We now consider the poem a delightfully sensuous and sensual "imitation of the ancients" embodying the theme of the nymph and the faun. Indeed, upon reading it shortly after it was written, Puškin's older contemporary Batjuškov—the poet whose sensuous poems "From the Greek Anthology" (published earlier in the same year, 1820) led immediately to the popularity of that genre in Russia—is said to have remarked: "How that young devil has learned to write."

We have noted that Puškin objected to the publication of this poem; he never published it himself. This is in sharp contrast to another lyric written in the same year, "The Nereid." The essential difference between the poems "To Jur'ev" and "The Nereid"—another "imitation of the ancients" that Puškin published and republished—is the conspicuous presence in the friendly epistle of the poet-persona directly identifiable as the author himself. One of the most complex problems with regard to Puškin has to do with the type and amount of self-revelation, or apparent self-revelation, he might allow to be reflected in a poem he would publish.[9]

6. THE THEME OF OTHELLO

It is not surprising that the theme of Othello the Moor would be in Puškin's consciousness. His friend Vigel' in his *Memoirs* says that while in Odessa (sometime in 1823–24) he "once told Puškin jokingly that by his African extraction I would like to compare him with Othello, and [Aleksandr N.] Raevskij with Othello's unfaithful friend Iago." He added that Puškin "only laughed" (Vacuro 1974 I: 226). Thus, at least from 1823–24 on, Puškin was aware of the literary theme of jealousy in relation to the love of a blackamoor and a white.

However, Puškin mentioned Othello only once—briefly—in the publications that appeared during his lifetime; this mention is contained in "Fragment from a Manuscript of Puškin's (*Poltava*)," a prose note written in 1830 and published in 1831 in such manner as to suggest that publication was not by him or at his wish. In response to those who objected that it was "unreasonable" for young Marija to fall in love with old Mazepa in *Poltava*, Puškin lists a number of myths and stories not "devoid of poetry," and specifically includes the love of Desdemona for Othello, "that old Negro who captivated her with stories of his wanderings and battles" (PSS XI: 164).[10]

The theme of Othello and jealousy is explicit in one of his pieces of "Table-Talk" (title in English) which he wrote in 1835–36, the last year or so of his life, and planned to publish: "Othello is not by nature jealous—on the contrary, he is trusting. Voltaire understood that, and developing Shakespeare's creation in his imitation, he placed in Orosmane's mouth the following verse: 'I am not at all jealous . . . If ever I were! . . . ' " (PSS XII: 157). The man who wrote this obviously did not think of himself as having a jealous disposition, though he might be capable of becoming jealous with cause; in that event, "African passion" might be manifested.

7. "MY GENEALOGY"

The next important published document with regard to Puškin's African heritage was neither written nor published by him; it was an attack on Puškin in the form of a transparent "foreign anecdote" published by Faddej Bulgarin, a Pole who fought with the French against the Russians in 1812 and then went over to the side of the Russians. Puškin made a rejoinder to that attack in his poem "My Genealogy."

Bulgarin is the most unsavory figure in Russian nineteenth-century literary life, and publishing this anecdote was perhaps the most unsavory deed of all.[11] According to his partner Nikolaj Greč, in memoirs written many years later, Bulgarin arbitrarily discharged an assistant, Orest Somov, and then when Somov began to work on Baron Del'vig's publications, the almanac *Northern Flowers* and the *Literary Gazette*, Bulgarin launched attacks on authors whose works appeared in them as the "literary aristocracy." Bulgarin's technique was to attack, often utilizing a pseudonym, in crude, coarse, but indirect fashion, in such manner that an effective answer would be difficult or impossible, but so as to get around the law against publishing a "personality" without that "personality's" consent. In 1830, Bulgarin attacked Puškin twice in "foreign anecdotes." The second of these refers transparently to Puškin's African ancestry. Here follows Bulgarin's anecdote (published in August 1830).[12]

The anecdote is told that a certain Poet in Spanish America, . . . the offspring of a Mulatto man or woman, I don't remember which, began to contend that one of his ancestors was a Negro Prince. In the town hall of the city it was discovered that in antiquity there was a lawsuit between a skipper of a ship and an assistant of his for this Negro, whom each of them wished to claim as his own, and that the skipper contended that he bought the Negro for a bottle of rum. Who would have thought then that a versifier would acknowledge connection with that Negro? Vanitas vanitatum!

We have seen that Puškin "acknowledged connection" with his "Negro" maternal great-grandfather in several works. Although Bulgarin does not use the word *slave*, the mention of purchase and possession of the "ancestor" clearly implies slavery, and alludes to Puškin's use of the word *rab* (literally "slave") in the poetic epistle "To Jazykov." The anecdote stops with the supposed initial status of the "Poet's" original black ancestor—nothing is said of his later career or accomplishments. What to Puškin was worst was bringing his mother into the affair; the mention in the anecdote of a Poet in Spanish America, an "offspring of a Mulatto man or woman," was an obvious allusion to his mother's being known as the "beautiful Creole."

Puškin was stung to the quick by Bulgarin's anecdote. The question was how to respond. Puškin's public rejoinder[13] was a two-part poem, "My Genealogy," which he at first proposed to publish but instead allowed to circulate in manuscript—so widely that, like some of his early poems, this amounted to a kind of "*public-ation*" (see PSS III: 1225–30, where sixty-four such surviving manuscript copies are described). The first part of the poem was a response to Bulgarin's previous attacks on "aristocratic authors": it compares the Puškin family genealogy with that of "new" families that became prominent in the eighteenth century. The part of the poem that is directly relevant to this essay—that dealing with Puškin's heritage on his mother's side—is called in it a "post-script":

Решил фиглярин, сидя дома,
Что черный дед мой Ганнибал
Был куплен за бутылку рома
И в руки шкиперу попал.

Сей шкипер был тот шкипер славный,
Кем наша двигнулась земля,
Кто придал мощно бег державный
Рулю родного корабля.

Сей шкипер деду был доступен,
И сходно купленный арап
Возрос усерден, неподкуплен,
Царю наперсник, а не раб.

И был отец он Ганнибала,
Пред кем средь чесменских пучин
Громада кораблей вспылала,
И пал впервые Наварин. (S:III.187.65–80; 1830)

[Figljarin decided, sitting at home, that my black granddad Gannibal was bought for a bottle of rum and fell into a skipper's hands. // That skipper was the glorious skipper by whom our land was set in motion, who in mighty fashion set the course of state to the rudder of his native ship. // That skipper was accessible to [my] granddad, and the blackamoor purchased cheaply grew up diligent, unpurchasable, a confidant to the tsar, and not a slave. // And he was the father of the Gannibal before whom amid the Chesma billows the armada of ships flamed up, and Navarino first fell.]

The poem does not respond to the supposition that Gannibal was "bought" but has a pointed rejoinder with regard to the themes of "skipper" (Peter the Great), "purchase" (and "purchasable"), and "slave." The poet-persona proudly responds that "that skipper was accessible to [my] granddad, and the blackamoor purchased cheaply grew up diligent, unpurchasable, a confidant to the tsar, and not a slave." Then, with regard to Abram Gannibal's son Ivan, it speaks of two feats in 1770: his being in charge of fire control in the Russian fleet that destroyed the Turkish fleet in Chesma Bay off the coast of Turkey, and his commanding Russian troops that landed and captured the important Turkish fortress on the Greek mainland at Navarino, *for the first time* (three years before the poem was written, Navarino had been conquered again by Allied forces in the Greek War for Independence).

In November 1831, Puškin sent a copy of the poem, and an explanation of its being circulated, to Count Benkendorf, to be shown to Nicholas I. The result is a rare example of a poet's explanation and a sovereign's response. Both deserve quoting. They are as follows:

About a year ago in one of our journals was printed a satirical article in which a certain man of letters was spoken of, who manifested pretensions of having a noble origin, whereas he was only a bourgeois-gentleman. It was added that his mother was a mulatto whose father, a poor pickaninny, had been bought by a sailor for a bottle of rum. Although Peter the Great little resembled a drunken sailor, I was the one referred to clearly enough, since no Russian man of letters except me can count a Negro among his ancestors. Since the article in question was printed in an official gazette, since indecency has been pushed to the point of speaking of my mother in a *feuilleton* which ought to be only literary, and since our gazetteers do not fight in duels, I believed it my duty to answer the *anonymous* satirist, which I did in verse, and very sharply. I sent my answer to the late Del'vig, asking him to insert it in his journal. Del'vig advised me to suppress it, calling to my attention that it would be ridiculous to defend oneself, pen in hand, against attacks of this nature and to flaunt aristocratic feelings, when everything considered, one is only a gentleman-bourgeois, if not a bourgeois-gentleman. I yielded to his opinion, and the affair rested there; however, several copies of this response circulated, at which I am not displeased, considering that there is nothing in it which I wished to disavow. I confess that I pride myself on what are called prejudices: I pride myself on being as good a gentleman as anybody whoever, though it profits me little; lastly, I greatly pride myself on my ancestors' name, since it is the only legacy that they have left me.

But inasmuch as my verses might be taken as an indirect satire on the origin of certain prominent families, if one did not know that they are a very moderate response to a very reprehensible provocation, I have considered it my duty to give you this frank explanation, and to enclose the piece in question. (PSS XIV: 242; Shaw 1967: 536)

Here follows the response (the original is in French) in Nicholas I's hand:

> You can tell Puškin from me that I am completely of the opinion of his late friend Del'vig; abuse so low, so vile as that with which he has been regaled dishonors the one who utters it rather than the one at whom it is directed; the only weapon against it is *contempt*, which is what I would have shown in his place. As for the verses, I find wit in them, but still more bile than in the other piece. It would do more honor to his pen and especially to his *reason* not to have them circulate. (Puškin, PSS XIV: 377)

Nicholas did not consider Puškin's response "moderate," whatever the provocation, and he was completely right about how others would look at the poem.

Thus Puškin reacted sharply to "Figljarin's" alluding to the initial status in Russia of his black ancestor rather than his accomplishments for the Russian state. In his letter to Benkendorf, Puškin shows how offensive it was to him that that his mother (a "mulatto woman") was brought into literary polemics (a *feuilleton*). The nature of Puškin's relationships with both parents, and especially his mother, was such that he would have objected at any time if an allusion to her were brought into a literary struggle; irrespective of Puškin's own relationship to his parents or his mother, strife in the presence of, or involving, a lady was unconscionable to him. The letter to Benkendorf clearly implies that Puškin would have challenged Bulgarin to a duel (in spite of the illegality of dueling at the time) if Bulgarin had belonged to Puškin's social class. However, Puškin was trapped: the "nobility around the throne" never forgave him for the first part of the poem, in which he ironically calls himself, a descendant of boyars, a "bourgeois," in contrast to the "new high nobility"—descendants of cooks, flunkies, foreign renegades, and adventurers. Much of the pain and difficulty of Puškin's final years can be attributed to this poem— to what provoked it and to Puškin's response.

Thus Puškin's black ancestry was directly involved in the personal-literary-social struggle with which he began the final stage of his life. Puškin did not cease to be proud of his black great-grandfather and great-uncle. His early comments about them are linked with feelings of exoticism, as well as with pride in their accomplishments in Russia. He reprinted the statements calling attention to exoticism; the comments written later emphasize his pride in their feats in their adopted land.

After 1831, Puškin published no new works dealing directly with his African heritage, though he continued to be interested in utilizing the theme in biographical or fictional works. He republished all the items we have dealt with that he was clearly responsible for publishing in the first place—that is, all those we have discussed except the poem "To Jur'ev" and the Note on *Poltava*. The only changes in these republications were in the long prose note about his great-grandfather in Chapter I of *Onegin*. When all the chapters of the novel in verse were combined in one book in 1833, the long note was replaced by the terse comment "The author, on his mother's side, is of African descent." When the entire novel was republished in early 1837, the note was changed again, to read: "See the first edition of *Evgenij Onegin*." The "first edition" of *Onegin* was the individual chapters published as separate books; Chapter I was so published in 1825.

Puškin's war with Bulgarin ended with a cease-fire—though not as a consequence of "My Genealogy." What proved effective was the tactic Bulgarin had employed—the use of a pseudonymous "author." Puškin succeeded in reducing Bulgarin to silence by publishing two articles signed "Feofilakt Kosičkin"—a persona with character, views, and style all quite different from Puškin's. The second "Kosičkin" article in devastating fashion "revealed" detailed information about the heredity and career of "Figljarin," beginning with his birth in a "kennel."

Perhaps nothing so clearly shows the paradoxical relationship between the *public* and the *private* question of Puškin and his African heritage as Puškin's diametrically opposed reactions to the *public* treatment of that heredity by Bulgarin, which resulted in "My Genealogy," and to a *private* or *personal* treatment of that heritage only a month after he wrote the above-cited letter to Benkendorf. The *personal* story has to do with a New Year's gift and accompanying greeting sent by Pavel Naščokin, perhaps Puškin's dearest friend in his final years. Naščokin, a man of the ancient high Russian nobility, was well acquainted with Puškin's difficulty with Bulgarin; indeed, he was the one who directly provided Puškin with the biographical materials that effectively silenced Bulgarin in the second of the "Feofilakt Kosičkin" articles.[14] Naščokin's gift was a bronze inkstand with a statuette of a black man leaning on an anchor and standing in front of two bales of cotton—two inkwells. In the letter accompanying the gift, Naščokin said: "I am sending you your ancestor with inkwells that open, and that reveal him to be a farsighted person (*a double vue*)" (Puškin PSS XIV: 250).

Puškin was obviously delighted with the gift, which suggests that his "farsighted" black ancestor had anticipated (by the inkwells) that a descendant of his would be a writer: so that not only did Puškin look backward with pride at his black great-grandfather, but that person looked forward to him. The answer to Bulgarin's rhetorical question, who could have predicted in the time of Peter the Great's blackamoor that a descendant would be a writer, was Gannibal himself. Upon receiving the gift, Puškin wrote to thank Naščokin "for the blackamoor," and he kept it on his working desk the rest of his life.

The lineage of most of the important ninteenth-century Russian authors includes a mixture of non-Russian and Russian blood—not only

Puškin but Žukovskij, Lermontov, Turgenev, Dostoevskij, Tolstoj, and others. However, Puškin is the only important Russian author known to have African heritage. Whatever his ancestry, there has never really been any question to the Russians that Puškin is their *own* most important author and cultural figure. To us, Puškin is the most European and cosmopolitan of Russian authors. To Russians, he is, paradoxically, the most "Russian" of authors, but at the same time not only one who had African heritage and temperament, but also one whose African temperament is reflected in his literary works and contributes to their nature. This essay has focused on the theme of Puškin and his African heritage in works published during his lifetime. How his "African temperament" affected his literary works beyond the explicit use of the theme is a subject for further investigation—and speculation.

WALTER VICKERY

Odessa—Watershed Year

Patterns in Puškin's Love Lyrics

"Itak ja žil togda v Odesse"—"Thus I lived then in Odessa." Puškin in fact spent, isolated visits apart, a year of his life in Odessa. He arrived there in early July 1823, and left in late July 1824. The relationships he established with women during that time and the love poems he wrote to them—then or later, over the next seven years—have given rise to much uncertainty. How serious were which relationships? Who were the addressees of which poems? I shall resist here the temptation to add to this confusion. Rather than targeting individual objects of Puškin's desires, I propose to examine briefly a number of lyrics (1823–1830) and to try to establish some general patterns of thought and attitude to the business of love.

The poems or parts of poems we will be considering are the following:

ODESSA

1. "Noč' " (Night), October 26, 1823;
2. "Pridet užasnyj čas" (There will arrive a terrible hour), October 22–November 3, 1823;
3. "Prostiš' li mne revnivye mečty" (Will you forgive me my jealous dreams), November 11, 1823;
4. "Želanie slavy" (Desire for Glory), ROUGH DRAFT UNFINISHED, November 1823;
5. "Vse končeno: mež nami svjazi net" (All is ended: between us there is no connection), January–not later than February 8, 1824;

MIXAJLOVSKOE EXILE

6. "Razgovor knigoprodavca s poètom" (Conversation between Bookseller and Poet), September 26, 1824;
7. "Nenastnyj den' potux" (The foul day has died out), probably September-November 1824;
8. "Sožžennoe pis'mo" (The Burned Letter), December 1824–January 5, 1825;
9. "Želanie slavy" (Desire for Glory), January–first half of May 1825;
10. "Vse v žertvu pamjati tvoej" (All in sacrifice to your memory), 1825;
11. "Pod nebom golubym strany svoej rodnoj" (Under the blue sky of her native country), July 25–31, probably July 29, 1826;

CAUCASUS

12. "Na xolmax Gruzii ležit nočnaja mgla" (On the hills of Georgia there lies a nocturnal darkness/haze), May 15, 1829;

PETERSBURG(?)

13. "Ja vas ljubil" (I loved you), 1829, not later than November;

BOLDINO

14. "Proščanie" (Farewell), October 5, 1830;
15. "Zaklinanie" (Incantation), October 17, 1830;
16. "Dlja beregov otčizny dal'noj" (For the shores of a distant fatherland), November 27, 1830.

On what principle were these poems and not others chosen for study? The idea of corpus was suggested to me by the example of the Soviet scholar G. P. Makogonenko (1974). Makogonenko uses ten poems (1823–1830) in support of his contribution to the debate on the identity of Puškin's Odessa love(s) (Makogonenko 1974: 30–95, esp. 82–83). To the ten Makogonenko items I have added a further six, because they shed additional light on Puškin's emotional attitudes. The requirement for selection—which all sixteen poems meet—is that they evidence a serious attitude to the woman addressed; they operate in that area of experience where feelings of love and passion intersect with feelings about the meaning and purpose of life.[1]

The first of the five Odessa poems, "Noč' " (Night; PSS I: 289), an eight-line poem in six-foot iambic rhymed couplets, is one of the very few serious Puškin love lyrics to express unalloyed happiness and fulfilment, happiness unmixed with questioning, sorrow, or resignation. The poem starts, characteristically, in a minor key: the candle burning by the poet's bed is described as sad ("pečal'naja sveča"). But a joyous note is then sounded: his verses gurgle forth, rivulets of love ("ruč'i ljubvi"), filled with the beloved ("tekut polny toboju"); he visualizes her eyes shining and smiling at him ("mne ulybajutsja")—one of only two occasions in Puškin's verse when a woman's eyes are specifically depicted as smiling.[2] We note that his composing poetry forms an inextricable part of his love. That the lovers are imagined as completely alone in a world of only two people is strongly suggested by the emphatic foregrounding of the first and second persons: "*moj* golos dlja *tebja* . . . *moi* stixi . . . polny *toboju* . . . *tvoi* glaza . . . predo *mnoju* (rhyming with *toboju*), *Mne* ulybajutsja . . . i zvuki slyšu *ja*: *Moj* drug, *moj* nežnyj drug . . . ljublju . . . *tvoja* . . . *tvoja*." The poem is all sound, all verse. And it is all *you* and *me*. It reaches a climax of happiness and fulfillment with the poet hearing the woman expressing her love and belonging. A reversal has taken place: at the start it is *his* voice, *his* verses; at the end it is *her* smiling-eyed voice proclaiming love and belonging.

If on October 26 ("Night") we had happiness and fulfillment, at nearly the same moment there sounds an ominous, sinister, macabre, almost necrophilic note, a total change of mood. The large Academy edition dates "Pridet užasnyj čas" (There will arrive a terrible hour; PSS II: 296) October 22–November 3. While the mood has changed very dramatically, from the joyful to the morbid, there are some similarities between this and the preceding poem—not merely that, like "Night," the present poem is written in six-foot iambs, with rhymed couplets at least through the first eight lines (the poem being unfinished, of course), but also that the backgrounds of both poems are silence (here "molčan'e večnoe") and night ("tumanom večnoj noči").[3] The difference is that while in "Night" darkness and silence indicate primarily the late hour, they are here used figuratively to describe death. And while in "Night" the minor key gives place to the major, in "There will arrive a terrible hour" the minor key persists unrelieved and unmitigated, to the end.

"Prostiš' li mne revnivye mečty" (Will you forgive me my jealous dreams; PSS II: 300) is dated November 11, 1823—only sixteen days after "Night." This poem is—let there be no doubt—a poem of agonizing jealousy. But for this assertion to stand, it must be defended against a thesis recently put forward by the eminent Soviet scholar V. E. Vacuro. Noting that the poem's five-foot iambic meter is the Russian equivalent of the French *décasyllabe*, much favored at the time for the elegy, Vacuro not only places "Will you forgive me" within the French elegiac tradition but convincingly establishes the predecessor to whom Puškin is here most indebted—Charles-Hubert Millevoye and his elegy "L'inquiétude." So far so good. But at this point Vacuro goes astray. He uses the Millevoye provenance in a logic-defying attempt to insist that Puškin's poem, far from being a poem of jealousy, is the expression of emotion of a happy, satisfied, and basically confident lover whose temporary aberration is caused by passion! Vacuro's line of reasoning is basically as follows: Millevoye's hero has nothing really to worry about, the paradox in his situation consisting in his being tormented by imagined past lovers when in fact his present love is fully shared by the woman:

Je suis jaloux, et jaloux sans rivaux!
Pardonne, hélas! dans mon trouble fatal,
Je te parais injuste, ingrat; mais j'aime!
Ah! songe bien que pour l'amour extrême
Un souvenir est encore un rival.

I am jealous, and jealous without rivals!
Forgive me, alas! in my fatal perturbation
I appear unjust, ungrateful; but I love you!
Ah! remember that for an overwhelming love
Even memory of the past is a rival.

But conceding that Vacuro is right about Millevoye's hero having nothing to worry about, this does not provide a certain clue to the "psychological collision" in Puškin's elegy, does not mean that Puškin too has nothing to worry about. To work within a tradition is often to change that tradition (see Vacuro 1978: 5–21). "No ja ljubim . . . . Na edine so mnoju / Ty tak nežna! Lobzanija tvoi / No ja ljubim, tebja ja ponimaju" (But I am loved. . . . Alone with me / You are so tender! . . . / But I am loved, I understand you). "No ja ljubim" is not the final pronouncement of an omniscient author. It is the hero's attempt to persuade himself, to reassure himself. "No ja ljubim" is represented speech.

We turn to the unfinished rough draft of "Želanie slavy" (Desire for Glory; PSS II: 934), dated November 1823, close in time, therefore, to the three poems already discussed. The draft, in six-foot iambs, shows three consecutive, abortive openings—of six, four, and seven lines each. Like "Will you forgive me," this poem, the difference in meter notwithstanding, belongs to the tradition of the elegy. And the poem contains one element which is central to the Millevoye elegy, namely, the two-part thought, the second part of which presents some sort of surprise or contrast to the first. This is what Vacuro calls the "psychological collision." In Millevoye's elegy there is the play between present satisfactions and jealousy of the past. In "Will you forgive me" the play is between the woman's neglect and indifference when in company and her passionate attentions when they are alone. And in the first of the three fragments which, with corrections and variants, constitute this poem's 1823 rough drafts, the play is between the tender lovemaking and, on the other hand, something which inexplicably casts a shadow over the happiness of the lovers. The second fragment, a mere four lines, doesn't get us beyond the turning point. The third fragment eliminates the "collision." But it is to the first fragment—when in spite of everything good there is something wrong—that I wish to call attention. Let us note too, for future reference, that the lyric hero is down on his knees ("kolenopreklonennyj"). This is not so unusual a position. But it does occur in other Puškin lyrics, and is often the position of the supplicant.

So far we have had four poems (counting the rough draft excerpt as a poem) in a short space of time—to be exact, within a maximum of thirty-eight days, from October 22 to the end of November (nineteen days only for the first three poems). Now comes a short pause: there is nothing recorded for December. And then, sometime in January or early February, not later than February 8, we have "Vse končeno: mež nami svjazi net" (All is ended: between us there is no connection).

> Все кончено: меж нами связи нет.
> В последний раз обняв твои колени,
> Произносил я горестные пени.
> Все кончено—я слышу твой ответ.
> Обманывать себя не стану [вновь],
> Тебя тоской преследовать не буду,

Про[шедшее] быть может позабуду—
Не для меня сотворена любовь.
Ты молода: душа твоя прекрасна,
И многими любима будешь ты. (PSS II: 309)

It's finished, yes; between us there's no tie.
Embracing for the last time your knees,
I've told you all my sorrow and complaint.
It's finished, yes; I hear, hear your reply.
No more henceforth will I deceive myself.
I will not persecute you with my grief,
And maybe too I shall forget the past.
For me—alas, love was not made for me.
You are so young, your soul is beauty's self,
And many they by whom you will be loved.

The message of the first line seems to indicate, though not conclusively, the end of an affair. The poet is here painfully weighing himself: "Ne dlja menja sotvorena ljubov' " (Love was not made for me). He is down on his knees—a position of supplication. He is not the one who has broken off the affair: he has been reproaching her, but everything is now over, he hears her answer: "ja slyšu tvoj otvet." In fact, his declaration that all is ended—"vse končeno," repeated—is to reassure her that he recognizes and accepts her verdict. The poem foreshadows to some degree Puškin's 1830 "Proščan'e" (Farewell): "*V poslednij raz* tvoj obraz milyj . . . Kak drug, *obnjavšij* molča druga . . . "(For the last time. . . . As a friend, silently embracing a friend . . .)—"*V poslednij raz obnjav* tvoi koleni" (Embracing your knees for the last time). It foreshadows to a far greater degree another poem of farewell, his 1829 "Ja vas ljubil: ljubov' ešče, byt' možet . . . " (I loved you . . .). In the two poems there is the same almost reluctant recognition that all is over; the same insistence that he will trouble her no more: "No pust' ona [moja ljubov'] *vas bol'še ne trevožit; Ja ne xoču pečalit' vas ničem*"(But let it [my love] no longer disturb you; I do not wish to cause you sorrow in anyway)—"*Tebja toskoj presledovat' ne budu*" (I will not persecute you with my anguish); the same suggestion that his love is not altogether extinguished: "*byt' možet,* / V duše moej *ugasla ne sovsem*" (perhaps, / In my soul is not quite extinguished)—"Prošedšee, *byt' možet,* pozabudu" (The past I shall, perhaps, forget); the same more or less resigned pondering of her future lover(s): "Kak daj vam Bog *ljubimoj byt' drugim*" (As God grant you to be loved by another)—"I *mnogimi ljubima budeš' ty*" (And you will be loved by many). There is also an important difference between these two poems. Our present 1824 poem, "All is ended," refers to an affair which is still, for all practical purposes, *in the present.* Certainly the poet speaks of the past ("Prošedšee"), but I would be inclined to paraphrase that as equivalent to "what has recently taken place between us." Note in this connection "Ja slyšu tvoj otvet"; i.e., the dialog has been or is still in progress between them. In "I loved you . . . " the time lapse between *the past*—the time of past loving, or at least the time when that loving was a current activity—and *the present* seems significantly greater.

There are two points about the Odessa poems that are worth carrying forward: (1) the short space of time in which they were written and the extraordinary variety of emotion expressed: love fulfilled, necrophilic musings, jealousy, a sorrow hard to explain, and termination; (2) the fact that they all deal with current love (we took note above of the fact that in "All is ended" the past, if that is the right term, is in fact contiguous with the present).

The next six poems on my list were all written in Mixajlovskoe or, in one case, Trigorskoe. Without exception they are poems of recollection, harking back to Puškin's Odessa experiences. The first of these, "Razgovor knigoprodavca s poètom" (Conversation between Bookseller and Poet), is dated September 26, 1824. We confine ourselves to that part of the poem—in either the final version or the drafts—which specifically relates to a beloved woman and therefore becomes our concern here (PSS II: 324; lines 129–59). We recall that the poet is polemicizing with the bookseller and that consequently the lyric passages to which we refer are brought in to help the poet score his points; they are subordinated to the poet's overall line of argument. With this caveat, we may take them here for what they are: the poet's thoughts about a love affair located in the past. Here we have, for the first time in this study, the use of four-foot iambs. Partly the shorter lines and partly the framing of the love passage in a larger polemically oriented context have combined to impart a no-nonsense, elliptical quality to the piece. There is no room for background, for setting. Only the bare essentials of the emotional situation are reported. Witness the magnificently elliptical ambiguity of the line "Vsja žizn', odna li, dve li noči?" (All of life, or one night, two nights?)—a line in its way without superior in poetry. Yet, notwithstanding this clipped staccato style, the reader is for two reasons reminded of the first poem discussed, the 1823 "Night"—first, because of the smiling eyes: "Kak nebo, ulybalis' mne?" (Like the heavens, smiled upon me?), and second, because of the close association between poetry and the poet's lov : "Ona odna by razumela / Stixi nejasnye moi" (She alone would have un erstood / My unclear verses). The obvious difference between this passaɟ,ɘ and the eight lines of "Night" is that whereas the latter describe reciprocity in present time, the "Conversation" passage describes rejection in the past: the suppliant poet has in vain entreated the woman to prolong the relationship.

"Nenastnyj den' potux" (The foul day has died out; PSS II: 348) is dated as probably written in September-November 1824. Puškin misleadingly dated it 1823. Puškin's dating is belied by the contrast made in the poem between the discomfortable dark northern nature of Mixajlovskoe and the moonlit warm southern seashore clime of the Odessa area. This poem of potential jealousy differs from "Will you forgive me" in, other things apart, the quality of the uncertainty. In "Will you forgive me" the hero can observe the acts and conduct of the woman: the uncertainty therefore rests on interpretation. How significant is her behavior in company? Is it offset by her behavior alone with him? In "The foul day" everything takes place in the hero's imagination—though clearly the woman's evening walk to the shore is habitual, and he has certainly in the past shared these walks. The uncertainty rests on whether or not she is alone. If she is alone and miserable, he is happy. But if . . . Note the effectiveness of the switch from third to second person: "Ne pravda l': ty odna . . . " (It's true, is it not, that you're alone). The "ty odna" fulfills here the same function as did "Ja ljubim" in the earlier poem: he is seeking to reassure himself.

"Sožžennoe pis'mo" (The Burned Letter; PSS II: 373) is dated the second half of December 1824–January 5, 1825. It is a contrived and ineffective little piece, which falls below the high standards characteristic of most of the lyrics under discussion. It is included here because Makogonenko included it in his cycle. I note, for what it may be worth in our discussion, that Puškin was instructed to burn the letter by its author; i.e., we may speculate that it is once more the woman who seeks to bring the relationship to a close.

We discussed earlier an incomplete draft of "Desire for Glory" (1823). We come now to the finished product (PSS II: 392), in six-foot iambic couplets, dated January–the first half of May 1825. The poetic tension of "Desire for Glory" rests on two stages in the relationship, the change from the earlier to the later stage having taken place in the past, with its effects extending into the present. The two different stages determine the poet's changed attitude to the desirability of glory: *then* we had reciprocal love, and I didn't care about glory; *now*, catastrophe having occurred, I desire glory so that you may be surrounded by my name and may remember my last entreaties. This poem marks the first occasion in the present corpus on which the intrusions of the outside world play a significant role: tears, torments, and betrayals ("Slezy, muki, izmeny") could be purely internal upheavals, between the lovers, but calumny ("kleveta") is surely from without. Clearly his poetry plays here an essential role. But it is a very different role from that observed in "Night" and in "Conversation between Bookseller and Poet," where it was an organic part of the relationship. Here it is a means through which he can obtain glory, thus, of course, getting the attention of the woman. In "Desire for Glory," we note briefly, he is again the supplicant ("čtob . . . Ty pomnila moi poslednie molen'ja").

"Vse v žertvu pamjati tvoej" (All in sacrifice to your memory), dated 1825, provides a curiously elliptical little list in four-foot iambs of the things the poet considers as having been sacrificed to "your" memory:

Все в жертву памяти твоей:
И голос лиры вдохновенной,

И слезы девы воспаленной,
И трепет ревности моей,
И славы блеск, и мрак изгнанья,
И светлых мыслей красота,
И мщенье, бурная мечта
Ожесточенного страданья. (PSS II: 433)

All sacrificed—to memory of you:
The voice of my inspiréd lyre,
The tears of an enfevered maid,
The trembling of my jealousy,
And glory's shine, and exile's murk,
The beauty of unclouded thoughts,
And vengeance and the stormy dream
Of rack-embittered suffering.

The list, though not altogether clear from the biographer's standpoint, pretty well speaks for itself as far as present needs go. His poetry ("golos liry vdoxnovennoj") is again involved. His jealousy is acknowledged. He mentions the glitter of glory ("slavy blesk"), which ties in loosely with "želanie slavy." His exile is connected in his mind with his love ("mrak izgnan'ja"). So too the beauty of his verse, and bitter suffering and thoughts of revenge.

"Pod nebom golubym strany svoej rodnoj" (Under the blue sky of her native country; PSS I: 20), the last of our Mixajlovskoe exile poems, dated July 25–31, 1826, was written shortly after Puškin heard of Amalia Riznič's death, probably on July 29. The poem consists of four quatrains of alternating masculine six-foot iambs and feminine four-foot iambs with criss-cross rhymes—an arrangement which obviously appealed to Puškin for poems of recollection; cf. "Vospominanie" (Recollection, 1828) and "Na xolmax Gruzii" (On the hills of Georgia, 1829).[4] The news of the woman's death leaves the poet entirely indifferent ("ravnodušno ej vnimal ja"[absorbed it without emotion]). His present indifference is contrasted with the intensity of his onetime feelings ("S takim tjaželym naprjažen'em"[with such heavy strain]), his madness and torment ("S takim bezumstvom i mučen'em" [with such madness and torment]).

To sum up briefly the emerging patterns of emotion relating to affairs of the heart, I noted above that the five pieces written in Odessa had in common that they all dealt with a current love relationship. I now note that the six pieces written during Puškin's Mixajlovskoe exile all hark back to past relationships, or at least to a period when the association was more actual than it is at the time of writing. In "The Burned Letter" we are, if you will, watching in present time the burning of the letter. The letter indicates that a relationship is still alive. But it also is a symbol of a time in the past when the relationship was more actual. By the same token, the imaginings of "The foul day" are in present time, and the relationship is still alive, but the poem is set in motion largely by memories of a past time when the lovers were together. The passage from "Conversation" recounts a parting at some time in the past, as does "Desire for Glory." "All in sacrifice to your memory" is a summary of past events. And in "Under the blue sky" the heroine who at one time in the past had so agitated him is dead, and he now feels only indifference. Only in the last poem, "Under the blue sky," does the poet declare himself liberated from the torments of past love. All the other five poems here discussed reveal in one way or another a present entanglement with the emotions of past time.

"Na xolmax Gruzii ležit nočnaja mgla" (On the hills of Georgia there lies a nocturnal darkness) is dated May 15, 1829. There are two versions—a four-stanza (16–line) draft version, and the two-stanza (8–line) canonical text. It has been plausibly suggested that both versions should be published in Puškin collections, separately, and with equal rights (Bondi 1971: 24), and less plausibly argued that the two versions are addressed to two different women (Blagoj 1977: 390–91).[5] Both versions are of interest to us here. First the canonical text:

> На холмах Грузии лежит ночная мгла;
>   Шумит Арагва предо мною,
> Мне грустно и легко; печаль моя светла;
>   Печаль моя полна тобою,
> Тобой, одной тобой . . . Унынья моего
>   Ничто не мучит, не тревожит,
> И сердце вновь горит и любит—оттого,
>   Что не любить оно не может. (PSS III: 158)

> On Georgia's hills there lies the mist of night,
> I hear Aragva's roar ahead,
> I am both sad and happy; my sadness is unclouded,
> My sadness is full of you,
> Of you, of you alone . . . My despondence
> Is untormented and untroubled,
> And my heart once more's afire and loves—because
> It cannot not love.

And now the sixteen-line draft version:

> Все тихо—на Кавказ идет ночная мгла
>   Восходят звезды надо мною
> Мне грустно и легко—печаль моя светла
>   Печаль моя полна тобою
>
> Тобой одной тобой—унынья моего
>   Ничто не мучит не тревожит
> И сердце вновь горит и любит от того
>   что не любить оно не может
>
> Прошли за днями дни—сокрылось много лет
>   Где вы, бесценные созданья

Иные далеко иных уж в мире нет
Со мной одни воспоминанья

Я твой попрежнему тебя люблю я вновь
И без надежд и без желаний
Как пламень жертвенный чиста моя любовь
И нежность девственных мечтаний (PSS III: 722–23)

All quiet—across the Caucusus the night mist moves,
The stars climb high above my head;
I am both sad and happy; my sadness is unclouded,
My sadness is full of you,

Of you, of you alone—My despondence
Is untormented and untroubled,
And my heart once more's afire and loves—because
It cannot not love.

Days have followed days—many years have passed.
Where are you, creatures, dear, so dear?
Some are far away, and some no longer live,
With me are only memories.

I'm yours as formerly, and you I love once more—
Quite without hope, without desire;
Just as the altar's flame, that pure is my love,
And the tenderness of my immaculate dreamings.

Puškin uses here the same alternating six-foot masculine and four-foot feminine rhyming iambs as in "Under the blue sky" (and in "Recollection," 1828); already noted is the tie between this arrangement and the theme of recollection. Recollection is more frequently spelled out in the original version, but is no less present in the final text. In both versions (line 7) we find the word *vnov'* "once more", indicating that the heart had at some point ceased burning and loving, but is now doing so again. In the original version (third stanza) the poet harks back to the people he once knew ("Inye daleko, inyx už v mire net" [Some are no more, others are far away]) (cf. *Evgenij Onegin*, VIII.51: "Inyx už net, a te daleče"), and to the memories which alone remain ("odni vospominan'ja"). And in the final, fourth, stanza, "po-prežnemu" and "vnov'" echo the "vnov'" of the second stanza. A significant difference between the original and final versions is the setting, the geographical location. In the original version it is the Caucasus. Puškin was in the Caucasus on May 15; he spent the night of May 15 in Georgievsk (Lerner 1903: 61). Whereas in the final version we are in Georgia—where Puškin had never been in his life before and whence therefore he could not claim to draw memories. And in fact, strictly speaking, he does not mention memories, except of love.

What we have, therefore, if we compare the two versions, is a movement away from an original, more accurate, more specific, more autobiographical version to a more generalized, less biographical final version. The year 1828 had been even for Puškin exceptionally bad; the end of the Chénier inquiry, the *Gavriliada* inquiry, his rejection by Olenina, his overall recognition that in various ways he was a marked man, finally in 1829 Gončarova's coldness to his suit: all these things added up to desperately bad news for Puškin—witness "Recollection," "Dar naprasnyj" (The Futile Gift), "Snova tuči nado mnoj" (Again clouds above me).[6] His 1829 journey to Arzrum was therefore a flight. "On the hills of Georgia," written early on in his journey, to some extent reflects the relief of the escapee. It can be interpreted as a happy poem—happiness oxymoronically mixed with sorrow; happiness brought in *the present* by the recollection of fond memories from the *past*. The reader cannot fail to note the reappearance of some of the same structural features which were present in "Night," that almost uniquely happy Puškin love lyric. We note the following: (1) night and darkness (both versions) ("nočnaja mgla" [night mist]), relieved by a not-too-bright light (original version only) ("Vosxodjat zvezdy" [The stars climb high])—cf "pečal'naja sveča" [sad candle]; (2) quietness (original version) ("Vse tixo"), broken by a not overly harsh sound (final version) ("šumit Aragva")—cf. "Moj golos . . . žurča, / Tekut, ruč'i ljubvi" [My voice . . . murmuring, / Flow, rivulets of love]; thus in both poems we have flowing water; (3) the following lexical items: *gorit*, (ne) *trevožit, pečal'/ pečal'naja*; (4) the idea of being full of some positive emotion, full of the loved one, precisely the same words here as in "Night" ("polny toboju") ending the line and giving the rhyme, in fact the rhymed endings are identical in the two poems, *nado mnoju* [above me] or *predo mnoju* [before me] / *polny* (*polna*) *toboju* [full of you]. (5) as in "Night," considerable play with the first- and second-person pronoun.

Let us note also some differences between "Night" and our 1829 poem: (1) the setting of the former is the indoors, while the setting of the latter is the outdoors ("sveča" [candle] against "zvezdy" [stars]); (2) in "Night" the poet's verses have an important function, whereas in "On the hills of Georgia" there is no mention of them; (3) in "Night" the beloved is imagined as being present and declaring her love; in 1829 she is not imagined as present, there is no fulfillment, no expectation of reciprocity ("I bez nadežd i bez želanij"). In this last respect, the rejection of hope of reciprocity, there is a move away from "Night" toward another link—that with "I loved you" of 1829. And, finally, let us emphasize that both versions of our 1829 poem make extremely effective use of symmetry: in the six-foot lines the caesura is syntactically reinforced, and there is repeated use of pairs, either close in meaning, augmenting each other ("Toboj, odnoj toboj . . . ne mučit, ne trevožit . . . gorit i ljubit . . . po-prežnemu . . . vnov' . . . bez nadežd i bez želanij"), or oxymoronically opposed ("grustno i legko" echoed and reinforced by the following oxymoron: "Pečal' moja svetla," topped and explained by "pečal' moja polna toboju"); note too the double negative with inversion: "ne ljubit' ono ne možet."[7]

"Ja vas ljubil" (I loved you; PSS III: 183) was written in 1829, not later than November. The meter is five-foot iambics, with masculine and feminine alternating rhymes, making up the poem's two quatrains. For the first and only time in the poems of our corpus we have the more formal form of the second-person pronoun (*Vas, vam* instead of *ty, tebja, tebe*). There is constant interplay of the first- and second-person pronouns, with the second person invariably an object, and the first person a subject. The poem is totally without background, without decor—without reference to any particular scene or event. It describes in the past the poet's attitude, his central concerns in the present, and his wish for the woman in the future. And it operates entirely without images ("poèzija bez obrazov," to use Roman Jakobson's characterization; Jakobson 1981 II: 72–75). In this respect, and in the poem's overall theme and tenor, it is clearly a development of the 1824 "All is ended: between us there is no connection." Excerpts from the two poems were juxtaposed, above, to demonstrate their similarities. In its theme of tender, timid, undemanding love, this poem is close also to "On the hills of Georgia"—especially to the original version: "I bez nadežd, i bez želanij." The two poems were written in the same year. Thematically, "I loved you" has points of contact with the three "poems of recollection" mentioned—"Under the blue sky," "Recollection," and "On the hills of Georgia." Although metrically it does not follow their six-foot, four-foot alternating pattern, it shares with them the symmetricality and tendency to emphasize the message by the use of pairs, close in meaning. This tendency was pointed out above for "On the hills of Georgia." So I merely note for "I loved you": " . . . ne trevožit; / Ja ne xoču pečalit' . . . bezmolvno, beznadežno, / To robost'ju, to revnost'ju . . . tak iskrenno, tak nežno. . . . " [. . . not disturb you; / I do not wish to cause you sorrow . . . silently, without hope, / Now by shyness, now jealousy . . . so sincerely, so tenderly]. We note as familiar lexical items "ne trevožit" (cf. "Night" and "On the hills of Georgia"—also in "All is ended": "Tebja toskoj presledovat' ne budu"); "pečalit' " (cf. "Night" and "On the hills"); "ugasla" (cf. "Night" and "On the hills"); "gorit"; "Beznadežno" (cf. in "On the hills": "bez nadežd"); "ljubil," "ljubov'," "ljubimoj," etc., passim. The closeness, noted above, of "I loved you" to "On the hills" serves to reinforce the idea of a lapse in time between the love in its active phase and the present moment of recollection; cf. in the original version of "On the hills": "sokrylas' mnogo let."

Above, we characterized the Odessa pieces as *current*, and the Mixajlovskoe pieces as *past* in the sense that they looked back to, put in perspective, or drew their nourishment from a relationship which had been in the past more actual, since at that time the lovers had been able to see and meet each other. How should we characterize "On the hills" and "I loved you"? They seem to me to be poems of reduced demandingness—in terms of the lover's rights and expectations. Past love is recalled, its continuance or reawakening is acknowledged, but the great emphasis is on the man's insistence, his reassuring the woman (more specifically in the original than in the final version of "On the hills") that he has no demands to make. He has therefore in his own mind reached some sort of elevated plateau of not disinterested but not demanding love. Characterize his newfound attitude how we will, we are bound to recognize that a qualitative change has taken place. And while "On the hills" expresses resignation, "I loved you" goes one step further—by looking into a future in which some other man will have replaced the departing lover. Both poems stand close together, on the threshold of being poems of farewell.

The last three lyrics on our list were all written in the fall of 1830 at Boldino. During this highly creative period, Puškin was, in part, as noted above, bidding farewell to his pre-married life. Leave-taking is the central theme of the three lyrics involved. Of these the first in time is entitled "Proščanie" (Farewell; PSS III: 233), dated October 5. This AbAAb-rhyming four-foot iambic stanza is used consistently in only two Puškin poems, "Farewell" and "Paž" (Page), the latter dated October 7, 1830, i.e., two days after "Farewell." The strophe in the case of "Page" was suggested by de Musset's "L'Andalouse," and it was used ten times in Sainte-Beuve's *Poésies de Joseph Delorme* (1829), which had favorably impressed Puškin. The strophe itself is regarded by B. V. Tomaševskij as thematically "neutral" (Tomaševskij 1958 II: 78). The idea espoused by some scholars that "Farewell" is addressed to a dead woman is patently wrong. Note that "*dlja* svoego poèta" and "dlja tebja" are in perfect symmetry—i.e., for *me* *you*'re dead, for *you* *I*'m dead, because our separation is final and decisive, not because either one of us is clinically dead. "I s negoj robkoj i unyloj"— applied to his own feelings—is a pretty good indication that the addressee is alive (cf. in "I loved you" *nežno, robost'*); it is a part of the poet's reassurance formula—his love will be undemanding. "Menjaja vse, menjaja nas" means changing both of us as the years change everything else—not changing *you* by death, and *me* in some less conspicuous way. The poem has been pruned of eroticism and is dominated by a mood of controlled gloom as the future is contemplated. In a draft we read "S negoj sladkoj" [with sweet voluptuousness], changed, of course, to "robkoj" [shy]. And in the final three lines we have two similes working together, which clearly militate against eroticism and in the direction of onetime love now recollected in tranquility.

To examine the two similes briefly: The idea of a widowed spouse is clear enough, and it enhances the overall melancholic tone of the poem; it also carries finality. But the addressee is seen also to be embracing a friend prior to his incarceration, which puts the poet-narrator in the position of facing imminent imprisonment! I don't think this is impossible. Puškin's views on his approaching marriage were not consistent—they varied with mood and with whom he was addressing. But one feeling that seems to constitute a strand in this emotional complex or composite is a feeling of being about to be tied, to be deprived of freedoms, in a sense imprisoned.

His "Elegija" (Elegy) ("Bezumnyx let ugaššee vesel'e" [The extinguished merriment of mad years]), dated September 8, 1830, is frequently cited as an expression of Puškin's courage, his positive view of life. But it also contains, in my view, a measure of self-pity:

> Но не хочу, о други, умирать;
> Я жить хочу, чтоб мыслить и страдать;
> И ведаю, мне будут наслажденья
> Меж горестей, забот и треволненья:
> Порой опять гармонией упьюсь,
> Над вымыслом слезами обольюсь,
> И может быть—на мой закат печальный
> Блеснет любовь улыбкою прощальной. (PSS III: 228)

> But no, my friends, I do not wish to die;
> I wish to live that I may think and suffer;
> And I know too that pleasures will be mine
> Amid my troubles and my tribulation:
> At times again the Muses will delight,
> Creation's work will cause my tears to flow;
> Perhaps once more my waning star will shine
> Beneath the farewell smile of love.

I.e., despite the odds, I may still squeeze out of life a little joy. The idea that a onetime love could be bidding him farewell before his incarceration is by no means far-fetched.

"Zaklinanie" (Incantation; PSS III: 246) was written on October 17, and is clearly addressed to a dead woman. This poem has its derivation in a forty-two-line poem by Barry Cornwall, "Invocation." Although "Invocation" and "Incantation" are both devoted to a beloved woman who has died, they differ markedly in tone and atmosphere. By and large, Cornwall is summoning a spirit, whereas Puškin has not entirely disincarnated the object of his love. He bids Leila to appear "as thou wast before we parted, pale, cold, like a winter day, contorted with thy final agony"—which fits what seems to be a Puškin pattern of fascination with fading and ailing charm. In this sense the poem is loosely reminiscent of the 1823 "There will arrive a terrible hour." The three stanzas of four-foot iambs follow a not particularly meaningful pattern—aBaBcDDc—with the *sjuda, sjuda!* refrain ending for each stanza (Tomaševskij 1958: II: 87–88).

Our last poem, "Dlja beregov otčizny dal'noj" (For the shores of a distant fatherland; PSS III: 257), is also written to a dead woman. It is dated November 27, 1830. This poem, three stanzas of four-foot iambs following the pattern AbAbCdCd, has created no little confusion. The definitive text would justify the assumption that the addressee is a foreigner returning to her distant homeland. But the draft gives the opposite picture: "Dlja beregov čužbiny dal'noj / Ty pokidala kraj rodnoj" [For the shores of a distant alien land / You left your native country]. According to this

version the addressee would seem to be a Russian woman going abroad—
not a foreign woman returning home. There is another feature in this poem
which may be of some general interest. Italy, most scholars agree, is the
land to which the beloved woman was summoning the poet, and the land
where she died. But Puškin has evoked Italy by recalling scenery with
which he was himself familiar from his southern sojourn, the scenery of the
Odessa area. As B. P. Gorodeckij so convincingly notes, this is the only
poem in which Puškin mentions—in fact, twice—the presence of olive
trees in connection with Italy. Gorodeckij links this to Puškin's personal
memories of Odessa and the South, and points out that the "Nereida"
(1820) line "Sokrytyj mež derev, edva ja smel doxnut' " [Concealed among
the trees, I scarcely dared to breathe] originally read "Sokrytyj mež oliv,
edva ja smel doxnut' " [Concealed among the olive trees, I scarcely dared
to breathe], thus referring to a bona fide olive grove near the Richelieu
house where Puškin was staying in 1820 with the Raevskijs (Gorodeckij
1962: 382–83). Also, in an early draft line 19 appears not as "Gde [ten' oliv
legla] na vody" [Where the shade of the olive trees lay across the waters]
but as "Gde pod skalami dremljut vody" [Where beneath the cliffs the
waters slumber]. It is difficult to believe that the "skaly" are not those near
Odessa, the same ones mentioned ("Pod golubymi nebesami . . . Tam, pod
zavetnymi skalami" [Beneath the blue heavens . . . There, beneath the
cherished cliffs]) in Puškin's 1824 "The foul day has died out." We note
that the poet had tried in vain to impede the woman's departure.

The last three poems discussed, those written in Boldino in the fall of
1830, are clearly poems of farewell.

What pattern, if any, emerges? The sixteen poems here studied cover a
space of seven years. It does not seem far-fetched to divide them into four
periods. These four periods correspond to the composition dates, but they
also, in the character of their respective lyrics, reflect a quality which dif-
ferentiates them from the other periods. Proceeding along these lines, it is
possible to characterize the periods as follows:

1. 1823–24, Odessa: poems involving current love affairs;
2. 1824–26, Mixajlovskoe: poems in which past love affairs are recollected;
3. 1829: two poems of recollection in which expectations have been reduced and there is a conscious effort to let go the past;
4. 1830, Boldino: poems of farewell.

Our study is posited on the belief that our post-Odessa lyrics refer back
to the Odessa period (or possibly in one or two cases to 1820–23 in the
Odessa area, i.e., to the pre-Odessa southern exile, but not Kišinev). This
means that in our view the Odessa experiences continued to be felt right up
to Puškin's marriage. That these experiences should in successive stages be
recollected with diminishing intensity is in the nature of things. Time has
its effect. But what is significant is that nothing in the years following

Odessa came to replace these memories. We do not forget Kern, Ušakova, Olenina. But relations with these women would seem not to have been of comparable intensity with the experiences which produced the five Odessa lyrics. And this makes Odessa a watershed year. From Odessa on, the road was all downhill—to February 18, 1831. This may sound a cynical comment, and indeed it is. But that is precisely the point—for the remark could very well have been made by Puškin himself!

We have already noted the emotional disorder of the Odessa period as expressed in the five lyrics: love fulfilled; necrophilic musings; jealousy; something amiss in the midst of an apparently satisfactory love relationship; supplication; termination.

Obviously these poems were not written to one woman only. For example, "There will arrive a terrible hour" and "All is ended" are mutually exclusive; you cannot describe in advance a woman's death through illness, and then two months later tell her she is young, and will be loved by many. But the question of how many women went into the making of the five Odessa pieces, though fascinating, is not my point. My point is the wide variety of intense, contradictory, and conflicting emotions that went into their making. The chaotic nature of the Odessa period also needs to be stressed, for it gives, with hindsight, to be sure, a clear indication of the non-viability of the attachments formed in 1823–24 in that city.

Second, and finally, there is one other feature of the sixteen pieces that attracts attention—the very considerable extent to which the pieces depict the man as a supplicant, as seeking to hold back or restrain the woman, to prolong a relationship which the woman is terminating. This can be seen in "Will you forgive me my jealous dreams," "All is ended: between us there is no connection," and "Conversation between Bookseller and Poet," in the 1825 final version of "Desire for Glory," in "I loved you" by implication (since he now wishes that his love no longer importune her or give her sorrow), and in "For the shores of a distant fatherland."

Our study appears—going up to 1830, at least—to substantiate Puškin's feeling that he was not made for love—at least not for love that stands the test of time: "Ne dlja menja sotvorena ljubov'." Or rather, more accurately, love was not made for him.

LESLIE O'BELL

Through the Magic Crystal
to *Eugene Onegin*

Many scholars have sought to find the "magic crystal" through which, Puškin says, he dimly glimpsed the "far horizon of his free novel," *Evgenij Onegin* (Eugene Onegin) (PSS VI: 190). Poring over manuscripts in dusty archives while intoning the metrical formula of the *Onegin* stanza, performing abstruse chronological calculations, creating dubious compounds of *Wahrheit* and *Dichtung*, we benighted but noble alchemists have yet to reach our gleaming objective. And what single "crystal" could bring *Onegin* into focus, a work that is so mutable and so elusive? By Puškin's own account, it took him seven years, four months, and seventeen days to finish the novel (PSS VI: 532). As Lotman once put it, *Onegin* was begun by the writer of *Baxčisaraj Fountain*, continued by the creator of *Boris Godunov,* and completed by the author of the *Little Tragedies.* Yet perhaps this is not only the problem but part of the solution as well. We have had the philosopher's stone in hand all along: *Eugene Onegin* is embedded in the larger and slowly developing crystal of those other works of Puškin which accompany and nurture it. Since *Onegin* required such long maturation, it should surely be considered in the process of its invention, growth, and change. The internal evolution of *Onegin*, from its drafts to the book which Puškin eventually published, is a fundamental part of the process, but the novel's inner dynamic is also intimately involved in the movement of his entire work. How did Puškin clarify ideas of the novel; how did he periodically reenvision it? Playing with Puškin's metaphor, we can say that he wrote *Eugene Onegin* by peering into a crystal ball that may very well have been his own inkwell.

Ideally, to reckon with this, we should take *Onegin* chapter by chapter, retelling it against the counterpoint of the works which form its context. I shall not be able to do so in the scope of this essay. Over the years a number of studies have accumulated which treat *Onegin*'s relation to one or another of Puškin's works. Yet no essay has ever integrated these particular observations, bringing out the latent picture that they form while simultaneously coordinating them with the inner dynamic of the novel. The critical overview that I will offer here represents only a first step toward chronicling the unfolding of *Onegin*.

What emerges when we step back from the individual studies are four major contexts or complexes in Puškin's work as a whole into which *Eugene Onegin* has been fit. They could be called first, the demon, second, the man of the world, third, the journey, and fourth, the farewell and homecoming. Actually, the four elements work together as parts of Puškin's continual preoccupation with one character and his fate, the man of the world in his demonic aspect, compelled to wander but doomed to nostalgia for his lost home. They also reflect the poet's increasing divergence from this character in an attempt to avoid sharing his fate and in the hope of accomplishing a different journey and winning for himself a homecoming. The demon and the man of the world are most important in the genesis of the novel, although they accompany it throughout. The journey, farewell, and homecoming naturally figure most prominently in the final chapters, especially when we include the "Wanderings" and the so-called Chapter X. But the journey theme was anticipated as early as the end of Chapter I, where Onegin and the poet were ready to set out for foreign parts. *Eugene Onegin* is a long farewell and the slow preparation of a nemesis.

Let us now consider in more detail how *Eugene Onegin* develops. We remember but seldom take effective cognizance of the fact that *Onegin* is addressed to "the friends of Ljudmila and Ruslan" (PSS VI: 15). In his introduction to Chapter I, Puškin wrote expressly that the first chapters "bear the imprint of the gaiety which marked the first works of the author of *Ruslan and Ljudmila*" (PSS VI: 638). Baevskij in a recent study has extended the reference to include the entire "tradition of light poetry in *Eugene Onegin*" as the source of the intimacy, informality, and banter which characterize the relationship between poet and reader in the novel. The conversational tone derives from genres of "light poetry" such as the friendly epistle and from the cultivated art of private correspondence. This is witnessed in the dedication and epigraph to the novel ("tiré d'une lèttre particulaire"). Puškin becomes increasingly critical of light poetry, and Baevskij traces the influence of genres such as album verse and the madrigal on parodic episodes which appear in later chapters of *Onegin*: the album of the provincial young ladies versus the album of the Petersburg grande dame, Onegin's "vulgar madrigal" to Ol'ga at the ball and M. Triquet's painfully inept birthday verses for Tat'jana. Baevskij omits to mention the important role which Puškin originally envisioned for Onegin's Album, or the way in which Tat'jana's visit to Onegin's library transforms the setting of "Gorodok," that friendly epistle from the author's country library. Baevskij concludes: "At the end of the introduction, Puškin indicates the other line of development which led him to *Eugene Onegin*, the romantic (*The Prisoner of the Caucasus* and the modern, melancholy elegies). Thus, the originality of *Onegin* was felt by Puškin against the background of the synthesis of all the artistic achievements of the first decade of his work" (1982: 113). Take Voltaire and Ariosto and add generous amounts of Byron and Sterne, Puškin's latest models for the free, authorial presence. The author in *Eugene Onegin*, though descended from the poet of *Ruslan and Ljudmila*, is not identical with him. If we were to reconstruct the whole story behind the creation of the authorial presence or "obraz avtora" in *Eugene Onegin*, we would need to know more about the Kišinev diaries which Puškin destroyed in 1826.

So far we have only an author. What of his search for a hero? *Kavkazskij plennik* (The Prisoner of the Caucasus) is the confident reply. D'jakonov has written that "*Eugene Onegin* redevelops *The Prisoner of the Caucasus* by other means" (1982: 80). It is generally recognized that the Prisoner is the first character sketch for Onegin; he is the prematurely disillusioned romantic, the young man from the capital marooned in the wilds, stirred to feeling and renewed by the love of a simple girl, which he cannot, however, reciprocate, and from which she ultimately perishes. Note here the lineaments of a shadowy Tat'jana. D'jakonov has commented on the plot similarities between *The Prisoner* with its passive hero and positive, self-sacrificing heroine and *Eugene Onegin* (1982: 72). In *The Prisoner*, the man of the world begins his long farewell to youth from his first place of exile, exile explored from a different point of view in Puškin's lyrics ("To Ovid" . . .). *The Prisoner* dramatizes ennui and the lament for lost youth. But it is also the source of what Puškin called the "ljubovnyj bred" (delirious passion) which erupts into the other southern poems right up to *Poltava*, and finally even into the last chapter of *Eugene Onegin* ("Benedetta," "Idol mio," PSS VI: 184). Puškin's preliminary epigraph from *Faust* "Gieb meine Jugend mir züruck!" (PSS IV: 286) might serve as the leitmotif for the lament. It migrated from the draft of *The Prisoner* known as *The Caucasus* to the draft of *Tavrida* (Fomičev 1982: 16). *Tavrida*, at times considered the predecessor of *Onegin*, eventually yielded stanzas of passionate reminiscence for Chapter I ("Ja pomnju more pred grozoju . . . " [PSS VI: 19]) which bring "ljubovnyj bred" and the theme of "hidden love" into *Onegin*. As we remember, Puškin learned from *The Prisoner* that he made a poor romantic hero ("ja ne gožus' v geroi romantičeskogo stixotvorenija" [PSS XIII: 52]). There was not enough distance in *The Prisoner*, too much submersion of the author into the character, a mistake not repeated in *Onegin*. Puškin's second Caucasian journey, along with his memories from *The Prisoner*, are reflected in the Caucasian episode in Onegin's "Wanderings," and perhaps most poignantly in the verse from Onegin's Album which returns us to the psychological springs of *The Prisoner*:

> Цветок полей, листок дубрав
> В ручье кавказкой каменеет.
> В волнении жизни так мертвеет
> И ветренный и нежный нрав. (PSS VI: 615)

> The flower of the field and the oak leaf
> Turn leaden in the icy Caucasian rill.

So, too, life's current deadens
A tender and flighty nature.

The "Prisoner of the Caucasus" is a romantically displaced young man from Petersburg society, a literary character known as the "man of the world," to emphasize his connection with good society (*le monde, svet*) and his pretensions to experience and sophistication. This is the contemporary hero as society has made him. *The Prisoner of the Caucasus* immediately contrasts him to the natural setting with its grandeur and energy, to the primitive passions of the native tribesmen and the ardent spirit of the Circassian girl. The first chapter of *Eugene Onegin*, on the other hand, takes place in the capital, as if to develop the *Vorgeschichte*. We witness the education and creation of the hero in his own milieu. The first stirrings of a conception like this may be attested in the June 1821 plan for the comedy "Skaži, kakoj sud'boj" (Fancy Meeting You). Here, as Vol'pert writes, "we find images and themes which will be further developed in *Onegin*, the type of the contemporary dandy and the description of social mores" (1979: 175). This was to be a comedy of manners with the sting of social satire. The tone of the piece and its setting seem to anticipate *Onegin*, but this hero has nothing of the demonic element which entered the novel from the end of the first chapter.

The demon is the most thoroughly explored context for *Onegin* in Puškin's work, and rightly so for its importance to the novel. *Onegin* has several personae, but even as man of the world or wanderer he is the demon. His vanity and pride, his egotism, his ennui, his very worldliness make the man of the world a fiend. When we hear repeatedly in the novel that Onegin is another Melmoth, the character in question is of course specifically Melmoth the Wanderer; and after the duel with Lenskij, Onegin undertakes his journey like an outcast Cain and murderer of his brother. The demon in Puškin has usually been considered in one of two aspects, either as the amorous seducer and betrayer or as the more philosophical "spirit of denial and doubt." The one appears as a tempter from without, the other tends to work from within (Vacuro 1976). But the two both bring on a serious crisis of faith. Certainly Onegin, as the spirit of doubt and denial, also possesses demonic powers of seduction both in friendship and in love. Tat'jana, Lenskij, and the poet are all drawn to him, though Tat'jana's dream hints at his demonic desire for possession ("moe!" [mine!] [PSS VI: 106]), and the duel with Lenskij reveals his capability for essentially mindless evil and the destructiveness latent in his ennui. The poet, too, often permits himself sarcasm toward love and friendship, whose ideal has been seriously undermined. The demon is actually a double, now a second self, now a magnetically attractive friend. His embodiment is a first step toward dealing with him and ultimately overcoming him.

We come to ask whether Onegin was truly demonic. "Who are you, angel or demon?" Tat'jana's letter asked. "Kto ty, moj angel li xranitel' / Ili kovarnyj iskusitel'?" (PSS VI: 67). Reading in Onegin's library, she stops short of pronouncing him a mere parody of the romantic demon ("uželi *slovo* najdeno?" [can the *word* have been found?] [PSS VI: 149]). The poet, launching Onegin on his journey, says in a draft that even the hero is tired of keeping up his reputation as a Melmoth ("Naskuča slyt' ili Mel'motom / Il' maskoj ščegoljat' inoj" [PSS VI: 475]). The Album, later omitted, showing us a diary of his past, calls his malice into question and humanizes him ("Vy sovsem ne tak opasny . . . prosto očen' vy dobry" [You are really not so dangerous . . . in fact, you are very kind] [PSS VI: 615]). In the final chapter the demonic seducer himself falls victim to love.

But let us return to the origins of Onegin. "Demonic" works accompany the novel throughout its development but decisively influence its initial stages. First we must consider the *Gavriiliada* (Gavriliada), and the plans for the story "Vljublennyj bes" (The Devil in Love), then the complex of poems surrounding "The Demon." The most recent treatment of their connection to *Onegin* belongs to Ospovat (1986). Puškin began Chapter I of *Eugene Onegin* on May 9, 1823, and completed it on October 22, immediately proceeding to Chapter II, which was largely finished by December 8. The *Gavriliada* dates to April of 1823, the period just before *Eugene Onegin*. Xodasevič noted that the situation of Chapter II echoes the *Gavriliada* where Puškin had written: "Let's talk about love's aberrations. . . . To reawaken the memory of it, we like to chatter with a confidant" (1924: 66). "Veteran of love," Onegin serves as the demonic confidant for Lenskij's effusions. Ospovat points to the fact that a passage characterizing Onegin's expertise in "the science of the tender passion" recasts several lines from the *Gavriliada* where Satan appears as the teacher (1986: 190). The demon as triumphant and carefree seducer is certainly the hero of the *Gavriliada*—and, as Ospovat observes, the author is his double. His speech most closely resembles the speech of Satan, and he declares himself "the demon's friend, a rake and a deceiver" ("drug demona, povesa i predatel' " [PSS IV: 136]). Thus, in the *Gavriliada* Puškin tries out the demon as double for author.

"I bešenoj ljubvi prokazy / V arxivax ada otyskal" (PSS II: 1, 199, draft dedication), this is how Puškin characterized the enterprise of the *Gavriliada*: unearthing the episodes of mad love in the archives of hell. The devil seduces a willing Virgin Mary, beating out his rival, Gabriel, and exposing the hypocrisy of God the Father. Onegin behaves exactly like the devil of the *Gavriliada*, instructing girls on the quiet. But the amorous adventures of the devil are also the reflection of the author's own past, of his "mad love." "A ja povesa večno prazdnyj . . . / Ja nravljus' junoj krasote / Besstydnym bešenstvom želanij" (But I, an eternally idle rake . . . / I please young beauty / with the shameless frenzy of my desires [PSS II: 1: 139–40; 1821; Ospovat 1986: 180]). The archives of hell are the memories of his Petersburg days, as attested by Puškin's sketches of carousing, inhabited by his acquaintances from the capital and a long-tailed devil (Cjavlov-skaja 1960: 115). "Strastej igru my znali oba" (We both knew how the passions play [PSS VI: 23]). Returning in memory to those times once more in the retrospective opening stanzas of Chapter VIII, Puškin wrote that his Muse had "sported like a Bacchante" (the drafts were more frank—"a kak vakxanočka besilas' "; "Ja Muzu pylkuju privel na igry ju-nošej razgul'nyx" (I brought my fervid Muse to the revels of boisterous youth [PSS VI: 621; Ospovat 1986: 193]). Compare Chapter I: "ljublju ja bešenuju mladost' " (I love mad youth [PSS 6: 7]).

The "Demon" poems of fall 1823 may be seen as the direct source of the pairing of Puškin and Onegin as the author and his familiar demon, a relationship so important to the structure of the novel and soon echoed in the friendship of Onegin and Lenskij. But the *Gavriliada* (April 1823) al-ready anticipates this, as does the plan called "The Devil in Love" (1821–23). Ospovat links the two as the "amorous adventures of the devil," on the one hand, and "the devil in love," on the other, and points out the striking plot similarities between the devil in love and Onegin, suggesting that indeed "The Devil in Love" might well have influenced the formation of the novel (1986: 185). To quote the plan:

> Старуха, две дочери, одна невинная, другая романическая—
> два приятеля к ним ходят. Один развратный, другой
> Влюбленный бес. Влюбленный бес любит меньшую и хочет
> погубить молодого человека.... старшая дочь сходит с ума
> от любви к Влюбленному бесу. (PSS VIII: 1: 429)

> An old woman, two daughters, one an innocent, the other a romantic—two friends visit the house. One is dissolute, the other the Devil in Love. The Devil in Love loves the younger daughter and wants to do in the young man. . . . The elder daughter goes mad over her love for the Devil in Love.

Ospovat (1986) comments:

> The two friends schema, one of which is a demon who tempts the other, goes back to the *Faust* plot. But the introduction into this schema of two sisters, the younger one (the innocent) the object of the demon's passion, the elder (the romantic) perishing from her love for him, not only introduces a love intrigue to complicate the schema but fundamentally transforms it. Essentially we have an original plot whose basic features coincide with the story of *Eugene Onegin*. (1986: 185)

However, the plan for "The Devil in Love" would seem to be a devel-opment from early graphic sketches and verse of 1821 which Annenkov called the "Adskaja poèma" (Hellish Poem) (Cjavlovskaja 1960: 104). The most relevant sketch depicts a devil in hell forlornly warming himself and gazing into the fire while above him, as it were in his mind's eye, wafts the figure of a woman. Thus he is the original "devil in love." Despite the nervous line drawing which might suggest satire, because of the accompanying lyrics Cjavlovskaja is probably correct that Puškin envisioned a romantic narrative (1960: 105–106). While the rest of hell keeps holiday, there is a remote corner where a contrasting scene is evidently in progress. Hell is a place "from which hope, peace, love and rest are forever exiled, where a terrible Satan laughs to hear the moans of sinners": "V Geene prazdnik . . . vo t'me kromešnoj / Est' udalennyj ugolok . . . Otkuda izgnanny naveki / Nadežda, mir, ljubov' i son, / Gde grešnika vnimaja ston / Užasnyj Satana xoxočet" (PSS II: 989; PSS II: 1: 469). Motifs of isolation, exile, lost hope, the mockery of Satan: it is as if *The Prisoner of the Caucasus* had been transported to the underworld. There, too, ennui reigns. In a neighboring verse fragment, devils joke about playing cards to while away eternity, "tol'ko b večnost' provodit' " (PSS II: 1: 382).

The *Gavriliada* and the plan "The Devil in Love" show what varied expressions the formant of the demonic double took in Puškin. Yet only "The Demon" is actually intertwined with the writing of *Eugene Onegin*, its drafts and related fragments interspersed with stanzas of the novel. As Medvedeva established in 1941, work on "The Demon" overlapped work on the end of Chapter I and the beginning of Chapter II (November–December 1823). Here Onegin becomes the gloomy and jaded companion of the poet and soon strikes up a friendship with Lenskij, whom he will eventually destroy. Nepomnjaščij has written, "The poem 'The Demon' can be called a metaphorical outline for the first chapter of the novel, a kind of mother cell containing the 'genetic code' of this 'beginning of a long poem' " (1983: 278). At the end of Chapter I, the poet and his demonic double, Onegin, attain their closest rapprochement ("S nim podružilsja ja v to vremja . . . ja byl ozloblen, on ugrjum" [I became friends with him at that time . . . I was embittered, he was glum] [PSS VI: 23]). Lotman has written in his analysis of the evolution of characters in *Onegin* that only when Onegin has taken on the aspect of the demon with all his philosophical skepticism does he gain the stature to become the poet's friend (1960: 143).

> Мне было грустно, тяжко, больно
> Но одолев меня в борьбе
> Он сочетал меня невольно
> Своей таинственной судьбе. (PSS VI: 277–78)

> It hurt, it was hard, it made me sad,
> But overpowering me in the fight,
> He involuntarily made me accomplice
> To his mysterious fate.

This fragment leading to "The Demon" is found among the drafts of *Onegin*, Chapter II (Medvedeva 1941: 61). In the person of Onegin, the "devil in love" joins the disillusioned hero of *The Prisoner of the Caucasus*.

Onegin seems to shed his worldliness for worldweariness, the demon displacing "the man of the world," and this attracts the poet. "Uslovij sveta svergnuv bremja, / Kak on otstav ot suety, / S nim podružilsja ja v to vremja" (Casting off the burden of worldly conventions, / Like him, in retirement from their vanity, / I became friends with him at that time] [PSS VI: 23]). Onegin, previously little more than the automaton of the social whirl, rushing through a single day to the chime of his pocket watch, gains depth of character through memory, the magical element of the poet. They share reminiscences, "Vospomnja prežnjuju ljubov' . . . tak unosilis' my mečtoj / K načalu žizni molodoj" (Remembering past love . . . we would be transported thus in fancy / To the beginnings of our young life) (PSS VI: 24). Now both express their readiness for the journey, which means escape for Onegin, freedom for the poet. Perhaps we should stress Onegin's *razdvoennost'* or divided personality at this point in the novel: "*Mečtam* nevol'naja predannost' . . . i rezkij oxlaždennyj *um*" (An involuntary dedication to *dreams* . . . and a sharp, cold *mind*). This corresponds to the famous sententia:

> Кто жил и *мыслил*, тот не может
> В душе не презирать людей;
> Кто *чувствовал*, того тревожит
> Призрак невозвратимых дней. (PSS VI: 24)

> He who has lived and *thought* cannot
> But despise people in his heart;
> He who has *felt*, is troubled by
> The ghost of days which can never return.

Stanzas 45 and 46 of Chapter I contain the principal elements of Puškin's famous poem "Vospominanie" (Recollection, 1828) and its manuscript continuation—the serpent of memory, remorse, the ghost of the past, the reference to slanderers and a ruined youth. "Oboix ožidala Zloba / Slepoj Fortuny i ljudej / Na samom utre našix dnej" (The malice of men and blind fortune lay in wait for both of us / At the very dawn of our days [PSS VI: 23–24]). Slander and betrayal precipitated the psychological crisis which brought the demon to Puškin's door, the spirit of negation and doubt. It is not surprising that he attributes the same experiences to Onegin, although there is nothing in Chapter I to substantiate the declaration.

Evidently, Puškin at first conceived of the conversations between Onegin and Lenskij as an opportunity for the demon to exercise his fascination. "Kto žil i myslil, tot ne možet v duše ne prezirat' ljudej / . . . vse èto často pridaet / Bol'šuju prelest' razgovoru" (He who has lived and thought cannot / But despise people in his heart / . . . all this often lends / A great charm to the conversation [PSS VI: 24]). The poem "The Demon" refers to "stinging speeches" ("ego jazvitel'nye reči"). In the drafts to

Chapter II we find the lines "ja neopisannuju sladost' / V ego besede nax-odil" (I took indescribable delight in his talk [Medvedeva 1941: 65]). "Sperva Onegina jazyk menja smuščal" (at first Onegin's talk disconcerted me [PSS VI: 24])—this remark from Chapter I is the only hint of the disturbing nature of the new friendship between the poet and Onegin. But Onegin's demonic traits do not really emerge until Lenskij enters the scene, that is, until Puškin creates a character from his past self to bear the brunt of Onegin's influence. The poet himself has moved on and sees the pair from a distance. The naive Lenskij replaces the poet as the demon's friend. Only the drafts have digressions in first person that Puškin recasts into poems such as "The Demon," digressions that remind us how close the poet originally was to his character, the poet Lenskij. "*Mne* bylo grustno, tjažko, bol'no" (It made *me* sad). The demonic skepticism is a caustic that eats away at all ideals—love, friendship, freedom. Lenskij is a believer and an innocent: "On serdcem milyj byl nevežda" (He was a dear ignoramus at heart [PSS VI: 34]). His characterization in Chapter II.8 stresses just those articles of faith which the demon mocks: romantic love expressing elective affinities, devoted friendship, the fellowship of genius. Note also the iden-tification of all this with "poetry." Cf. Puškin: "Byvalo v sladkom osleplen'e / Ja veril izbrannym dušam" (Once in sweet blindness / I be-lieved in chosen spirits [PSS II: 1: 294]).

But Lenskij is constructed as a "pure" poet, unlike the persona of the author; for Lenskij, Onegin is an opposite, not a double. (See the drafts: Lenskij "ne slavil seti sladostrast'ja . . . " [didn't praise the snares of con-cupiscence] [PSS VI: 270]). The demonic in *Eugene Onegin* is rather toned down in Chapter II—Onegin, though jaded himself, does not attempt to disillusion Lenskij: "On oxladitel'noe slovo / V ustax staralsja uderžat" (He tried to hold back the chilling word upon his lips); "Snosnee mnogix byl Evgenij . . . I včuže čuvstvo uvažal" (Eugene was more decent than most . . . and respected feeling in others) (PSS VI: 37–38). Eugene's sup-pressed passion and his disdain for altruistic values are relegated to the drafts.

Но вырывались иногда
Из уст его такие звуки
Такой глубокий, чудный стон . . . (PSS VI: 562)

But sometimes there escaped
From his lips such sounds,
Such a marvelous, deep moan . . .

Хоть думал, что добро, законы
Любовь к отечеству, права—одни условные слова . . . (PSS VI: 561)

Though he thought that the good, the law,
Patriotism and rights were nothing but empty words . . .

What happened was a purging of the demonic. Only the author's mocking irony toward Lenskij's idealism remains. In the lyrics: "Vzgljanul na mir ja vzorom jasnym . . . Uželi on kazalsja mne / Stol' veličavyim i prekrasnym?" (I looked with clear eyes at the world . . . Could it really have seemed to me / So magnificent and so beautiful? [PSS II: 1: 293]). Of Lenskij:

> Цель жизни нашей для него
> Была заманчивой загадкой,
> Над ней он голову ломал
> И чудеса подозревал. (PSS VI: 34)

> For him the aim of our life
> Was an enticing riddle,
> He wracked his brains over it
> And suspected wonders.

Lenskij is not aware that a demon is near. The demonic side of Onegin emerges only as the plot progresses—foreshadowed in Tat'jana's dream and revealed in the duel, Onegin's demonic betrayal of love and friendship.

What "The Demon" did in a nutshell was to add conflict, struggle, and drama to the static disillusionment of *The Prisoner of the Caucasus*. In a poem such as "Ty prav, moj drug" (You're right, my friend) of fall 1822, the transition from youth to embittered experience is unmotivated: "No vse prošlo!—ostyla v serdce krov', / V ix nagote ja nyne vižu / I svet, i žizn', i družbu i ljubov' " (But all is over!—the blood has cooled within. / I now see in their nakedness, / The world, and life and friendship and love [PSS VI: 265]). When the Demon appears, he objectifies the feeling "I am a different person, something else has taken possession of me." Without the separation of a Demon, plot is hardly conceivable. Only when a conflict has been discovered can the situation progress further, and *Onegin* is one of the works through which this conflict is clarified and played out. As has often been observed, in the writing of the lyric Puškin quickly goes from fascination by the Demon to a sense of sad oppression by him; he no longer declares their existences to be united forever (Lakšin 1979: 142; Ospovat 1986: 186). In Chapter I of *Onegin* the author's closeness to his demon is already in the past, and attached to particular circumstances: "S nim podružilsja ja v to vremja" (I became friends with him at that time [Ospovat 1986: 172]). Puškin's treatment of the demonic would pass through several more stages ("A Scene from *Faust*," "The Angel," "Devils"). The novel breaks off on an "ill moment" for Onegin. After Tat'jana makes her exit, he stands "thunderstruck," a parody of Don Juan. The seducer is foiled, and the spirit of denial and doubt is himself cast into confusion. At the same time, however, during the Boldino autumn of 1830, in *Kamennyj gost'* (The Stone Guest) another "demon in love" is left more tragically perplexed with his demonic aura intact (Cjavlovskaja 1960: 125).

But *Onegin* had to originate from a demonic fascination. His hold on the imagination was inexplicable and unsanctioned. For Puškin, at least in his early years, the very workings of the imagination could well hold something demonic. Remembering his beginnings as a poet, in the "Conversation of the Bookseller with the Poet," the preface to Chapter I of the novel, Puškin speaks of the "demon" who had pursued him, whispering the marvelous sounds of poetry:

> Какой-то демон обладал
> Моими играми, досугом;
> За мною всюду он летал,
> Мне звуки дивные шептал,
> И тяжким, пламенным недугом
> Была полна моя глава. (1824, PSS II: 1: 325)

> Some demon possessed
> My games and leisure;
> He flew after me everywhere,
> Whispered marvelous sounds to me,
> And my head was filled
> With this grave, burning malady.

As Onegin was ending, in another reminiscence of first youth, Puškin wrote "v načale žizni školu pomnju ja" (I recall school in the beginning of life, 1830), with its two mysterious pagan "demons" ("To bylo dvux besov izobražen'ja . . . Bezvestnyx naslaždenij temnyj golod / Menja terzal . . . vse kumiry sada / Na dušu mne svoju brosali ten' " [There were the representations of two demons . . . The dark hunger of undiscovered pleasures / Tormented me . . . All the idols of the garden / Cast their shadow upon my soul] [PSS III: 1: 255]). Ospovat is right to say that "love and art had entered Puškin's life full of demonic charm" (1986: 193).

At this point it may be useful to provide at least a schematic picture of where the remaining chapters of *Onegin* fall in the progression of the rest of Puškin's work. Chapter III of *Onegin*, "Baryšnja" (The Young Lady), was written in alternation with *The Gypsies*; both cover the period approximately January—October 1824. Although Chapter IV was begun soon after, *Boris Godunov* consumed most of 1825, and Puškin laid aside *Onegin* for nearly a year, returning to finish Chapter IV at the end of 1825. As he completed Chapter IV he also wrote *Count Nulin* (December 13–14, 1825). We might note that the so-called Odessa stanzas of Onegin's Journey date to 1825 as well. The year 1826 marked a rededication to *Eugene Onegin*: Chapters V and VI were written in their entirety over the course of the year, although Puškin continued to polish Chapter VI into 1827. Some of Chapter VII was written in 1827, alternating with work on the unfinished "Arap Petra Velikogo" (Blackamoor of Peter the Great) (August-

September). In 1827, however, Chapter VII differed from its present form. Most important, it was projected to include Onegin's Journey. It began directly from Tat'jana's journey to Moscow and did not as yet contain the introductory reflections on the fate of Lenskij or Tat'jana's visit to Onegin's library. Early in 1828, Puškin revised Chapter VII, writing the opening stanzas and reaching the point of insertion for Onegin's journey, but he apparently changed his mind and finished the chapter without it. Work on the final version of Chapter VII was completed on November 4, 1828.

In the meantime, Puškin had dedicated much of the year to *Poltava* (April-October) and worked sporadically at fragments for society tales. In March 1828 he had published Chapter VI of *Eugene Onegin* as "the end of part I"—the reader remembers the summarizing reflections concluding Chapter VI, "Daj ogljanus'" (Let me look back), an apparent semi-cadence. Presumably, the plan was for another six chapters. Off and on in 1829, Puškin worked on Onegin's Journey, as a separate chapter then called Chapter VIII. The best evidence is that the so-called Decembrist stanzas which Puškin eventually enciphered, and which have become known as fragments of Chapter X, were originally part of Onegin's Journey and date to 1829. At the same time he wrote his own travel diary, "Voennaja gruzinskaja doroga" (Georgian Military Road), the cycle of poems based on the same journey, and, on his return, the unfinished "Novel in Letters" along with some of "Rusalka" (The Water Nymph) and the fragment *Tazit*. Chapter VIII as Onegin's Journey was finished only in 1830, during the first Boldino autumn. By that time, Puškin hesitated between two plans, finishing *Onegin* in nine chapters or excluding the Journey entirely and doing the novel in eight, as attested by the draft preface to the final chapters (PSS V: 547–49).

Ultimately, he excluded the Journey, working some necessary transitional material on Onegin into the last chapter, today's Chapter VIII. We now have only fragments of Onegin's Journey left. Chapter VIII, begun in late December 1829, was completed along with the Journey at Boldino on September 25, 1830, though Puškin did revise it later. *Onegin* seemed to be finished. Puškin noted that he had "burned Chapter X," some of which he nevertheless enciphered. However, on October 5, 1831, Puškin put the final touch to the novel by writing Onegin's letter to Tat'jana. There is no evidence that Puškin ever wrote any material for further chapters of *Onegin*. We have no text, only the legend that Onegin was to have perished either with the Decembrists or in the Caucasus. The most that we can say is that there is the published *Eugene Onegin* such as we know it, and that there existed the undeveloped idea for an Onegin not for publication.

Puškin's rhythm of composition in writing *Eugene Onegin* is schematically represented in the table. It is worth highlighting certain facts. The "first half" of the novel up to the climax of Onegin's duel with Lenskij came relatively easily—Chapters I, II, III in quick succession, a break for *Boris Godunov*, and then Chapters IV, V, VI. The years 1823 and 1826 were

Eugene Onegin: Rhythm of Composition

I, II, III	1823 I, II
	1824 III
break IV	1825 IV
V, VI	1826 V, VI
VII	1827 VII
break	1828 VII
Journey	1829 Journey
VIII	1830 Journey, VIII
	1831 Onegin's letter

particularly intense, with two chapters each. It was the *razvjazka* or resolution that came hard. Puškin spent two years on Chapter VII, two on Onegin's Journey. Actually, the question of how to deal with the Journey occupied him for all four years, since originally it was to be part of Chapter VII. There was a break for *Poltava*, then the Journey and Chapter VIII. In 1830 Puškin again wrote two chapters, bringing *Onegin* to a close. Toward the end he had reconceptualized its structure as a novel in three parts (see his balance sheet from Boldino, 1830): Part I—I, II, III; Part II—IV, V, VI; Part III—VI, Journey, VIII (PSS VI: 532). In terms of plot dynamics, Part I corresponds to the development, including Tat'jana's letter; Part II corresponds to the climax, including Onegin's answer and the duel with Lenskij; Part III covers the consequences or aftermath. The development of the novel was closely intertwined with Puškin's life: Chapters I, II, III were written in southern exile on the basis of reminiscences of Petersburg and country life. No sooner had Onegin been sent to the provinces than Puškin was dispatched there himself; the "country chapters," IV, V, and VI, were written at Mixajlovskoe. In September 1826 Puškin returned to Moscow from exile, and Chapters VII, the Journey, and VIII follow his peregrinations—Moscow, the journey of 1829, and the return to Petersburg society. The rhythm of *Eugene Onegin* thus reflects both the rhythm of Puškin's life and the rhythm of his creative work.

Only the second concerns us here. The four contexts for Onegin which have received the most attention (man of the world, demon, journey, farewell and homecoming) speak mostly to the beginning and the end of the novel. Some work, however, has been done on the middle chapters in their creative setting, much of it by L. D. Sidjakov (1977), which unfortunately I will not be able to consider here. Solovej has advanced the view that it was while working on Chapter VII (in October 1828) that Puškin decided on a nine-chapter plan for the novel. At least the plan for an edition of Puškin's works prepared in February-March 1829 seems to reflect this (1977: 109). Onegin's Journey, initially conceived, according to D'jakonov, as the "leisurely introduction to the second half of the novel" (1982: 97) (that is, Chapter VII of XII), was displaced from Chapter VII to Chapter VIII of IX and finally to fragments which found a place as an extended footnote to the final chapter, today's Chapter VIII. Chapter VII now dealt with the end of the Lenskij-Ol'ga plot and with Tat'jana (Solovej 1977: 103). Puškin had provided a point of transition to Onegin's Journey in Chapter VII after Tat'jana's reflections on his library (PSS VI: 442). This was a possibility in late October 1828 (after *Poltava*).

However, very soon, probably within the week, Puškin had rejected this solution. About the same time Puškin was also considering what to do with Onegin's Album. The Journey and the Album, like the sequence in Onegin's library, were both devices for the self-revelation of the hero. Lotman now speculates that the famous enciphered stanzas of Chapter "X," which probably derived from the Journey, are written from Onegin's point of view, in his voice, and perhaps were part of his diary. The hero is not named, and Puškin is mentioned once in the third person (1986: 140). Simultaneously, Puškin excluded both the Album and the inner transition to the Journey from Chapter VII (Solovej 1977: 106–107). Now it is Tat'jana's Journey to Moscow which occupies the analogous position. Puškin's final plan for the close of Chapter VII ended with the following items: "Doroga, Moskva, General, Odessa" (The Road, Moscow, the General, Odessa [Solovej 1977: 107]). That is, the Odessa stanzas, "Ja žil togda v Odesse pyl'noj" (Then I lived in dusty Odessa), etc., as a final digression in Chapter VII, were to lead into Onegin's Journey, Chapter VIII, which would bring the hero and the poet together after their separation in Chapter I. But the Odessa stanzas were to migrate further. As for Onegin's Album, which Puškin excluded, Solovej has suggested that it became the germ for the development of Onegin in Chapter VIII (1977: 113–14). Thus, Chapter VII had simply been too big, and it had anticipated too much too soon. The Journey and Chapter VIII grew out of it. This inner evolution accompanied Puškin's return to *Eugene Onegin* after *Poltava*.

We do not have the complete manuscripts to Onegin's Journey. The "Odessa stanzas" had existed since 1825. Levkovič has noted (following Cjavlovskaja 1960) that on his way to the Caucasus Puškin gave a copy of Scott's *Ivanhoe* to the Poltoratskijs, with inscriptions including part of a stanza to the so-called Chapter X. This confirmed D'jakonov's hypothesis that the "Decembrist" stanzas were first meant for the Wanderings chapter (then Chapter VIII) and were written in Petersburg before Puškin's departure for the Caucasus (1986: 249). The enciphered stanzas could have provided the ideological motivation for Onegin's journey of discovery in his own land, whose first episode is a journey from Saint Petersburg to Moscow. In other drafts to the Journey, Puškin initially gave him a civic impulse—*Mel'mot* wittily rhymed with *patriot*: "Naskuča ili slyt' Mel'motom / Il' maskoj ščegoljat' inoj / Prosnulsja raz on patriotom" (Tired of being known as Melmoth / Or sporting some other mask / He woke up one day a patriot [PSS VI: 495]). The manuscripts that we have for the Journey date to Puškin's return from Arzrum, when in the fall of 1829 he disengaged himself from his Caucasian impressions and returned to *Onegin*. Note the continuity with the end of Chapter VII, Tat'jana's arrival in Moscow, and the narrator's Moscow impressions. Levkovič suggests that in fall 1829 Puškin removed the patriotic aureole from his hero's Moscow life. His journey thus will not fit him to be reborn as a political activist. (But Puškin marked the Melmoth Stanza "to Chapter X" in 1830.)

This changed perspective coincides significantly with Puškin's return from Arzrum to his *ingrata patria*, from a journey which began in the desire to rejoin his Decembrist friends on the battlefield but which turned out to be a sequence of anti-climaxes. The hero of the *Journey to Arzrum*, a work based on the impressions of 1829, is driven by his "demon." There, too, we often seem to hear the refrain of Onegin's Journey: "toska, toska!" (anguish, anguish!). For Puškin, the journey to Arzrum was also a journey into reminiscence, back to *The Prisoner of the Caucasus* and lost youth, a revisiting of scenes of romantic inspiration. Work on Onegin's Journey broke off at a psychological turning point, after taking Onegin to the Caucasus and the Crimea: "Kakie čuvstva ne tailis' / Togda vo mne—teper' ix net. / Oni prošli il' izmenilis' . . . / Mir vam, trevogi prošlyx let!" (Whatever feelings I then cherished—they are no more. / They are gone or changed . . . / Peace unto you, cares of bygone years [PSS VI: 200]). Puškin returned to the Journey a year later, in the Boldino autumn of 1830. In early November 1829, after a break, he had written his last lines of that year for the Journey, the stanza "Ne dolgo vmeste my brodili" (Not long did we wander together [PSS VI: 505; Levkovič 1986: 264]), which prepares for Onegin's return to Petersburg and the narrator's journey to Mixajlovskoe (PSS V: 564). This stanza presupposed the Odessa stanzas, completing Onegin's sequence Caucasus, Crimea, Odessa, and keeping him ever one step behind the narrator. It was the natural transition to Chapter VIII, "High Society," which Puškin began shortly.

If Onegin's Journey represented the wanderings of Melmoth turned patriot, Puškin was simultaneously exploring the spiritual itinerary of the Russian prodigal son. Petrunina has noted the parallel between Onegin's Journey (along with Vjazemskij's "Stancija" [The Station]) and Puškin's fragment "Zapiski molodogo čeloveka" (Notes of a Young Man). She comments that ennui links Onegin and the youth, though the causes of it in each are quite different (1986: 79–80). As the predecessor of the narrator in "The Stationmaster," the youth is the first to view the parable of the prodigal son in pictures. Petrunina remarks that the theme of the road or journey ("dorožnaja tema") is a crucial one in Puškin's work of the late 1820s and early 1830s and becomes especially active under the influence of the journey to Arzrum (1986: 79–80).

The journey to Arzrum had led Puškin once again to his demon, "demon neterpen'ja" (the demon of impatience [PSS VIII: 1: 462]). Compare Onegin: "I žit' toropitsja, i čuvstvovat' spešit" (He hastens to live and hurries to feel [PSS VI: 5]). The draft to the poem "Besy" (Demons) dates to the return from Arzrum, the second half of September 1829 (Levkovič 1986:

276; revised Sept. 7, 1830). It is significant that the demons appear on the road, to the traveler. In fact, devils lead him into the storm, but these devils are themselves in torment in the final version. About two months later, Puškin wrote his note on Goethe and Byron, putting the lesser demon firmly in his place. "Goethe had a great influence on Byron. Faust troubled the imagination of the creator of *Childe Harold*. Several times he tried to wrestle with this giant of romantic poetry but kept limping behind" (Levkovič 1986: 267, emended text). We note that Puškin does not belittle *Faust* itself. He well understood the restless spirit, ever striving, never happy in the moment, goaded by his ennui instead of deadened by it. To the extent that this is Faust, there is something Faustian in Onegin's Journey, an element that is compositionally unresolved.

Čumakov tries to argue against D'jakonov and with Tynjanov that the fragments from a journey are actually the end or "last lines" of Onegin, the "real finale of the novel on a par with the finale of Chapter VIII" (1976: 9). Graphically, they do follow the body of the text, appearing in the footnotes. This conception appeals to the modern reader; the form becomes open-ended and cyclical (returning us to the end of Chapter I). However, the conscientious reader does not actually arrive at the Journey last; he mentally inserts it where the footnote falls within Chapter VIII, a position which reflects Puškin's decision to telescope the journey into a background element for the final chapter. The effort to see the Journey as following Onegin's last interview with Tat'jana instead of preparing his return to Petersburg is meant to buttress the "Decembrist" interpretation of the novel whereby Onegin seeks a worthy alternative to ruined love or at least accomplishes "closure" by his death. Although it amounts to a major change in plan, this might make some sense if Puškin had not persisted in placing the Journey as the penultimate chapter as late as September 1830, when writing his last preface to *Onegin*, and if he had not assigned the fragments the role of footnote to Chapter VIII. A less doubtful hypothesis is that the Journey seemed to motivate whatever might have followed from *Onegin* and established a historical dynamic for future events. The exclusion of the Journey chapter from *Onegin*, because of the frankness with which it treated history and politics, forced the restructuring of the novel and effectively closed the door on its development. D'jakonov maintains that the Journey was meant to lead up to December 1825 and beyond, and when it could not, Puškin omitted it as the "gun which didn't go off," to use Čexov's argument for artistic economy (1982). Yet Puškin attempted to keep the Journey as Chapter VIII in a finished text of nine chapters for publication, after drawing up his balance sheet and writing seven years, four months, seventeen days as the "bottom line." He certainly sacrificed it reluctantly, probably in 1831 after personal censorship by Nicholas.

But didn't Puškin mean to use at least part of the Journey as the basis for further chapters to *Onegin*? Yes and no. The question of a tenth chapter or continuation of *Onegin* is a controversial one. Puškin's preface of 1830 remarks pregnantly, "Here are two more chapters of *Onegin*—the last, at least for print . . . " (PSS VI: 541). This was after Puškin had jotted in the margin of the manuscript to "The Snowstorm," "Burned Canto X" (PSS VIII: 1: 622). Puškin had marked the "Melmoth-into-patriot" stanza for transposition "to Canto X" (PSS VI: 496). He recited some of the enciphered stanzas to his friends, who thought that they were hearing material for a projected Chapter X. These stanzas originated as part of the Journey. Both their time of composition as evidenced by the *Ivanhoe* inscription of 1829 and their place in the inner chronology of the novel convince us this is so (they discuss conditions in Russia up to 1823, when Onegin and the narrator were to meet again in Odessa). D'jakonov has argued persuasively that Chapter X was a shortlived conception and that all we have is what Puškin extracted from Onegin's Journey. When he saw, it seems in 1831, that it would be impossible to publish the Journey as he wished, the Journey and Chapter X again fell together (D'jakonov 1963: 60–61).

The commonplace has been that Puškin does not sufficiently prepare the reader for Tat'jana's transformation from provincial girl to mistress of Petersburg salon, although he does motivate her changed view of Onegin through the library episode. Yet, without the Journey, we realize that Onegin's life from the duel to the moment when he amazedly recognizes Tat'jana is a total blank. His transformation in Chapter VIII is equally abrupt. But we must admit that whatever Puškin sacrificed in the Journey, its remaining drafts and fragments do not serve to advance the plot. The Journey, punctuated by the refrain "toska, toska," simply returns Onegin to his point of departure. No doubt, Puškin regretted the waste of such good material, and the cipher shows that he hoped to make use of it in the future. As Tomaševskij reports, perhaps fragmentary lines found by Bondi in Puškin's last notebook show that in 1834 or 1835 Puškin was still working on a Chapter X, but perhaps he was just adapting it, using viable material from it as he had for the 1830 poem "Geroj" (The Hero) (Tomaševskij 1961: 226).

The important thing, as sober-minded scholars have long recognized, is, in Lotman's words, that "we do not really know what the so-called tenth chapter of *Eugene Onegin* represents. If you think of it, the text is very strange and in many ways unlike the texture of the rest of the novel. Habit makes the contemporary reader perceive the remaining parts of 'Chapter X' as an unqualified apology for Decembrism" (1986: 149). Tomaševskij, too, had said that where Puškin was tending with Chapter X was hardly clear (1961: 234).

The only text that we have for *Onegin* ends with Chapter VIII, subtitled "High Society" (*bol'šoj svet*), in Puškin's 1830 summation. The society setting, the issue of the social self, and the genre of the society tale are all involved. High society exerts a contradictory push and pull upon the author, who first idealizes Tat'jana's salon but then comes to satirize the rest of its inhabitants. Solovej (1977) has shown that in the relevant stanzas, Puškin first makes use of his "Letter to the Editor of the *Literary Gazette*," a document reflecting his views as one of the party of literary aristocrats. According to Solovej, the next stage of work on the society setting fell in 1831 and was influenced by "Moja rodoslovnaja" (My Genealogy), that is, by Puškin's polemics with the *novaja znat'* or *parvenu* aristocracy. The author's efforts to define the society which he wished to create, on the one hand, and to distance himself from society as it existed, on the other, ran parallel to his explorations in the genre of the society tale begun in 1828 with fragments such as "Gosti s"ezžalis' na daču" (The Guests Gathered at the Dacha). Sidjakov has written that in the dialectic of Puškin's work, the idea for the society tale which appeared in conjunction with the development of *Onegin* returned to influence Chapter VIII (1977: 120, 124). In the context of the society tale, the hero, who is very much his social persona, "l'homme du monde malheureux" (PSS VIII: 2: 554), contrasts with the woman, much more the creature of her passionate nature. Their heroine is, as Axmatova put it, the "anti-Tat'jana." She strays into Chapter VIII in stanza xvi, where the brilliant Nina Voronskaja sits next to Tat'jana without eclipsing her neighbor. Yet Chapter VIII is emphatically not a society tale; that is its secret. Tat'jana has made herself the mistress of social convention, not its slave, although her nature remains intact. As for the unhappy man of the world, Onegin, no predictable liaison awaits him. His situation is more like that of the Prince in "The Water Nymph." The simple girl has become a queen, and now the hero, after abandoning her for his social role, desires her. But he has found true love too late. This motif also binds Chapter VIII of *Onegin* with Puškin's *Stone Guest*, another product of the Boldino autumn of 1830 (Axmatova 1977: 189). In the last chapter of *Onegin*, the man of the world and the demon both turn out to be masks.

But what if we pass from the story of the heroes to the end of the poet's novel which encompasses it and ask how that lyrical frame emerges? As the journey modulated into the final Petersburg chapter, Puškin's lyrics took a similar turn. On December 23, 1829, he was still writing an *invitation au voyage*, "Poedem, ja gotov" (Let us go, I am ready), the day before beginning Chapter VIII. But starting the next day, December 24, he changed direction, returning to his first home, in reminiscences of the Lyceum and working through a translation of Southey's "Hymn to the Penates," the spirits of home. He questions his final destination ("Brožu li ja . . . " [Wherever I roam . . .]) hoping to find his resting place close to familiar abodes. Where am I going, what is my home, where is my end? These are the meditations that accompany the beginning of Chapter VIII (Levkovič 1986: 267–68). The retrospective digression that opens the chapter, which also begins with memories of the Lyceum, reflects this movement toward summation. By the end of Chapter VIII, the author has bid farewell to *Onegin*, a moment made possible by the conclusion of a long farewell to his own youth and past. It is well known that the mood of *Onegin* is echoed in the haunting series of love elegies from 1830 about the final farewell: "Proščan'e" (Farewell), "Zaklinanie" (Incantation), and "Dlja beregov otčizny dal'noj" (For the shores of a distant homeland). The final stanza of *Onegin* intones, "Inyx už net, a te daleče" (Some are gone and others far away), striking the elegiac note from *The Fountain of Baxčisaraj* which had come to be applied to the fate of the Decembrists. Vetlovskaja has noted that the source of Puškin's lines may well not be Moore (or not only Moore) but Žukovskij's translation of Goethe's dedication to *Faust* (1986: 107). This is remarkable poetic closure. Puškin had modeled his preface to Chapter I on Goethe's *Vorspiel auf dem Theater* (Prologue in the Theater), and now with the final stanzas of his novel he returns to the author's position in *Faust*.

Parting from a work, Puškin naturally arrives at this theme as he finishes *Onegin*: Goethe's sorrowful parting from *Faust*, then Gibbon's "sober melancholy" on penning the last lines of his monumental history. Puškin's poem "Trud" (Labor), written in connection with the completion of *Onegin* on the night of September 25–26, 1830, was based on Gibbon's memoirs. "Mig voždelennyj nastal: okončen moj trud mnogoletnij. / čto ž neponjatnaja grust' tajno trevožit menja?" (The longed-for moment has come: my labor of many years is accomplished. / Why then does an incomprehensible sorrow secretly trouble me? [PSS III: 184; Kibal'nik 1986: 157–58]). The classical meter pays tribute to Gibbon and antiquity and also solemnizes the poetic occasion. Along with the first stanzas of his Chapter VIII, Puškin had written a note on the publication of Gnedič's *Iliad* which reworks his earlier letter to Gnedič of 1825 couched in these terms: "While your ship is sailing into port laden with the riches of Homer, there is no use talking about my Trifle Shop No. 1. I have a lot started, but nothing completed" (Levkovič 1986: 269; emended text). Now that *Onegin* was finished, Puškin measured it one last time against the classics.

In 1833 the first complete edition of the novel came out; in 1835, the second. On each occasion, Puškin attempted to frame a reply to the urgings of his friends—and his publisher—that he go on with the book. As Levkovič puts it, the fragmentary epistles of 1833 and 1835 are the author's Afterword to *Onegin* (1974: 277). One fragment clearly echoes "The Conversation of the Bookseller and the Poet," the Preface to Chapter I. Yet whether Puškin casts his thought in octaves, in Alexandrines, or in the *Onegin* stanza, we hear only the voice of the public and the counsels of expediency. The poet answers nothing, but his irony is evident. *Onegin* has successors in Puškin, but no continuation.

I have tried to present the context of Puškin's works as something like the magic crystal through which he glimpsed *Onegin*. Perhaps, after all, the best image of this magic crystal is the kaleidoscope, in which one form blossoms out of another and finally explodes to collapse and rearrange itself into a shape unforeseen at the beginning. But we have only just begun to distinguish within the kaleidoscope the gemlike bits of glass which play so brilliantly in the light, and to follow a little the hand which turned the cylinder.

STEPHANIE SANDLER

Solitude and Soliloquy in
Boris Godunov

"*They* were the players, and we who had struggled at the game
Were merely spectators, though subject to its vicissitudes
And moving with it out of the tearful stadium, borne on shoulders, at last.
Night after night this message returns . . . "
—John Ashbery, "Soonest Mended"

Praise for Puškin has become a central fact of Russian literary life. Readers admire Puškin's elegant lucidity and return to his poems, plays, and stories in expectation of renewed pleasure and deep satisfaction. Puškin's status as Russia's national poet takes on a daily meaning in this capacity to create a continuing community of readers. Yet some Puškin texts participate uneasily in a tradition where to read Puškin is to fall imperceptibly under his spell. Among the most problematic is the 1825 drama *Boris Godunov*. The play makes difficult the notion of a community of readers for, as I shall explore in this paper, *Boris Godunov* exudes a sense of inexpressible solitude.

Critics have never been quite sure what to do with *Boris Godunov*. At least since Belinskij, most energy has been spent among Puškinists trying to explain why the play was not a popular success and writing commentaries that translate archaic words and track down historical references; there have also been comparative studies, most notably on the Shakespearean elements of *Boris Godunov* (Arxangel'skij 1930; Bayley 1971: 165–85; Gorodeckij 1969; Alekseev 1984: 253–92; and Verxovskij 1937). Each approach has diverted attention away from the text itself: those who seek to explain its failure consider the audience, the construction of stages, the changing political climate; those who write commentaries position themselves as prior to any act of interpretation by doing the work which should make reading easier. My goal is neither to annotate nor to defend *Boris Godunov*, but instead to see how it anticipates these approaches. The play's incomprehensibility, its need for scholarly apparatuses or for comparative studies that seek analogies in other texts—these are effects of its strategies to keep readers at their distance. It is the play's guarantee that *Boris Godunov* will, as a text, have a worldly existence as solitary as that of its central characters and, as I shall suggest at the conclusion of this essay, of Puškin himself at the time he composed the play.

Yet *Boris Godunov* has found its readers, some of them quite certain as to what, if not how, the play means. A standard and influential interpretation among Soviet scholars holds that the play shows Puškin's incipient historical realism, particularly an appreciation for the power of Russia's common folk to change history (Filonov 1899; Gorodeckij 1953). Because of the kind of observations that this interpretation has stressed, a certain avoidance of the play again occurs: more attention is paid to one stage direction, the much-discussed conclusion, where the people (the *narod*) do not hail their new tsar, than to what is said in the preceding twenty-three scenes.[1] During the last ten years, *Boris Godunov* has attracted a less canonical set of readers, some concerned to explain the play's structure (Frejdin 1979), its use of point of view (Poljakov 1978), its generic innovations (Emerson 1986; Nepomnjaščij 1983), its psychological and historical complexity (Aranovskaja 1984; Konick 1982; Rassadin 1977). Although these groupings simplify the rich interpretations of quite diverse scholars, all of whom have brought great intelligence to the play, my intention in pointing to their work is to indicate still another curiosity in the play's reception: modern readers have been drawn to *Boris Godunov*. Some have sensed how its silences have left them so much to say; others have been challenged to make sense of the play because they have felt palpably its resistances to interpretation. Here, indeed, is my concern, which I propose to read in the play's scenes of misunderstanding and misrepresentation. *Boris Godunov* exudes solitude, I suggest, by showing us characters who cannot mean what they say and who thus speak so as to shield their thoughts and feelings from curious listeners.

I turn to *Boris Godunov* in order to ask what kind of audience it imagines for itself, to see how the idea of an audience (or its disappearance) motivates the play's rhetorical and dramatic strategies. My task is to discover how Puškin's representation of particular kinds of listeners transforms the idea of dramatic speech in *Boris Godunov*, both its conversations and its soliloquies. The play is profoundly lyrical, both in its desire to find a language that lets characters bespeak their deepest emotions and in its capacity to transmit to its audience the feelings and attitudes of its author. As a genre, drama arouses expectations of connections among characters on the stage and between spectacle and audience. In *Boris Godunov*, Puškin presents unsuccessful and isolated characters and produces a dramatic structure where conflicts do not lead to confrontation and where the very anxiety about audience is itself an indicator of generic bewilderment. Caryl Emerson (1985) has written beautifully about later plays that "undo" Puškin's *Boris Godunov*, yet the lesson of the play is that it undoes itself. The play does not ignore conventions of connection and community in drama; it shows, repeatedly, their impossibility. As I discuss the rhetorical work of discontinuity in *Boris Godunov*, my purpose is to understand how the play creates a sense that we are as alone when we read it as Puškin was when he wrote it.[2]

Boris Godunov offers guidance to readers in a manner so deft that one might confuse help with intentional bewilderment. This is neither accident nor error, for the assistance emerges in warnings about false signs, false rulers, and true rhetoric. In the opening scenes, one character busily observes another but draws conclusions that are proven wrong; others extravagantly announce their success in penetrating a ruse even as their own words bespeak guile. These exchanges offer readers information, not about the play's events (the speakers are maddeningly elliptical) but about how to read characters' ellipses. There are two lessons: read rhetoric when reference fails, and acknowledge incomprehension rather than feigning understanding.

Consider the talk of two boyar princes, Vorotynskij and Šujskij. In the first scenes, they trade information about what they do not see and cannot yet know. They read the blank spaces around them quite differently: Vorotynskij believes that Boris is reluctant to rule, while Šuiskij insists that the ritual of refusing the throne is a ruse. If told that Boris irrevocably refuses the throne, Šujskij will say: "Skažu, čto ponaprasnu / Lilasja krov' careviča-mladenca; / Čto esli tak, Dimitrij mog by žit' " (PSS VII: 6; "I will say that the blood / Of the infant Tsarevich was spilled in vain; / That if that is so, then Dimitrij could have lived"). Šujskij thus introduces the play's recurrent interest in the death of the Tsarevich: his refusal to provide further information will define the structure of that recurrence. "Kto podkupal naprasno Čepčugova? / Kto podoslal oboix Bitjagovskix / S Kačalovym?" (PSS VII: 6; "Who bribed Chepchugov in vain? / Who sent both Bitjagovskijs/ With Kachalov?"). Here the rhetorical signs are crucial: by creating a chain of rhetorical questions, Šujskij gains the usual advantage of this trope, intensified attention from his listener. Moreover, Šujskij's rhetorical questions turn the issue. They fail to respond to Vorotynskij's direct question (did Boris kill the Tsarevich?), instead substituting more names into a scene where the issue had been only Boris. A short list of proper names swells to fill the gap left by Šujskij's evasion of Vorotynskij's question, yet it is not just a case of fullness covering over emptiness.

"Empty," to be sure, is a crucial epithet in *Boris Godunov*. The play's first sentence includes the phrase "Moskva pusta" (PSS VII: 5; "Moscow is empty"), so that *Boris Godunov* opens with two boyar princes discussing the fact that there is no dramatic spectacle, only their own speculation about an unseen event of momentous political consequence. The stage has had to be emptied in order for the performance to begin. Moscow's throne, too, is empty; what is more, the new tsar will be threatened by a pretender whose appearance implies that a grave is empty. The specter of emptiness haunts *Boris Godunov* and will sometimes force it toward a false sense of plenitude: scenically, when the stage is filled with masses of the Russian people, and rhetorically, in exchanges which are overdetermined because characters have emptied their words of any finite meaning except that which signifies facade.

Such is the case when Šujskij speaks to Vorotynskij about the death of the Tsarevich, only to find that he must undo his allegations against Boris once Boris is named tsar. Šujskij again diverts Vorotynskij from the topic of Dimitrij's death, this time by claiming that he was only pretending to say slanderous things about the Tsar: "A vpročem ja zlosloviem pritvornym / Togda želal tebja liš' ispytat', / Vernej uznat' tvoj tajnyj obraz myslej" (PSS VII: 16; "But in any case I, with made-up slander / Was merely trying to test you, / To know more surely your secret mode of thought"). Penetrating the pretenses of others becomes a necessary form of acquiring power in *Boris Godunov*, and penetration occurs through various forms of denial and passivity: to cite one further instance, retracting what one has just said when it proves troublesome or ineffective is also chosen by Dimitrij when he makes love to Marina near the fountain (scene 15).

Although Šujskij and Vorotynskij seem to teach nothing beyond how not to read events, their evasions and self-corrections are quite instructive. One learns from reading their rhetoric (the lists, the rhetorical questions, the use of epithets) and from comparing them to the play's other exemplary on-stage audiences. Most memorable among these are the Russian people who, in the fourth scene, await Boris's emergence as tsar with an extraordinarily comic sense of their own marginality.[3] The people try to cry and bow on command, acting the part of audience, but Puškin lets their pretense show through: they grope for an onion to help along their tears, or throw down a baby as if it were a stage prop to make it cry with them. The profound realism of these spectators is brought briefly to the foreground when one of them mutters, just before the cheers for Boris close the scene, "A kak nam znat'? to vedajut bojare, / Ne nam četa" (PSS VII: 13; "How should we know? that's for the boyars to know, / We're no match for such a task").

In the Novodevičij Monastery scene, the *narod* comment on their own exclusion from the arenas of power even as they pretend to cheer Boris's ascension to the throne. Because the stage shows us listeners creating their own commentary, while the rise of Boris to power occurs offstage, what Puškin does in the opening of *Boris Godunov* is to dramatize not Boris's drama but the process of trying to "figure out," as the people call it, the drama. We watch mostly those who watch. Audiences and listeners have immense influence not on what takes place in the arenas of public consequence but on how these events come to have meaning. The audience has a hermeneutic function, one could say, which means that the listeners, depending on how they listen and then on how they retell each other what they have heard, control how an event takes on meaning. When we see and hear Boris, in scene 3, the presence of an audience requires his posture of openness, even as his words reveal great falseness.

Boris speaks his first lines with an openness meant to disarm: "Ty, otče patriarx, vy vse, bojare, / Obnažena moja duša pred vami" (PSS VII: 15; "You, father patriarch, all of you, boyar princes, / My soul is bared before you"). The two lines emphasize both the importance of Boris's listeners and his need to have them believe his sincerity. Yet the investiture serves largely to make Boris's legitimacy seem false from the start. His slowness to accept the throne has been discredited by Prince Šujskij ("Boris ešče pomorščitsja nemnogo, / Čto p'janica pred čarkoju vina" [PSS VII: 5; "Boris will wrinkle his brow a bit, / Like a drunkard before a chalice of wine"]); his accession to power was also described allusively as a transgression (directly in Šujskij's tales about the dead Tsarevich, indirectly when Šujskij predicts that Boris will take power—"perešagnet" [PSS VII: 7; "he will step across"], a word in which one hears "perestupit," "he will transgress"). Words intended by Boris to bolster his claims to authenticity forewarn disaster and death. Boris's milieu is, from the beginning, sepulchral. He goes to the coffins of past tsars to pray, a living ruler seeking an authority endowed by the dead: "Teper' pojdem, poklonimsja grobam / Počijuščix vlastitelej Rossii" (PSS VII: 15; "Now let us go and bow before the coffins / Of the deceased rulers of Russia"). All tsars in the Rjurik dynasty would have paid homage to the tombs of their predecessors, but their deference would have signified dynastic continuity. Boris disrupts the legitimate transfer of power from father to son. His desire to derive legitimacy from the dead will be grotesquely literalized in scene five, where the monk Grigorij first hears of the dead Tsarevich, whom he decides to impersonate. Indeed, the ghost of the dead Dimitrij already haunts the coronation scene, where Boris cannot pledge to work for his people without being drawn to a tomb. For Boris, these coffins are yet powerful signifiers, and he vainly invokes their fullness of meaning as if he could incorporate it.[4]

The investiture scene, though its falseness comes partly from its status as a public ritual, prepares for Boris's two soliloquies by establishing that the only self Boris has to reveal is one driven by fear of its own inauthenticity. Soliloquies are rare in *Boris Godunov*. In a play in which the *dramatis personae* engage in elaborate acts of pretense, the actors demand an on-stage audience for whom they consciously perform, and the readers or viewers benefit from that internal audience as it guides them in deciphering the actors' ambiguous behavior and speech. What is remarkable about Boris's first soliloquy ("Dostig ja vysšej vlasti" ["I have attained the highest power"]), as well as his second, shorter one, is that he provides his own audience.

Boris begins the first soliloquy by a kind of clearing away of all distractions, which works much like the emptying of the stage that begins *Boris Godunov*. The speech opens with a recognition of emotional emptiness: achieved glory yields no pleasure. One thus expects a moment of introspection, an exploration of why, after six years of rule, Boris still feels like a failure. The morbid tone of the speech and its omnipresent allusions to death more than answer that question, but a sense persists that Boris is using language to conceal rather than to reveal.

One source is the intrusion of an audience into this private moment.

Boris's long lament about his failed attempts to win his subjects' love and loyalty sounds like someone seeking pity from his listener.

> Мне счастья нет. Я думал свой народ
> В довольствии, во славе успокоить,
> Щедротами любовь его снискать—
> Но отложил пустое попеченье:
> Живая власть для черни ненавистна.
> Они любить умеют только мертвых—
> Безумны мы, когда народный плеск
> Иль ярый вопль тревожит сердце наше!
> Бог насылал на землю нашу глад,
> Народ завыл, в мученьях погибая;
> Я отворил им житницы, я злато
> Рассыпал им, я им сыскал работы—
> Они ж меня, беснуясь, проклинали!
> Пожарный огнь их домы истребил,
> Я выстроил им новые жилища.
> Они ж меня пожаром упрекали!
> Вот черни суд: ищи ж ее любви. (PSS VII: 26)

> There is no happiness for me. I thought to calm my people
> With satisfaction and glory,
> To attract their love with generosity—
> But I have put aside that empty hope;
> Living power is hateful to the mob.
> They know how to love only the dead—
> We're mad if we let the people's clapping
> Or raging howl disturb our heart!
> God sent famine to our land,
> The people started to wail, they were perishing in torment;
> I opened the granaries to them, scattered
> Gold to them, found them work—
> Then they cursed me in their rage!
> Fires laid waste to their homes,
> So I built them new dwellings.
> Then they reproached me for the fires!
> That is the judgment of the mob: go try to win its love.

Boris catalogues the protective gestures that he has made toward the Russian people, but they see in him a source of harm. The *narod*, as audience, demonstrates here its great interpretive powers, even when they are absent. Boris confirms the decisiveness of their judgments as the morbidity for which he condemns the people infects his own language. As the soliloquy continues, Boris finds his conscience eating away at itself, poisoning his body with the death that seems to be everywhere around him. He twists that which is life-affirming into morbidity and failure, especially in the second half of the soliloquy when he turns from popular adulation to the love of his family. The family would seem a less vexed topic for Boris to explore, but nothing is new as he turns to his family's failures. The metaphors do not change. Death comes like a "storm," thus recalling in a more aggressive way the clapping sound (as of waves against a shore, "plesk") made by the people in the first half of the speech. The crowd itself does not disappear, as its rumors get repeated for more evidence that Boris is forever blamed.

В семье моей я мнил найти отраду,
Я дочь мою мнил осчастливить браком—
Как буря, смерть уносит жениха . . .
И тут молва лукава нарекает
Виновником дочернего вдовства—
Меня, меня, несчастного отца! . . .
Кто не умрет, я всех убийца тайный:
Я ускорил Феодора кончину,
Я отравил свою сестру царицу—
Монахиню смиренную . . . все я!
Ах! чувствую: ничто не может нас
Среди мирских печалей успокоить;
Ничто, ничто . . . едина разве совесть.
Так, здравая, она восторжествует
Над злобою, над темной клеветою—
Но если в ней единое пятно,
Единое, случайно завелося;
Тогда—беда! как язвой моровой
Душа сгорит, нальется сердце ядом,
Как молотком стучит в ушах упрек,
И все тошнит, и голова кружится,
И мальчики кровавые в глазах . . .
И рад бежать, да некуда . . . ужасно!
Да, жалок тот, в ком совесть нечиста. (PSS VII: 26–27)

I imagined finding joy in my family,
I imagined making my daughter happy in marriage—
Like a storm, death carries away the groom . . .
And here rumor slyly censures me
Guilty of my daughter's widowhood—
Me, me, the unlucky father! . . .
No matter who dies, I am everyone's secret murderer:
I hastened Feodor's demise,
I poisoned my sister, the Carica,
The humble nun . . . it is always I!
Ah! I feel it: nothing can soothe us
Amid worldly sorrows;
Nothing, nothing . . . except perhaps conscience alone.
Thus, when healthy, it triumphs
Over malice, over dark slander.
But if there is a single spot on it,
One, it appeared accidentally,

Then—disaster! As if with the plague,
The soul catches fire, poison pours into the heart,
Reproach pounds at the ears like a hammer,
And one is ever sickened, and the head spins,
And there are bloodied little boys before one's eyes . . .
And one would gladly flee, but there is nowhere to go . . . horror!
Yes, piteous is he whose conscience is unclean.

Does the evocation of an audience diminish Boris's courage in naming the causes for his discontent? Boris's evasiveness is eloquent enough an answer. The "spot" on his conscience is represented as only that, a threat so grave that it cannot be named (as were the more preposterous crimes, that Boris "hastened Feodor's demise," poisoned his sister, killed his future son-in-law). The dead Tsarevich is armed with a name too terrible to utter, as Boris will later say to his son (PSS VII: 89). Boris even has trouble settling upon a satisfactory metaphor to represent the death of the Tsarevich figuratively. It is, serially, a "spot," a "plague," a soul on fire, a poison-flooded heart, ears pounded by hammers. This rhetorical display dizzies Boris until bloody children, a near-representation of the dead Dimitrij but, as if to continue the lines' excesses, a multiplicity of children, loom before his eyes.

Boris seems to revel in the horror of his life, but the play reveals in him a sense of interiority that "discovers itself as too monstrous to be revealed."[5] The syntax in the end of the soliloquy contains a revealing clue as to how Puškin creates in Boris a character who wants to flee his own oppressive sense of self. Boris now refers to himself in the accusative case for the first time, and then repeatedly, as if literalizing the etymological hint of accusation in the name for this grammatical category (*vinitel'nyi*). The accusations intensify a sense of guilt, but with them responsibility becomes easier to evade. Rather than sentences that place Boris as the agent of his actions, the play gives us sentences where things are done to him. He is the victim of the dead little boys' dizzying appearance rather than the possible cause of their death.

As the judgment of the *narod* was disruptive in the first half of the speech, so self-judgment is Boris's fear in the end. At the conclusion of the speech he stops beginning his sentences with "I" and avoids self-reference altogether.[6] In the last line, he talks about conscience as if it could be anyone else's, and increases the distance between himself and his words when he feels pity for "him" who has an unclean conscience. From first person, through sentences where he is the victim of others' actions, to impersonal constructions, Boris finally brings himself around to a self-conceptualization which divorces its pathos from any admission of self-reference. The shift to a third-person outcry about pity makes us hear that last line ("Da, žalok tot, v kom sovest' nečista" ["Yes, piteous is he whose conscience is unclean"]) either as Boris talking about someone else or as if someone else were speaking about Boris. What Puškin has done, then, in

Boris's first soliloquy, is to take apart the conventions of dramatic soliloquy: the actor speaks, but as if about someone else. He is alone, but overcome by his thoughts of an audience. Rather than revealing himself to himself, he has performed a spectacle of his desire to flee from the self he is too frightened to confront.

In Boris's second soliloquy, the final line of which is "Ox, tjažela ty, šapka Monomaxa!" (PSS VII: 49; "Oh, you are heavy, crown of Monomax!"), there is less opportunity for evasiveness. Boris has just heard that a young man claiming to be Dimitrij has appeared in Poland, and he is terrified. The final line would immediately seem much less a distancing summation than an impersonal conclusion about an unclean conscience.

> Ух, тяжело!.. дай дух переведу . . .
> Я чувствовал: вся кровь моя в лицо
> Мне кинулась—и тяжко опускалась . . .
> Так вот зачем тринадцать лет мне сряду
> Все снилося убитое дитя!
> Да, да—вот что! теперь я понимаю.
> Но кто же он, мой грозный супостат?
> Кто на меня? Пустое имя, тень—
> Ужели тень сорвет с меня порфиру,
> Иль звук лишит детей моих наследства?
> Безумец я! чего ж я испугался?
> На призрак сей подуй—и нет его.
> Так решено: не окажу я страха—
> Но презирать не должно ничего . . .
> Ох, тяжела ты, шапка Мономаха! (PSS VII: 49)

> Oh, this is oppressive! . . . let me catch my breath . . .
> I felt it: all my blood rushed
> To my face and then heavily receded . . .
> So this is why for thirteen years in a row
> I keep dreaming about a murdered child!
> Yes, yes—this is it. Now I understand,
> But who is he, my terrible adversary?
> Who is against me? An empty name, a shade—
> Will a shade really tear the porphyry from me,
> Or a sound deprive my children of their inheritance?
> I am a madman! What am I afraid of?
> Just blow on this ghost—and he will vanish.
> So it is resolved: I will show no fear—
> Though one should not disdain anything . . .
> Oh, you are heavy, crown of Monomax!

Boris gazes inward and momentarily finds a peculiar satisfaction in the sure knowing of what he beholds. He is, indeed, as badly off as he had previously feared. Earlier dreams of murdered children are now interpreted as foreshadowing. Paradoxically, Boris is relieved that his apprehensions were justified, even though the satisfaction of knowing that nightmares were not causeless brings a heightened sense of anxiety about Dimitrij.

As soon as Boris looks beyond himself, however, all certainty vanishes. Questions overpower the exclamations of the first six lines. Boris mixes rhetorical with genuine questions, so confused is he in stance. He cannot distinguish syntactically between what he wants to know (who is he? why am I afraid?) and what he wishes to persuade himself to believe (that Dimitrij, because "shade" or "sound," cannot possibly deny Boris his right to rule). How can Boris believe that he understands anything at all? Boris's speech turns back upon itself in a way which once again denies him any authentic power as a speaker. He claims to understand the significance of his recurring dream, but he denounces as void of significance the very event that has enabled his apparent comprehension. As in the first soliloquy's avoidance of the death in Uglič, the Tsar cannot here name the pretender. Dimitrij, the enemy, is an empty name, a shade, a sound and a ghost. "Ghost" and "shade" recall the ubiquitous dead child. Dimitrij is also a "terrible adversary" (*groznyi supostat*), where the word "terrible" repeats the epithet for Ivan the "Terrible," as if Dimitrij were himself of royal lineage.

The "empty name" and the "sound" define the False Dimitrij (as opposed to the dead child) as someone who has no identifiable origin or name, as a mystery devoid of knowable significance. Both words ("empty name" and "sound") are empty shells, ghostlike in their own linguistic vagueness, suggestions of Boris's vain belief that Dimitrij the Pretender has no personality which will win him followers, only the magnet of a rumored identity. There is little space in this play to consider seriously the possibility that the name "Dimitrij" is empty:[7] Everyone, especially Boris, has burdened the name with emotional overtones. It is not the "šapka" ("crown") that is oppressive by the end of the speech, it is the unspeakable name, so that the absence of a specific referent in the opening line, "Ux, tjaželo!" ("Oh, this is oppressive!"), seems in retrospect particularly ominous.

Boris reacts to these various forms of oppressiveness by reasserting an imaginary power over them. He stresses his ability to pretend, to hide his emotions, as part of his strategy. "Ne okažu ja straxa" ("I will show no fear"), he resolves, saying not that he will feel no fear but that he will not show it. The appearance of the pretender is treated as an emotional, not political, crisis, and it is emotional authenticity which Boris reaches for desperately in this scene.

Were there an achievement of emotional intensity here, it would need to be felt in the famous last line, "Oh, you are heavy, crown of Monomax!" Despite its lexicon of weightedness, the exclamation rhetorically seeks an elevated conclusion for the soliloquy. What makes the line so memorable, perhaps, is that it feels both natural and incredibly staged. The line is an effective mechanism of repression by its very tropes. The "crown" lets Boris refer to his imperial power without really naming it in a way that reminds us of his many ways of not naming Dimitrij. The expression "crown of Monomax" already hints at the unmentionable name, since the reference to Vladimir Monomax is also an invocation of the Rjurik dynasty, of which Dimitrij was the last descendant. The "crown" is also significant. Boris refers to Dimitrij's threat as "tearing the porphyry" from him, a more striking usage of almost the same metonymy where costumes stand in for the power they signify. Boris can invoke his power only via articles of clothing, themselves bodily coverings which impersonally signify sovereign might.

When it is heard at last, the epithet "heavy" is also reduced in force by the very echoes that have given it resonance in the play. It recurs a fateful third time: Boris is oppressed by the news of Dimitrij's appearance (I.1); he feels his blood sinking weightily within him (I.3); and he finally exclaims that the symbol of his rulership, his cap, weighs heavily on him (I.14).[8] Elsewhere in the play, the adjective finds several revealing contexts. The monk Pimen uses it with reference to the press of public duties which force tsars to withdraw into monastic seclusion (PSS VII: 20). Pimen's words suggest that where responsibilities become oppressive, they soon end, a possibility which changes the exclamation ("Oh, you are heavy, Crown of Monomax!" from a sigh of exhaustion amid renewed determination into a proleptic vision that Boris's reign will shortly collapse. Perhaps more damning, though, is Boris's investiture speech, where he exclaims, "Skol' tjažela objazannost' moja!" (PSS VII: 15; "How heavy is my obligation!"). The sincerity of that speech was undercut by Šujskij's imputations, and, what is more, rulership is a much-sought-after and very new burden which scarcely could have begun to weigh on the just-named tsar. One wonders, as a result, if the second complaint about feeling oppressed is similarly uttered for dramatic effect. Perhaps not, since the ruling tsar now has cause for complaint, but the complaints are not heard here; they are figured as things as light as a shade or an empty name.

All of which suggests that when Boris tries to bring everything down to a sense of heaviness, we are inclined to disbelieve him, even though his assessment could be made plausible were the speech a different speech. As elsewhere in the play, the audience is at once drawn in by expectations of insight and put off by the inevitable language of self-deception. In its very gesture of summation, distance is imposed in this final line, and what is heard is an attempt at mastery rather than a release of emotion. Boris is frequently aphoristic. Earlier he has told his son that habit is the soul of sovereignty (PSS VII: 90), and Boris, enclosed in his own patterns, eagerly connects habit with might. Epigrammatic discourse presents itself as its own end, and covers a desire for control over a situation which inherently escapes summary.[9] Boris's introspection remains insular, emptied out of any sense of discovery or even disclosure. We read that well-known final

line as if it were an exhalation of breath, a natural release of pent-up
emotion. A physicality normally avoided in the play is nearly suggested in
the speech's emphasis on breath, yet breath is an image which by its very
insubstantiality does not add to Boris's might. Boris wishes to blow Dimitrij away in one breath, and he begins the speech by hoping to catch his
breath. The desires are in both instances paradoxically expressed; both
seek to stifle the rhythm of life despite the suggested "breath" of air.

There is one other bodily detail that subverts Boris's claims to authority and, at the same time, could tell us what it is that makes Boris feel the
crown so heavy on his head. To assure Boris that the child Dimitrij died,
Šujskij has just described his peaceful face. Boris then mentions his own
face as reddened by the blood of emotion. When Boris speaks of the blood
rushing to his own face, he appropriates the image of blood normally reserved for the dead child that his adversary now claims to incarnate. The
dead child's face leads to Boris's face, then to the crown heavy on his head:
the itinerary of description in this speech brings the Tsar ever closer to
identifying with his apparent past victim and imminent adversary.

Such a reading of this soliloquy is dizzying, since nothing could be
more threatening to Boris's sense of self-identity than for a listener to find
in his words the suggestion that he is somehow like Dimitrij. Others have
suggested that Boris, too, is a pretender, thus undermining any possible
sense of authority available to him in the play (Rassadin 1977; Nepomnia-
ščij 1983: 226–31; Emerson 1986: 99–105). Named in the play's title, the
character so obviously framed as the play's hero, Boris seems finally uncomfortable in the limelight. He is at his best when he talks to himself (or
when he seems to, as in the farewell scene with his son), yet in the two
soliloquies, Boris uses his words as much to hide from as to probe the self
he claims to seek. Split into actor and audience, Boris wants to run from
the self who would listen, but, as he himself says, there's nowhere to go.
Listening carefully to his words, watching him consider the possibility of
running away from himself, we as the play's readers gain insight not into
Boris's character but into why the play as a whole is so uncomfortable to
read. The hero would gladly escape from the text, which contains him
oppressively and yet cannot provide him with satisfying means of self-
discovery and self-expression. What we see in Boris, then, we come to
recognize as characteristic of the play in its entirety. He is a character
painfully compressed into roles that he pretends to play while the drama
continually faces him with a self-demanding recognition for its personal
authenticity. The character is, then, an allegory for the play, which, in its
loneliness, seems only to have itself as an audience. There is a further
allegory to be read here, that of Puškin's act of authorship.

Puškin's attitudes toward his audience were in turmoil at the time that
Boris Godunov was written. Biographers have noted the extreme isolation
of Puškin's months of exile in Mixajlovskoe (Lotman 1981: 128), and Puškin's letters amply confirm their judgment. Yet the play's lessons about

solitary acts of speech cannot be ignored: even distant audiences have powers over how one speaks, and even when alone one inevitably speaks before an audience.

The imagination of an audience for *Boris Godunov* was for Puškin problematic and filled with change. A self-consciously innovative work intended to reform the state of Russian theater, *Boris Godunov* could not but feature the sense of an audience learning new lessons about art from its performances.[10] More narrowly, the play might have had personal implications for Puškin's daily life, living as he was in political disfavor. Žukovskij predicted that the play would bring about an end to Puškin's long exile: "Write *Godunov* and things like it: they will open the doors of freedom" (PSS XIII: 271).[11] Puškin is alternately eager to believe such predictions (PSS XIII: 237) and sanguine about the unlikelihood that *Boris Godunov* will bring him public recognition. His rueful comments about his political honesty sticking out of the play like the Holy Fool's ears are well known (PSS XIII: 239–40).

One can conclude, then, that Puškin could not, finally, believe that his play would please an imperial audience. By 1830 he seems to have given up on reaching popular audiences as well. His drafted prefaces for *Boris Godunov* predict its failure, but they re-imagine the play as a success by recalling yet another possible audience. "Written by me in strict isolation, far from society's coldness, the fruit of constant labor, this tragedy has given me everything that a writer is permitted to enjoy: a living and inspired sense of occupation, an inner conviction that I have applied all my forces, and, finally, the approval of a small number of chosen people" (PSS XI:140). There is only one more paragraph in this drafted preface, and it ends with the words "solitary labor."

Puškin thus makes of *Boris Godunov* one long soliloquy, a speech act where the most palpable hearer is the speaker himself, encouraged by thoughts of other hearers (a small circle of friends) but aware that the most intense relationship at hand is between the speaker and his words. Even in 1825 Puškin had foreseen how much he was writing for himself alone: "My tragedy is finished; I reread it aloud to myself and clapped my hands and cried, good for you, Puškin, good for you, you son of a bitch!" (PSS XIII: 239). In this letter to Vjazemskij, Puškin, alone, reads the play for his own pleasure, and claps his hands as if in applause, thus acting out the role of audience. In that single stroke, several apparently separate strands of meaning in *Boris Godunov* come together. Puškin is like the boyars or the *narod*, both focused on the spectacle before him and aware that his own solitary performance is already part of the play; he is like Boris as well, not in the discoveries about self and pretense but in his position as a speaker, strangely alone all the while that imagined audiences impinge upon his words. The speeches written for himself alone will, inevitably, be taken up by others who will see themselves as the play's momentary audience. In its silences and evasions, the play offers readers extraordinary freedom: by showing how actors' speeches make and unmake meanings, *Boris Godunov* invites conclusions not only about history, personality, theater, and pretense, but also about the workings of language itself. *Boris Godunov* may well be a Puškin text that does little to foster a community of readers, but it permits solitary and creative readings that take us a long way toward seeing how complex are all acts of speaking, writing, and listening.

GEORGE J. GUTSCHE

Puškin and Nicholas: The Problem of "Stanzas"

A fascinating issue in biographical studies of Puškin is the poet's relationship with Nicholas I in the years following the Decembrist revolt. The issue serves as a focal point of numerous complex questions, literary and biographical. Scholars are still debating the content, significance, and implications of the famous 8 September 1826 meeting between tsar and poet—a crucial event in Puškin's life. The "facts" are by no means unquestionable—we have a number of accounts (twenty-nine; see Ejdel'man 1985: 193) of varying length; we have Puškin's correspondence, poetry, and other writings, including his "note" on popular education; and we have memoirs of acquaintances and government officials. But all of these materials, which to varying degrees suggest what may have happened during the meeting, are susceptible to an enormous range of interpretation, and in the case of memoir accounts especially, to questions of reliability as well.

The content of the 8 September meeting is just one of the puzzles. Determining Puškin's views about Nicholas and post-Decembrist Russia on the basis of his poetry is even more challenging. Claims that appeal to the facts or the "texts themselves" seem ludicrous when the facts and the texts have so much potential for multiple meanings. Of course, it is just this potential of multiple meanings relating to Puškin's political views that has given his works of these years an enduring vitality and interpretational richness.

Three poems that occupy, even preoccupy, attention for their significance in defining Puškin's political and moral position in the late 1820s are "Stansy" (Stanzas; written in December 1826, printed in *Moskovskij vestnik* [Moscow Herald] in 1828; PSS III: 40), "Vo glubine sibirskix rud . . . " (In the depth of Siberian ores; written in early 1827, and not printed during Puškin's lifetime; PSS III: 49), and "Druz'jam" (To Friends; written in 1828, approved for "circulation" but not publication by Nicholas; PSS III: 89–90). The first poem, referred to here as the epistle to Nicholas, has been viewed as an expression of both Puškin's support of the government and his hopes that Nicholas would follow Peter's example in promoting education (or "enlightenment"), in working hard to fulfill Russia's destiny, and in being firm but at the same time forgiving and merciful. By extension, the poem may be and has been read (by Blagoj 1967; Tomaševskij 1977; Makogonenko 1985; Mejlax 1959; and numerous others) as Puškin's appeal to Nicholas to grant amnesty to the exiled Decembrists.

The second poem, the epistle to the Decembrists, scholars usually view as expressing Puškin's moral support and sympathy for the Decembrists, as well as his confidence that their cause was not totally lost and that their political goals would someday be realized. The third poem, the epistle to "friends," represents the poet's response to accusations that he was ingratiating himself with Nicholas, flattering the sovereign in gratitude for past favors, with the hope of receiving similar favors in the future. The poem not only confronts these accusations directly but also indirectly affirms a program of state action for Nicholas and criticizes the "real" flatterers around him, whose actions and behavior actually harm the state.[1]

The focus of this study is the first of the three poems, the epistle to Nicholas, but the other works of the period, because they are such an important part of the context, will also play a role. By focusing attention on the first of the epistles, I hope to clear an opening into the tangled net of political, literary, and biographical issues that make this period so fascinating and problematic to Puškinists. Moreover, the new reading of "Stanzas" offered here should shed light on the other two poems, especially the epistle to the Decembrists. An underlying thesis of this study is that our understanding and appreciation of these three poems—and in particular the epistle to Nicholas—will benefit from a perspective that assumes "Stanzas" is a complex, multidimensional, poetic text that utilizes subtexts and polysemic potential to achieve several distinctly different purposes. In fact, reducing the poem (or in fact all three of the poems) to a single meaning in order to unify and harmonize Puškin's political views in the post-Decembrist years deprives it of considerable power and effectiveness. "Stanzas" shows Puškin as a careful tactician, using his poetic and linguistic talents to achieve complex literary and extra-literary goals.

Broadly stated, Puškin's "messages" were aimed at two groups. On the one hand, "Stanzas" was designed to encourage Nicholas's pretensions of becoming a new "Peter"; moreover, Puškin exploited the parallel with Peter to direct Nicholas into a moderate attitude toward political dissent. But the poem was also designed to reassure Puškin's liberal friends that he continued to support their goals, was not afraid to mention politically dangerous subjects, and in fact was willing and able to "educate" Nicholas without servility.

That he was not altogether successful in determining the response of all of his readers (both contemporary and of later generations) undoubtedly says more about the sometimes prejudicial assumptions of these readers (and reflects Puškin's underestimation of the good will of the public) than about his verbal skill.

"Stanzas" marked the appearance of a "new" Puškin (Lev Sergeevič Puškin's words, according to the Decembrist Lorer [1984: 205])—no longer the critic of the government and of official religion and author of impious and incendiary verse, but a loyal and grateful supporter of the tsar's new programs who was willing to serve the government with his writing.

After finally being allowed to return from the south of the empire—a punishment meted out by Alexander I which Puškin regarded as overly harsh in view of his "crimes"—Puškin continued his exile at his family estate, Mixajlovskoe, until summoned to Moscow by the new tsar in September of 1826. Although he was not under arrest, he was hardly free to refuse a summons to Moscow. And he could only fear the worst: that his requests to be freed from exile on his estate would be ignored, that he was to be interrogated and accused of complicity with the Decembrists, and that his punishment was to be continued at best in Mixajlovskoe and at worst in Siberia.

The outcome of his unprecedented personal meeting with Nicholas was unexpectedly different:[2] now, instead of exile, Puškin was given relative freedom of movement; now, instead of an even stricter censoring of his works by ignorant and insensitive officials, he had Nicholas as his personal censor; and now, instead of isolation and ignominy, he had social attention and fame. His fortunes were radically reversed, and he was presumably on the threshold of a new life.

Grateful to the new tsar, hopeful about the future, and perhaps with an expectation of playing an important role in regard to the new government (see below), he wrote the five quatrains of "Stanzas" (PSS III: 40). But there is much more than the poet's gratitude and hope reflected in this poem. The analysis that follows will show that its tone, allusions, and various subtexts make it quite different from a servile panegyric:

В надежде славы и добра
Гляжу вперед я без боязни:
Начало славных дней Петра
Мрачили мятежи и казни.

Но правдой он привлек сердца,
Но нравы укротил наукой,
И был от буйного стрельца
Пред ним отличен Долгорукой.

Самодержавною рукой
Он смело сеял просвещенье,
Не презирал страны родной:
Он знал ее предназначенье.

То академик, то герой,
То мореплаватель, то плотник,
Он всеобъемлющей душой
На троне вечный был работник.

Семейным сходством будь же горд;
Во всем будь пращуру подобен:

Как он неутомим и тверд,
И памятью, как он, незлобен. (PSS III: 40)

With hope for glory and good deeds
I look ahead without misgiving:
Rebellions and executions also shrouded
The start of Peter's glorious days.

But he attracted hearts with justice,
But he used learning to tame customs.
For him a Dolgorukii was distinguished
From the ungovernable streletz.

With autocratic hand
He boldly sowed enlightenment;
He did not hate his native land:
He knew its predestination.

Now academic, now hero,
Now navigator, now carpenter,
With all-encompassing soul, he was
Eternal worker on the throne.

Be proud of your family likeness;
Be like your ancestor in everything:
Untiring and firm like him,
And of past wrongs forgiving.

As Ejdel'man remarks (1985: 208), Puškin did not hurry to publish the poem, possibly because he thought Nicholas would not like "Stanzas" any more than he liked Puškin's note "On Popular Education" (which the tsar had commissioned him to do but which Nicholas subsequently criticized severely) or because he felt offended by Nicholas and Benkendorf's critical reaction to *Boris Godunov*; furthermore, Puškin was beginning to realize—after only two to three months—that having the tsar as his personal censor meant having more, not fewer, restrictions on his poetry and actions. Apparently begun in Pskov, where Puškin had returned to gather his things from Mixajlovskoe for the move to Moscow, and finished in Moscow shortly before the new year (22 December 1826, at V. P. Zubkov's, according to Puškin's note on the manuscript), the poem was not published until January of 1828, though permission was given 6 July 1827 by Benkendorf (the circumstances are discussed by Ejdel'man [1985: 209]). The poem represents the first "published" view of the "new" Puškin (since he had given numerous readings of his works); it would have, in its public context, mostly negative reverberations.[3]

In the first stanza the poet offers his feelings: he is hopeful and unafraid, expecting glory and good from the new tsar. He invokes historical precedent—revolts and punishments also cast a pall over the beginning of Peter's reign, but glorious times followed. The connection between the glory (hoped-for) of Nicholas and the glorious days of Peter is firmly made, and with it the key analogy is established. What is unsaid but merely implied is what could not be said explicitly: the Decembrist revolt and the executions and exiles that followed are presumably counterparts to the executions administered by Peter. The rhyming of "fear" and "executions" could not help but reinforce the evocation of contemporary parallels. It is inconceivable that readers would fail to understand the import of these lines.

The implication of this stanza is that the situation that met Nicholas in 1825 was not unlike that which met Peter in the late seventeenth century. Peter dealt with revolt and went on to glorious achievements; Nicholas could do the same by emulation. Indeed, as scholars have noted (Lincoln 1978: 95–104; Ejdel'man 1985: 210–12; Mejlax 1959: 100–101), the prospects for meaningful reform were good in 1826 and 1827. Even liberals such as Aleksandr Bestužev (who compared Nicholas to Peter) were hopeful in the beginning (Mejlax 1959: 101).

The second stanza begins with the strong conjunction "but" (*no*), made even more prominent by repetition in the second line of the stanza. Since the word indicates "contrariness to expectation," the implication is that the opposite of "justice" and "learning" (perhaps unjust, arbitrary punishment and ignorance) would be the expected response to "revolts" (*mjateži*): Peter, however, attracted hearts with justice and tamed "customs, morals, and manners" (*nravy*) with learning and education (*nauka*). (The word *nravy* refers to behavior, a way of life corresponding with the moral norms of a society; *Slovar' jazyka Puškina* II: 888.) The strong initial anaphora of the first two lines is followed by the mild connective "and," which introduces an important distinction: for Peter the "furious," "ungovernable" strelets differed from Dolgorukij.

This is a key stanza in the poem. Puškin in effect tells Nicholas that Peter did the unexpected, that he responded to revolt with his positive program of reforms, not with vindictiveness. Furthermore, Peter discriminated between presumably reasoned opposition (that of Dolgorukij) and mindless opposition (that of the streltsy). But the allusions to Peter's time are controversial if they are understood as analogy: if we connect them with analogy of the first stanza, are the Decembrists then to be understood (as Lerner understood them) as streltsy? And is Puškin himself—who had expressed opposition to the government and was pardoned by the tsar—to be understood as Dolgorukij? Or is it Nicholas's brother Alexander whom Puškin criticizes here, as someone who could not tolerate reasoned opposition (as suggests Eremin [1976: 112–13])? Interpreting the analogy is perhaps the most puzzling problem the poem raises. Several possibilities present themselves, but surely one reasonable hypothesis is that there may not be a single "correct" solution, that the distinction's very suggestiveness serves the poet's purposes.

The third stanza carries the analogy of the two reigns deeper: Peter "sowed enlightenment" with an autocratic hand. The image reaffirms autocratic power, and at the same time links it with an ideal that in turn echoes the reference to learning in the preceding stanza. Knowing the "predestination" of his native land, Peter (like the Peter of *The Bronze Horseman*) did not despise Russia. Thus the poet affirms Peter's sense of mission, his notion of Russia's place in history, and his bold leadership, devoid of personal rancor and anchored in belief in the beneficial power of enlightenment. Although one may question the historical accuracy of Peter's description (as Lerner did), and the correspondence between the positive depiction and Puškin's real views of Peter (see Lednicki 1955: 57–72; Driver 1981: 10), such questions are not relevant to Peter's function in the poem.[4] The main point is that Peter in this poem serves as an ideal, a gauge against which Nicholas's own stature could be measured.

The fourth stanza lists Peter's personal qualities, his skills, both theoretical ("academic") and practical ("hero," navigator, and carpenter). Moreover, he was a tireless ("eternal") worker with an "all-embracing soul." The ideal monarch is not arrogant, nor is he to be exalted above all others; the lexicon and imagery of tsar-farmer and tsar-carpenter (Blagoj 1967: 131), far from formal high style, also underline an openness, a willingness to accept ideas and all people—not just those who surround the throne.

The final stanza turns the poem back to the addressee; in fact, it apostrophizes Nicholas in the familiar form of address characteristic of verse addressed to the monarch (such as the coronation and "advisory" poetry of Deržavin and Karamzin). The poet tells the new tsar to be proud of his family resemblance, to be like his ancestor in everything, to be tireless and firm, and also forgiving, without rancor. The final line gains prominence by its position: it marks closure and also, through the anaphora of "kak on," reinforces the kinship between Peter and what Puškin hopes Nicholas will be.

But the poem is not simply an expression of the poet's hopes through an instructive analogy. Beneath the surface there is an intricate web of literary, historical, and biographical subtexts. Puškin, of course, knew Russian history as well as the history of his own family members and their relations with Russian monarchs; moreover, he was undoubtedly familiar with historical events involving treason and clashes with authority. There can be little question that the stormy events of Peter's reign had a personal dimension for the poet. With Peter in particular, Puškin's own family history suggested two possible outcomes to encounters with the tsar. On the one hand, his great-grandfather Gannibal played a role in the new state as a valued and privileged adviser to the tsar; on the other, Fedor Puškin was hanged in 1697 for taking part in a conspiracy against the throne (the poet refers to him in "Moja rodoslovnaja" [My Genealogy, 1830]).

When summoned by Nicholas to Moscow, Puškin insisted on bringing his pistols, undoubtedly believing, as Ejdel'man notes (1985: 190), that to insist on taking them reinforced his nobility and made it clear to all that his status was not that of a prisoner. Surely in his consciousness were thoughts not only of Fedor Puškin, but also of Peter's dealings with his son Aleksej (the "brother" of Peter's adopted son Gannibal), who had been required to appear without sword when summoned by Peter in early February of 1718. Aleksej's appearance before the emperor resulted in his formal disinheritance and a pardon by Peter that was conditional on his naming accomplices and advisers. Even after implicating numerous others, including Vasilij Dolgorukij (of the same family as the referent of "Dolgorukij" in "Stanzas"; see below), he could not escape further interrogation, torture, and death. (Puškin, too, had problems with a father suspicious of his loyalty, and the two had quarreled badly in Mixajlovskoe. The unhappy outcome of that confrontation could have intensified Puškin's anxieties.) What if Nicholas, doubting the poet's loyalty, wished Puškin to implicate others in the Decembrist conspiracy?

To the list of personal and historical parallels could be added other figures whom Puškin may have contemplated as he traveled to Moscow to meet with the tsar, and whom he subsequently would allude to when writing "Stanzas." We know from Puškin's writings that he was familiar with biographies of members of the Dolgorukij family—in particular Vasilij and Jakov—and their relationship to Peter. Vasilij Vladimirovič Dolgorukij (1667–1746) had supported Tsarevich Aleksej, and for his support had been arrested by Menšikov (on Peter's orders); he is said to have responded bravely and nobly (Weber 1723: I: 204). Moreover, even after admitting that he had sympathy for Aleksej (and less than positive feelings about many of Peter's reforms), Dolgorukij suffered a sentence which could be termed mild when compared to the brutal punishments meted out to others: his rank of general was taken away and he was exiled to Solikamsk. His milder punishment was largely the result of appeals by his relatives— especially Jakov, who reminded Peter of the family's long record of service to the state (*Enciklopedičeskij slovar'* 1903: 921–22). Some years later, following the name of Vasilij Dolgorukij in the materials of *Istorija Petra* (History of Peter; PSS IX: 388), Puškin wrote "NB," suggesting his importance to Puškin's account; perhaps he wished to discuss in more detail Dolgorukij's role or his subsequent fate.

The more obvious referent of Dolgorukij in "Stanzas," however, is Prince Jakov Dolgorukij (1659–1720), whom he had referred to (as a representative of opposition not punished by Peter) in two other poetic works, "Mordvinovu" (To Mordvinov) and "My Genealogy." Jakov, too, had shown opposition to some of Peter's reforms, as well as some sympathy for Aleksej, and despite his outspokenness and opposition, he suffered no punishment (see *Russkij biografičeskij slovar'* 1905 VII: 575–77, and *Modern Encyclopedia of Russian and Soviet History* 1961 IV: 204–206 for stories of his opposition). Puškin mentions him explicitly in his *Istorija Petra* (PSS

IX: 386) as well as in his "Moja rodoslovnaja," where Dolgorukij is contrasted with Fedor Puškin:

> Упрямства дух нам всем подгадил.
> В родню свою неукротим,
> С Петром мой пращур не поладил
> И был за то повешен им.
> Его пример будь нам наукой:
> Не любит споров властелин.
> Счастлив князь Яков Долгорукой,
> Умен покорный мещанин. (PSS III: 262)

> A stubborn spirit caused us all some problems.
> Intractable in his own family,
> My ancestor did not get on with Peter,
> And for this was hanged by him.
> Let his example be a lesson to us:
> The sovereign does not like arguments.
> Prince Jakov Dolgorukij is fortunate,
> The humble commoner intelligent.

Puškin purportedly discussed him with Nicholas (according to A. O. Smirnova's account [1929 I: 71, 267]) when Nicholas asked Puškin about Jakov Dolgorukij's relationship with Peter.

Jakov Dolgorukij was noted for his sharply worded criticism of Peter's ukazes; such opposition stimulated numerous anecdotes with which Puškin was undoubtedly familiar. When Puškin in "Mordvinovu" (unpub., 1826) called N. S. Mordvinov—who had boldly opposed the execution of the Decembrists—a "new Dolgorukij," he was surely referring to the man's courageous and articulate opposition to state policy.

Invoking the name Dolgorukij in "Stanzas" functioned to affirm the legitimacy of reasoned opposition, but it also served to exemplify imperial restraint, for Dolgorukij was allowed by Peter to state his opposition. Such restraint is consistent with the description of Peter in "Stanzas" as *nezloben*, "forgiving" or "without rancor."

The contrast between Dolgorukij and the strelets is, as noted above, strongly marked in Puškin's poem. While the former's opposition was only verbal and presumably rooted in principles, the latter's revolt was violent and motivated primarily by more concrete goals: a desire to burn Moscow, expel the Germans, and elevate Sof'ja to the throne. The streltsy uprising was, like the Decembrist revolt, quickly put down (see *Istorija Petra*, PSS IX: 73–74, for Puškin's description of it). Half of the rebels, some four thousand, fell in the skirmish and in its aftermath. But the analogy with the Decembrists seems less apt when the focus is turned from the circumstances of the revolt to motivating ideals. It is hardly flattering to Decembrist idealists to compare them to wild and ungovernable troops, though the general confusion and lack of central authority in the Senate Square revolt certainly could have given observers that impression. The fact remains that it would be horribly tactless for Puškin to say this explicitly—even if true—considering the severity of the punishments meted out to his friends.

Clearly reacting to the negative import of this analogy (as well as other political aspects of the poem), Lerner (xxii) remarked that the poem was one of Puškin's "first and most decisive steps" on the "road of compromise." Not only did Puškin violate history with his reference to Peter's mercy, but he violated tact and civil duty in his comparison of the Decembrists to the streltsy. For Lerner the Decembrists were analogous to Peter: they had the progressive ideas of Peter, not "streltsy" ideals of a Byzantine or Tatar Moscow. But it is possible to take Lerner's observation in a different direction: if the Decembrists were closer in motivation, social standing, and education to Jakov and Vasilij Dolgorukij, then by implication Nicholas was hardly like Peter, i.e., forgiving, bearing no ill will, in his punishment of them. This is certainly one valid inference that can be made from allusions in the poem, and shows once again how strongly the poem resists a "single" meaning or interpretation. The poem's allusions, analogies, and suggestive ambiguities all illustrate a general feature of Puškin's semantics: its multifocal orientation (Davydov 1985: 31).

Affinities between the streltsy revolt and the Decembrist revolt are also undeniable—though such connections cannot be made without reservation. Puškin frequently referred to open revolt against the government as a kind of madness: this and like expressions were applied in published and unpublished writings in reference to Radiščev, for example, as well as to the Decembrists. (See Blagoj 1931: 279–91 for the meanings of "madness" in Puškin's works.)

In an unpublished essay (which was written for publication) on Radiščev (PSS XII: 30–40; 1836), Puškin used such phrases as "insane audacity," "rashness," "act of a madman," and "mad delusions" to characterize the rebellion of the eighteenth-century writer.[5] Moreover, in his letters and other writings (which of course must be evaluated carefully in view of their intended audience) he left similar suggestions about the Decembrists—viz., that the means employed to bring about their possibly worthwhile ends were indeed "mad." He said as much to the tsar in his note on popular education (XI: 43–44); and it is known that from 1823 on he was noticeably cooler toward the ideas of his Decembrist friends (Blagoj 1967; Nečkina 1938; Driver 1981). Furthermore, in his efforts to gain freedom from exile, he sincerely voiced his belief that opposition to the general order of things was a kind of madness.[6] Despite the frequent claim made in Puškin scholarship of Puškin's political unity (edinomyslie) with the Decembrists, there is no doubt that he did not approve of their "means," and could only in the most general sense (in terms of principles relating to progress, education, a less restrictive censorship, more humane treatment of the peasants, and rule by law) approve of their ideals. As Driver (1981:

2–3) and Nepomnjaščij (1985: 144) observe, there are many ideas—some of them mutually contradictory—that could be associated with the Decembrists; and it was not so much on the basis of shared ideas that he told Nicholas he would have been on Senate Square alongside his friends on 14 December, but because his sense of honor required it (Ejdel'man 1985: 200).[7] Indeed, distinguishing between Puškin's sympathy for former comrades as men rather than as bearers of a political program helps us to achieve a coherent view of his political position.

Puškin's sense of honor required him to do what he could to ease the fate of his friends. There can be no question that his epistle to Nicholas represents, with its references to Peter's distinction between types of opposition and its emphasis on Peter's absence of rancor, an indirect appeal for mercy for the Decembrists. In fact, the poem is daring (Blagoj 1967: 135; Mejlax 1959: 103; Nepomnjaščij 1984: 155–56) by its oblique reference to the revolt as analogous with the revolts during Peter's time, as well as to the distinction between honorable, principled opposition and ignorant, unthinking revolt (Dolgorukij vs. the streltsy). And it is daring and perhaps even dangerously patronizing in its exhortations to Nicholas to adopt the high ideals of enlightenment and to work tirelessly in behalf of his country with an awareness of its predestined place in history—in short, to be like Peter "in everything." It is not really important that the historical Peter may not have been as "merciful" or as positive a figure as the poem presents him as being—nor, for that matter, that Puškin's political views, as expressed in his poetry, be consistent.[8] Poetry for Puškin was not necessarily the bearer of important ideas, as such: he has left a well-known expression of his views on this subject in a letter to Vjazemskij (1826), where he said that poetry must be a bit "stupid" (*glupovata*). This disclaimer need not be construed, however, as any diminishment of poetry's importance in achieving important personal goals.

What undoubtedly prepared the way for Puškin's frank exhortations of Nicholas was their previous meeting, during which some of the same issues the poem raises were discussed (the immediate past of Russia, its present state, and its future; Ejdel'man 1985: 198); also contributing was the poetic tradition in Russia: Blagoj rightly notes (1967: 130–32) that Lomonosov's court poems could have served as models for Puškin, as could poems of Deržavin, a poet who could speak the truth to tsars, who could praise them or criticize them and, of course, instruct them. Karamzin, however, was an even better model for Puškin.

The image of the poet-adviser to the emperor exemplifed by Karamzin, with his boldly instructive verse to Alexander I, was undoubtedly attractive to Puškin (Vickery, forthcoming). Not only did Karamzin respectfully instruct Alexander on the value of knowledge and enlightenment, he also invoked historical models to make his point. Indeed, in his poetry to Alexander, Karamzin made use of Peter as an exemplar, referring not only to Peter's enlightened policies but also to the similar problems

Alexander and Peter faced at the outset of their reigns: to overcome threats
to the state's stability and punish those who were responsible while showing moderation and restraint in the use of punishment.

For example, in Karamzin's "Na toržestvennoe koronovanie ego im-
peratorskogo veličestva Aleksandra I, samoderžca vserossijskogo" (On the
August Coronation of His Imperial Highness Alexander I, All-Russian Autocrat, 1801), the poet refers positively to Peter in recommending learning
(the "kingdom of light") and the elimination of evil with limited recourse
to physical punishment (Karamzin 1966: 268, stanza 13). He also advises
Alexander to work in behalf of the state (stanza 17): "Trudis' . . davaj us-
tavy nam / I budeš' *Pervyj* po delam!" (Work . . give us regulations / And
you will be *First* in deeds!).

In Karamzin's coronation poem to Alexander, "Ego imperatorskomu
veličestvu Aleksandru I, samoderžcu vserossijskomu, na vosšestvie ego na
prestol" (To His Imperial Highness Alexander I, All-Russian Autocrat, on
the Occasion of His Rise to the Throne, also 1801), the poet ends (stanzas
11–14) with a warning to the new tsar (in terms similar to those used by
Puškin in his epistle to "friends") to beware of flatterers and to heed those
who are sincere and who dare to speak the truth; to value education and
poets; to have an open mind and to use restraint, especially in dealing with
opposition. Here the name Dolgorukij is placed next to that of the heroic
Požarskij:

> Довольно патриотов верных,
> Готовых жизнь ему отдать,
> Друзей добра нелицемерных,
> Могущих истину сказать!
> У нас *Пожарские* сияли,
> И *Долгорукие* держали
> Петру от сердца говорить:
> Великий соглашался с ними
> И звал их братьями своими.
> Монарх! Ты будешь нас любить!
>
> Ты будешь солнцем просвещенья—
> Наукой счастлив человек,—
> И блеском твоего правленья
> Осыпан будет новый век.
> Се музы, к трону приступая
> И черный креп с себя снимая,
> Твоей улыбки милой ждут!
> Они сердца людей смягчают,
> Они жизнь нашу услаждают
> И доброго царя поют! (1966: 263–64)

It is enough to have faithful patriots,
Prepared to give their life for him,
Unhypocritical friends of the good,

Who are able to tell the truth!
Our *Požarskijs* have shone brightly,
And *Dolgorukijs* have spoken
To Peter from their heart:
He, the great one, agreed with them
And called them his brothers.
Monarch! You will love us!

You will be the sun of enlightenment—
Fortunate is a man with learning,—
And the brilliance of your rule
Will adorn the new age.
Those muses, advancing toward the throne
And removing their black mourning crepe,
Await your kind smile!
They soothe people's hearts,
They sweeten our life
And sing of the new tsar!

What we see emphasized are the same ideals Puškin later invoked in his epistle to Nicholas: knowledge as a guide in government (for the good of the people) and enlightened treatment of opposition (Peter called those who, like the Dolgorukijs, dared to speak the truth—those who spoke from the heart—his "brothers").

Karamzin was highly valued by Nicholas, and undoubtedly his positive feelings for Puškin, which he expressed to Nicholas on several occasions before he died, relieved some of the suspicion that may have fallen on Puškin after the revolt. Nicholas, who strongly desired the support of the educated aristocracy, gave considerable attention to Karamzin; and the latter, in turn, as a firm believer in the virtues of education, advised Nicholas to attract educated people to the court and to treat Puškin favorably (Ejdel'man 1985: 192).

There can hardly be a question that Puškin's career was moving in a direction roughly comparable to Karamzin's. Puškin had been giving more and more attention to historical study (for example, with his work on *Boris Godunov*), and now, on the basis of an understanding he and Nicholas had reached in their meeting on 8 September, Puškin may have perceived himself as a successor to Karamzin—poet, historian, and adviser to the emperor. Puškin certainly showed an awareness of Karamzin's verse (noted above) and historical writing, and he indicated in his writing his high regard for Karamzin; and he also willingly—and clearly with the hope of serving in an advisory role to the tsar—accepted an assignment from Nicholas to write on education; finally, Puškin embarked upon a course of historical studies which suggest he found amenable the activities Karamzin had pursued in his later years (Vacuro [with Gillel'son] 1972).

Besides Karamzin, there were other poets with subtexts to "Stanzas." The poem contains verbal and thematic echoes of Vladimir Raevskij's "K druz'jam" (To Friends, 1822) and Kondratij Ryleev's "Videnie" (A Vision, 1823) (Mejlax 1959: 104–106). Furthermore, Ryleev, too, used Dolgorukij as a model of constructive political opposition both in his *duma* "Volynskij" (published first in 1822), and again in his ode "Graždanskoe mužestvo" (Civic Courage, written in 1823 or 1824, not published until 1856), which Puškin may have known in manuscript.

Whatever functions Puškin had planned "Stanzas" to fulfill, the results could not have been to his liking. Contemporaries reading the poem apparently attached unwarranted significance to the expressions "glory" and "good," concluding that the poem was in praise of Nicholas. Presumably overlooked was the qualification that this "glory" and "good" represented the poet's hope: Puškin did not say that Nicholas had already achieved glory and brought about "good." As has often been noted (Nepomnjaščij 1984: 155–56), the poem exhorts and hardly flatters.

This is not to say that the poem contains no suggestion of praise for Nicholas; otherwise it would be difficult to account for his approving its publication and the negative reactions of some of Puškin's contemporaries. More than misreading is undoubtedly involved. The poem, after all, makes assumptions about the poet's relationship with the tsar and about the perceived potential of Nicholas. The act of comparing the two emperors—if only on a potential basis—may be perceived as flattering to Nicholas, for it suggests he has the potential to be like Peter. Moreover, the poet in writing this poem shows himself as being close enough to the sovereign to offer advice. To those who regarded Nicholas as a tyrant and murderer beyond salvation (a view Puškin may have gravitated toward later in his life), Puškin's relationship could easily be seen in a negative light. Moreover, any poem by Puškin about Nicholas appearing in print could prima facie be viewed as an expression of the poet's gratitude, for all knew that Nicholas had pardoned Puškin and allowed him to return from exile.

The poem has been read and understood in so many ways because it is both an expression of encouragement and praise and also a daring exhortation of the tsar which hints that his behavior to that moment may not have had any semblance to that of the somewhat idealized Peter. Despite its references to hope for a glorious future and its analogies between the time of Peter and the time of Nicholas, the poem does not really praise Nicholas, but rather urges him to resemble Peter in more than physical appearance. The violence that occurred at the outset of Peter's reign did not prevent him from being merciful: Nicholas, the poem implies, has yet to respond to the violence in his reign in an analogous way. What constitutes praise here is the implication that Nicholas is capable of emulating Peter.

It is reasonable to suppose that in post-Decembrist Russia, Puškin believed that the only hope for effecting change lay in influencing government policy (Tomaševskij 1977: 504; Mikkelson 1980: 10–11; Driver 1981: 9). Having been convinced by Nicholas that the government was moving in the direction of reform, and that Nicholas sincerely valued his thinking on

Russia's future, Puškin felt that he could speak to the tsar frankly as a representative of the enlightened nobility. In this role of noble and poet, Puškin urged Nicholas to be like Peter—forward-thinking, progressive, hard-working, and dedicated to the welfare of Russia. Furthermore, he reminded Nicholas that Peter could show tolerance for and extend mercy to the opposition. Obviously Puškin nursed the hope that his influence on the government might bring back the exiled Decembrists. Puškin's role then involved multiple functions: adviser, historian, poet, noble, and intercessor (Ejdel'man 1985: 200).

Determining Puškin's politico-ideological position is a complex task (Gutsche 1982; Driver 1981), primarily because Puškin showed himself as striving to maintain relations with the authorities without betraying his liberal friends and the liberal ideas he had embraced throughout his youth. Certainly foremost among his personal problems was preserving his integrity while at the same time ensuring that his creative tranquility not be jeopardized.

It was not the purpose of this study to examine all the complex factors involved in determining Puškin's political views, especially as they are expressed in his poetry. What can be said, however, on the basis of what was shown above concerning the epistle to Nicholas, is that drawing out the implications of Puškin's political verse may not result in one unambiguous conclusion demonstrable on the basis of the poetry alone. Puškin's epistle to Nicholas is certainly suggestive in many different ways, and this suggestiveness may very well have been by the poet's design. The conscious use of ambiguity allowed Puškin to accomplish honorably two tasks: (1) he could secure his position as a replacement for Karamzin, with all of the honor and personal tranquility such a position entailed, and (2) he could guide Nicholas toward what Puškin conceived of as reasonable goals—goals which included government reform and amnesty for the Decembrists. At the same time, in order to make his exhortations more palatable to Nicholas, Puškin used a language of hope and glory and positive individual virtues, all leading to (but not quite reaching) an identification of Peter and Nicholas; only with a careful reading is it apparent that Puškin was not really praising Nicholas for anything he had done already. Here, as in the case of the epistle to the Decembrists (Nepomnjaščij 1984: 159), readers, including the authorities, could be misled by the lexicon into making conclusions of their own.

The connecting link between the epistles to Nicholas, to the Decembrists, and to "friends" is not, as Makogonenko maintains (1985: 175), the notion of mercy—for the epistle to Siberia, even if construed to mean that Puškin is nurturing the exiles' hopes for amnesty, has little to do with Nicholas's personal qualities. What the poems have in common is courage manifested in different ways. The epistle to the Decembrists showed courage in an obvious way: Puškin avoided the censorship and the tsar by secretly sending to Siberia poetry that was highly suggestive of the eventual overthrow of autocracy by violent means. That the poem could be understood in less radical ways is undoubtedly true as well (Nepomnjaščij 1984). From this it hardly follows, however, that the poem is either radical or moderate, expressing the violent and inevitable victory of the Decembrists, or, less radically, the imminent amnesty of the exiles by a new tsar who can show himself to be merciful by freeing them (as he freed the exiled poet) and returning to them their rights as citizens (their "swords"). The poem is probably both, but this will be unsatisfying only if we insist on one and only one meaning. And "Stanzas" can be viewed similarly.

The deep resonance and suggestiveness of Puškin's poetry is often perceived as a merit; there is no reason to object to such interpretational richness here, too—especially considering the difficulty of Puškin's position with respect to the government and his exiled friends.

"Stanzas" is noteworthy for its bold, imperial tone of advice, a tone bolstered and justified by the tradition of poet-tsar advisory relations *in verse*, most notably represented by Karamzin. But whether or not justified and approved by tradition and convention, there is always the risk that the tsar will take the poet's advice in the wrong way. Moreover, Puškin, in this case, faced the possibility that anything positive he said about Nicholas, especially so soon after the hanging of the Decembrists, could be understood by his contemporaries as an attempt to curry favor, to repay a debt, cynically to seek personal advantage with the enemy.

What Puškin managed to do was to tell, or perhaps remind, the tsar of a historical parallel. Peter too was challenged at the beginning of his reign; he too ended the revolt with executions. But he was also capable of showing mercy to those who opposed him, who honestly and in a principled manner disagreed with his policies. The references to the streltsy and Dolgorukij are troublesome because the analogy is not clear: perhaps it is, as Lerner saw it, a comparison of the Decembrists with the streltsy, and Puškin himself with Dolgorukij, or perhaps it is a finer distinction between different Decembrists: those who in violent and mindless rage carried on the revolt, and those who through noble and unrealistic idealism planned the rebellion and supported it once it began. To Nicholas it made clear the importance of distinctions (and a forgiving spirit) without denying that the Decembrist revolt had something in common with the streltsy uprising; for the exiled Decembrists, the poem left open the possibility that they represented the tradition of principled opposition to the government.

Nepomnjaščij (1985: 151) is undoubtedly correct in suggesting that something other than the works themselves determines whether we perceive Puškin as a hypocritical manipulator, an idealistic, politically naive, and well-meaning poet who out of gratitude (and it seems clear that he was sincerely grateful to Nicholas [Ejdel'man 1985: 198]) was willing to believe anything Nicholas told him, or something in between—a man who, well aware of necessity and the need to survive with honor, to work and to deal nobly with friends in a far-from-perfect society, made small compromises with the government without betraying his own sense of integrity. Within Puškin's own system of values, a hard-headed realism about the limited possibilities of political change played as important a role as the obligation to be loyal to friends, no matter how imprudent or impractical their views might be. Whether one is charitable toward Puškin and his motives is probably dependent on how one reacts to his words about the "assignment" on popular education Nicholas gave him; these words contain much of what I take to be Puškin's understanding of his task in the post-Decembrist years—a willingness to use any opportunity to accomplish a limited end, even if it meant risking being misunderstood: "It would have been easy for me to write what was wanted, but I couldn't let pass the opportunity to do good."

PAUL DEBRECZENY

Puškin's Reputation in Nineteenth-Century Russia

A Statistical Approach

Measuring the place a writer occupies in the public consciousness is a difficult task because the evidence available is usually subjective or slanted. One consults, first of all, the literary critics of the writer's own time, and the scholars or essayists of later periods, with the assumption that they represent the reading public vis-à-vis the author. But critics are usually members of literary coteries, subject to cultural fads and prejudices as are the authors themselves; and their judgments can be accepted as expressions of public opinion only to a certain extent. One can turn to diaries, letters, reminiscences of private individuals, each of whom is of course subjective but may offer opinions that can become highly revealing when set alongside the opinions of a fair number of other individuals. Such an approach is perhaps the most interesting, but also the most time-consuming because of the difficulty of tracking down and scanning relevant materials. It is also possible to gather data—more reliable, "factual," and quantifiable—by surveying the records of publishers, holdings of libraries, information on the reading habits of library patrons if available, school curricula, inclusions in anthologies and chrestomathies, and so forth. In this essay I would like to explore still another method that has some pretensions to tangible measurements.

What the literary critic says in an essay devoted to a particular author is of crucial importance, but it is equally significant when he brings up the name of the author outside the context of the author's own work. In an attempt to assess to what extent a particular author is on the critic's mind, one can count how many times he mentions the name of that author—for comparison, contrast, or whatever—in reviews or essays devoted to others. The Swedish sociologist Karl E. Rosengren has counted, for example, how many times internationally known authors, including Turgenev, Tolstoj, and Dostoevskij, were mentioned in the Swedish press in reviews of other writers' works from 1876 through 1891 and from 1953 through 1965 (Rosengren 1968: 94–101 and 173–96). A writer might be mentioned as having influenced a certain author or as being very different from another one: the significant fact from Rosengren's point of view is not what was said about him but the mere fact that his name was invoked. A reference to him outside the context of his own work implies that the critic regarded him as a standard against which other authors could be measured, that his name was sufficiently at the forefront of cultural consciousness to be called up from memory through certain associations. Rosengren compares his method to statistical stylistics, in which marked features falling outside the normal flow of a writer's discourse are counted. One could go a step further and say that computing a critic's references to authors outside the immediate context at hand is like putting him on the historian's couch and observing his free associations. The names he brings up will reveal the cultural frame of reference within which he is operating; and conversely, being invoked means for the author that his name has been firmly lodged in that frame of reference. Naturally, one particular critic's references reflect his personal proclivities, but if quite a few critics contribute to a journal, their combined references can add up to a network of codes shared by at least a segment of society.

In this paper five Russian journals at different periods are examined from the point of view of associative literary references. The first two are *Vestnik Evropy* (The European Herald) from 1820 through 1828 and *Syn otečestva* (Son of the Fatherland) from 1820 through 1829. The former has been selected as the leading conservative periodical, and the latter as the chief journal supporting the romantic trend, during a crucial decade in Puškin's own lifetime.[1] The remaining three selections represent "thick journals" from later periods, and therefore it was thought that scanning one year of each would provide enough material to be meaningful. The 1862 volume of *Sovremennik* (The Contemporary) was selected for its twenty-five-year distance from Puškin's death; although as the organ of the "revolutionary democrats" it is somewhat one-sided in its literary views, it is still the most significant journal of the time; and 1862, the year following the publication of Alexander II's manifesto about the emancipation of the serfs, is a significant juncture. The next two journals surveyed are spaced twenty years apart. The 1882 volume of *Otečestvennye zapiski* (Annals of the Fatherland) has been chosen because that journal had in certain ways succeeded *The Contemporary;* and 1882, two years after the unveiling of the Puškin monument in Moscow and one year after the assassination of Alexander II, is a crucial year. Finally, the 1902 volume of *Russkoe bogatstvo* (Russian Treasures)—the most encyclopedic journal of the turn of the century, and a successor to *Annals of the Fatherland*—comes three years after the large-scale centennial Puškin celebrations of 1899 and also represents a period of social and cultural fermentation.

One departure in this paper from Rosengren's method is that I have included in the survey not only literary reviews in the strict sense but any kind of writing having to do with literary or general cultural issues. Biographical essays, reminiscences about a late author, satirical comments on the literary attitudes of other journals (as in *Svistok* [The Whistler], a supplement to *The Contemporary*) have all been scanned for references; even those parts of the various surveys of domestic and foreign affairs which deal with cultural questions have been included. The reasoning behind this decision has been, simply, that the wider you cast your net, the more fish you are likely to catch; but such a broadening of the areas surveyed has presented its problems. What do we do, for instance, with a historical essay such as A. Skabičevskij's "Outline of the History of Russian Censorship" (*Annals of the Fatherland*, 1882, Nos. 3, 4, 6, 8, 10–12)? If the essay were devoted solely to Puškin, it would not count as a reference to him, but if in the course of a survey fifty different authors become the essayist's subject, should they all be excluded? After all, the very fact that an author is mentioned, or not mentioned, in a survey can be significant. After some thought and some false starts, it was decided that in such a case the segment of the article dealing with a particular author should be counted as one reference, even if it ran to sixteen pages. Similarly, an extended reference should be counted as one only, even in a conventional critical essay. A review of a novella by G. Jurko begins, for example, with an eight-page analysis of *Hamlet*, and the play is being referred to all through the next twelve pages (*Annals of the Fatherland*, 1882, Vol. 265, No. 12, pp. 219–34): since this amounts to a comparison of Jurko's novella with one literary classic, it has been counted as one reference. By contrast, if *The Prisoner of the Caucasus* is brought into the argument on one page, and *Boris Godunov* is mentioned on the next one, these amount to two references. It must be added, on the other hand, that if both works had been mentioned on the same page, they would have been counted only once; the line has been drawn at one reference per page to any one author.

All this leads one to admitting that the technique of counting references lacks precision in a strictly scientific sense. One person counting might include what another one has excluded; even the same person may make decisions, when confronting new problems, which are not entirely in line with his previous practice. Another problem is that hidden references, such as a phrase or a line of poetry quoted, can be easily identified if they belong to a major poet but may be missed if the source is a lesser-known author. Further, in order to gain greater reliability of data, one ought to survey several periodicals over decades and decades, which would be a highly unwieldy and time-consuming job. Given these limitations, I can claim only that the data presented in this essay correctly represent general trends, but not without a margin of error.

The characteristic reference found in the course of this investigation has been of the type: "Longfellow, like our Puškin, moved from romanticism to realism" (*Annals*, 1882, No. 6, p. 266); "Although Gleb Uspenskij was not endowed with the talents of a Puškin, a Gogol', or a Lev Tolstoj, to us his significance is just as great" (*Russian Treasures*, 1902, No. 5, p. 166);

"He [Nekrasov] is higher, higher than Puškin or Lermontov" (*Russian Treasures*, 1902, No. 11, p. 45); "An effort has been made to supply [village libraries] with at least one work each of our great writers, such as Puškin, Lermontov, Gogol', and L. N. Tolstoj" (*Russian Treasures*, 1902, No. 7, p. 71), and the like. Such references, along with more elaborate comparisons of literary merits, occur with great regularity, and their relative frequency, I submit, can be assumed to be typical for Russian cultural discourse beyond the confines of our samples.

THE EUROPEAN HERALD (VESTNIK EVROPY), 1820–28

Established in 1802, *The European Herald* was at first edited by N. M. Karamzin (1802–1804), later by V. A. Žukovskij (1808–10) and by V. V. Izmajlov (1814), and, although it did not engage in sharp debates with the Šiškovites, it generally supported the trend of new sensibility.[2] Puškin's very first published poem, "To a Versifier Friend" (K drugu stixotvorcu), appeared in it in 1814 (No. 13). From 1815 on, however, M. T. Kačenovskij became its sole editor, and he gradually transformed it into a champion of "good sense" according to the neoclassical model. It was in this journal that *Ruslan and Ljudmila* was most severely criticized (1820, No. 11) and where conservative tastes were generally defended against such champions of the new as P. A. Vjazemskij and A. S. Griboedov. After the Decembrist uprising, literary debates generally subsided, but in 1828 a new contributor to the journal, N. I. Nadeždin, took up the cudgel against Puškin and other presumed romantics once more. With several adverse reviews of his work, *The European Herald* devoted a large enough number of its pages to Puškin, yet, as Table 1 shows, it contained relatively few references to him outside the context of articles dealing directly with him.

The table reveals that contributors to the journal operated chiefly within a classical or neoclassical frame of reference, with some recognition of outstanding romantics such as Byron, Walter Scott, and Schiller. Karamzin's high ranking is a tribute more to the historian than to the poet or writer of fiction. It has been necessary to cite quite a long list in order to get as far as Puškin, who shares twenty-third place with Ossian (MacPherson), Pliny, and Schiller.

Since the number of references counted for the nine years is 1,741, even the highest number related to a single author (to Homer) amounts only to 5.34 percent of the total. The percentage for Puškin is 0.86.

Puškin's standing improves, of course, if we discount foreign authors and eighteenth-century Russian classics: among his Russian contemporaries he is in third place, behind Karamzin and the sentimentalist poet I. I. Dmitriev.

This, however, is not the full story. Looking at the source of Puškin references, one is struck by the fact that all but four of the fifteen fall in the period prior to December 1825. For the six years from 1820 through 1825,

TABLE 1 *The European Herald* (Vestnik Evropy), 1820–28

Total number of references counted: 1,741

Authors most frequently referred to	Number of references
Homer	93
Horace	67
Virgil	65
Karamzin	34
Cicero	34
Lomonosov	32
Byron	30
Shakespeare	27
Pindar	26
Boileau	25
Voltaire	24
Petrarch	22
I. I. Dmitriev	21
Sophocles	21
Nestor (chronicler)	19
Racine	18
Walter Scott	18
Dante	17
Molière	17
Deržavin	16
Tasso	16
Ossian (James MacPherson)	15
Pliny	15
Puškin	15
Schiller	15

Puškin shares seventeenth place with Schiller, Tasso, and Žukovskij. The clear implication is that after the Decembrist uprising, references to Puškin, at least in this particular journal, declined for political rather than literary reasons. Even if the tsar had concluded a private truce with the poet, to critics it must have seemed safer to leave him alone. Three of the four post-1825 references to him represent unidentified citations from his poetry in Nadeždin's essay "Literary Forebodings about the Coming Year" (1828, Nos. 21–22).

SON OF THE FATHERLAND (SYN OTEČESTVA), 1820–29

First established in 1812 as a champion of patriotic sentiments engendered by the Napoleonic War, *Son of the Fatherland* was gradually expanded in scope by its editor, N. I. Greč, and by 1820 it had become the main promoter of new literary trends. It carried some of Puškin's poetry and several friendly reviews of his works. After 1825, Greč gradually shifted to politically conservative positions, and the standards of the journal were somewhat lowered, but the change was not so abrupt as to cause a break in the number of Puškin references. As one would expect, references to the poet gradually increased over the decade, as his fame grew.

As Table 2 shows, Puškin occupies fifth place, which is in keeping with the journal's policy to promote new trends. Byron's being in third place (rather than seventh, as in *The European Herald*) and the high ranking of Schiller and Žukovskij point in the same direction. The heavy presence of ancient Greek and Latin authors as well as pre-romantic Western writers indicates that even a romantic journal operated in a general milieu of classical and neoclassical culture.

The forty-three references to Homer amount to 4.17 percent of the total; the Puškin references represent 3.01 percent. Fourteen out of the thirty-one Puškin references fall into the period 1820–25. Among Russian writers, Puškin occupies second place (next to Lomonosov), and among his Russian contemporaries he comes in first. This is an extraordinary achievement by a poet still in his youth (he was only thirty at the end of the period surveyed), unparalleled, as we shall see, by any of the great writers of the latter half of the century.

THE CONTEMPORARY (SOVREMENNIK), 1862

Established by Puškin in 1836, *The Contemporary* was probably the best-known nineteenth-century Russian journal. It was taken over by N. A. Nekrasov and I. I. Panaev as new editors in 1847, and V. G. Belinskij contributed to it in his last years. It was in this journal that Tolstoj's *Childhood* first appeared (1852, No. 9) and that Turgenev published most of the stories which

TABLE 2 *Son of the Fatherland* (Syn otečestva), 1820–29

Total number of references counted: 1,031

Authors most frequently referred to	Number of references
Homer	43
Voltaire	40
Byron	33
Lomonosov	33
Puškin	31
Žukovskij	30
Schiller	29
Shakespeare	29
Racine	27
Virgil	26
Karamzin	24
Tasso	24
Horace	21
La Fontaine	20

were to form *A Sportsman's Sketches.* After N. G. Černyševskij, N. A. Dobroljubov, and M. E. Saltykov-Ščedrin joined the staff of the journal (in 1854, 1856, and 1857, respectively), it shifted to the left and became more and more radical in both its political and literary attitudes. The year 1862 represents the last period when the journal still functioned as the organ of the "revolutionary democrats" to full extent: in June of that year Černyševskij was arrested, and the journal was prohibited for eight months.

Although this truncated year of *The Contemporary* offers less material than the other journals included in the present survey, it is still a rich source for associative literary references. It contains M. A. Antonovič's well-known review of *Fathers and Sons* (Vol. 92, March), an essay on Turgenev's female characters (Vol. 93, May), a major article by Černyševskij on Tolstoj's pedagogical journal *Jasnaja Poljana* (Vol. 92, March), and reviews of certain volumes of collected works by I. V. Kireevskij, A. S. Xomjakov, and K. S. Aksakov (Vol. 91, January and February). Although these writings are not counted as references to the author under review, they yield a large number of references to other authors. The journal's satirical supplement, *Svistok* (The Whistler), is also included in our survey.

This year of the journal was chosen for our survey under the assumption that it would reveal a low point in Puškin's reputation, a period when he had been eclipsed by Gogol', especially in the estimation of civic-minded literary critics. Černyševskij had indeed said as much in his "Sketches of the Gogolian Period in Russian Literature" (1855, No. 12, and 1856, Nos. 1–12) and in his reviews of P. V. Annenkov's edition of Puškin (1855, Nos. 2–3 and 7–8). Dobroljubov, especially in his essay "The Contribution of the People's Point of View to the Development of Russian Literature" (1858, No. 2), echoed Černyševskij's opinion that Puškin, more an artist than a thinker, was a poet of the past. The ground was being prepared for D. I. Pisarev's notorious 1865 essay "Belinskij and Puškin," in which the critic declared that it was best to leave Puškin untouched on the bookshelf, along with Lomonosov, Deržavin, Karamzin, and Žukovskij (Pisarev 1956 III: 295).[3] Similarly, in the 1862 articles surveyed, whenever a critic mentions an author with veneration, as though holding up his party's banner, the names are always those of Gogol' and Belinskij. Yet when it comes to establishing a general frame of reference for Russian culture, it is Puškin whose name is invoked.

The twenty-one references to Puškin represent 5.11 percent of the total number of references, which is close to the 5.36 percent accorded to Homer in *The European Herald* during the 1820s—the highest figure relating to a single author which we have seen so far.

Hegel, though no author of imaginative literature, has been included in our survey because he is often mentioned in literary contexts. N. I. Kostomarov, a professor at St. Petersburg University, is frequently referred to because he expressed Slavophile views on Russian history, which the contributors to *The Contemporary* tried to ridicule on every available occa-

Table 3 *The Contemporary* (Sovremennik), 1862

Total number of references counted: 411

Authors most frequently referred to	Number of references
Puškin	21
Gogol'	19
Hegel	17
Černyševskij	16
N. I. Kostomarov	14
Turgenev	12
V. I. Askočenskij	10
Lermontov	8
Belinskij	8

sion. V. I. Askočenskij was the author of an 1858 novel, *An Asmodeus of Our Time*, with which Antonovič compared Turgenev's *Fathers and Sons*.

Apart from Černyševskij's article on *Jasnaja Poljana*, Tolstoj is referred to only once (in Antonovič's review of *Fathers and Sons*), which reflects his withdrawal from the literary scene in this period. Dostoevskij's journal *Time* is the frequent target of attacks, but by name he is mentioned only once (in *The Whistler*).

Annals of the Fatherland (Otečestvennye zapiski), 1882

The history of *Annals of the Fatherland* goes back to 1818, but the journal did not achieve prominence until its editorship was assumed by A. A. Kraevskij in 1838. It was here that Belinskij published most of his essays up until 1847. After that date *Annals* was eclipsed by *The Contemporary*, but in 1867, the year after the government had finally closed down *The Contemporary*, Kraevskij offered his somewhat attenuated journal to Nekrasov, and thus *Annals* became a successor to the radicals' organ. From 1868 on it employed N. K. Mixajlovskij and A. M. Skabičevskij as its leading literary critics, and as political events evolved at a rapid pace, it became more and more closely associated with the populist movement. In 1878, after Nekrasov's death, Mixajlovskij entered into co-editorship with Saltykov-Ščedrin. The year 1882 was the last one under the two writers' joint editorship, for in 1883 Mixajlovskij was arrested, and in 1884 *Annals* was closed down by the government.

In the 1882 volume we find Mixajlovskij's famous essay on Dostoevskij as a writer endowed with a "cruel talent" (Nos. 9–10), a major article on John Stuart Mill and Renan (Nos. 2–3), and Skabičevskij's survey of Russian censorship, already mentioned. We come across reviews of Leskov, Garšin, Hugo, and Zola, and of A. Nezelenov's book *A. S. Puškin in His Poetry: The First and Second Periods in His Life and Works, 1799–1826* (No. 12).

If one read only the critics' overt statements, one would assume that

Puškin continued to be underappreciated as he had been by the "revolutionary democrats." Skabičevskij wrote, for instance, that the poetry of Puškin and Lermontov "did not present any profound, salutary ideas capable of fostering society and moving it forward" (1868, No. 1, "Sovremennoe Obozrenie," p. 15); and an 1878 essay, entitled "New Prognostic Signs in Our Literature," relegated not only Puškin's works but also those of Gogol', Turgenev, and Ostrovskij to "social mementos of Russian life," in which "one cannot feel the pulse of the people" (No. 8, "Sovremennoe obozrenie," pp. 165–66). Despite such statements, however, the 1882 volume yielded the data shown in Table 4.

Ever since the romantic revival of Shakespeare in the earlier decades of the century, he had been frequently performed on the Russian stage and constantly referred to by literary critics, especially those, like Belinskij, who had been brought up on German idealist philosophers. Turgenev's essay "Hamlet and Don Quixote" and his stories "Prince Hamlet of the Ščigrovo District" and "The Lear of the Steppe" testify to how central a place Shakespeare occupied in Russian aesthetic consciousness from about the fourth decade of the century on. To be second to Shakespeare on the scale of references is surely no shame for Puškin.

It must be observed, on the other hand, that the twenty-five references to Shakespeare amount to only 3.53 percent of the total number of references; and those to Puškin (21) represent 2.96 percent—lower than the percentages either for *Son of the Fatherland* (3.01) or for *The Contemporary* (5.11). Whatever that might imply, Puškin certainly stands first among Russian writers referred to.

M. N. Katkov and Ivan Aksakov are mentioned so often because, as leading figures in conservative, Slavophile-oriented circles, they were the frequent targets of satirical comments in *Annals of the Fatherland*.

The evidence seems to indicate that although *War and Peace* and *Anna Karenina* had drawn much comment during the preceding fifteen years, Tol-

TABLE 4 *Annals of the Fatherland* (Otečestvennye zapiski), 1882

Total number of references counted: 709

Authors most frequently referred to	Number of references
Shakespeare	25
Puškin	21
M. N. Katkov	18
Goethe	17
Gogol'	17
I. S. Aksakov	16
Byron	12
Nekrasov	10
Voltaire	10

stoj (with only five references) was still viewed as a contemporary, not as a classic. The same is true of Dostoevskij (four references), who had died the year before and whose career was surveyed by Mixajlovskij in his "Cruel Talent." In 1882, when a critic invoked "our great writers," "our best literature," the names mentioned were almost invariably Puškin, Gogol', and Lermontov, with the occasional addition of Turgenev (eight references).

RUSSIAN TREASURES (RUSSKOE BOGATSTVO), 1902

Established in 1875 for the purpose of disseminating scientific and technological information, *Russian Treasures* was acquired in 1879 by a group of populist writers, who undertook publishing it as a cooperative venture. The enterprise did not last very long, however, and the editorship of the journal passed into the hands of L. E. Obolenskij in 1882. An adherent primarily of Auguste Comte's positivist philosophy, Obolenskij nevertheless provided an outlet for Tolstojan ideas, and we see quite a few articles by and about Tolstoj appear in the journal under Obolenskij's editorship, up to 1892. At that time a populist group, headed by N. K. Mixajlovskij, took over *Russian Treasures* once more, to be joined by V. G. Korolenko as Mixajlovskij's co-editor in 1895. Although leaning toward populism, *Russian Treasures* could be considered a mainstream, middle-of-the-road journal that reflected the chief concerns of Russian society and culture at the turn of the century.

The 1902 volume contains major essays on Victor Hugo (No. 2), Gleb Uspenskij (Nos. 3, 4, 5), Stanislaw Przybyszewski (No. 4), H. G. Wells (No. 4), A. A. Bestužev-Marlinskij (Nos. 5, 8, 12), Afanasij Fet (No. 7), the Yiddish poet S. G. Trug (No. 8), Emile Zola (No. 10), and Nekrasov (Nos. 11, 12). There is an article each on mass readership in Russia (Nos. 6, 7, 8) and on village libraries in Vjatka Province (No. 7). Since 1902 was the fiftieth

TABLE 5 *Russian Treasures* (Russkoe bogatstvo), 1902

Total number of references counted: 1,760

Authors most frequently referred to	Number of references
Puškin	92
L. N. Tolstoj	79
Turgenev	56
Belinskij	41
Shakespeare	38
Dostoevskij	35
Gogol'	35
Lermontov	34
G. I. Uspenskij	27
Nekrasov	24
Saltykov-Ščedrin	24

anniversary of Gogol's death, there are several essays devoted to him in the first four issues for the year.

The ninety-two references to Puškin amount to 5.23 percent of the total number, close to the 5.36 percent for Homer in *The European Herald* during the 1820s. (It is interesting to note that one year of a turn-of-the-century "thick journal" yields almost the same overall number of references as nine years of the largest journal in the 1820s.) These figures indicate how integral Puškin had become to the thinking of educated Russians. The references range from comparison of Puškin with other poets through statements about "our greatest classics" to almost unconscious citations of lines or phrases from his poetry. At least at the turn of the century he was more clearly at the forefront of Russian cultural consciousness than Tolstoj, Dostoevskij, or Turgenev.

A few caveats must be mentioned in this context. For one thing, the canonization of Puškin as the anointed poet of Holy Russia (a result of the 1899 celebrations) had brought with it a certain simplification of his poetic identity. In the eyes of some lesser-educated Russians, he was simply a symbol of national greatness with no regard for the aesthetic complexity of his works. We read, for instance, that the mayor of Nižnij Novgorod, by the name of Memorskij, responded to a higher directive to hold Gogol' celebrations by calling together all the teachers and administrators of the city's schools. "In his opening remarks to the assembly," relates the report, "Mr. Memorskij developed two ideas: one, 'that Gogol' is no Puškin,' and two, that there was no need to celebrate him as Puškin had been celebrated; in other words, there was no need for 'Gogol' days' as there had been 'Puškin days,' and if there was to be a program of reading at schools in memory of Gogol', such a program must have 'a general pedagogic character, leaving Gogol's works in the background,' because," as was added later at the meeting, "acquainting the pupils with Gogol' may even be harmful, since he paid too much attention to the negative aspects of life" (*Russian Treasures*, 1902, No. 3, pp. 159–60). Little did the good mayor of Nižnij Novgorod realize that one of Gogol''s teachers at Nežin High School had been dismissed in 1827 for possessing some works by Puškin!

Another fact to be borne in mind is that by 1902 Puškin had still not reached more than the thin upper layer of society. Provincial teachers and librarians who tried to read him and other classics to illiterate peasants and workers reported that the response of their audience was disappointing. "I tried to read Puškin and Gogol', Lermontov and Nekrasov, Turgenev, and Dostoevskij," reports one teacher, "but each of these attempts left a deep sense of pain and sorrow in my soul. . . . My listeners not only did not understand what I was reading to them, but they didn't even try, didn't even wish to" (*Russian Treasures*, 1902, No. 6, p. 90). Similarly, we can see from provincial librarians' reports that Puškin's works were not among volumes needing to be frequently replaced because of heavy use (*Russian Treasures*, 1902, No. 7, p. 69).

Finally, the difference between Puškin's reputation at home and abroad could be seen already at the turn of the century: a survey of French readers turned up some references to Tolstoj and Dostoevskij, but none to Puškin (see the report in *Russian Treasures*, 1902, No. 1, pp. 29–30).

Tolstoj—to turn back to the evidence of Table 5—had at last received his rightful ranking by 1902, although it must be observed that a good many of the references are to his controversial religious and pedagogical views rather than to his fictional works. The rest of Table 5 more or less corresponds to later twentieth-century perceptions of who were the most outstanding nineteenth-century authors.

One of the most remarkable aspects of our list is that, apart from Shakespeare, no foreign author appears on it. This is not because *Russian Treasures* was a parochial journal—indeed, it reported on foreign political and cultural developments more broadly than did the other journals surveyed—but Russian culture had become so rich during the nineteenth century that interpreting it had evidently become the most important task for literary journals.

A disappointing fact revealed by our survey of *Russian Treasures* is that there are only four references to Čexov. Although in a brief review of his works in No. 2 of the journal Mixajlovskij retracts his earlier view that Čexov was an amoral writer and describes him as one of the leading authors of the period, his name is rarely invoked in reviews of other contemporary writers. This lack of canonization by his contemporaries is even more striking than the low ranking of Tolstoj and Dostoevskij was in 1882.

Our findings are summarized in Table 6. Puškin's high ranking in *Son of the Fatherland* shows that he had achieved already in his twenties the kind of recognition that was to be granted to Tolstoj only in his seventies, and to Dostoevskij, Turgenev, and Čexov only after their deaths. The data gathered from *The Contemporary* indicate that, contrary to the commonly accepted notion, Puškin's fame did not go into decline during the decades immediately following his death. *Annals of the Fatherland* shows him maintaining a lead among Russian writers, and *Russian Treasures* demonstrates that by the turn of the century he had become the timeless national

TABLE 6 **Puškin's Ranking in the Five Journals Surveyed**

	Number of refs.	General ranking	Among Russians	% total ranking
The European Herald	15	23rd	3rd	0.86
Son of the Fatherland	31	5th	2nd	3.01
The Contemporary	21	1st	1st	5.11
Annals of the Fatherland	21	2nd	1st	2.96
Russian Treasures	92	1st	1st	5.23

poet of Russia. The term "Russia's Shakespeare" is not an empty cliché: by the 100th anniversary of his birth Puškin had become an integral part of the "personality" of the educated Russian, springing to the mind as spontaneously as Shakespeare does among English-speaking people.

VICTOR TERRAS

Puškin's Prose Fiction in a Historical Context

Now things are quite different: now our literature has changed to novels and short stories. The ode, the verse epic, the ballad, the fable, even the so-called, or rather the once so-called, *romantic verse epic*, the Puškinian verse epic, which once overflowed and flooded our literature, all this is today no more than a memory of a merry but long-gone time. The novel has killed all, swallowed all, and the short story, which arrived together with it, smoothed out the very traces of it all, and the novel itself has respectfully ceded the right of way to it. (Belinskij 1953–59 I: 261; my translation)

So wrote Vissarion Belinskij in his essay "On the Russian Short Story and the Short Stories of Mr. Gogol'" (1835). His essay puts Puškin's prose fiction into a context in which it rarely has been seen since. In this context, Puškin is one of a number of writers who were responsible for the ascendancy of prose fiction described by Belinskij. In an earlier essay, "Literary Reveries" (1834), Belinskij had said that the year 1830 had launched "an entirely new period" of Russian literature (1953–59 I: 87). Indeed, 1830 was not only the year of *Povesti pokojnogo Ivana Petroviča Belkina* (The Tales of Belkin). Bestužev resumed publishing in 1830, and Dal' published his first story that same year. Pogodin published a book of short stories in 1832, Polevoj in 1833, and Pavlov in 1835. Orest Somov, Vladimir Odoevskij, and Vladimir Sollogub also started their careers as writers of prose fiction at about the same time. A division into a "romantic" and a "naturalist" branch of fiction developed almost immediately—so in *The Tales of Belkin*.

How important was Puškin's role in this development? "Pikovaja dama" (The Queen of Spades) is of course one of the best romantic short stories, and *Kapitanskaja dočka* (The Captain's Daughter) is by far the best Waverley novel of Russian literature, but neither of these genres is very important in the general cast of Russian literature. Puškin's contemporaries did not think highly of his prose. Certainly the age of prose was "the age of Gogol'." However, the twentieth-century view which puts a very high value on Puškin's prose was fully anticipated in almost every detail by Apollon Grigor'ev, a member of the generation immediately following Puškin's. Grigor'ev saw Puškin as the father of Russian Realism, a position to which Vasilij Rozanov returned in the 1890s.[1] Grigor'ev (1967: 183) quite specifically saw in Puškin's story "Grobovščik" (The Undertaker) no more and no less than "the seed of the entire school," and the sensibility of Ivan Petrovič Belkin (which Grigor'ev allowed to subsume Grinev's of *The Captain's Daughter*) as "the seed of the writer's rapprochement to everyday reality" (Grigor'ev 1970: 47). Grigor'ev finds reincarnations of Ivan Petrovič Belkin in the works of Turgenev and Tolstoj, to mention only the most important (1967: 337–38, 519).

It must be understood that Grigor'ev does not operate as an empirical comparatist when he makes these assertions, but rather as a Hegelian phenomenologist. He perceives Ivan Petrovič Belkin as a manifestation of "the process of negation" (1967: 517) by which native Russian common sense[2] sublates the Western ideas which the Russian elite had so ardently embraced. Belkin, says Grigor'ev, is the side of Puškin that fears Sil'vio, though still believing that he exists. Tolstoj will then simply deny that such a type exists (1967: 183). Of course, Belkin is only one aspect of Puškin's all-encompassing spirit which embraced "all the *genuine, true* strivings" that were to become manifest in the writings of the next generation (Grigor'ev wrote this in 1859; 1967: 517). Here Grigor'ev obviously anticipated Dostoevskij's "Puškin Speech" (1880).

An early confrontation of the "Puškinian" and "Gogolian" trends of Russian literature appears in Dostoevskij's *Bednye ljudi* (Poor Folk, 1846), whose hero vehemently disapproves of "Šinel' " (The Overcoat), while wholeheartedly approving of "Stancionnyj smotritel' " (The Stationmaster). Devuškin sincerely sympathizes with Samson Vyrin. He recognizes himself in Akakij Akak'evič, but still feels that the image drawn of the poor clerk is not fair. Dostoevskij accordingly "corrects" Gogol' by humanizing Gogol''s metaphysical grotesque (Terras 1984) and letting his story drift from "The Overcoat" into "The Stationmaster"—Devuškin, like Vyrin, will not overcome the loss of Varen'ka, will take to drink, and will die. Dostoevskij intentionally or unintentionally misinterprets Gogol' and sidesteps the issue of the human reduced to the subhuman in "The Overcoat." It does not necessarily follow from this that Dostoevskij failed to see the irony in "The Stationmaster," since we have only Devuškin's reading of it, but Dostoevskij's grafts of Puškin's plot and psychology on the character of Gogol''s "poor clerk" make it likely. At any rate, in Dostoevskij's *Poor Folk*, at least as read and welcomed by Belinskij, Russian prose fiction has abandoned the detachment which marks Puškin's and even Gogol''s prose. In Devuškin's reading, "The Stationmaster" is an example of what

Grigor'ev called "sentimental humanitarianism," a label which he applied to *Poor Folk* and other, less remarkable works of the natural school.[3] It is a distinct possibility that in Dostoevskij's reading, "The Stationmaster" and *The Tales of Belkin* as a whole served as a paradigm of that writer's own early manner: a narrative generated by transformation, often bordering on travesty, of familiar literary themes, images, characters, and styles. An important point, demonstrated by Paul Debreczeny (1983b) in meticulous detail,[4] is that virtually every single motif in Puškin's prose fiction is of literary origin. In many instances we are dealing with a patent literary subtext which is often pointed out by an epigraph. Obviously this trait interferes with "realism." Similarly, the early Dostoevskij used themes from Puškin, Gogol', Rousseau, Hoffmann, George Sand, Sue, and many other authors, making them serve specific ideal or parodic ends. Often the result was a *parodie sérieuse*—in the sense that Sil'vio of "The Shot" may be a *parodie sérieuse* of the Byronic hero.

Dostoevskij's *Poor Folk* is a paradigm of the phenomenological as well as of the empirical relation of Puškin's prose fiction to later Russian literature. Many observations regarding both types of relation are on the record for some important works by major authors. It is remarkable that in an ambience where originality is at a premium, Gogol' claimed that he owed the ideas of his two greatest works to Puškin. He created a powerful precedent which has a parallel in the mythical *My vse vyšli iz 'šineli' Gogolja* (We all have emerged/come from Gogol''s "Overcoat"). One is used to reading statements such as the following, which combines an empirical and a phenomenological conception of the Puškinian presence in Russian prose fiction:

> Dostoevsky borrowed from it ["The Queen of Spades"] heavily: its central character, Hermann, served as a model for both Aleksei Ivanovich of *The Gambler* (1866) and Raskolnikov of *Crime and Punishment* (1875), and the hero of *The Adolescent* (1875), Arkadii Dolgorukii, characterized him as "a colossal personality, an extraordinary type born entirely of St. Petersburg; a type of the Petersburg period." (Debreczeny 1983b: 186)

The fame of Puškin the poet and legend has caused every line he wrote to be highly visible regardless of its intrinsic value or interest. Hence the question may be raised how much of the reputation of Puškin's prose fiction, so little regarded in his lifetime, is a side effect of his total stature. Also, it ought to be considered that the privilege of having many attentive and ingenious readers results in an enhancement of the content of the text, as all possible angles and nuances are discovered and added to the initial impression. Only a few select texts get the exhaustive interpretation accorded, for example, "The Stationmaster" by J. Thomas Shaw (1977: 3–29).

How distinctive is Puškin's prose style? Some quite specific observations have been made on this score. First of all, Puškin's prose has been seen in antithesis to his poetry, so by Puškin himself. This is an exceptional situation, not met with in the case of other major figures who wrote prose as well as poetry, say Goethe or Hugo, or even Lermontov, to take an example from Russian literature. Puškin's very special case may be the ultimate reason why some scholars, notably Ju. M. Lotman, have decided to deal with prose as a form of "anti-poetry."

Adolf Stender-Petersen characterizes Puškin's prose style as follows:

> The language which Puškin used in his stories and novels was also an eloquent expression of his striving for a realistic effect. Compared with the stylistic efforts of contemporary prose writers, it was wholly unromantic. It lacked all emotional and rhetorical elements and was aimed at not mood-creating stylistic effects. . . . And so the conjunction of romantic thematics and classical linguistic norm led to the creation of a new realistic style. (1978: 148–49)

This characterization, which reflects the prevailing view in Soviet scholarship, disregards the ironic detachment of Puškin's prose, the "verbal gestures" which tell the reader that the story should not be taken too seriously, for example, the flippant details inserted in the scene of the old countess's funeral in "The Queen of Spades." Such a show of detachment is characteristic of Russian (and Western) "romantic realism." It is precisely this trait which prevents the Russian natural school from reaching full-fledged realism. While Puškin's poetry often reaches a high level of immediacy, his prose rarely escapes the magic circle of romantic irony. It may be argued that Puškin never got as close to reality in any of his prose works as he did in some of his poetry.

Nor is it to be taken for granted that Puškin's prose style was the perfect expression of his creative vision. D. S. Mirsky writes: "Prose was to him a foreign tongue, acquired by more or less laborious learning. . . . There is always in his prose a sense of constraint, a lack of freedom, a harking back to some outer rule" (1958: 121). Stender-Petersen may also be overestimating the originality of Puškin's prose. In fact, he observes himself: "It is obvious that the manner of composition of Puškin's first stories, *The Tales of Belkin*, came directly out of Walter Scott" (1978: 146).[5] Walter Scott was of course widely imitated in Russian prose fiction of the 1830s and 1840s. If Scott's direct influence on the whole manner of *The Tales of Belkin* is granted, the very close connection between *The Captain's Daughter* and Scott's Waverley novels can hardly be overlooked.

The notion that Puškin's prose is "objective" is hardly tenable in view of the multiple layers of irony and ambiguity found in it. The "Chinese box" type composition of *The Tales of Belkin* (and there are elements of it present in Puškin's other prose works) is common in the romantic fiction of the period, abroad and in Russia. Bestužev offers some good examples, and so does Vel'tmann. This kind of composition has stylistic implications. Nevertheless, there may be some truth in Stender-Petersen's suggestion that Puškin's stories were "stages on the road to a great realist novel." It does seem likely that Puškin was indeed groping for a new form, the prose novel, in which he would give expression to his most cherished concerns and convictions. He had, albeit marginally, touched upon one of these concerns in "Egyptian Nights": the threatened dignity and freedom of the Russian nobleman, and had approached another quite explicitly: the conflict between the man and the poet within himself. Another vital concern, the anticipation of a new *pugačevščina*, is stated in *The Captain's Daughter*. The tragedy of an unhappy marriage emerges from the sketches which are credited with being the model for *Anna Karenina*.

It may be asked whether the isomorphism of content ("life") and literary form, which some structuralists have observed in so much detail in *Evgenij Onegin* (Eugene Onegin),[6] extends to Puškin's prose, and also whether the transition to prose was "organically" motivated by a change in the life which Puškin lived and of which he was a part. Lotman's observations on the period before the transition to prose make this a logical corollary:

> The clear differentiation between the poetic and the prosaic in human behavior and actions is characteristic of the period we have been considering. . . . The sphere of poetry in real life was the world of "daring."
> The individual living in the age of Puškin and Vjazemskij moved freely back and forth from the sphere of prose to that of poetry. In literature only poetry "counted." Similarly, in judging a person the prosaic sphere of behavior was in a sense discounted, as if it did not exist.
> The Decembrists brought unity to human behavior, not through the rehabilitation of life's prose but by filtering life through heroic texts. (Lotman 1985: 148)

As Todd has pointed out, Puškin took the step from literature as a pastime of "polite society" to literature as a profession, but explicitly refused to participate in the move to make literature into a social institution (for which he was chided by Belinskij). This seems consistent with Lotman's conception. Puškin, a committed *poet* of the aristocratic Decembrist movement, was after 1830 an uncommitted *littérateur*.[7] It is consistent with this notion if one sees Puškin's prose as detached, even aloof, seeking to put a certain distance between the author and his text. There are some exceptions, to be sure. The beginning of "Egyptian Nights" is almost a "confession." But certainly any "involved" *socialité* could not be a trait of Puškin's prose.

It was only natural that a story by the manumitted serf Pavlov should lack the quality of detachment if it dealt with the plight of the educated serf. In fact, Pavlov's story "The Nameday Party" (1835) "comes on" as strongly as any American abolitionist piece, striking the detached reader as sentimental and too transparently tendentious. Likewise, it was to be expected that women writers of the period should lack detachment when describing the misery of an educated woman left without a chance to exert her intellectual faculties. By the same token, Puškin would lose his detachment when his subject was the freedom and dignity of a Russian nobleman—as when Čarskij lectures his Italian visitor on the independence of Russian poets.

Yet it is also true that among the writers of the natural school who were very much "involved" with the social underdog, one finds Count Vladimir Sollogub, very much a member of high society. And it could be argued that some of the tales of Jakov Butkov, whose heroes are poor devils like their author, are ironically detached. Still, the fact remains that Puškin does gravitate toward a narrative manner which is in one way or another detached from its subject. This detachment is obtained in various ways: through a pointedly—one is tempted to say "artfully"—terse and artless narrative manner, through irony, or through the creation of a dummy narrator. All of these manners are common in romantic prose. I do not believe that there really is such a thing as a distinctive "Puškinian" prose style.[8] I submit that the whole notion that Russian realist prose "came straight from Puškin" is at least as suspect as that according to which it "came straight out of Gogol''s 'Overcoat.' "

The prose fiction of Puškin's contemporaries, with the exception of Gogol', is rarely read and rarely discussed in scholarly literature. Much of it has not been reprinted since the mid-nineteenth century. Meanwhile, Puškin's prose fiction continues to be read by millions of readers and to be studied by hundreds of scholars. The point of my remarks is that an assessment of the value of Puškin's prose fiction in context and in comparison with the works of his contemporaries is in order. Whether this will lead to a revision of the prevailing view that makes Puškin one of the pillars of Russian prose fiction is a different question.

Notes

INTRODUCTION

1. Berberova 1960: 229. This sententia was then taken by Xodasevič as epigraph to his book on Puškin, *Poètičeskoe xozjajstvo Puškina* (1924).
2. The Puškin Symposium was the culmination of a semester-long university-wide Puškin Festival. Among the various events in that festival were the following: a production of Tchaikovsky's opera *Eugene Onegin*, based on Puškin's novel in verse, by the University of Wisconsin Opera (6, 7, 13, 15 February 1987); a performance of Russian music by the Milwaukee Symphony Orchestra (6 February 1987); two exhibitions at the Elvejhem Art Museum ("Russian Paintings in the Davies Collection," 7 February–8 March 1987; and "Popov, Vilner, and Utenkov: Contemporary Russian Printmakers," 21 February–5 April 1987); Puškin exhibits in the Memorial Library (the Rare Book Room and the Music Library) and at the Cooperative Children's Book Center (10 February 1987 to the end of the semester); a program featuring Russian music given by the University of Wisconsin Symphony Orchestra and the Choral Union (28 February 1987); three programs of dances featuring Russian music (5 and 7 May and 21 November 1987)—the last of these included the premiere of an original choreographed solo ballet based on Puškin's lyric "The Demon"; a Russian chamber music concert broadcast live over the state (15 March 1987); and a four-evening series of Russian films on Puškin's works (2, 9, 16, 23 April 1987). Finally, at the Puškin Symposium there was a special exhibition featuring copies of all the U.S. dissertations on Puškin completed at U.S. institutions up to that time, and books on Puškin and/or his time by participants at the symposium.
   The Puškin Symposium itself included 25 papers by American Puškinists (all on faculties of U.S. institutions, except one who earned his Ph.D. in the U.S.). The complete list of participants is as follows (together with their institutional affiliation at that time): Walter Arndt (Dartmouth Coll.), David Bethea (Univ. of Wisconsin, Madison), James Brown (Univ. of Minnesota), Brett L. Cooke (Texas A.&M. Univ.), Sergej Davydov (Bryn Mawr Coll.), Paul Debreczeny (Univ. of North Carolina), J. Clayton Douglas (Univ. of Ottawa), Caryl Emerson (Cornell Univ.), Monika Frenkel (Stanford Univ.), Antonia Glasse (Duke Univ.), George Gutsche (Northern Illinois Univ.), William Harkins (Columbia Univ.), Sona Hoisington (Univ. of Illinois, Chicago), Simon Karlinsky (Univ. of California, Berkeley), Lauren Leighton (Univ. of Illinois, Chicago), Gerald Mikkelson (Univ. of Kansas), Leslie O'Bell (Univ. of Texas), Daniel Rancour-Laferriere (Univ. of California, Davis), Roberta Reeder (Harvard Univ.), Savely Senderovich (Cornell Univ.), J. Thomas Shaw (Univ. of Wisconsin, Madison), Victor Terras (Brown Univ.), William Mills Todd III (Stanford Univ.), and Walter Vickery (Univ. of North Carolina).
3. This situation (religious intolerance in the Soviet Union) has changed radically (for the better) in recent years under the impact of *glasnost'*.

"THE RUSSIAN TERPSICHORE'S SOUL-FILLED FLIGHT"

1. Leon Stilman (1958) provides a discussion of these two "realities" (characters' and authors'). In an earlier study (Todd 1986) I analyzed the ways in which

Puškin related these two ontological levels to others by treating each in terms of convention, choice, and autonomy.

2. Unless otherwise noted, I shall use Arndt's translation (Puškin 1981), indicating chapter and stanza in the form [I.3]. The square brackets and roman numeral will distinguish these references to the novel from references to the "large Academy" edition of Puškin's works (PSS).

3. Turgenev's essay, a taxonomy of dance forms, gives valuable insights into the state of dance theory in early nineteenth-century Russia. Distinguishing dance forms according to the dominant emotion that each expresses, Turgenev's essay reveals the impact of Sentimentalist poetics, which classified verse forms by their dominant emotions.

4. It lies beyond the scope of this essay to comment on the vicious theatrical politics of which there is a hint in these lines. Slonimskij (1974) has several excellent chapters on the subject.

5. V. S. Baevskij (1986: 140) notes that for Puškin and his contemporaries Istomina was indeed "the Russian Terpsichore."

6. Krasovskaja (1958: 157) identifies the dance movements here as a *rond de jambe*, a *renversé*, and a *battement battu*. Slonimskij (1974: 33–34), following an unpublished manuscript by L. D. Blok, prefers to describe them as a *grand fouetté de face* on *demi-pointe*, performed to an andante violin or cello solo and followed by a series of *brisés* (*jetés battus*).

7. "Odnoj nogoj kasajas' pola"; "I vdrug pryžok, i vdrug letit"; "Letit, kak pux ot ust Eola"; and "I bystroj nozkoj nožku b'et." The two-stress line begins the passage "Blistatel'na, polovuzdušna" [I.20].

On the prosody of *Eugene Onegin* see Tomaševskij (1918), Vinokur (1941), and Nabokov (1975 III: 448–540).

8. The sense of social dance as ritual that I am advancing here is derived from Claude Lévi-Strauss (1966: 30–33), who distinguishes conjunctive ritual from competitive, disjunctive game.

9. In a manuscript note Puškin acknowledged the inaccuracy of the spurs—the cavalier guards wore low shoes to balls—but kept them in the stanza for their "poetic" quality (PSS VI: 528).

10. The translator's "unbridle" somewhat reverses the sense of the Russian *vlečet* ("draw," "attract"); desire here is aroused and directed by the dancing feet.

11. Flora, in Didelot's *Zephyr and Flora*, was one of Istomina's best-known roles; it has been argued that Puškin intended his sketch on Acteon and Diana (PSS V: 154) to become a Didelot ballet (Baevskij 1986: 141–42).

12. Nabokov (1975 II: 148) reminds us that this phrase is "an old French cliché . . . a standardized echo of Rome and her poets." Within the context of *Eugene Onegin*, however, the phrase acquires new life and concreteness from the clamor of the ballroom scenes that I have just discussed. Within the novel, "noise" and "clamor" stand in binary opposition to the "magic" sounds of poetry and music.

13. Chapters II and III touch upon the choral dance of the folk; Chapter IV compares the ice on which some boys are skating to the polished parquet of a ballroom floor; Chapters V and VI feature a ball at the Larins; Chapter VII takes Tat'jana to a Moscow ball. In the final chapter, however, reference to the dance is only implicit, as the poet recalls the bacchanal revels of his youthful days. To assume that this stanza refers to the Green Lamp Society's discussion of the ballet is not far-fetched, but the reference is not explicit. On this point, see Slonimskij (1974: 48).

14. For further information on the serf ballets see Krasovskaja (1958: 67–80).

15. Puškin includes two other forms of folk dance in the novel. Tat'jana's dream, which shows how thoroughly the gentry could assimilate both folk and European culture, features a windmill dancing the "squat-jig" (*pljašet vprisjadku*, PSS V: 17),

as Nabokov translates it. In the stanzas from "Onegin's Journey," which Puškin appended to the novel, the poet includes the "drunken stomping of the *trepak*" among the prosaic scenes that he would like to describe (PSS VI: 201).

16. Lotman (1983: 85–86) notes the connotations of eroticism, modernity, and romanticism that were linked with waltzing in the 1920s.

17. Lotman (1983: 81) makes the important point that salons also differed from balls in the more intellectual quality of their talk.

18. I am most grateful to my colleagues Carol Anschuetz, Victoria Bonnell, Gregory Freidin, Herbert Lindenberger, and John Malmstad for their valuable comments on earlier drafts of this essay.

"THE QUEEN OF SPADES" AND THE OPEN END

This essay is developed out of ideas generated through discussion with Gary Saul Morson on a larger co-authored work in progress on parodic strategies in Puškin.

1. In an excellent, as yet unpublished essay, Felix Raskolnikov summarizes the major Soviet contributions to this debate on "the real versus the irrational" in "The Queen of Spades," regretting that earlier studies have not "admitted the possibility of a *serious* attitude on Puškin's part toward the irrational."

2. This aspect of the Onegin-Tat'jana relationship received provocative treatment by Sergej Bočarov in a paper prepared for—but not delivered at—the Kennan Institute's Conference on Russian Classic Literature, "Puškin: The Shorter Prose Works" (January 20–21, 1986, Washington, D.C.). Bočarov points out that Onegin's first reference to Tat'jana is already provisional and twice displaced, "not from himself nor for himself" ("I would have chosen the other / If I were a poet like you"). The fact that he is *not* a poet but a sceptic effectively bars him from satisfying any of the definitions Tat'jana craves; for most of the novel he represents openness, potential, whereas Tat'jana is forever the symbol of resoluteness and irreversible decision. The tension between the hero and heroine, Bočarov suggests, is the tension between "dal' svobodnogo romana" (distance of a free novel) (which Onegin represents) and the more teleological variant of that line in the notebooks, "*plan* svobodnogo romana" (plan of a free novel), which is the realm of Tat'jana's equilibrium and quest for answers. See Bočarov 1986.

3. From Puškin's review of the second volume of Polevoj's *Istorija russkogo naroda* (History of the Russian People, 1830), in PSS XI: 127.

4. Interestingly enough, this subtext of real gambling—which Puškin so cunningly hides from Germann himself—is revealed to the hero in Čajkovskij's much-maligned operatic version of the tale. In the main, of course, Čajkovskij sentimentalizes the plot, creating a banal love story between Liza and Germann and stripping away Puškin's cool irony as surely as he strips it from his operatic *Onegin*. But on close inspection, Čajkovskij's Germann is a surprisingly self-conscious character. Perhaps because he must sing arias about himself, he has perspective on his dilemma—which Puškin's hero does not.

Consider, for example, Germann's ruminations at the beginning of Act II, scene 4, as he enters the old Countess's bedroom and vows to extract her secret. "A esli tajny net?" (And if there is no secret?) he suddenly sings. "I èto vse pustoj liš' bred moej bol'noj duši!" (And it is all merely the empty delirium of my sick soul!). Even more telling is the nervous song Germann performs at the gaming tables (Act III, scene 7) while he is still in his winning phase, that is, before he draws the fatal queen of spades. Surrounded by stunned friends and watched maliciously by Prince Eleckij—the injured ex-fiancé, from whom Germann had stolen Liza—Germann calls for wine and "giggles hysterically." He then sings: "Čto žizn' naša?

Igra! Dobro i zlo—odni mečty! Trud, čestnost' —skazki dlja bab'ja! Kto prav, kto
sčastliv zdes', druz'ja? Segodnja ty a zavtra ja!" (And what is our life? A game!
Good and evil—both are only dreams! Labor, honor—old wives' tales! Who is
right, who is happy here, friends? Today it's you, tomorrow it's I!).

Both Puškin's and Čajkovskij's heroes are close to being obsessive paranoids, to
be sure. But only the operatic Germann is granted the right to question and mock
his own pathology. He has clearly glimpsed by the end of the opera what real
gambling requires, and the realization kills him.

PUŠKIN'S EASTER TRIPTYCH

1. The eventual shape of this cycle was discussed by Izmajlov (1954: 553–55;
1958: 29–40), Stepanov (1959: 30–34), and Alekseev (1967: 122–27). A slightly
expanded Russian version of this article appeared in *Revue des études slaves* 59
(Paris, 1987): 157–72.

2. E. Etkind, in the French edition of Puškin, published the four poems under
the title "Les deux pouvoirs" (Puškin 1983).

3. At the time this essay was written, I was not familiar with the excellent work
of V. P. Stark (1982), who analyzes the poem ("Hermit fathers . . . ") in a similar
context, and E. A. Toddes (1983), who interprets the cycle in a broader Christian
framework.

4. My calculation is based on K. Taranovsky's table of stressed vowel frequen-
cies (Taranovsky 1965: 116). See also Cherry, Halle, and Jakobson (1953: 34–46).
If one were to read the poem with the Old Church Slavic pronunciation, that is,
without a reduction of the unstressed "o's," the first segment would become even
more marked.

5. Annenkov (1855: 312). The poem is also quoted by Lerner (Puškin 1907–15
VI: 491) and Tomaševskij (1930: 78–79).

6. There is really no simple way to translate the difference in English between
besy (devils) and *diavol* (devil, the devil). Hence we have decided in the interest of
clarity to leave the Russian terms when describing this "infernal trinity."

7. By calling Judas "vsemirnyj vrag" (universal foe), Puškin endows him with
Satan's attributes. "Satan" in Hebrew is a descriptive title meaning "adversary."
When the Old Testament was translated into Greek, Satan became *diabolos*, which
meant "accuser, slanderer" (Fishwick 1963: 18 and Cavendish 1975: 185).

8. An analogous plot (though contrary to that of "Imitation of the Italian") can
be found in Puškin's "Prorok" (Prophet) (1826), based on Isaiah 6:1–13, in which a
six-winged Seraph enlivens the senses of a dying man and places a burning coal in
his chest, whereupon God resurrects the man and turns him into a prophet.

9. I include both graphic and phonetic occurrences. The average incidence of
this anagram in other Puškin texts of the same length is only 2, 3. My calculation is
based on 40 samples of Puškin's Alexandrines.

10. It is said in the Gospel that Satan planted betrayal in the heart of Judas (John
13:2, 27). But evil presupposes freedom of consent. It is, perhaps, interesting to
note that the inversion of the word "ad" (hell) is the affirmative "da" (yes). Most
meaningful, the anagram "da" figures, of course, in the name of Iu*da*, who is not
named in the poem but is referred to as "pre*DA*tel'," containing the same anagram.

11. Dante, too, meted out punishment for his sinners, identical with their transgression (*contrapasso*): they are doomed to suffer the harm they committed in life.
This notion is not accepted by the Catholic Church at large and is unique to Dante.
Both Satan and Judas, having betrayed God and Christ, are reunited in the lowest,
ninth circle of Hell, where Judas's head is being chewed by Satan ("Measure for
measure, or one good kiss deserves another").

12. In order to avoid the "orthographic atheism" of post-revolutionary editions, I capitalize certain words, as was the custom in Puškin's time. According to the manuscript reproduced and described by Izmajlov (1954), Puškin crossed out two epithets in line 5 without replacing them: "Stojali [, blednye,] dve [slabye] ženy" (Stood [, pale,] two [weak] women). The poem was published in censored form by Annenkov in 1855 and 1857 (without the title and with the omission of lines 12–13 and 19–22), and later by Gercen in London in *Poljarnaja zvezda* (Polar Star) (1856). The full version appeared in Russia in 1870.

13. The other relevant subtext for this line is Matt. 6:19–20: "Ne sobirajte sebe sokrovišč na zemle, gde mol' i rža istrebljajut i gde vory podkoryvajut i kradut; No sobirajte sebe sokrovišča na nebe, gde ni mol', ni rža ne istrebljaet i gde vory ne podkoryvajut i ne kradut" (Do not collect for yourselves treasures on earth, where moth and rust destroy and where thieves break in and steal; But collect for your- selves treasures in heaven, where neither moth nor rust destroys and where thieves do not break in and steal).

BESTUŽEV-MARLINSKIJ'S *JOURNEY TO REVEL'* AND PUŠKIN

1. Russian literary travelogues and their Western sources are discussed in Wilson 1973. There are separate chapters devoted to Bestužev's models Sterne, Dupaty, and Karamzin. There is also a brief account of *Journey to Revel'* in Chapter IX, "The Epigones" (meaning the epigones of Karamzin, whose *Pis'ma russkogo putešestvennika* [Letters of a Russian Traveler] is the subject of the preceding Chapter VIII). Wilson cites the same six lines of the prefatory poem that Nikolaj Mordovčenko quoted in his edition of Bestužev's poetry (Bestužev-Marlinskij 1948 and 1961). Unlike Mordovčenko, Wilson does perceive that "the tone [of this poem] is not unlike that of Puškin's *Eugene Onegin*" (Wilson 1973: 87).

I am grateful to my colleague Hugh McLean for bringing Wilson's book to my attention after the present study was completed.

2. Evgenij Baratynskij, in his poems of 1820–21, associated *dosug* and *dosugi* with erotic situations rather than poetry. Konstantin Batjuškov, the direct prede- cessor of Puškin, Baratynskij, and Bestužev in the sphere of light poetry, did con- nect leisure and friendship with the genesis of poetry in his 1806 poem "K Gnediču" (To Gnedič): "Pel ot leni i dosuga; / Muza mne byla podruga" (Batjuš- kov 1964: 76–77; Shaw 1975a: 2, 3).

3. Baratynskij's numerous instances of the inchoative *Byvalo* all occur in poems written after 1828 (Shaw 1975b: 3).

4. Boris Modzalevskij's catalogue of Puškin's personal library shows that he had a number of issues of the journal *Sorevnovatel'* (The Contender), where *Journey to Revel'* first appeared, though the issue of February 1821 is not listed in the cata- logue (Modzalevskij 1910: 132). Considering the fate of Puškin's library as de- scribed by Modzalevskij (xiff.) and later by Arnol'd Gessen (1965), the absence of a particular edition from a twentieth-century catalogue can in no way indicate that Puškin did not own a copy of it in his lifetime.

THE COUVADE OF PETER THE GREAT

I wish to thank Barbara Milman and Galya Diment for their constructive sugges- tions. All translations of passages in *The Bronze Horseman* are from Walter Arndt's

Pushkin Threefold (New York: E. P. Dutton, 1972), pp. 401–27. Other translations are my own.

1. Izmajlov (Puškin 1978: 259) goes so far as to apply the verb "roždat'sja" (to be born) in its figurative sense: " . . . v mae 1703 g. v soznanii Petra roždaetsja derzkaja, no genial'naja mysl' ob osnovanii novogo goroda . . . ." But this metaphor is not extended, and there is no suggestion that the poem contains a fantasy of male childbirth.

At one point Makogonenko speaks of the "vse novye i novye storony goroda— narodnogo i Petrova *detišča*" (1982: 169, emphasis added). This metaphor too is not developed.

Gutsche describes the origin of St. Petersburg in these terms: "Its very *birth* was morally tainted by the anonymous graves of its builders" (1986: 17, emphasis added). Again the metaphor is not extended.

2. I wish to thank Simon Karlinsky for bringing these lines to my attention. They are quoted in Karlinsky 1985: 257.

3. I borrow the *verx/niz* opposition from the Soviet semioticians (e.g., Ivanov 1976: 336; see also Belyj 1929: 190). The contrast of high and low in the passage is just one more example of what Knigge calls "das Kontrastprinzip" in the poem (1984: 72).

4. The myth of the birth of Athena is directly alluded to in *Egipeckie noči* (Egyptian Nights) (Cooke 1983: 253).

5. An association of water with *horses* as well has been discussed by psychoanalyst Ernest Jones: "In general the ideas of horse and water have always been closely associated, suggesting that something about a horse instinctively brings to mind the idea of water" (1951: 291–92). In Puškin's poem the horse of Peter stands immovably over the waters of the Neva and is tied to the Neva in other ways, as we have seen. Jones's examples of the horse-water association include the Centaurs with their "essentially watery origin" (1951: 293), the aquatic Hippocampen, the sea god Poseidon, who begat horses and discovered the riding art, the Hippocrene spring, etc. Belyj believes that the waves of the flooding Neva represent Neptune's (i.e., Poseidon's) horses (1929: 274). Jones adduces evidence for his thesis that "the actual link between the ideas of Horse and Water is the *reproductive powers* of both" (1951: 296). The exercise of reproductive power is of course precisely what the couvade of Peter the Great means.

6. Perhaps, following the structural scheme of Žolkovskij (1979: 46), the couvade of Peter as well as the couvade of Puškin's poetic creativity could be regarded as manifestations of the abstract notion of "vyxod iz sebja" (coming out of oneself).

In a handout provided to all participants in the conference "Pushkin Scholarship in America Today," Professor Shaw made the following observation:

> It turns out that [Pushkin] rhymes *voln-poln* in eleven different rhyme sets; three of them are sets of three with the word *čoln*. None of these three words is used (in this form) as a rhymeword with any other word [see Shaw 1974]. Does this mean that [Puskin] had eleven pregnancies with the word, some of which he attributed to a swan, to Napoleon, to Peter?

A psychoanalyst's answer to this question would occupy many pages. Each of the eleven rhyme sets would have to be examined in context, just as the opening rhyme in *The Bronze Horseman* has here been examined in the context of the poem.

In another context the *voln-poln* rhyme could conceivably have an entirely different psychoanalytic meaning. Here, for example, is the final quatrain of "K morju" (To the Sea): "V lesa, v pustyni molčalivy / Perenesu, toboju [morem] poln, / Tvoi skaly, tvoi zalivy, / I blesk, i ten', i govor voln" (To forests, to silent wildernesses / I will transport, full of you [the sea], / Your cliffs, your bays, / And the glitter and shade and murmur of waves) (PSS II: 333). In this particular case the persona expresses an intense identification with the personified sea. Psychoanalytically speaking, the persona is identifying with the lost object. What the *poln-voln* rhyme does is reinforce the identification by making a word that refers to the persona match up with a word that refers to the lost object itself, the sea, or its metonymically functioning waves (*voln*). The phonological (rhyme) similarity bolsters the semantic similarity implicit in the psychological process of identification. The rhyme thus has a completely different psychoanalytic function in "To the Sea" than it has at the beginning of *The Bronze Horseman*. The "eleven pregnancies" whimsically proposed by Professor Shaw therefore have to be reduced to ten, and would probably have to be reduced even further if each of the poems possessing the *voln-poln* rhyme were to be examined in psychoanalytic detail.

7. The meaning of the reference to Aleksandrov is not clear.

8. Kučera (1956: 281) suggests that in each of the works *The Bronze Horseman*, *The Stone Guest*, and *The Tale of the Golden Cockerel* there is a "tired man" who is involved in an Oedipal triangle with a desired woman, and a statue that functions as a "father-image." Unfortunately, Kučera concentrates his analysis on *The Stone Guest*, but his valuable insight would obviously be the starting point for any future study of the Oedipal dynamics of *Bronze Horseman*.

THE REJECTED IMAGE

1. See also Kvjatkovskij (1966: 189–90).

THE ROLE OF THE *EQUES* IN PUŠKIN'S *BRONZE HORSEMAN*

1. An extensive overview of Russian/Soviet scholarship on *Bronze Horseman* is found in Makarovskaja 1978. For full recent interpretations/critical treatments, see Borev 1981 and Knigge 1984. Perhaps the two finest single works on *Bronze Horseman* are Lednicki 1955 and Puškin (Izmajlov) 1978. See as well Ospovat and Timenčik 1985, a study which is particularly helpful for its wealth of information about the subsequent reception of Puškin's work.

2. See, for example, Sergej Davydov's study in this volume of the religious motifs in Puškin's last poems ("Puškin's Easter Triptych"). The situation with regard to religious intolerance in the Soviet Union has of course changed fundamentally in the *glasnost'* era, especially since the Puškin conference (April 1987; see Introduction), which provided the impetus for the present volume. Two recent Soviet works linking Puškin's text to the Book of Job, the Ten Commandments, Revelation, and various Old Testament themes are Tarxov 1977 and Nemirovskij 1990.

3. For more on the links between Puškin's *poèma* (narrative poem) and the later explicitly *apocalyptic* connotations associated with Peter as horseman of doom, see Ospovat and Timenčik 1985, Bethea 1989, and Nemirovskij 1990.

4. Much of the following section on the role of the equestrian in European statuary is taken from my book *The Shape of Apocalypse* (see note 3). I have been particularly aided in this discussion by the articles of Janson 1974, Levitine 1972, and Watson 1983. The most complete study to date of Falconet and his work on the statue of Peter is Kaganovič 1975.

5. Here I follow the chronology and emphasis of Janson (1974: 166–67), who singles out Bernini as the turning point in this tradition. Kaganovič (1975: 82) suggests that Pietro Tacca's equestrian of Phillip IV of Spain, created in the mid-seventeenth century, is the most likely predecessor/model for Falconet. Janson, however, who mentions the Tacca equestrian, is the better informed about the

European tradition of equestrians. His point is that Bernini represents the logical *culmination* of a tradition which includes the works of Giovanni da Bologna, Tacca, and Francesco Mochi and which may be expressed as a move away from an emphasis on *virtù* (the prowess of the individual hero) and toward an emphasis on dynastic authority (166).

6. These words belong to Giles Fletcher, an envoy of England's Queen Elizabeth I who visited Russia during the reign of Fedor Ivanovič. See Durov 1977: 4. It is intriguing to note that on some of these medals there was simply a horseman, *without the defeated dragon*, or a *unicorn*. Some scholars attest that the dragon *came later*—that is, after the solitary horseman—during the late fifteenth century, when Moscow was considering the significance of the fall of Constantinople and adopting as state emblem the two-headed eagle. For more on the history of the St. George medal and order on Russian soil, see Lakier 1855 I: 228–31, 290–91; and Speransov 1974: 25–26.

7. "An additional iconographic manifestation of the changed [i.e., more secularized—DMB] image of the ruler is provided by numismatic evidence: Throughout the sixteenth and seventeenth centuries, the Moscovite coins bore the representation of St. George. At the same time, the image of the saint was modified by an imperial radiate crown and by a portrait of the reigning tsar; i.e., the 'Moscow rider' of Moscovite coinage was, simultaneously, St. George and the Tsar. With Peter, the tsar gives way to the saint and the coins were not regarded as portraits of the tsar-saint; by the end of Peter's reign even the saintly symbol loses its significance and a decree of 1724 refers to the representation simply as 'rider with spear' " (Cherniavsky 1961: 82, n23). See also Spasskij 1955: 266–67.

8. Blok, for example, makes explicit reference in his "Petersburg Poem" to an apocalyptic confrontation between Moscow horseman and Petersburg horseman. See Hackel 1975: 41.

9. Here and elsewhere I use the literal translation of *Bronze Horseman* found in Arndt 1972: 400–27.

10. Puškin clearly did not have what today would be called an apocalyptic "turn of mind." But he did take for granted a knowledge of the last book of the Bible on the part of his readers and correspondents. There are in all five indisputable mentions of the apocalypse in Puškin's literary works (including drafts) and letters. (See the "large" Academy edition: PSS I: 162–63, III: 860, XII: 174, XIII: 29, XIV: 121.) Most of these references are parodic; that is, Puškin tended to use them in a comic rather than serious context, referring to himself during the first Boldino autumn (1830), for example, as sending regards from his "Patmos" (letter to M. P. Pogodin of November 1830 in XIV: 121). On another occasion, Puškin includes an allusion to the Pale Horse of Revelation in a draft of the poem "Stixi, sočinennye noč'ju vo vremja bessonnicy" (Verses composed at night during insomnia) (1830), but then removes it, presumably because he does not want the elements of this mythological system to invade his art on a serious level. In an interesting recent study ("The Apocalyptic Theme in Puškin's 'Count Nulin' ") the émigré scholar Boris Gasparov argues for the presence of an apocalyptic subtext in *Graf Nulin* (1825). The Russian eschatological tradition, especially as it relates to the equine motif, is treated at some length in Bethea 1989.

11. The important point to be made here is that, in carefully studying the biography of Peter and in insisting on the greatest possible verisimilitude allowable within the sculptural conventions of the time, Falconet the foreigner was trying to get at his own, fully dimensionalized understanding of the Petrine myth. His visual conception went against the "classicism" being imposed upon him "from within," just as Puškin's verbal conception would to a significant degree go against the unquestioning "panegyric tradition" established by Kantemir, Trediakovskij, Sumarokov, Lomonosov, and others (see Vickery 1963). That the cliff juts out into

space (and by analogy time) and the steed and rider are perched in mid-stride atop it gives the entire ensemble a "revolutionary character" (i.e., this is no simple, straightforward "progress" but a great "turning-point") within the context of eighteenth-century statuary, leading Diderot to comment in a letter of 6 December 1773 to the sculptor, "May I be stricken dead if I suspected that you had anything like that in your head" (cited in Levitine 1972: 60). And as shall be shown presently, it is precisely this *revolt against classicism* which the raised steed epitomizes that Puškin chooses to focus on in his "poetic" *concetto*.

12. See the excellent studies on the lack of a "middle ground" in Russian history and the role of tsar as revolutionary in Lotman and Uspenskij 1975 and 1985.

13. The statue of a triumphant Lenin arriving at the Finland Station *in his armored car* (*bronevik*) is of course further evidence that even the Soviets have felt compelled to tap into a transparently similar version of the imperial equestrian.

14. Puškin himself on several occasions made remarks about Peter's essentially *revolutionary* character. See, e.g., his notes for a planned work about the nobility (1830): "Pierre I est tout à la fois Robespierre et Napoléon (la Revolution incarnée)" (PSS XII: 205).

15. Falconet, by contrast, kept Peter's clothing simple (a loose-fitting shirt such as that worn by the Volga boatmen—see Levitine 1972: 55) but did give him a crown of laurels.

16. Cf. the opening scenes of Shakespeare's *Julius Caesar*, where Icarus/Phaeton imagery, in conjunction with that of the passing chariot and the fawning crowd, plays an important role (I.i.69–75).

17. This word is of course especially marked, with connotations of doom, in *Bronze Horseman*. Depending on whether the poet/speaker views the subject as a "hero" or "tyrant," the word can mean either "awesome" or "awful, terrible" in Puškin's vocabulary. The paradox in *Bronze Horseman* is that Peter is both "awesome" for his creation of the beautiful city and "awful, terrible" for his "execution" of Paraša and his degradation of Evgenij. See, e.g., the discussion of Peter and Mazepa in *Poltava* in Shaw 1985b: 659.

18. Recall the important lines in *Bronze Horseman* when the narrator, surveying the rising tide of floodwaters, exclaims, "Narod / Zrit božij gnev i kazni ždet. / Uvy! Vse gibnet . . . " (The people / gaze on the wrath of God and bide [their] doom. / Woe! All is perishing . . . ") (PSS V: 141).

19. Puškin compares the poet to his opposite, the *zemnye kumiry* (earthly idols), in his first draft of *Bronze Horseman* ("Pervaja černovaja rukopis'," in Puškin (Izmajlov) 1978: 36).

20. Puškin is not an author who is likely to use scapegoats. His victims are almost always endowed with larger ideological and artistic concerns.

21. All references to Puškin's use of *gerb* (coat-of-arms) have been checked against the four-volume *Slovar' jazyka Puškina* (Vinogradov 1956–61).

22. *Son* (sleep, dream) is a very important word and theme in *Bronze Horseman* (see below).

23. See as well the closely related "Moja rodoslovnaja" (My Genealogy, 1830).

24. The image complex of boyars' domicile + overgrown grass + coat-of-arms reappears a few years later in "Putešestvie iz Moskvy v Peterburg" (Journey from Moscow to Petersburg, dated 1834–35) (PSS XI: 246), where the basic meaning of "hereditary nobility in eclipse" is further reinforced.

25. The emblems of Jaroslav', Nižnij Novgorod, Rostov, and Perm' may be older than that of Vladimir, but their exact age has not been firmly established (Speransov 1974: 22).

26. For a description of the way the house and square looked at the time of the great flood of 1824, see "Primečanija k tekstu poèmy," in Puškin (Izmajlov) 1978: 173.

27. In this regard, it may be appropriate to recall that in one of the early sketches for *Bronze Horseman*, Evgenij's ancestor fought on the side of the Old Believers against Peter (noted in Jakobson 1975: 41).

28. Evgenij is now "seized with a dark force" (*obujannyj* siloj černoj) as the people (*narod*) were earlier "struck mad with fright" (straxom *obujalyj*) during the flood. A form of the same word is used in each case (PSS V: 141, 148).

29. It is possible, upon careful reading, to demonstrate how Puškin's "panegyric" style in the "Introduction" already contains thematic and semantic elements that potentially undermine it. In any event, it is not a simple reproduction of the odic manner of various eighteenth-century writers (Kantemir, Trediakovskij, Sumarokov, Lomonosov, Deržavin, etc.).

30. "Mode of address" is something of a play on words in this context since the Bronze Horseman does not actually speak in the poem. However, in Evgenij's mind, at least, the statue's "silence" changes from one of *indifference* to one of threatening *attentiveness*.

PUŠKIN ON HIS AFRICAN HERITAGE

1. The most extensive treatment of the question of the precise homeland of Abram Gannibal is that of Vladimir Nabokov (1975). S. S. Gejčenko (1977: 332–34) gives an interesting account of a Russian journalist visiting in 1960 what he takes to be Puškin's ancestral home in Ethiopia. Interest in Puškin's black ancestry has been shown by biographers and scholars since 1855, when Annenkov's biography first appeared (Annenkov 1984). The most thorough recent studies are those of Teletova (1981), Fejnberg (1983), and Leec (1984). Among the important earlier studies, one should mention those of Auslender (1910), Modzalevskij (1929), Vegner (1937), and Paina (1962).

2. In this essay, citations directly from Puškin's text are from the "large Academy" textual edition (Puškin 1937–59), and are indicated by PSS plus volume and page, except that poems are cited by volume and number according to the system in *Slovar' jazyka Puškina* (Vinogradov 1956–61). Factual information regarding dating, titles, and publication is drawn from the notes to that edition. For precise timing of publications, PSS has been supplemented by Sinjavskij and Cjavlovskij (1938). Reliance for biographical information has been placed mainly on Cjavlovskij (1951) and Čerejskij (1975). Translations from the letters are from Shaw (1967). Translations from Puškin's prose fiction are from Debreczeny (1983a); plain translations of the verse and other translations from the prose are mine.

3. The specific reference here is to Negro slaves in the Americas; those slaves were from south of the Sahara. Puškin uses the term in a letter in which he is less than enthusiastic about the modern Greeks he had seen during the early part of the effort at independence from Turkey: "About the fate of the Greeks, one is permitted to reason, just as of the fate of my brothers the Negroes—one may wish both groups freedom from unendurable slavery" (Letter to P. A. Vjazemskij of 24–25 June 1824; PSS XII: 99; Shaw 1967: 161). It should be noted that the kind of "brotherhood" Puškin speaks of here did not preclude the possibility of social distinctions. Russian peasant serfs, like all other Russians, were also his "brothers," but that hardly made them his social equals, however much he may have favored the liberation of the serfs. In Odessa, according to I. I. Liprandi, Puškin thought of Morali (the "Moor Ali"), a ship captain originally from Tunis, as possibly a descendant of a close relative of his own great-grandfather—so that the Moor very well might be a relative (Vacuro 1974 I: 338).

4. The lithograph was of Puškin as a blackamoor boy, some 13–15 years old. Puškin was obviously unenthusiastic at the publication of this lithograph; he commented as follows: "Alexander Puškin is masterfully lithographed, but I do not

know whether it resembles him" (Letter to N. I. Gnedič of 27 Sept. 1822; Shaw 1967: 102; PSS XIII: 48).

5. In 1824, in addition to the prose note to EO.I.50 and the verse epistle to his friend Jazykov, Puškin also wrote of his "blackamoor" great-grandfather in an uncompleted poem which exists only in rough draft and which was first published sixty years later. It is one of Puškin's earliest experiments in imitating Russian folk poetics and diction: "When the Tsar's Blackamoor Took a Notion to Get Married" (Kak ženit'sja zadumal carskij arap). It ends, in plain translation, as follows: "The blackamoor has chosen a lady (*sudarušku*) for himself; the black raven, a white swan, but he is a black blackamoor (*arap čerešenek*), and she is a white darling (*duša belešen'ka*)."

6. Puškin's surviving papers show that he retained his interest in biographical information about his ancestors and apparently thought of publishing a biography or autobiography including information about them (see PSS XI: 310–14). The closest he comes to dealing with the question of his black ancestry in works he completed after 1830–31 and himself wished to publish is in a number of individual items (mainly anecdotes) in his "Table Talk" (title in English, written 1835–36); there are mentions of *arapy* in Russia, and one of the items, as noted above, is about Othello. If Puškin had lived longer, apparently he would have published them; they appeared only after his death, like the uncompleted *Blackamoor of Peter the Great*, except for the two chapters he published and which are treated here.

7. The south-north, north-south theme here may be compared with his poem "To Ovid," in which the poet-persona, on exile from St. Petersburg to a place close to where Ovid had been exiled so many years ago, identifies himself with Ovid and at the same time—as both being poets in exile in the same general place, Ovid from south to north (like the enforced movement of old Gannibal from Africa), and Puškin from north to south (St. Petersburg to the Black Sea area). The contrast of north and south—and of thinking of or remembering one from the other—recurs in Puškin's verse, particularly in "Nenastnyj den' potux . . . " (Odessa and Mixajlovskoe), and, curiously enough, in *The Stone Guest* (Paris and Madrid).

8. In reading memoirs about Puškin, one can never be sure whether he might not have suggested both the term and the perception. Contemporaries, in memoirs written after Puškin's death, spoke of his "blackamoor profile." An example is the novelist I. I. Lažečnikov, who uses the term in his account of meeting Puškin in 1819 or 1820, some eight or nine years before this poem (Vacuro 1974 I: 178; Veresaev 1936 I: 119). In this essay, citations from the memoir literature of Puškin's contemporaries are, for convenience, from these two compilations: Vacuro has particularly useful notes and introductions evaluating the accuracy and importance of the materials included.

9. There is a curious history of the printing of this poem. Jur'ev himself privately printed the poem when it was first written, in a very limited number of copies. Obviously Puškin considered the first *publication* to be the unauthorized one of 1829. See Annenkov (1984: 55n).

10. Debreczeny (1983b: 34) interestingly compares Puškin's characterizations of Ibragim and Mazepa as "explorations of how disadvantaged men might fare in love—one disadvantaged by the color of his skin, the other by his age." One major contrast might, however, be mentioned. In the full form, as we now have it, of *The Blackamoor of Peter the Great*, there is no hint that Gannibal thinks it will be possible for him to inspire a real love that will be faithful—*respect* is the most he can hope for. However, Mazepa, like Othello, inspires a young woman's intense and faithful love. The irrationality of Desdemona's love for Othello is specifically mentioned in the lack of "laws" for the wind, the eagle, a maid's heart, and the poet in the unfinished *Ezerskij* (EZ.168–82; 1833–36), and the passage from it inserted in the unfinished *Egyptian Nights* (PSS VIII: 269; 1835?).

11. But only barely so. Puškin and his friends were convinced that Bulgarin read

Boris Godunov for Count Benkendorf, head of the Secret Police, through whom Puškin had to communicate with Nicholas I, supposedly his "only censor." Before Nicholas I allowed *Boris Godunov* to be published, Bulgarin's historical novel *Dimitrij the Pretender* (*Dimitrij Samozvanec*, 1829) appeared, containing some of Puškin's own fictional inventions. However, when Puškin's play was finally published, Bulgarin accused Puškin of plagiarizing from him, citing points in common between the two works. For details, see Shaw (1963), and references there.

12. It is in his article "Vtoroe pis'mo iz Karlova na Kamennyj Ostrov" (in *The Northern Bee* [Severnaja pčela], 1830, No. 104). For a detailed study of Puškin's use of a fictional journalistic persona, Feofilakt Kosičkin, so as to succeed in publishing an unanswerable response, see Shaw 1963. The second of the two articles, "Feofilakt Kosičkin," gives details of Bulgarin's life, beginning with his birth in a kennel (making clear *his* maternity). According to Greč, Bulgarin heard the anecdote told by by Count S. S. Uvarov in the home of A. O. Olenin (Veresaev 1936 II: 121). Olenin was the father of the O[lenina] whose beauty is contrasted to Puškin's "blackamoor profile" in "To Dawe, Esq.," treated above.

13. Before writing "My Genealogy," Puškin wrote of Bulgarin's attacks in one of his notes which he never published; these notes were combined as "Rebuttal to Criticisms" and published after his death (PSS XI: 152). In the note, as in the poem, Puškin does not deny the possibility that his great-grandfather was "purchased"; in both places he insists that people should be remembered for what they do, specifically their important service to the nation.

14. For Naščokin's sources, see Bartenev (1925: 35).

ODESSA—WATERSHED YEAR

1. There is in my mind the strong possibility that not all sixteen poems refer to attachments formed in 1823–1824 in Odessa. But we are close in place; i.e., all attachments referred to in the sixteen poems originated during the poet's southern exile.

2. See "Razgovor knigoprodavca s poètom" (Conversation between Bookseller and Poet, 1824), to be discussed, and close, his use of the noun: "Ulybka ust, ulybka vzorov" (Smile of the lips, smile of the eyes), from an 1823 excerpt (PSS II: 471); perhaps also *Ruslan i Ljudmila* (Ruslan and Ljudmila, PSS IV: 50): "ulybka, oči golubye" (Their smiles and their blue eyes).

3. Without pushing parallels too far, let us note for what it's worth that the sorrowful candle ("pečal'naja sveča") relieving the darkness of "Noč' " (Night) is loosely echoed in "Pridet užasnyi čas" (There will arrive a terrible hour), in a draft variant: "Lampada blednaja tvoj xladnyj trup osvetit" (A pale lamp will throw light on your cold corpse).

4. For further comments on this arrangement see Tomaševskij 1958 II: 67–68.

5. Blagoj wants to have the original dedicated to Marija Raevskaja Volkonskaja, and the final version to Puškin's future wife.

6. See the situation excellently described in Levkovič 1974: 107–20; see also Axmatova 1977: 207–22.

7. See the excellent analysis in Xolševnikov 1985: 98–105.

SOLITUDE AND SOLILOQUY IN
BORIS GODUNOV

I am grateful to Caryl Emerson and Susan Amert for critical comments on earlier versions of this essay.

1. Whether that final stage direction should be considered Puškin's has been

disputed. See Alekseev 1984: 221–52 and Vinokur 1935: 430–31. Their positions are summarized in Emerson 1986: 243, n120.

2. I refer throughout to the experience of "reading" the play, an imperfect but necessary choice meant to suggest two things: first, since I am not writing a review of any particular performance of the play, nor can I assume that readers of my words will have anything more than a visualization of a performance in mind, I necessarily work from the published, printed script of the play. Yet Puškin clearly wished for his play to exist as a performed piece of drama, and I will address myself throughout to the implications for performance of various features of the written text. Second, I "read" the play as a way to name my own cognitive activity of reacting to the play in writing. The term "reading" has taken on particular meanings in recent criticism, in opposition to the idea of "interpretation." "Reading" strives less for closure and seeks more actively to account for textual moments that make "interpretation" impossible. For a good description of the difference as well as a fine example of such a "reading," see Burt 1985.

3. Comedy was Puškin's touch. Compare the indignant tones of Karamzin's *Istorija gosudarstva rossijskogo* (History of the Russian State): "In the manuscript document: 'women threw their suckling infants down to the ground, with crying sobs.' In one chronicle, it is said that some people, afraid not to cry, but unable to feign tears, wiped saliva into their eyes!" (Karamzin [1852], Notes to XII: 121). On Puškin's reliance upon Karamzin, to whom he dedicated the play, for historical facts and descriptive details, see Luzjanina (1972, 1974), Vacuro, and Emerson 1986: 82–87.

4. My sense of the empty grave as a sign which gives everything else the possibility of meaning derives much from the work of Jacques Lacan (1979; 1982).

5. The reference is to Racinean tragedy, though it describes Boris's plight perfectly. See Kurrik 1979: 40.

6. Compare the observations about the "strange impersonality" of Boris's speech in Konick 1982: 58.

7. Boris has a particular terror of empty language because he thinks it is inappropriate for a tsar to speak unless his words be weighty. Compare his farewell speech to his son, where Boris advises him to be taciturn.

8. The evidence of the *Slovar' jazyka Puškina* (Vinogradov 1956–61 IV: 611–15) suggests that Puškin used the adjectives *tjaželyj* and *tjažkij* interchangeably: both words show several kinds of usage and appear often.

9. The effects of epigrammatic discourse as a defense mechanism are explored in Cameron 1979: 32–35.

10. Puškin's hoped-for innovations in *Boris Godunov* can be recognized in many of his writings about drama, including draft prefaces to *Boris Godunov* (XI: 140–42). For an excellent discussion of these innovations, see Emerson 1986: 91–99.

11. Here and in all prose citations to follow, translations from the Russian originals are mine.

PUŠKIN AND NICHOLAS

1. Puškin presented this poem to Nicholas himself, who responded, through Benkendorf, that he was pleased with the poem but nonetheless did not want it published, possibly because it might appear unseemly to allow the publication of a poem praising him. Critics have subsequently speculated that Nicholas did not want it published because of the last three quatrains, where Puškin presumably expressed his beliefs that the autocracy should be limited, that people should have the right of free expression of their views, and that enlightenment and human rights should serve as principal values in Nicholas's reign (see commentary in 10–vol. edition; PSS [1963–68] III: 486).

2. The content of this audience with the tsar is still the subject of considerable

discussion; see Ejdel'man (1985) for a recent treatment which utilizes previously neglected memoir material.

Puškin found himself in an unusual situation: six years of efforts by his friends had failed to free him from an exile to which he had been sentenced without any clear political crime and in the absence of any real evidence. Now there was politically incriminating evidence—the testimony of Decembrists on the revolutionary meaning of Puškin's poetry, his friends and acquaintances sent to exile or hanged—and the government freed him from exile and offered him support as well (Vacuro 1974: 16–17).

3. N. O. Lerner's commentary on the poem (1910, xxi-xxii) gives some of the reactions: N. M. Jazykov called the verses cold; Aleksandr Mixajlovič Turgenev said they were composed impromptu in the tsar's chamber. See also Mejlax (1959: 99–100).

4. Puškin's interest in the reign of Peter is of course documented in other ways; he mentioned to his friend Vul'f in 1827 that he planned to write a history of Peter (in *A. S. Puškin v vospominanijax* . . . , PSS I: 416). Several years later (1831), Puškin requested permission to use the archives to study the reigns of Peter I through Peter III. Formal permission, through Benkendorf, was given the same year. Puškin's contemporaries understood this as meaning that Puškin had become official historiographer of Peter I. (See commentary in the small academy edition, PSS [1963–68] IX: 514.) Puškin, of course, was interested in Russian history before this time (Ejdel'man 1984).

5. Vickery (1989 and forthcoming) has many valuable comments on Puškin's affinities with and attitudes toward Radiščev.

6. Puškin's post-Decembrist political views are partially reflected in his essay on popular education, and his letter to Žukovskij of 7 March 1826 (PSS XIII: 265), which he assumed would be shown to Nicholas; a relevant passage of this letter, which was written so that it could be shown to Nicholas, is the following: "Whatever may have been my political and religious way of thinking, I am keeping it to myself, and I have no intention of insanely opposing the generally accepted order of things, and necessity" (Shaw 1967: 307).

Driver (1981) and Mikkelson (1980) have particularly good discussions of Puškin's political views in the post-Decembrist period; Driver (1981: 8–9) convincingly argues for a continuity with Puškin's pre-Decembrist thinking.

7. The Decembrist Lorer said that Puškin did not sympathize with their task (*delo*), was critical of their ideas, but nonetheless maintained a warm personal relationship with many of them. Although Puškin's real convictions may not have been clear, it was clear (according to Lerner) that the Decembrists in exile expected more from swords than from love and friendship. And in his epistle to them, Puškin was promising only amnesty and the restoration of their rights, not the realization of their political ideals (xxiii). Commiseration with their fate and hope for amnesty, not sympathy for their ideals, was the principal message of the epistle. Nepomnjaščij (1984) argued along these lines in order to bring it politically and morally closer to "Stansy."

8. Mejlax (1959) argues against "smoothing over" the rough edges, and urges that Puškin's occasional political lapses, such as "Stansy" (which he calls a "tragic mistake" [99]), not be given undue importance.

PUŠKIN'S REPUTATION IN NINETEENTH-CENTURY RUSSIA

1. I am grateful to my former graduate students Kate Dubina, Terry Kersey, and Amy Miller for helping me in surveying these two periodicals.

2. A detailed description of nineteenth-century Russian journals can be found in Evgen'ev-Maksimov 1950 and Zaxarova 1965.

3. V. B. Sandomirskaja, in her survey of Puškin criticism during the 1850s and 1860s, concludes that "Pisarev's article for fifteen years obliterated Puškin as a topic of contemporary interest for critics and publicists, unequivocally declaring the great poet's heritage to be an outmoded, even retrograde phenomenon, which had no vital connection with the present" (Gorodeckij 1966: 72).

PUŠKIN'S PROSE FICTION IN A HISTORICAL CONTEXT

1. "Eto on est' istinnyj osnovatel' *natural'noj školy*, vsegda vernyj prirode čeloveka, vernyj i sud'be ego. Ničego naprjažennogo v nem net, nikakogo boleznennogo voobraženija ili nepravil'nogo čuvstva" (*Legenda o velikom inkvizitore*, in Rozanov 1906: 225).

2. " . . . [P]rostoj zdravyj tolk i zdravoe čuvstvo" (Grigor'ev 1967: 182).

3. The question whether or not a deep irony lurks even in *Poor Folk* need not concern us here.

4. See also Tamarčenko 1972 and 1973.

5. Stender-Petersen identifies Scott's *Tales of My Landlord* as the immediate source.

6. For example: "Onegin's nonchalant rebellion—bringing a valet as his second and showing up inexcusably late—runs parallel to the author-narrator's invocation of the muse in the last stanza of chapter 7" (Todd 1986: 134).

7. It ought to be mentioned that a social commitment could be expressed in poetry as well as prose. Note, for example, Nekrasov's civic poetry.

8. It might appear that the "Puškinian" strain in Russian realist prose is represented by writers who came from Puškin's milieu: Aksakov, Turgenev, Tolstoj, Bunin. But what about Gončarov or Pisemskij? And is not Dostoevskij's habit "not to show his own mug" but to create dummy narrators also "Puškinian"?

Works Cited

Alekseev, M. P.
1930 "Puškin i Bestužev." *Puškin i ego sovremenniki* 38–39: 241–51.
1967 *Stixotvorenie Puškina 'Ja pamjatnik sebe vozdvig . . . '* Leningrad: Nauka.
1984 *Puškin. Sravnitel'no-istoričeskie issledovanija.* 1st ed., 1972. Leningrad: Nauka.

Alpatov, M.
1937 "'Mednyj vsadnik' Puskina." *Slavia* 14: 361–75.

Anciferov, Nikolaj Pavlovič
1924 *Byl' i mif Peterburga.* Petrograd: Izd. Brokgauz-Efron.

Annenkov, P. V.
1984 *Materialy dlja biografii A. S. Puškina.* Ed. A. A. Karpov. Moscow: Sovremennik. [Facsimile of the original publication, vol. 1 of Annenkov's edition of *Sočinenija Puškina.* St. Petersburg: Author, 1855.]

AN SSSR
1950–65 *Slovar' sovremennogo russkogo literaturnogo jazyka.* 17 vols. Moscow, Leningrad: Nauka.

Anučin, D. N.
1899 "A. S. Puškin (Antropologičeskij èskiz)." *Russkie vedomosti* 99: 3; 106: 2–3; 114: 2–3; 120: 2–3; 127: 2; 134: 2–3; 143: 4–8; 163: 2–3; 172: 2–3; 180: 2–3; 193: 2–3; 209: 2–3.

Aranovskaja, O. R.
1984 "O vine Borisa Godunova v tragedii Puškina." *Vestnik russkogo xristianskogo dviženija* 143: 128–56.

Arnt, Walter
1972 *Pushkin Threefold: Narrative, Lyric, Polemic, and Ribald Verse.* New York: E. P. Dutton.

Arxangel'skij, K. P.
1930 "Problema sceny v dramax Puškina (1830–1930)." *Trudy Dal'nevostočnogo pedagogičeskogo instituta,* Series 7, 106: 5–16.

Auslender, Sergej
1910 "Arap Petra velikogo." In Vengerov, ed. 4: 104–12.

Axmatova, A. A.
1977 *O Puškine.* Leningrad: Sovetskij pisatel'.

Baevskij, V. S.
1982 "Tradicija 'legkoj poèzii' v 'Evgenii Onegine.'" *Puškin: Issledovanija i materialy* 10: 106–21.
1986 "O teatral'nyx strofax 'Evgenija Onegina.'" *Vremennik puškinskoj komissii* 20: 139–50.

Banerjee, Maria
1978 "Pushkin's *The Bronze Horseman:* An Agonistic Vision." *Modern Language Studies* 8: 47–64.

Baratynskij, E. A.
1957 *Polnoe sobranie stixotvorenij.* Ed. E. N. Kuprejanova. (Biblioteka poèta, Bol'šaja serija, 2-e izd.) Leningrad: Sovetskij pisatel'.

Bartenev, P. I.
1925 *Rasskazy o Puškine zapisannye so slov ego druzej P. I. Bartenevym v 1851–1860 godax.* Ed. M. Cjavlovskij. Moscow: Sabašnikovy.

Batjuškov, K. N.
1934 *Sočinenija.* Ed. D. Blagoj. Moscow: Academia.
1964 *Polnoe sobranie stixotvorenij.* Ed. N. V. Fridman. (Biblioteka poèta, Bol'šaja serija, 2-e izd.) Moscow, Leningrad: Sovetskij pisatel'.

Bayley, John
1971 *Pushkin: A Comparative Commentary.* Cambridge: Cambridge University Press.

Bazanov, V. G.
1949 *Vol'noe obščestvo ljubitelej rossijskoj slovesnosti.* Petrozavodsk. (Cited by Kuprejanova in Baratynskij 1957: 382.)

Belinskij, V. G.
1953 *Polnoe sobranie sočinenij.* 13 vols. Moscow: AN SSSR, 1953–59.

Belyj, Andrej
1929 *Ritm kak dialektika i "Mednyj vsadnik."* Moscow: Izd. Federacija.

Berberova, N. N., ed.
1960 "Pis'ma M. O. Geršenzona k V. K. Xodaseviču." *Novyj žurnal* 60: 222–35.

Bestužev, A.
1821 *Poezdka v Revel'.* St. Petersburg: V tipografii Aleksandra Pljušara.

Bestužev-Marlinskij, A. A.
1937 *Izbrannye povesti.* Ed. G. V. Proxorov. Leningrad: GIXL.
1948 *Sobranie stikhotvorenij.* Ed. N. Mordovčenko. Leningrad: Sovetskij pisatel'.
1958 *Sočinenija v dvux tomax.* Ed. N. N. Maslin et al. Moscow: GIXL.
1961 *Polnoe sobranie stixotvorenij.* Ed. N. I. Mordovčenko. (Biblioteka poèta, Bol'šaja serija, 2-e izd.) Leningrad: Sovetskij pisatel'.

Bethea, David M.
1989 *The Shape of Apocalypse in Modern Russian Fiction.* Princeton: Princeton University Press.

Bettelheim, Bruno
1954 *Symbolic Wounds: Puberty Rites and the Envious Male.* Glencoe, Ill.: Free Press.

Bjalik, B.
1985 "Da byli li gory-to? . . . " *Voprosy literatury* 7: 114–41.

Blagoj, Dmitrij
1929 *Sociologija tvorčestva Puškina: Ètjudy.* Moscow: Federacija.
1931 *Sociologija tvorčestva Puškina.* Moscow: Mir.
1967 *Tvorčeskij put' Puškina (1826–1830).* Moscow: Sovetskij pisatel'.
1977 *Duša v zavetnoj lire.* Moscow: Sovetskij pisatel'.

Bočarov, Sergej
1986 "Real'noe i vozmožnoe v romane Puškina: 'Evgenij Onegin' i buduščee russkogo romana." Paper prepared for the Kennan Institute's Conference on Russian Classic Literature, "Pushkin: The Shorter Prose Works" (January 20–21, 1986, Washington, D.C.).

Bogoslovskij, N. B., ed.
1934 *Puškin-kritik. Puškin o literature.* Moscow, Leningrad: Academia.

Bondi, Sergej
1935 Commentary to *Sceny iz rycarskix vremen.* In A. S. Puškin, *Polnoe sobranie sočinenij,* vol. 7: *Dramatičeskie proizvedenija,* pp. 639–58. Moscow, Leningrad: AN SSSR.
1971 *Černoviki Puškina. Stat'i 1930–1970 gg.* Moscow: Prosveščenie.

Borev, Ju.
1981 *Iskusstvo interpretacii i ocenki: Opyt pročtenija 'Mednogo vsadnika'.* Moscow: Sovetskij pisatel'.

Briggs, A. D. P.
1976 "The Hidden Qualities of Pushkin's *Mednyj vsadnik.*" *Canadian-American Slavic Studies* 10: 228–41.

Brjusov, V.
1909 "Mednyj vsadnik." In Vengerov, ed. 3: 456–72.
1929 *Moj Puškin: Stat'i, issledovanija, nabljudenija.* Moscow: Gos. izd.

Burgin, Diana Lewis
1974 "The Mystery of 'Pikovaja dama': A New Interpretation." In *Mnemozina: Studia litteraria russica in honorem Vsevolod Setchkarev,* pp. 46–56. Munich: Wilhelm Fink Verlag.

Burt, E. S.
1985 "Developments in Character: Reading and Interpretation in 'The Children's Punishment' and 'The Broken Comb.'" *Yale French Studies* 69: 192–210.

Byron, George Gordon Lord
1935 *Don Juan and Other Satirical Poems.* Ed. Louis I. Bredvold. New York: The Odyssey Press.

Cameron, Sharon
1979 *Lyric Time: Dickinson and the Limits of Genre.* Baltimore: Johns Hopkins University Press.

Cavendish, R.
1975 *The Powers of Evil in Western Religion, Magic and Folk Belief.* New York: Putnam's.

Cherniavsky, Michael
1961 *Tsar and People: Studies in Russian Myths.* New Haven: Yale University Press.

Cherry, E. C.; M. Halle; and R. O. Jakobson
1953 "Toward the Logical Description of Languages in Their Phonemic Aspect." *Language* 29: 34–46.

Cjavlovskaja, T. G.
1960 "Vljublennyj bes." *Puškin: Issledovanija i materialy* 3: 101–31.

Cjavlovskij, M. A., ed.
1951 *Letopis' žizni i tvorčestva A. S. Puškina*. Vol. 1. Moscow: AN SSSR.

Cooke, Leighton Brett
1983 *Poèt: Aleksandr Puškin and the Creative Process*. Ann Arbor: University Microfilms International.

Corbet, Charles
1966 "Le symbolisme du *Cavalier de bronze*." *Revue des études slaves* 45: 129–44.

Černov, Aleksej
1949 *Narodnye russkie pesni i romansy*. In two parts. New York: Rausen Bros.

Čirejskij, L. A.
1975 *Puškin i ego okruženie*. Leningrad: Nauka.

Čumakov, Ju. I.
1976 "'Otryvki iz Putešestvija Onegina' kak xudožestvennoe edinstvo." *Voprosy poètiki literaturnyx žanrov* 1: 3–12.

Dante, A.
1972 *La Divina Commedia*. Ed. C. H. Grandgent. Cambridge, Mass.: Harvard University Press.

Davydov, Sergej
1983 "The Sound and the Theme in the Prose of A. S. Puškin: A Logo-Semantic Study of Paranomasia." *Slavic and East European Journal* 27: 1–18.
1985 "Pushkin's Merry Undertaking and 'The Coffinmaker.'" *Slavic Review* 44: 30–48.
Forthcoming "The Ace in Puškin's 'The Queen of Spades.'" Unpublished ms.

Debreczeny, Paul
1983a *Alexander Pushkin: Complete Prose Fiction*. Ed. and trans. Stanford, Calif.: Stanford University Press.
1983b *The Other Pushkin: A Study of Alexander Pushkin's Prose Fiction*. Stanford: Stanford University Press.

Deržavin, G. R.
1957 *Stixotvorenija*. Biblioteka poèta, bol'šaja serija. Leningrad: Sovetskij pisatel'.

Driver, Sam
1981 "Puškin and Politics: The Late Works." *Slavic and East European Journal* 25: 1–23.

Durov, V.
1977 *Russkie i sovetskie nagradnye medali*. Moscow: Gos. Istor. Muzej.

D'jakonov, I.
1963 "O vos'moj, devjatoj i desjatoj glavax 'Evgenija Onegina.'" *Russkaja literatura* 3: 37–62.
1982 "Ob istorii zamysla 'Evgenija Onegina.'" *Puškin: Issledovanija i materialy* 10: 70–106.

Èjdel'man, N. Ja.
1984 *Puškin. Istorija i sovremennost' v xudožestvennom soznanii poèta.* Moscow: Sovetskij pisatel'.
1985 "Sekretnaja audiencija." *Novyj mir:* 190–217. Rpt. in *Puškin iz biografii i tvorčestva, 1826–1837.* Moscow: Xud. lit., 1987.

Emerson, Caryl
1985 "Pretenders to History: Four Plays for Undoing Pushkin's *Boris Godunov.*" *Slavic Review* 44: 257–79.
1986 *Boris Godunov: Transpositions of a Russian Theme.* Bloomington: Indiana University Press.

Ènciklopedičeskij slovar'. 41 vols. St. Petersburg: Brokgauz i Èfron, 1890–1904.

Epštejn, M.
1981 "Faust na beregu morja." *Voprosy literatury* 6: 89–110.

Eremin, M.
1976 *Puškin publicist.* 2nd ed. Moscow: Xud. lit.

Evgen'ev-Maksimov, V. E., et al., eds.
1950 *Očerki po istorii russkoj žurnalistiki i kritiki.* Vol. 1: *XVIII vek i pervaja polovina XIX veka.* Leningrad: Izd. LGU.

Faletti, Heidi E.
1977 "Remarks on Style as Manifestation of Narrative Technique in 'The Queen of Spades.'" *Canadian-American Slavic Studies* 11: 114–33.

Fejnberg, I. L.
1983 *Abram Petrovič Gannibal, praded Puškina.* Moscow: Nauka.

Filonov, A.
1899 *"Boris Godunov" A. S. Puškina.* St Petersburg: Glazunov.

Fishwick, M. W.
1963 *Faust Revisited: Some Thoughts on Satan.* New York: The Seabury Press.

Fomičev, S. A.
1982 "Periodizacija tvorčestva Puškina (K postanovke problemy)." *Puškin: Issledovanija i materialy* 10: 5–22.

Frejdin, Jurij
1979 "O nekotoryx osobennostjax kompozicii tragedii Puškina *Boris Godunov.*" *Russian Literature* 7: 27–44.

Freud, Sigmund
1953–65 *Standard Edition of the Complete Psychological Works of Sigmund Freud.* Trans. and ed. J. Strachey. 24 vols. London: Hogarth Press.

Gasparov, Boris
1987 "The Apocalyptic Theme in Puškin's 'Count Nulin.'" In *Text and Context: Essays in Honor of Nils Åke Nilsson,* ed Barbara Lönnqvist et al., pp. 16–25. Stockholm: Almqvist & Wiksell.

Gejčenko, S. S.
1977 *U lukomor'ja.* Izd. 3-e, dop. Leningrad: Lenizdat.

Geršenzon, M. O.
1926 "Plagiaty Puškina." In *Stat'i o Puškine,* pp. 114–22. Moscow: Gosudarstvennaja Akademija Xudožestvennyx Nauk.

Gessen, A. I.
1965 *Vse volnovalo nežnyj um . . . : Puškin sredi knig i druzej.* Moscow: Nauka.

Giamatti, A. Bartlett
1976 "Headlong Horsemen: An Essay in the Chivalric Epics of Pulci, Boiardo, and Ariosto." In *Italian Literature: Roots and Branches,* ed. Giose Rimanelli and Kenneth John Atchity, pp. 265–307. New Haven: Yale University Press.

Gippius, V. V.
1930 "K voprosu o puškinskix plagiatax." *Puškin i ego sovremenniki* 38–39: 37–46.

Golubov, Sergej
1960 *Bestužev-Marlinskij,* M. (Žizn' zamečatel'nyx ljudei, 2-e izd.) Moscow: Molodaja gvardija.

Gorodeckij, B. P.
1953 *Dramaturgija Puškina.* Moscow, Leningrad: AN SSSR.
1962 *Lirika Puškina.* Moscow, Leningrad: AN SSSR.
1966 *Puškin: Itogi i problemy izučenija.* Ed. B. P. Gorodeckij. Moscow: Nauka.
1969 *Tragedija A. S. Puškina Boris Godunov.* Kommentarij. Leningrad: Izd. "Prosveščenie."

Gregg, Richard
1977 "The Nature of Nature and the Nature of Eugene in *The Bronze Horseman.*" *Slavic East European Journal* 21: 167–79.

Grigor'ev, Apollon
1967 *Literaturnaja kritika.* Ed. B. F. Egorov. Moscow: Xud. lit.
1970 *Sočinenija.* Ed. V. S. Krupič. Villanova, Penn.: Villanova University Press.

Gutsche, George
1982 "Puškin and Belinskij: The Role of the 'Offended Provincial.'" In *New Perspectives on Nineteenth-Century Russian Prose,* pp. 41–59. Columbus, Ohio: Slavica Publishers.
1986 *Moral Apostasy in Russian Literature.* DeKalb: Northern Illinois University Press.

Hackel, Sergei
1975 *The Poet and the Revolution: Aleksandr Blok's "The Twelve."* Oxford: Oxford University Press.

Hammond, N. G., and H. H. Scullard, eds.
1970 *The Oxford Classical Dictionary.* 2nd ed. Oxford: Oxford University Press.

Horace
1952 *The Odes and Epodes of Horace.* Ed. Clement Lawrence Smith. 2nd ed. Washington, D.C.: Catholic University of America Press.

Iser, Wolfgang
1978 *The Act of Reading: A Theory of Aesthetic Response.* Baltimore: Johns Hopkins University Press.

Ivanov, G. K., ed.
1969 *Russkaja poèzija v otečestvennoj muzyke.* Vyp. 2. Moscow: Sovetskij kompozitor.

Ivanov, V. V.
1976 "The Significance of M. M. Bakhtin's Ideas on Sign, Utterance, and Dialogue for Modern Semiotics." In *Semiotics and Structuralism: Readings from the Soviet Union,* ed. H. Baran, pp. 310–67. White Plains, N.Y.: IASP.

Izmajlov, N. V.
1954 "Stixotvorenie Puškina 'Mirskaja vlast'' (Vnov' najdennyj avtograf)." *Izvestija Akademii Nauk SSSR. Otdelenie literatury i jazyka* 13(6): 548–56.
1958 "Liričeskie cikly v poèzii Puškina 30-x godov." *Puškin: Issledovanija i materialy* 2: 7–48. Moscow, Leningrad: AN.

Jakobson, R.
1975 *Puškin and His Sculptural Myth.* Trans. and ed. John Burbank. The Hague: Mouton.
1981 *Selected Writings.* The Hague: Mouton.

Janson, H. W.
1974 "The Equestrian Monument from Cangrande della Scala to Peter the Great." In *Sixteen Studies,* pp. 159–87. New York: Harry N. Abrams.

Jones, Ernest
1951 *On the Nightmare.* New York: Liveright.

Kaganovič, A.
1975 *'Mednyj vsadnik': Istorija sozdanija monumenta.* Leningrad: Iskusstvo.

Karamzin, N. M.
1852 *Istorija gosudarstva rossijskogo.* 12 vols. 6th ed. St. Petersburg: Tip. "Eduarda Praca."
1966 *Polnoe sobranie sočinenij.* Ed. Ju. M. Lotman. (Biblioteka poèta, Bol'šaja serija, 2-e izd.) Moscow, Leningrad: Sovetskij pisatel'.

Karlinsky, Simon
1985 *Russian Drama from Its Beginnings to the Age of Pushkin.* Berkeley: University of California Press.

Kibal'nik, S. A.
1986 "Antologičeskie èpigrammy Puškina." *Puškin: Issledovanija i materialy* 12: 152–75.

Knigge, Armin
1984 *Puškins Verserzahlung "Der eherne Reiter" in der russischen Kritik: Rebellion oder Unterwerfung.* Amsterdam: Adolf M. Hakkert.

Konick, Willis
1982 "The Secrets of History: Pushkin's *Boris Godunov.*" *Occasional Papers in Slavic Languages and Literature* (Summer): 53–62. Department of Slavic Languages, University of Washington, Seattle.

Kornilovič, A. S.
1960 "O pervyx balax v Rossii." In *Poljarnaja zvezda, izdannaja A. Bestuževym i K. Ryleevym,* ed. V. A. Arxipov et al. Moscow, Leningrad: AN SSSR.

Krafcik, Patricia
1976 "The Russian Negative Simile." *Slavic and East European Journal* 20.1: 18–26.

Krasovskaja, V. M.
1958 *Russkij baletnyj teatr: Ot vozniknovenija do serediny XIX veka.* Leningrad: Iskusstvo.

Kurrik, Marie Jaanus
1979 *Literature and Negation.* New York: Columbia University Press.

Kučera, Henry
1956 "Puškin and Don Juan." In *For Roman Jakobson,* ed. M. Halle, H. Lunt, H. McLean, and C. H. Van Schooneveld, pp. 273–84. The Hague: Mouton.

Kvjatkovskii, A.
1966 *Poetičeskij slovar'.* Moscow: Sovetskaja enciklopedija, 1966.

Lacan, Jacques
1979 "Signification of the Phallus." In *Écrits,* trans. Alan Sheridan, pp. 281–91. New York: W. W. Norton.
1982 "Desire and Interpretation of Desire in *Hamlet.*" In *Literature and Psychoanalysis,* ed. Shoshana Felman, pp. 11–52. Baltimore: Johns Hopkins University Press.

Lacroix, Paul
1865 *Histoire de la vie et du règne de Nicolas Ier Empereur de Russie.* Vol. 2. Paris: Librairie de L. Hachette et Compagnie.

Laferriere, Daniel (see also "Rancour-Laferriere")
1977 *Five Russian Poems: Exercises in a Theory of Poetry.* Englewood, N.J.: Transworld.

Lakier, A. B.
1855 *Russkaja geral'dika.* 2 vols. St. Petersburg.

Lakšin, Vladimir
1979 "Sputnik strannyj." In *Biografija knigi,* pp. 72–223. Moscow: Sovremennik.

Lanham, Richard A.
1968 *A Handlist of Rhetorical Terms: A Guide for Students of English Literature.* Berkeley: University of California Press.

Lednicki, Waclaw
1955 *Pushkin's "Bronze Horseman."* Berkeley: University of California Press.

Leec, Georg
1984 *Abram Petrovič Gannibal: Biografičeskoe issledovanie.* 2-e izd. Tallin: Eèsti Raamat.

Leighton, Lauren G.
1969a "Bestuzhev-Marlinsky as a Lyric Poet." *Slavonic and East European Review* 47, No. 109.

1969b "Marlinskij's 'Ispytanie': A Romantic Rejoinder to Puškin's *Evgenij Onegin.*" *Slavic and East European Journal* 13: 200–16.
1972 "Marlinsky." *Russian Literature Triquarterly* 3: 249–68.
1975 *Alexander Bestuzhev-Marlinsky.* Boston: G. K. Hall & Co.
1977 "Gematria in 'The Queen of Spades': A Decembrist Puzzle." *Slavic and East European Journal* 21: 455–69.
1983 "Puškin and Marlinskij: Decembrist Allusions." *Russian Literature* 14: 351–382.

Lerner, N. O.
1903 *Trudy i dni.* Moscow: Skorpion.
1909 "Posle ssylki v Moskve." In Vengerov, ed. 3: 335–52.
1910 "Primečanija k stixotvorenijam 1826–1828 gg." In Vengerov, ed. 4: i–lxxi.

Lévi-Strauss, Claude
1966 *The Savage Mind.* Chicago: University of Chicago Press.

Levitine, George
1972 "The Problem of Portraits, Late Allegory, and the Epic of the Bronze Horseman." In *The Sculpture of Falconet,* trans. Eda M. Levitine, pp. 51–60. Greenwich: New York Graphic Society.

Levkovič, Ja. L.
1974 *Stixotvorenija Puškina 1820–1830-x godov.* Ed. N. V. Izmajlov. Leningrad: Nauka.
1986 "Rabočaja tetrad' Puškina PD No. 841 (Istorija Zapolnenija)." *Puškin: Issledovanija i materialy* XII: 243–78.

Liddell, H. G., and Robert Scott
1940 *A Greek-English Lexicon.* 9th ed. Oxford: The Clarendon Press.

Lincoln, W. Bruce
1978 *Nicholas I: Emperor and Autocrat of All the Russias.* London: Allen Lane.

Lorer, N. I.
1984 *Zapiski dekabrista.* Ed. M. V. Nečkina. 2nd ed. Irkutsk: Vostočno-sibirskoe knižnoe izdatel'stvo.

Lotman, Jurij M.
1960 "K èvoljucii postroenija xarakterov v romane 'Evgenii Onegin.'" *Puškin: Issledovanija i materialy* 3: 131–74.
1973 "Teatr i teatral'nost' v stroe kul'tury načala XIX veka." In his *Stat'i po tipologii kul'tury: Materialy k kursu teorii literatury.* 2 Tartu.
1975 "Tema kart i kartočnoj igry v russkoj literature načala XIX veka." *Trudy po znakovym sistemam* 7 (Tartu). Translation by C. R. Pike as "Theme and Plot: The Theme of Cards and the Card Game in Russian Literature of the Nineteenth Century." *PTL* 3 (1978): 455–92.
1981 *Aleksandr Sergeevič Puškin: Biografija pisatelja.* Leningrad: Prosveščenie.
1983 *Roman A. S. Puškina "Evgenij Onegin": Kommentarij.* Leningrad: Prosveščenie.
1985 "The Decembrist in Daily Life (Everyday Behavior as a Historical-Psychological Category)." In Nakhimovsky and Nakhimovsky, pp. 95–149.

———, and Mixail Ju. Lotman
1986 "Vokrug desjatoj glavy 'Evgenija Onegina.'" *Puškin: Issledovanija i materialy* 12: 125–51.

———, and Boris Uspenskij
1975 "Spory o jazyke v načale XIX v. kak fakt russkoj kul'tury." *Trudy po russkoj i slavjanskoj filologii* 24: 168–254.
1985 "Binary Models in the Dynamics of Russian Culture (to the End of the Eighteenth Century)." In Nakhimovsky and Nakhimovsky, pp. 30–66.

Luzjanina, L. N.
1972 *Problemy istorii v russkoj literature pervoj četverti XIX veka (Ot "Istorii gosudarstva rossijskogo" N. M. Karamzina do tragedii A. S. Puškina "Boris Godunov").* Candidate's Dissertation, Leningrad State University.
1974 "*Istorija gosudarstva rossijskogo* N. M. Karamzina i tragedija Puškina *Boris Godunov* (K probleme xaraktera letopisca)." *Russkaja literatura* 1: 45–57.

Makarovskaja, V.
1978 *"Mednyj vsadnik': Itogi i problemy izučenija.* Saratov: Izd. Saratovskogo Univ.

Makogonenko, G. P.
1974 *Tvorčestvo A. S. Puškina v 1830-e gody.* Leningrad: Xud. lit.
1982 *Tvorčestvo A. S. Puškina v 1830-e gody (1833–1836).* Leningrad: Xud. lit.
1985 "Obratimsja k puškinskomu tekstu." *Voprosy literatury* 7: 160–75.

Medvedeva, I. N.
1941 "Puškinskaja èlegija 1820-x godov i 'Demon.'" *Vremennik puškinskoj komissii* 6: 51–71.

Mejlax, B. S.
1959 "Iz istorii političeskoj liriki Puškina." In *Iz istorii russkix literaturnyx otnošenij XVIII-XX vekov,* pp. 96–107. Moscow, Leningrad: AN SSSR.

Mickiewicz, Adam
1944 *Poems by Adam Mickiewicz.* Ed. G. R. Noyes. New York.

Mikkelson, Gerald
1980 "Puškin's 'Arion': A Lone Survivor's Cry." *Slavic and East European Journal* 25: 1–13.

Mirskij, D. S.
1934 "Problema Puškina." *Literaturnoe nasledstvo* 16–18: 91–112.
1958 *A History of Russian Literature from Its Beginnings to 1900.* New York: Vintage Books.
1963 *Pushkin.* New York: E. P. Dutton.

Modern Encyclopedia of Russian and Soviet History. Ed. Joseph L. Wieczynski. Vol. IV. Gulf Breeze, Fla.: Academic International Press, 1961.

Modzalevskij, B. L.
1910 "Biblioteka A. S. Puškina." *Puškin i ego sovremenniki* 9–10.
1929 "Rod Puškina." In *Puškin,* pp. 19–63. Leningrad: Priboj.

Molitvoslov
1907 *Pravoslavnyj tolkovyj molitvoslov.* St. Petersburg: Sinodal'naja Tipografija.

Monas, Sidney
1984 "Unreal City: St. Petersburg and Russian Culture." In *Russian Literature and American Critics,* ed. K. Brostrom, pp. 381–91. Ann Arbor: University of Michigan, Dept. of Slavic Languages and Literatures.

Morson, Gary Saul
1981 *The Boundaries of Genre: Dostoevsky's "Diary of a Writer" and the Traditions of Literary Utopia.* Austin: University of Texas Press.

Muratova, K. D., ed.
1962 *Istorija russkoj literatury XIX veka. Bibliografičeskij ukazatel'.* Moscow, Leningrad: AN SSSR.

Nabokov, Vladimir
1975 Aleksandr Pushkin, *Eugene Onegin.* Trans. and ed. Vladimir Nabokov. 4 vols. 2nd ed. Princeton: Princeton University Press.

Nakhimovsky, Alexander D., and Alice Stone Nakhimovsky, eds.
1985 *The Semiotics of Russian Cultural History.* Ithaca: Cornell University Press.

Nečkina, M. V.
1938 "Puškin i dekabristy." In *Sto let so dnja smerti A. S. Puškina* (Trudy puškinskoj sessii Akademii nauk SSSR, 1837–1937), pp. 37–56. Moscow, Leningrad: AN SSSR.

Nemirovskij, I. V.
1990 "Biblejskaja tema v 'Mednom vsadnike.'" *Russkaia literatura* 3: 3–17.

Nepomnjaščij, B.
1983 *Poèzija i sud'ba.* Moscow: Sovetskij pisatel'.
1984 "Sud'ba odnogo stixotvorenija." *Voprosy literatury* 6: 144–81.
1985 "Opirat'sja na dostignutoe naukoj." *Voprosy literatury* 7: 142–59.

Niederland, William G.
1956–57 "River Symbolism." *Psychoanalytic Quarterly* 25–26: 469–504; 50–75.

Ospovat, A. L.
1986 "'Vljublennyj bes.' Zamysel i ego transformacija v tvorčestve Puškina 1821–1831 gg." *Puškin: Issledovanija i materialy* 12: 175–200.

Ospovat, A. L., and R. D. Timenčik
1985 *'Pečal'nu povest' soxranit': ob avtore i čitateljax 'Mednogo vsadnika.'* Moscow: Kniga.

Paina, E. S.
1962 "Ob obstojatel'stvax otstavki A. P. Gannibala." *Puškin: Issledovanija i materialy* 4: 413–48.

Petrunina, N. N.
1986 "O povesti 'Stancionnyj smotritel'.'" *Puškin: Issledovanija i materialy* 12: 78–104.

Pisarev, D. I.
1955–56 *Sočinenija v 4-x tomax.* Moscow: Gos. izd. xud. lit.

Poljakov, M.
1978 *Voprosy poètiki i xudožestvennoi semantiki.* Moscow: Sovetskij pisatel'.

Poljakova, E.
1974 "Real'nost' i fantastika 'Pikovoj damy.'" In *V mire Puškina: Sbornik statej,* pp. 373–412. Moscow: Sovetskij pisatel'.

Proffer, Carl
1968 "Pushkin and Parricide: *The Miserly Knight.*" *American Imago* 25: 347–53.

Puškin, A. S.
1907–15 *Puškin.* Ed. S. A. Vengerov. 6 vols. St. Petersburg (Petrograd): Brokgaus-Èfron.
1935 *Polnoe sobranie sočinenij.* Vol. 7. Moscow: AN SSSR.
1937–59 *Polnoe sobranie sočinenij.* 17 vols. Ed. V. D. Bonč-Bruevič. Moscow: Akademija Nauk SSR.
1959–62 *Sobranie sočinenij.* 10 vols. Ed. D. D. Blagoj et al. Moscow: Gos. izd. xud. lit.
1963–68 *Polnoe sobranie sočinenij v desjati tomax.* Moscow: AN SSSR.
1978 *Mednyj vsadnik.* Ed. N. V. Izmajlov. Leningrad: Nauka.
1981 *Eugene Onegin: A Novel in Verse.* Trans. Walter Arndt. 2nd ed., rev. New York: Dutton.
1982 *Perepiska A. S. Puškina v dvux tomax.* Moscow: Xud. lit.
1983 *Oeuvres poétiques.* 2/1 Ed. E. Etkind. Lausanne: L'age d'homme.

Rancour-Laferriere, Daniel (see also "Laferriere")
1985 *Signs of the Flesh: An Essay on the Evolution of Hominid Sexuality.* Berlin: Mouton de Gruyter.

Rank, Otto
1964 (1914) *The Myth of the Birth of the Hero and Other Writings.* Ed. P. Freund. New York: Vintage Books.

Raskolnikov, Felix
Forthcoming "Irracional'noe v 'Pikovoj dame.'" Article ms.

Rassadin, St.
1977 "Dva samozvanca." In *Dramaturg Puškin: Poètika, ideja, evoljucija,* pp. 3–58. Moscow: Izd. "Iskusstvo."

Rosen, Nathan
1975 "The Magic Cards in the 'The Queen of Spades.'" *Slavic and East European Journal* 19: 255–75.

Rosengren, Karl E.
1968 *Sociological Aspects of the Literary System.* Stockholm: Natur och Kultur.

Rowland, Beryl
1965–66 "The Horse and Rider Figure in Chaucer's Works." *University of Toronto Quarterly* 35: 249–59.

Rozanov, M. N.
1930 "Ob istočnikax stixotvorenija Puškina 'Iz Pindemonte.'" In *Puškin: Sbornik vtoroj,* ed. N. K. Piksanov. Moscow, Leningrad: Gos. izd.

Rozanov, V. V.
1906 "Puškin i Gogol'." In *Legenda o velikim inkvizitore F. M. Dostoevskogo . . . s priloženiem dvux ètjudov o Gogole,* 3rd ed., pp. 253–56. St. Petersburg: Pirožkov.

Russkij biografičeskij slovar'. St. Petersburg: Obščestvennaja Pol'za, 1905.

Schwartz, Murray M., and Albert Schwartz
1975 "'The Queen of Spades': A Psychoanalytic Interpretation." *Texas Studies in Literature and Language* 17: 275–88.

Shapiro, Michael
1979 "Pushkin's Modus Significandi: A Semiotic Exploration." In *Russian Romanticism: Studies in Poetic Codes,* ed. Nils Ake Nilsson, pp. 110–32. Stockholm Studies in Russian Literature 10. Stockholm: Almqvist and Wiksell.

Shaw, J. Thomas
1963 "The Problem of the *Persona* in Journalism: Puškin's Feofilakt Kosičkin." In *American Contributions to the Fifteenth International Congress of Slavists, Sofia, 1963,* pp. 301–26. The Hague: Mouton.
1966 "Pushkin on America: His 'John Tanner.'" In *Orbis Scriptus: Dmitrij Tschizewskij zum 70. Geburtstag,* ed. Dietrich Gerhardt et al. pp. 739–56. Munich: Wilhelm Fink.
1967 *The Letters of Alexander Pushkin.* Trans. and ed. J. Thomas Shaw. Madison: University of Wisconsin Press. [1st ed., 1963.]
1974 *Pushkin's Rhymes: A Dictionary.* Madison: University of Wisconsin Press.
1975a *Batiushkov: A Dictionary of the Rhymes and a Concordance to the Poetry.* (Wisconsin Slavic Publications, 2.) Madison: University of Wisconsin Press.
1975b *Baratynskii: A Dictionary of the Rhymes and a Concordance to the Poetry.* (Wisconsin Slavic Publications, 3.) Madison: University of Wisconsin Press.
1977 "Pushkin's 'The Stationmaster' and the New Testament Parable." *Slavic East European Journal* 21: 3–29.
1985a *Pushkin: A Concordance to the Poetry.* 2 vols. Columbus: Slavica Publishers, Inc.
1985b "Alexander Pushkin." In *The Romantic Century,* ed. Jacques Barzun and George Stade, pp. 659–91. New York: Charles Scribner's Sons.

Sidjakov, L. S.
1977 "'Evgenij Onegin' i zamysel 'Svetskoj povesti' 30-x godov XIX v. (K xarakteristike Onegina v sed'moj glave romana)." In *Zamysel, trud, voploščenie . . . ,* ed. V. I. Kulešov, pp. 118–24. Moscow: MGU.

Simmons, E. J.
1971 *Puškin.* 2nd ed. Gloucester: Peter Smith. [1st ed., Cambridge: Harvard University Press, 1937.]

Sinjavskij, N., and M. Cjavlovskij
1938 *Puškin v pečati: 1814–1837.* Izd. 2-e isp. Moscow: GSEI.

Slonimskij, A.
1963 *Masterstvo Puškina.* Moscow: Gos. izd. xud. lit.

Slonimskij, Ju. I.
1974 *Baletnye stroki Puškina.* Leningrad: Iskusstvo.

Smirnova, A. O.
1929 *Zapiski, dnevnik, vospominanija, pis'ma.* Moscow: Federacija.

Smith, Clement Lawrence, ed.
1952 *The Odes and Epodes of Horace.* 2nd ed. Vol II. Washington, D.C.: Catholic University of America Press.

Solovej, N. Ja.
1977 "Iz istorii raboty A. S. Puškina nad sjužetom 'Evgenija Onegina.'" In *Zamysel, Trud, Vplošćenie . . .* , ed. V. I. Kulešov, pp. 101–17. Moscow: MGU.

Spasskij, I. G.
1955 "Denežnoe obrašćenie v Moskovskom gosudarstve." *Materialy i issledovanija po Arxeologii SSSR* 44: 266–67.

Speransov, N. N.
1974 *Zelem'nye gerby Rossii.* Moscow: Sovetskaja Rossija.

Stark, V. P.
1982 "Stixotvorenie 'Otcy pustynniki i ženy neporočny . . . ' i cikl Puškina 1836 g." *Puškin: Issledovanija i materialy* 10: 193–203.

Stender-Petersen, Adolf
1978 *Geschichte der russischen Literatur.* Munich: Beck.

Stepanov, N. L.
1959 *Lirika Puškina.* Moscow: Xud. lit.

Stilman, Leon
1958 "Problemy literaturnyx žanrov i traditsii v 'Evgenii Onegine' Puškina." *American Contributions to the Fourth International Congress of Slavists,* Moscow, September 1958, pp. 321–67. The Hague: Mouton.

Tamarčenko, N. D.
1973 "O žanrovoj obšćnosti *Pikovoj damy* A. S. Puškina i *Prestuplenija i nakazanija* F. M. Dostoevskogo." *Gercenovskie čtenija* 26: 44–48.
1972 *"Pikovaja dama" A. S. Puškina i "Prestuplenie i nakazanija" F. M. Dostoevskogo.* Leningrad: Leningradskij gos. ped. inst.

Taranovsky, K. F.
1965 "The Sound Texture of Russian Verse in the Light of Phonemic Distinctive Features." *International Journal of Slavic Linguistics and Poetics* 9: 114–24.

Tarxov, A. E.
1977 "Povest' o peterburgskom Iove." *Nauka i religija* 2: 62–64.

Teletova, N. K.
1981 *Zabytye rodstvennye svjazi A. S. Puškina.* Leningrad: Nauka, 1981.

Terras, Victor
1984 "'Šinel'' Gogolja v kritike molodogo Dostoevskogo." *Transactions of the Association of Russian-American Scholars in the U.S.A.* 17: 75–81.

Todd, William Mills III
1986 *Fiction and Society in the Age of Pushkin: Ideology, Institutions, and Narrative.* Cambridge, Mass.: Harvard University Press.

Toddes, E. A.
1968 "K izučeniju *Mednogo vsadnika.*" (Puškinskij sbornik, 1.) *Učenye zapiski Latvijskogo gos. universiteta* 106: 92–113. Riga: LGU.
1983 "K voprosu o kamennoostrovskom cikle." In *Problemy Puškinovedenija.* Riga.

Tomaševskij, B. V.
1918 "Ritmika četyrexstopnogo jamba po nabljudenijam nad stixom 'Evgenija Onegina.'" *Puškin i ego sovremenniki* 29–30: 144–87.
1930 "Meloči o Puškine." *Puškin i ego sovremenniki* 38–39: 78–81.
1956 *Puškin. Kniga pervaja (1813–1824).* Moscow, Leningrad: AN SSSR.
1958 "Strofika Puškina." *Puškin: Issledovanija i materialy* 2: 49–184. Moscow, Leningrad: Akademija Nauk.
1961 "Desjataja glava 'Evgenija Onegina' (Istorija razgadki)." In *Puškin,* Vol. 2, pp. 200–44. Moscow, Leningrad: AN.
1977 *Puškin. Kniga vtoraja (1824–1837).* Moscow, Leningrad: AN SSSR.

Turbin, V. N.
1968 "Xaraktery samozvancev v tvorčestve A. S. Puškina." *Filologičeskie nauki* 6: 85–95.

Turgenev, A. I.
1810 "Orxestika. O pljasan'e i tancax." *Vestnik Evropy* 23: 207–17.

Turner, Victor
1977 *The Ritual Process: Structure and Anti-Structure.* Ithaca: Cornell University Press.

Vacuro, V. E.
1972 (with M. I. Gillel'son) "Podvig čestnogo čeloveka." In *Skvoz' umstvennye plotiny,* pp. 100–108. Moscow: Kniga.
1974 *A. S. Puškin v vospominanijax sovremennikov.* Intro. by V. E. Vacuro. Moscow: Xud. lit.
1976 "K genezisu puškinskogo 'Demona.'" In *Sravnitel'noe izučenie literatur. Sbornik statej k 80-letiju akademika M. P. Alekseeva,* pp. 253–59. Leningrad: Nauka.
1978 [1981] "K istorii elegii 'Prostiš' li mne revnivye mečty . . . .'" *Vremennik puškinskoj komissii* 16: 5–21.

Vegner, M.
1937 *Predok Puškina.* Moscow: Sovetskij pisatel'.

Vengerov, S. A.
1892 "Bestužev, Aleksandr Aleksandrovič." In *Kritiko-biografičeskij slovar' russkix pisatelej i učenyx,* Vol. 3, pp. 147–77. St. Petersburg, 1889–1904.

Vengerov, S. A., ed.
1907–15 *Puškin.* 6 vols. St. Petersburg: Brokgauz-Èfron.

Veresaev, V., ed.
1936 *Puškin v žizni.* 6-e izd. Moscow: Sovetskij pisatel'.

Verxovskij, N. P.
1937 "Zapadnoevropejskaia istoričeskaja drama i *Boris Godunov* Puškina." In *Zapadnyj sbornik,* ed. V. M. Žirmunskij, pp. 187–226. Moscow, Leningrad: AN SSSR.

Vetlovskaja, V. E.
1986 "'Inyx už net, a te daleče . . .'" *Puškin: Issledovanija i materialy* XII: 104–24.

Vickery, Walter N.
1963 "'Mednyj vsadnik' and the Eighteenth Century Heroic Ode." *Indiana Slavic Studies* 3: 140–62.
1989 "Catherine II and Puškin in the Radiščev Affair." *Russian Language Journal* 43 (144): 187–98.
Forthcoming "Puškin's 'Aleksandr Radiščev': La Grande Illusion." To be published in *Puškin Symposium III.* Columbus: Slavica.

Vinogradov, V. V.
1934 "O stile Puškina." *Literaturnoe nasledstvo* 16–17: 136.
1956–61 *Slovar' jazyka Puškina.* Ed. V. V. Vinogradov. 4 vols. Moscow: Gos. izd. inostrannyx nacional'nyx slovarej.

Vinokur, G. O.
1941 "Slovo i stix v 'Evgenii Onegine.'" In *Puškin: Sbornik statej,* ed. A. Egolin. Moscow: Gos. lit. izd.
1935 See Puškin, A. S., 1935.

Vol'pert, L. I.
1979 "Puškin i francuzskaja komedija XVIII v." *Puškin: Issledovanija i materialy* 9: 168–88.

Watson, Robert N.
1983 "Horsemanship in Shakespeare's Second Tetralogy." *English Literary Renaissance* 13: 274–300.

Weber, Friedrich Christian
1723 *The Present State of Russia.* 2 vols. London: W. Taylor.

Wilson, Reuel K.
1973 *The Literary Travelogue.* The Hague: Martinus Nijhoff.

Xarlap, M.
1961 "O 'Mednom vsadnike' Puškina." *Voprosy literatury* 7: 87–101.

Xmel'nickaja, T. Ju.
1966 "Poèzija Andreja Belogo." In Andrej Belyj, *Stixotvorenija i poèmy,* ed. T. Ju. Xmel'nickaja, pp. 5–66. (Biblioteka poèta, Bol'šaja serija, 2-e izd.) Moscow, Leningrad: Sovetskij pisatel'.

Xodasevič, V.
1924 *Poètičeskoe xozjajstvo Puškina.* Leningrad: Mysl'.

Xolševnikov, V. E., ed.
1985 *Analiz odnogo stixotvorenija.* Leningrad.

Zaxarova, N. A., ed.
1965 *Očerki po istorii russkoj žurnalistiki i kritiki.* Tom 2: *Vtoraja polovina XIX veka.* Leningrad: Izd. LGU.

Zilboorg, Gregory
1944 "Masculine and Feminine." *Psychiatry* 7: 257–96.

Žolkovskij, Aleksandr
1979 "Materialy k opisaniju poètičeskogo mira Puškina." In *Russian Romanticism: Studies in the Poetic Codes,* ed. N. A. Nilsson, pp. 45–93. Stockholm: Almqvist and Wiksell.

Index